T0212035

Lecture Notes in Computer Science 9519

Commenced Publication in 1973
Founding and Former Series Editors:
Gerhard Goos, Juris Hartmanis, and Jan van Leeuwen

More information about this series at http://www.springer.com/series/7407

Xipeng Shen · Frank Mueller
James Tuck (Eds.)

Languages and Compilers for Parallel Computing

28th International Workshop, LCPC 2015
Raleigh, NC, USA, September 9–11, 2015
Revised Selected Papers

 Springer

Editors
Xipeng Shen
North Carolina State University
Raleigh, NC
USA

James Tuck
North Carolina State University
Raleigh, NC
USA

Frank Mueller
North Carolina State University
Raleigh, NC
USA

ISSN 0302-9743   ISSN 1611-3349   (electronic)
Lecture Notes in Computer Science
ISBN 978-3-319-29777-4   ISBN 978-3-319-29778-1   (eBook)
DOI 10.1007/978-3-319-29778-1

Library of Congress Control Number: 2016930546

LNCS Sublibrary: SL1 – Theoretical Computer Science and General Issues

Printed on acid-free paper

This Springer imprint is published by SpringerNature
The registered company is Springer International Publishing AG Switzerland

Preface

This volume presents the papers accepted for the 28th International Workshop on Languages and Compilers for Parallel Computing (LCPC), held during September 9–11, 2015, in Raleigh, North Carolina, USA. Following a long tradition, LCPC 2015 offered a valuable forum for sharing research on all aspects of concurrency: parallel languages, parallel programming models, compilers, runtime systems, and tools. LCPC 2015 in addition encouraged work that went beyond the scope of scientific computing and enabled parallel programming in new areas, such as mobile computing and data centers.

LCPC 2015 received 44 abstract submissions, 37 of which turned into full submissions. Each full submission received three independent reviews from the Program Committee, and some submissions received an additional review from an external expert reviewer. The Program Committee met to discuss each of the full submissions, and decided to accept 19 regular papers. The accepted papers cover a range of important topics on parallel computing, including programming models, communication and latency, optimizing frameworks, parallelizing compilers, correctness and reliability, applications and data structures. LCPC 2015 additionally included four posters on preliminary research results and reflection of past experiences.

LCPC 2015 was fortunate to include two keynote talks. Paul H.J. Kelly from Imperial College, London, gave a talk titled "Synthesis Versus Analysis: What Do We Actually Gain from Domain-Specificity?" Kelly reflected on the extensive experiences that he and his collaborators had in domain-specific performance optimizations, and offered a series of insights on the profitability of domain-specific optimizations. The second talk, presented by Padma Raghavan from Pennsylvania State University, was titled "Toward Programming Models for Parallel Processing of Sparse Data Sets." Raghavan discussed the utilization of fine-grain parallelism while reducing the latencies of data accesses for data sets with many dimensions that are sparse.

LCPC 2015 held a panel on "Implications of Emerging Memory Technology (e.g., Persistent Memory, Stacked Memory, Processing in Memory) to the Research on Compilers and Programming Systems." The panelists include five experts on the topic: Dhruva R. Chakrabarti from HP Labs, Rudolf Eigenmann from Purdue University, David Padua from UIUC, Yan Solihin from NCSU, and Youtao Zhang from the University of Pittsburgh. The panel stimulated discussions on the new challenges and opportunities that emerging memory technology brings to compilers and programming systems research.

We would like to thank all the participants of LCPC 2015 for making it a success. The hard work by the Program Committee and external reviewers in reviewing the submissions is key to ensuring a high-quality technical program. We are indebted to the Steering Committee for the strong support. We give our special thanks to Lawrence Rauchwerger for helping us with the workshop registration and many other organizational issues. We are grateful for the financial support by Cisco, Huawei, Intel,

NVIDIA, and NetApp. Finally, the workshop would not have been a success without the excellent work by the volunteers: Amir Bahmani, Richa Budhiraja, Guoyang Chen, Anwesha Das, Anwesha Das, Yufei Ding, Neha Gholkar, Neha Gholkar, Lin Ning, Xing Pan, Apoorv Parle, Shanil Puri, Tao Qian, Tao Wang, Tiancong Wang, Zhipeng Wei, Bagus Wibowo, and Qi Zhu.

December 2015   Xipeng Shen
Frank Mueller
James Tuck

Organization

Workshop Chairs

Xipeng Shen	North Carolina State University, USA
Frank Mueller	North Carolina State University, USA
James Tuck	North Carolina State University, USA

Workshop Committee

James Brodman	Intel Corporation, USA
Calin Cascaval	Qualcomm Research Silicon Valley Center, USA
Marcelo Cintra	Intel Corporation, USA
Chen Ding	University of Rochester, USA
Michael Garland	NVIDIA Research, USA
Mike Hind	IBM Research, USA
Hironori Kasahara	Waseda University, Japan
Xiaoming Li	University of Delaware, USA
Sam Midkiff	Purdue University, USA
Pablo Montesinos Ortego	Qualcomm Research Silicon Valley Center, USA
Peng Tu	Intel Corporation, USA
Bo Wu	Colorado School of Mines, USA
Qing Yi	University of Colorado, Colorado Springs, CO, USA
Jidong Zhai	Tsinghua University, China
Huiyang Zhou	North Carolina State University, USA

Poster Selection Committee

Aparna Chandramowlishwaran	University of California, Irvine, CA, USA
Xu Liu	College of William and Mary, USA
Xipeng Shen	North Carolina State University, USA
Zhijia Zhao	University of California, Riverside, CA, USA

Steering Committee

Rudolf Eigenmann	Purdue University, USA
Alex Nicolau	University of California, Irvine, CA, USA
David Padua	University of Illinois, USA
Lawrence Rauchwerger	Texas A&M University, USA

Contents

Programming Models

Size Oblivious Programming with *InfiniMem*

Sai Charan Koduru$^{(\boxtimes)}$, Rajiv Gupta, and Iulian Neamtiu

Department of Computer Science and Engineering,
University of California, Riverside, USA
{scharan,gupta,neamtiu}@cs.ucr.edu

Abstract. Many recently proposed BigData processing frameworks make programming easier, but typically expect the datasets to fit in the memory of either a single multicore machine or a cluster of multi-core machines. When this assumption does not hold, these frameworks fail. We introduce the *InfiniMem* framework that enables *size oblivious processing* of large collections of objects that do not fit in memory by making them *disk-resident*. *InfiniMem* is easy to program with: the user just indicates the large collections of objects that are to be made disk-resident, while *InfiniMem* transparently handles their I/O management. The *InfiniMem* library can manage a very large number of objects in a uniform manner, even though the objects have different characteristics and relationships which, when processed, give rise to a wide range of access patterns requiring different organizations of data on the disk. We demonstrate the ease of programming and versatility of *InfiniMem* with 3 different probabilistic analytics algorithms, 3 different graph processing *size oblivious frameworks*; they require minimal effort, 6–9 additional lines of code. We show that *InfiniMem* can successfully generate a mesh with 7.5 million nodes and 300 million edges (4.5 GB on disk) in 40 min and it performs the PageRank computation on a 14 GB graph with 134 million vertices and 805 million edges at 14 min per iteration on an 8-core machine with 8 GB RAM. Many graph generators and processing frameworks cannot handle such large graphs. We also exploit *InfiniMem* on a cluster to scale-up an object-based DSM.

1 Introduction

BigData processing frameworks are an important part of today's data science research and development. Much research has been devoted to scale-out performance via distributed processing [8,12,13,17] and some recent research explores scale-up [1,6,11,15,16,21]. However, these scale-up solutions typically assume that the input dataset fits in memory. When this assumption does not hold, they simply fail. For example, experiments by Bu et al. [4] show that different open-source Big Data computing systems like Giraph [1], Spark [21], and Mahout [19] often crash on various input graphs. Particularly, in one of the

---

This work was supported by NSF Grant CCF-1524852, CCF-1318103, CNS-1157377, CCF-0963996, CCF-0905509, and a Google Research Award.

© Springer International Publishing Switzerland 2016
X. Shen et al. (Eds.): LCPC 2015, LNCS 9519, pp. 3–19, 2016.
DOI: 10.1007/978-3-319-29778-1_1

experiments, a 70 GB web graph dataset was partitioned across 180 machines (each with 16 GB RAM) to perform the PageRank computation. However, all the systems crashed with java.lang.OutOfMemoryError, even though there was less than 500MB of data to be processed per machine. In our experiments we also found that GTgraph's popular R-MAT generator [2], a tool commonly used to generate power-law graphs, crashed immediately with a *Segmentation Fault* from memory allocation failure when we tried to generate a graph with 1M vertices and 400M edges on a machine with 8 GB RAM.

Motivated by the above observations, in this paper, we develop *InfiniMem*, a system that enables *Size Oblivious Programming* – the programmer develops the applications without concern for the input sizes involved and *InfiniMem* ensures that these applications do not run out of memory. Specifically, the *InfiniMem* library provides interfaces for transparently managing a large number of objects stored in files on disk. For efficiency, *InfiniMem* implements different read and write policies to handle objects that have different characteristics (fixed size vs. variable size) and require different handling strategies (sequential vs. random access I/O). We demonstrate the ease of programming with *InfiniMem* by programming BigData analysis applications like frequency estimation, exact membership query, and Bloom filters. We further demonstrate the *versatility* of *InfiniMem* by developing size oblivious graph processing frameworks with three different graph data representations: vertex data and edges in a single data structure; decoupled vertex data and edges; and the shard representation used by GraphChi [11]. One advantage of *InfiniMem* is that it allows researchers and programmers to easily experiment with different data representations with minimal additional programming effort. We evaluate various graph applications with three different representations. For example, a quick and simple shard implementation of PageRank with *InfiniMem* performs within ∼30 % of GraphChi.

The remainder of the paper is organized as follows: Sect. 2 motivates the problem and presents the requirements expected from a *size oblivious programming* system. Section 3 introduces the programming interface for size oblivious programming. Section 4 describes the object representation used by *InfiniMem* in detail. Section 5 describes the experimental setup and results of our evaluation. Related work and conclusions are presented in Sects. 6 and 7, respectively.

2   Size Oblivious Programming

The need to program processing of very large data sets is fairly common today. Typically a processing task involves representing the data set as a large collection of objects and then performing analysis on them. When this large collection of objects does not fit in memory, the programmer must spend considerable effort on writing code to make use of disk storage to manage the large number of objects. In this work we free the programmer from this burden by developing a system that allows the programmer to write *size oblivious* programs, i.e., programs where the user need not explicitly deal with the complexity of using disk storage to manage large collections of objects that cannot be held in available memory. To enable the successful execution of size oblivious programs, we propose a general-purpose programming interface along with an *I/O efficient* representation of objects on disk. We now introduce a few motivating applications and identify requirements to achieve I/O efficiency for our *size oblivious programming* system.

Motivating Applications: Consider an application that is reading continuously streaming input into a Hash Table in heap memory (lines 1–3, Algorithm 1); a website analytics data stream is an excellent example of this scenario. When the memory gets full, the `insert` on line 3 could fail, resulting in an application failure. Similarly, consider the GTGraph [2] graph generator which fails to generate a graph with 1M edges and 400M vertices. Consider a common approach to graph generation which assumes that the entire graph can be held in memory during generation, as illustrated by lines 8–15 in Algorithm 1. First, memory for NUM-VERTICES is allocated (line 8) and then the undirected edges are generated (lines 11-13). Note that the program can crash *as early as line 8* when memory allocation fails due to a large number of vertices. Finally, consider the problem of graph processing, using SSSP as a proxy for a large class of graph processing applications. Typically, such applications have three phases: (1) input, (2) compute, and (3) output. The pseudocode for SSSP is outlined in lines 16–31 in Algorithm 1, highlighting these three phases. *Note that if the input graph does not fit in memory, this program will not even begin execution.*

Algorithm 1. Motivating applications: Membership Query, Mesh Generation and Graph Processing.

```
1  HashTable ht;                              16  Graph g;
2  while read(value) do                       17  while not end of input file do
3      ht.insert(value);                      18      read next;
                                              19      g.Add( α(next) );
4  while more items do
5      if ht.find(item) then                  20  repeat
6          print("Item found");               21      termCondition ← true;
                                              22      forall the Vertices v in g do
7  ─────────────────────────                 23          for int i=0; i<v.nbrs(); i++ do
8  Mesh m(NUM-VERTICES)                       24              Vertex n = v.neighbors[i];
                                              25              if v.dst>n.dst+v.wt[i] then
9  foreach node n in Mesh m do                26                  v.dst←(n.dst+v.wt[i]);
10     i ← rand(0, MAX);
11     for j=0; j < i; j++ do                 27      if NOT converged then
12         n.addNeighbor(m[j]);               28          termCondition ← false;
13         m[j].addNeighbor(n);
                                              29  until termCondition is true;
14 foreach Node n in Mesh m do                30  foreach Node n in Graph g do
15     Write(n)                               31      Write(n);
```

Our Solution: We focus on supporting size oblivious programming for C++ programs via the *InfiniMem* C++ library and runtime. Examples in Algorithm 1 indicate that the data structures that can grow very large are represented as *collections* of objects. Size Oblivious Programming with *InfiniMem* simply requires programmers to *identify potentially large collections of objects* using very simple abstractions provided by the library and these collections are transparently made *disk-resident* and can be efficiently and concurrent accessed. We now analyze these representative applications to tease out the requirements for *size oblivious programming* that have influenced the architecture of *InfiniMem*.

Let us reconsider the pseudocode in Algorithm 1, mindful of the requirement of efficient I/O. Lines 5–6 will execute for *every* key in the input; similarly, lines 9 and 14 indicate that lines 10–13 and line 15 will be executed for *every* node in the mesh. Similarly, line 22 indicates that lines 23–26 will be performed on *every* vertex in the graph. It is natural to read a contiguous *block* of data so that no additional I/O is required for lines 24–26 for the vertices and is an efficient disk I/O property. Moreover, this would be useful for any application in general, by way of decreasing I/O requests and batching as much I/O as possible. Therefore, we have our first requirement:

Support for Efficient Block-Based IO.

Consider next, the example of the hash table where the input data is *not* sorted; then, line 3 of Algorithm 1 motivates need for random access for indexing into the hash table. As another example, observe that line 24 in Algorithm 1 fetches every neighbor of the current vertex. When part of this graph is disk-resident, we need a way of efficiently fetching the neighbors, much like *random access* in memory. This is important because any vertex in a graph serves two roles: (1) vertex and (2) neighbor. For the role (1), if vertices are contiguously stored on disk block-based I/O can be used. However, when the vertex is accessed as a neighbor, the neighbor could be stored anywhere on disk, and thus requires an imitation of random access on the disk. Hence our next requirement is:

Support for Efficient, Random Access to Data on Disk.

To make the case for our final requirement, consider a typical definition of the HashTable shown in Fig. 1a. Each `key` can store multiple values to support *chaining*. Clearly, each `HashTableEntry` is a variable sized entity, as it can hold multiple `values` by chaining. As another example, consider the definition for a *Vertex* shown in Fig. 1b: the size of `neighbors` array can vary; and with the exception of the `neighbors` member, the size of a *Vertex* can be viewed as a fixed-size object. When reading/writing data from/to the disk, one can devise very fast block-based I/O for fixed-size data (Sect. 4). However, reading variable-sized data requires remembering the size of the data and performing n reads of appropriate sizes; this is particularly wasteful in terms of disk I/O bandwidth utilization. For example, if the average number of neighbors is 10, every time a distance value is needed, we will incur a 10x overhead in read but useless data. As a final example, Fig. 1c is an example of an arbitrary container that showcases the need for both fixed and variable sized data. Hence we arrive at our final requirement from *InfiniMem*:

Support to speed up I/O for variable-sized data.

The goal of *InfiniMem* is to transparently support disk-resident versions of object collections so that they can grow to large sizes without causing programs to crash. *InfiniMem*'s design allows size oblivious programming with little effort as the programmer merely identifies the presence and processing of potentially large object collections via *InfiniMem*'s simple programming interface. The details of how *InfiniMem* manages I/O (i.e., uses block-based I/O, random access I/O, and I/O for fixed and variable sized data) during processing of a disk-resident data structure are hidden from the programmer.

```
template <typename K, typename V>
struct HashTableEntry {
  K key;
  V* values; /* for chaining */
};
```
(a) Hash Table

```
struct Vertex {
  int distance;
  int* weights; /*Edge weights*/
  Vertex* neighbors;   /*Array*/
};
```
(b) Graph Vertex

```
template<typename T>
struct Container{
  T stackObjects[96]; /* Fixed */
  T *heapObjects;  /* Variable */
};
```
(c) Arbitrary container

Fig. 1. Common data structure declarations to motivate the need for explicit support for fixed and variable sized data, block based and random IO.

3 The *InfiniMem* Programming Interface

InfiniMem is a C++ template library that allows programmers to identify size oblivious versions of fixed- and variable-sized data collections and enables transparent, efficient processing of these collections. We now describe *InfiniMem*'s simple application programming interface (API) that powers *size oblivious programming*. *InfiniMem* provides a *high-level* API with a default *processing* strategy that hides I/O details from the programmer; however the programmer has the flexibility to use the *low-level* API to implement any customized processing.

Identifying Large Collection of Objects: In *InfiniMem*, the programmer identifies object collections that potentially grow large and need to be made disk-resident. In addition, the programmer classifies them as fixed or variable sized. This is achieved by using the Box and Bag abstractions respectively. The Box abstraction can be used to hold fixed-size data, while the Bag holds flexible-sized data. Figure 2 illustrates an example and lists the interface. The programmer uses the Box or Bag interface by simply inheriting from the Box (or Bag) type and provides an implementation for the update() method to process each object in the container. Here, Container is the collection that can potentially grow large,

```
template<typename T>                        template<typename T>
struct Container: public Box<T> { // or Bag<T>    T Box::fetch(ID);
  T data;
  void update() {  /* for each T */          template<typename T>
    ...                                       T* Box::fetchBatch(ID, count);
  }
                                             template<typename T>
  void process();                            void Box::store(ID, const T*);
};
                                             template<typename T>
typedef Container<int> intData;              void Box::storeBatch(ID, count);

typedef Container<MyObject> objData;         template<typename T>
                                             T Bag::fetch(ID);
int main() {
  Infinimem<intData> idata;                  template<typename T>
  idata.read("/input/file");                 T* Bag::fetchBatch(ID, count);
  idata.process();
                                             template<typename T>
  Infinimem<objData> odata;                  void Bag::store(ID, const T*);
  odata.read("/input/data/");
  odata.process();                           template<typename T>
}                                            void Bag::storeBatch(ID, count);
```

Fig. 2. Programming with *InfiniMem*: the `Box` and `Bag` interfaces are used for *fixed size* and *variable sized* objects; `process` drives the computation using the user-defined `update()` methods and the low-level `fetch()` and `store()` API.

as identified by the programmer. `Infinimem` is the default processing engine; *InfiniMem*'s `process()` function hides the details of I/O and fetches objects as needed by the `update()` method, thereby enabling *size oblivious programming*.

Processing Data: The `process()` method is the execution engine: it implements the low-level details of efficiently fetching objects from the disk, applies the user-defined `update()` method and efficiently spills the updated objects to disk. Figure 3 details the default `process()`. By default, the `process()`-ing engine `fetches`, `processes` and `store`-es data in batches of size `BATCH_SIZE` which is automatically determined from available free memory such that the entire batch fits and can be processed in memory.

While *InfiniMem* provides the default implementation for `process()` shown in Fig. 3, this method can be overridden: programmers can use the accessors and mutators exposed by *InfiniMem* (Fig. 2) to write their own processing frameworks. Notice that *InfiniMem* natively supports both sequential/block-based and random accessors and mutators, satisfying each

```
// SZ = SIZEOF_INPUT; BSZ = BATCH_SIZE;
Box<T>::process() { // or Bag<T>
  for(i=0; i<SZ; i+=BSZ) {
    // fetch a portion of Box<T> or Bag<T>
    cache = fetchBatch(ID(i), BSZ);
    for(j=0; j<BSZ; j++)
      cache[j].update();
  }
}
```

Fig. 3. *InfiniMem*'s generic batch `process()`-ing.

of the requirements formulated earlier. For block-based and random access, *InfiniMem* provides the following intuitively named fetch and store APIs: `fetch()`, `fetchBatch()`, `store()` and `storeBatch()`.

Illustration of* InfiniMem *for Graph Processing: We next demonstrate *InfiniMem*'s versatility and ease of use by programming graph applications using *three* different graph representations. We start with the standard declaration of a `Vertex` as seen in Fig. 1b. An alternate definition of `Vertex` separates the fixed sized data from variable sized edgelist for IO efficiency, and used in many vertex centric frameworks [11,12]. Finally, we program GraphChi's [11] shards.

Figure 4a declares the `Graph` to be a `Bag` of vertices, using the declaration from Fig. 1b. With this declaration, the programmer has identified that the collection of vertices is the potentially large collection that can benefit from size oblivious programming. The `preprocess()` phase partitions the input graph into disjoint intervals of vertices to allow for parallel processing. These examples use a vertex-centric graph processing approach where the `update()` method of `Vertex` defines the algorithm to process each vertex in the graph. The `process()` method of `Graph` uses the accessors and mutators from Fig. 2 to provide a *size oblivious programming* experience to the programmer. Figure 4b declares a `Graph` as the composition of a `Box` of `Vertex` and a `Bag` of EdgeLists, where `EdgeList` is an implicitly defined list of neighbors. Finally, Fig. 4c uses a similar graph declaration, with the simple tweak of creating an array of `N` `shard` partitions; a `shard` imposes additional constraints on the vertices that are in the shard: vertices are partitioned into intervals such that all vertices with neighbors in a given vertex interval are all available in the same shard [11], enabling fewer random accesses by having all vertices' neighbors available before processing each shard. Note that representing shards in *InfiniMem* is very simple.

```
void Vertex::update() {        void Vertex::update() {        void Vertex::update() {
  foreach(neighbor n)            foreach(neighbor n)            foreach(neighbor n)
    distance = f(n.distance);      distance = f(n.distance);      distance = f(n.distance);
}                              }                              }

template <typename V>          template <typnam V,typnam E>   template <typename V,typename E>
class Graph {                  class Graph {                  class Graph {
  Bag<V> vertices;               Box<V> vertices;               Box<V> vertexShard[N];
                                 Bag<E> edgeLists;              Bag<E> edgeShard[N];

public:                        public:                        public:
  void process();                void process();                void processShard(int);
};                             };                             };

int main() {                   int main() {                   int main() {
  Graph<Vertex> g;               Graph<Vertex, EdgeList> g;     Graph<Vertex, EdgeList> g;
  g.read("/path/to/graph");      g.read("/path/to/graph");      g.read("/path/to/graph");
  g.preprocess(); //Partition    g.preprocess(); //Partition    g.createShards(N);//Preprocess
  g.process();                   g.process();                   for(int i=0; i<N; i++)
}                              }                                  g.processShard(i);
                                                              }
```

(a) Graph for Vertex in Figure 1b. (b) Decoupling Vertices from Edgelists. (c) Using Shard representation of graphs.

Fig. 4. Variations of graph programming, showcasing the ease and versatility of programming with *InfiniMem*, using its high-level API.

```
// SZ = SIZEOF_INPUT;          // SZ = SIZEOF_INPUT;          // NS = NUM_SHARDS;
// BSZ = BATCH_SIZE;           // BSZ = BATCH_SIZE;           // SS = SIZEOF_SHARD;
// vb = vertices;              // v = vertices;               // vs = vertexShard;
                              // e = edgeLists;

Graph<V>::process() {         Graph<V, E>::process() {       Graph<V, E>::process() {
  for(i=0; i<SZ; i+=BSZ) {      for(i=0; i<SZ; i+=BSZ) {       for(i=0; i<NS; i++) {
    // fetch a batch             // fetch a batch               // fetch entire memory shard
    vb=fetchBatch(ID(i), BSZ);   vb=v.fetchBatch(ID(i), BSZ);   mshrd = vs[i].fetchBatch(..,SS);

                                 // fetch corr. edgelist         // fetch sliding shards
                                 eb=e.fetchBatch(ID(i), BSZ);    for(j=0; j<NS; j++)
                                                                   sshrd += vs[j].fetchBatch(.,.);

                                                                 sg = buildSubGraph(mshrd,sshrd);

  for(j=0; j<BSZ; j++)           for(j=0; j<BSZ; j++)            foreach(v in sg)
    vb[j].update();                vb[j].update(eb[j]);            v.update();

  storeBatch(vb, BSZ);           storeBatch(vb, BSZ);            storeBatch(mshrd, SS);
  }                              }                              }
}                              }                              }
```

(a) `process()`-ing graph in Figure 1b. (b) `process()` for decoupled Vertex. (c) Custom `process()` for shards.

Fig. 5. Default and custom overrides for `process()` via low-level *InfiniMem* API.

Figure 5a illustrates the default `process()`: objects in the `Box` or `Bag` are read in batches and processed one at a time. For graphs with vertices decoupled from edgelists, vertices and edgelists are read in batches and processed one vertex at a time (Fig. 5b); batches are concurrently processed. Figure 5c illustrates custom shard processing: each memory shard and corresponding sliding shards build the subgraph in memory; then each vertex in the subgraph is processed [11].

4   *InfiniMem*'s I/O Efficient Object Representation

We now discuss the I/O efficient representation provided by *InfiniMem*. Specifically, we propose an *Implicitly Indexed* representation for fixed-sized data (`Box`); and an *Explicitly Indexed* representation for variable-sized data (`Bag`).

As the number of objects grows beyond what can be accommodated in main

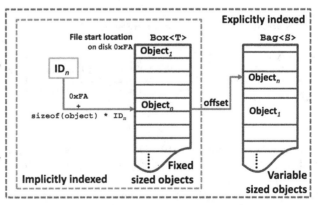

Fig. 6. Indexed disk representation of fixed- and variable-sized objects.

memory, the frequency of object I/O to/from disk storage will increase. This warrants an organization of the disk storage that reduces I/O latency. To allow an object to be addressed regardless of where it resides, it is assigned a unique numeric ID from a stream of non-negative, monotonically increasing integers. Figure 6 shows the access mechanism for objects using their IDs: fixed-sized data is stored at a location determined by its ID and its fixed size: FILE_START + (sizeof(Object) * ID). For variable-sized data, we use a *metafile* whose fixed-sized address entries store the offset of the variable-sized data into the *datafile*. The Vertex declared in Fig. 4a for example, would only use the *explicitly indexed* Bag notation to store data, while the representations in Fig. 4b and c use both the Box and Bag for the fixed size Vertex and the variable sized EdgeList respectively. Thus, fixed-sized data can be fetched/stored in a *single logical* disk seek and variable-sized data in *two logical* seeks. This ensures fetch and store times are nearly constant with *InfiniMem* and independent of the number of objects in the file (like random memory access), and enabling:

- **Efficient Access for Fixed-Sized Objects:** Using the object ID to index into the datafile, *InfiniMem* gives fast access to fixed-sized objects in 1 logical seek.
- **Efficient Access for Variable-Sized Objects:** The metafile enables fast, random-access access to objects in the datafile, in at most 2 logical seeks.
- **Random Access Disk I/O:** The indexing mechanism provides an imitation of random access to both fixed and variable sized objects on disk.
- **Sequential/Batch Disk I/O:** To read n consecutive objects, we seek to the start of the first object. We then read sizeof(obj)*n bytes and up to the end of the last object in the sequence for fixed- and variable-sized objects, respectively.
- **Concurrent I/O:** For parallel processing, different objects in the datafile must be concurrently and safely accessed. Given the large number of objects, individual locks for each object would be impractical. Instead, *InfiniMem* provides locks for groups of objects: to decrease lock conflicts, we group non-contiguous objects using modulo ID modulo a MAX_CONCURRENCY parameter set at 25.

5   Evaluation

We now evaluate the programmability and performance of *InfiniMem*. This evaluation is based upon three class of applications: probabilistic web analytics, graph/mesh generation, and graph processing. We also study the scalability of size oblivious applications written using *InfiniMem* with degree of parallelism and input sizes. We programmed size oblivious versions of several applications using *InfiniMem* and are listed in Table 1. We begin with data analytics benchmarks: frequency counting using *arrays*, membership query using *hash tables*, and probabilistic membership query using *Bloom filters*. Then, in addition to mesh generation, in this evaluation, we use a variety of graph processing algorithms from diverse domains like graph mining, machine learning, etc. The *Connected Components* (CC) algorithm finds nodes in a graph that are connected to each other by at least one path, with applications in graph theory. *Graph Coloring*

Table 1. Between 6 and 9 *additional* lines of code are needed to make these applications *size oblivious*. Graph processing uses decoupled version (Fig. 4b).

Application	Additional LoC	Application	Additional LoC
Probabilistic Web Analytics		Graph Processing	
Freq. Counting	$2 + 3 + 3 = 8$	Graph Coloring	
Member Query	$2 + 3 + 3 = 8$	PageRank	
Bloom Filter	$2 + 4 + 3 = 9$	SSSP	$1 + 3 + 2 = 6$
Graph/Mesh Generation		Num Paths	
Mesh Generation	$2 + 2 + 2 = 6$	Conn. Components	

(GC) assigns a color to a vertex such that it is distinct from those of all its neighboring vertices with applications in register allocation etc. In a web graph, *PageRank* (PR) [14] iteratively ranks a page based on the ranks of pages with inbound links to the page and is used to rank web search results. *NumPaths* (NP) counts the number of paths between a source and other vertices. From a source node in a graph, *Single Source Shortest Path* (SSSP) finds the shortest path to all other nodes in the graph with applications in logistics and transportation.

5.1 Programmability

Writing size oblivious programs with *InfiniMem* is simple. The programmer needs to only: (a) initialize the *InfiniMem* library, (b) identify the large collections and `Box` or `Bag` them as necessary, and (c) use the default `process()`-ing engine or provide a custom engine. Table 1 quantifies the ease of programming with *InfiniMem* by listing the number of additional lines of code for these tasks to make the program size oblivious using the default processing engine. At most 9 lines of code are needed in this case and *InfiniMem* does all the heavy lifting with about 700 lines for the I/O subsystem, and about 900 lines for the runtime, all of which hides the complexity of making data structures disk-resident from the user. Even programming the shard processing framework was relatively easy: about 100 lines for simplistic shard generation and another 200 lines for rest of the processing including loading memory and corresponding sliding shards, building the subgraph in memory and processing the subgraph; rest of the complexity of handling the I/O etc., are handled by *InfiniMem*.

5.2 Performance

We now present the runtime performance of applications programmed with *InfiniMem*. We evaluated *InfiniMem* on a Dell Inspiron machine with 8 cores and 8 GB RAM with a commodity 500 GB, 7200RPM

Table 2. Inputs used in this evaluation.

Input Graph	$|V|$	$|E|$	Size
Pokec	1,632,804	61,245,128	497 M
Live Journal	4,847,571	68,993,773	1.2 G
Orkut-2007	3,072,627	223,534,301	3.2 G
Delicious-UI	33,778,221	151,772,443	4.2 G
RMAT-536-67	67,108,864	536,870,912	8.8 G
RMAT-805-134	134,217,728	805,306,368	14 G

SATA 3.0 Hitachi `HUA722050CLA330` hard drive. For consistency, the disk cache is fully flushed before each run.

Size Oblivious *Graph Processing:* We begin with the evaluation of graph processing applications using input graph datasets with varying number of vertices and edges, listed in Table 2. Orkut, Pokec, and LiveJournal graphs are directed graphs representing friend relationships. Vertices in the Amazon graph represent products, while edges represent purchases. The largest input in this evaluation is rmat-805-134 at 14 GB on disk, 805M edges and 134M vertices.

We first discuss the benefits of decoupling edges from vertices. When vertex data and edgelists are in the same data structure, line 22 in Algorithm 1 requires fetching the edgelists for the vertices even though they are not used in this phase of the computation. Decoupling the edge-lists from vertex data has the benefit of avoiding wasteful I/O as seen in Table 3. The very large decrease in running time is due to the extremely wasteful I/O that reads the variable sized edgelists along with the vertex data even though only the vertex data is needed.

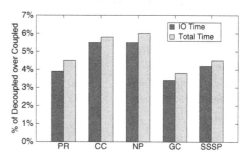

Fig. 7. Percentage(%) of IO and execution time for decoupled over coupled representations for various applications on the 'Delicious-UI' input.

Figure 7 shows the I/O breakdowns for various benchmarks on the moderately sized Delicious-UI input. While the programming effort with *InfiniMem* is already minimal, switching between representations for the same program can be easier too: with as little as *a single change* to data structure definition (Fig. 4a–b), the programmer can evaluate different representations.

Tables 4 and 5 show the frequencies and percentage of total execution time spent in various I/O operations for processing the *decoupled* graph representation with *InfiniMem*, as illustrated in Fig. 4b. Observe that the number of batched vertex reads and writes is the same in Table 4 since both vertices and edgelists are

Table 3. Decoupling vertices and edgelists avoids wasteful I/O (runtime time shown is in seconds). 'Co' and 'DeCo' refer to coupled and decoupled respectively.

Input Graph	PageRank		Conn Comp		Numpaths		Graph Coloring		SSSP	
	Co	DeCo	Co	DeCo	Co	DeCo	Co	DeCo	Co	DeCo
Pokec	2,228	172	352	60	37	8	277	28	48	7
Live journal	8,975	409	1,316	122	106	14	602	58	133	70
Orkut	3,323	81	3,750	277	459	11	3,046	140	660	154
Delicious-UI	32,743	1,484	15,404	904	1,112	67	9,524	365	1,453	65
rmat-536-67	23,588	3,233	12,118	2,545	1,499	861	5,783	1,167	1,853	584
rmat-805-134	25,698	3,391	>8h	3,380	3,069	1,482	11,332	2,071	>8h	2,882

Table 4. Frequencies of operations for various inputs for PageRank.

I/O Operation	LiveJournal	Orkut	Delicious-UI	rmat-536-67	rmat-805-134
Vertex batched reads	7,891	421	40,578	12,481	24,052
Edge batched reads	7,891	421	40,578	12,481	24,052
Vertex individual reads	865e+6	188e+6	2.8e+9	1.8e+9	2.5e+9
Vertex batched writes	7,883	413	40,570	12,473	24,044

Table 5. Percentage of time for I/O operations for various inputs for PageRank.

I/O Operation	LiveJournal	Orkut	Delicious-UI	rmat-536-67	rmat-805-134
Vertex batched reads	0.05 %	0.02 %	0.31 %	0.12 %	0.13 %
Edge batched reads	8.48 %	2.75 %	11.25 %	7.75 %	9.72 %
Vertex Individual Reads	54.80 %	71.59 %	76.96 %	86.47 %	81.73 %
Vertex batched writes	0.12 %	0.03 %	0.37 %	0.04 %	0.10 %
Total IO	63.45 %	74.39 %	88.89 %	94.38 %	91.68 %

read together in batches. There are no individual vertex writes since *InfiniMem* only writes vertices in batches. Moreover, the number of batched vertex writes is less than the reads since we write only updated vertices and as the algorithm converges, in some batches, there are no updates. Observe in Table 5 that as described earlier, the maximum time is spent in random vertex reads.

***Sharding with* InfiniMem:** In the rest of this discussion, we always use the decoupled versions of Vertex and EdgeLists. We now compare various versions of graph processing using *InfiniMem*. Table 6 compares the performance of the two simple graph processing frameworks we built on top of *InfiniMem* with that of GraphChi-provided implementations in their 8 thread configuration. *InfiniShard* refers to the shard processing framework based on *InfiniMem*. In general, the slowdown observed with *InfiniMem* is due to the large number of random reads generated, which is $O(|E|)$. For PageRank with Orkut, however, we see speedup for the following reason: as the iterations progress, the set of changed vertices becomes considerably small: ∼50. So, the number of random reads generated also goes down considerably, speeding up PageRank on the Orkut input. With Connected Components, our *InfiniMem* runs slower primarily because the GraphChi converges in less than half as many iterations on most inputs. Table 6 also presents the data for PageRank that processes shards with our *InfiniMem* library as compared to the very fine-tuned GraphChi library. The speedup observed in Table 6 from *InfiniMem* to *InfiniShard* is from eliminating random reads enabled by the shard format. Notice that even with our quick, unoptimized ∼350 line implementation of sharding, the average slowdown we see is only 18.7 % for PageRank and 22.7 % for Connected Components compared to the highly tuned and hand-optimized GraphChi implementation. Therefore, we have shown that *InfiniMem* can be used to easily and quickly provide a *size oblivious programming* experience along with I/O efficiency for quickly evaluating various representations of the same data.

Table 6. *InfiniMem* (decoupled) vs. *InfiniShard*; Speedups over GraphChi.

Input Graph	PageRank time (sec)			Conn. Comp. time (sec)		
	InfiniMem (speedup)	*InfiniShard* (speedup)	GraphChi	*InfiniMem* (speedup)	*InfiniShard* (speedup)	GraphChi
Pokec	172 (0.72)	121 (1.02)	124	60 (0.40)	26 (0.92)	24
LiveJournal	409 (0.90)	488 (0.76)	371	122 (0.49)	80 (0.75)	60
Orkut	81 (1.91)	190 (0.82)	156	277 (0.44)	142 (0.87)	123
Delicious-UI	1,484 (0.43)	730 (0.89)	652	904 (0.17)	191 (0.78)	149
rmat-536-67	3,233 (0.36)	1,637 (0.70)	1,146	2,545 (0.21)	746 (0.71)	529
rmat-805-134	3,391 (0.44)	2,162 (0.69)	1,492	3,380 (0.30)	1,662 (0.61)	1,016

Size-Oblivious Programming *of Probabilistic Apps:* Here, we present the throughput numbers for the probabilistic applications in Table 7. We evaluated these applications by generating uniformly random numeric input. Frequency counting is evaluated by counting frequencies of random inserts while membership query and Bloom filter are evaluated using uniformly generated random queries on the previously generated uniformly random input. Jenkins hashes are used in Bloom filter. Bloom filter achieves about half the throughput of Frequency Counting since Bloom filter generates twice as many writes.

We also experimented with querying. We searched for entries using the Orkut input file (3.2 GB on disk) as an input file. Using a naive, sequential scan and search took 67 s. Using *InfiniMem* with 1 thread took 15 s, while using 4 threads took 5 s for the *same*

Table 7. QPS for the probabilistic apps.

Application	Throughput (qps)
Frequency counting	635,031
Membership query	446,536
Bloom filter	369,726

naive implementation. The highly optimized GNU Regular Expressions utility took an average of 4.5 s for the same search. This shows that in addition to ease of programming, *InfiniMem* performs well even with very simple implementations.

5.3 Scalability

Next, we present data to show that *InfiniMem* scales with increasing parallelism. Figure 8a shows the total running times for various applications on the 14 GB rmat-805-134 input: for most applications *InfiniMem* scales well up to 8 threads.

However, given that the performance of applications is determined by the data representation and the number of random accesses that result in disk I/O, we want to study how well *InfiniMem* scales with increasing input size. To objectively study the scalability with increasing number of edges with fixed vertices and controlling for variations in distribution of vertex degrees and other input graph characteristics, we perform a controlled experiment where we resort to synthetic inputs with 4 M vertices and 40 M, 80 M, 120 M, 160 M and 200 M edges.

Figure 8c shows the time for each of the for these inputs. We see that with increasing parallelism, *InfiniMem* scales well for increasing number of edges in the graph. This shows that *InfiniMem* effectively manages the limited memory resource by orchestrating seamless offloading to disk as required by the application. The performance on real-world graphs is determined by specific characteristics of the graph like distribution of degrees of the vertices etc. But for a graph of a specified size, Fig. 8c can be viewed as a practical upper bound.

Figure 8b illustrates the scalability achievable with programming with *InfiniMem* with parallelism for the Frequency counting, Exact membership query and Probabilistic membership query using Bloom filters. Notice that these applications scale well with increasing number of threads as well as increasing input sizes. The execution time for Bloom filter is significantly larger since Bloom filter generates more random writes, depending on the number of hash functions utilized by the filter; our implementation uses two independent hashes.

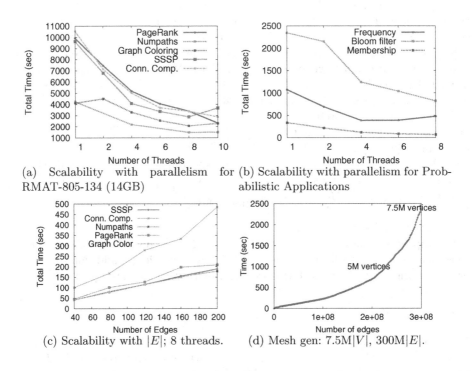

(a) Scalability with parallelism for RMAT-805-134 (14GB)

(b) Scalability with parallelism for Probabilistic Applications

(c) Scalability with |E|; 8 threads.

(d) Mesh gen: 7.5M|V|, 300M|E|.

Fig. 8. Scalability of *InfiniMem* with parallelism and input size.

Figure 8d illustrates that very large graph generation is feasible with *InfiniMem* by showing the generation of a Mesh with 7.5 M vertices and 300M edges which takes about 40 min (2400 s). We observe that up to 5 M vertices and 200 M edges, the time for generation increases nearly linearly with the number of edges generated after which the generation begins to slow down. This slowdown is not due to the inherent complexity of generating larger graphs: the number of type of disk operations needed to add edges is independent of the size of the graph – edge addition entails adding the vertex as the neighbor's neighbor and accessing the desired data in *InfiniMem* requires a maximum of 2 logical seeks. The reason for the observed slowdown is as follows: modifications of variable sized data structures in *InfiniMem* are appended to the datafile on disk; this data file, therefore, grows very large over time and the disk caching mechanisms begin to get less effective. Compare this with the fact that GTGraph crashed immediately for a graph with just 1 M vertices and 400 M edges.

5.4   Integration with Distributed Shared Memory (DSM)

Next we demonstrate the applicability of Size Oblivious Programming in the context of Distributed Shared Memory. While clusters are easy to *scale out*, multi-tenant environments can restrict memory available to user processes or certain inputs may not fit in the distributed memory. In either case, it would be beneficial to have the programs run successfully without rewrites. We applied the *InfiniMem* framework to seamlessly make our object based DSM [9]

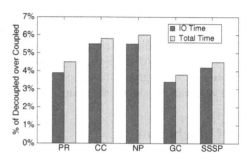

Fig. 9. Extra overhead of RocksDB over *InfiniMem* in our DSM.

size oblivious. When the data allocated to the node does not fit in available memory, the DSM system spills data to local disk and fetches it back to local memory as demanded by the application. When running distributed software speculation with 75 % of the input in memory and the rest spilt to disk, *InfiniMem* has much lower overhead as compared to an alternative solution based upon RocksDB [7]: Fig. 9 shows that RocksDB based programs run up to ~20.5 % slower than using *InfiniMem*. Compared to when all the data fits in memory, *InfiniMem* introduces a small overhead of 5 % over our baseline DSM, i.e. at this small cost, *InfiniMem* makes our DSM size oblivious.

6   Related Work

The closest file organization to that used by *InfiniMem* and illustrated in Fig. 6 is the B+ tree representation used in database systems. The primary differences in our design are the following: (1) *InfiniMem* uses a flat organization, with at most one level index for variable sized data. (2) *InfiniMem* provides O(1) time I/O operations for random access while the B+ trees require O(log n) time.

Out-of-Core Computations – In this paper, we enable applications with very large input data sets to efficiently run on a single multicore machine, with minimal programming effort. The design of the *InfiniMem* transparently enables large datasets become disk-resident while common out-of-core algorithms [5,10,20] *explicitly* do this. As demonstrated with shards, it should be easy to program these techniques with *InfiniMem*.

Processing on a Single Machine – Traditional approaches to large-scale data processing on a single machine involve using machines with very large amounts of memory, while *InfiniMem* does not have that limitation. Examples include Ligra [16], Galois [15], BGL [18], MTGL [3], Spark [21] etc. FlashGraph [6] is a semi-external memory graph processing framework and requires enough memory to hold all the edgelists; *InfiniMem* has no such memory requirements.

GraphChi [11] recently proposed the Parallel Sliding Window model based on *sharded* inputs. Shard format enables a complete subgraph to be loaded in memory, thus avoiding random accesses. GraphChi is designed for and works very well with algorithms that depend on static scheduling. *InfiniMem* is general-purpose and recognizes the need for sequential/batched *and* random input for fixed *and* variable sized data and provides simple APIs for rapid prototyping.

7   Conclusion

We have presented the *InfiniMem* system for enabling *size oblivious programming*. The techniques developed in this paper are incorporated in the versatile general purpose *InfiniMem* library. In addition to various general purpose programs, we also built two more graph processing frameworks on top of *InfiniMem*: (1) with a simple data format and (2) to process GraphChi-style shards. We have shown that *InfiniMem* performance scales well with parallelism, increasing input size and highlight the necessity of concurrent I/O design in a parallel set up. Our experiments show that *InfiniMem* can successfully generate a graph with 7.5 million vertices and 300 million edges (4.5 GB on disk) in 40 min and it performs the PageRank computation on an RMAT graph with 134M vertices and 805M edges (14 GB on disk) an 8-core machine in about 54 min.

References

1. Avery, C.: Giraph: large-scale graph processing infrastructure on hadoop. In: Proceedings of Hadoop Summit. Santa Clara, USA: [sn] (2011)
2. Bader, D.A., Madduri, K.: Gtgraph: A synthetic graph generator suite. Atlanta, GA, February 2006
3. Berry, J., Mackey, G.: The multithreaded graph library (2014)
4. Bu, Y., Borkar, V., Xu, G., Carey, M.J.: A bloat-aware design for big data applications. In: Proceedings of ISMM 2013, pp. 119–130. ACM (2013)
5. Chiang, Y.J., Goodrich, M.T., Grove, E.F., Tamassia, R., Vengroff, D.E., Vitter, J.S.: External-memory graph algorithms. In: Proceedings of SODA 1995, pp. 139–149 (1995)

6. Da Zheng, D.M., Burns, R., Vogelstein, J., Priebe, C.E., Szalay, A.S.: Flashgraph: processing billion-node graphs on an array of commodity SSDs. In: FAST (2015)
7. Facebook: RocksDB Project. http://RocksDB.org
8. Gonzalez, J.E., Low, Y., Gu, H., Bickson, D., Guestrin, C.: Powergraph: Distributed graph-parallel computation on natural graphs. In: OSDI 2012, pp. 17–30 (2012)
9. Koduru, S.-C., Vora, K., Gupta, R.: Optimizing caching DSM for distributed software speculation. In: Proceedings of Cluster Computing (2015)
10. Kundeti, V.K., et al.: Efficient parallel and out of core algorithms for constructing large bi-directed de bruijn graphs. BMC bioinform. **11**(1), 560 (2010)
11. Kyrola, A., Blelloch, G., Guestrin, C.: Graphchi: Large-scale graph computation on just a PC. In: Proceedings of the 10th USENIX Symposium on OSDI, pp. 31–46 (2012)
12. Low, Y., Gonzalez, J., Kyrola, A., Bickson, D., Guestrin, C., Hellerstein, J.M.: Graphlab: A new framework for parallel machine learning. (2010). arXiv:1006.4990
13. Malewicz, G., et al.: Pregel: a system for large-scale graph processing. In: Proceedings of the 2010 ACM SIGMOD ICMD, pp. 135–146. ACM (2010)
14. Page, L., Brin, S., Motwani, R., Winograd, T.: The pagerank citation ranking: Bringing order to the web (1999)
15. Pingali, K., Nguyen, D., Kulkarni, M., Burtscher, M., Hassaan, M.A., Kaleem, R., Lee, T.H., Lenharth, A., Manevich, R., Méndez-Lojo, M., et al.: The tao of parallelism in algorithms. ACM SIGPLAN Not. **46**, 12–25 (2011)
16. Shun, J., Blelloch, G.E.: Ligra: a lightweight graph processing framework for shared memory. In: Proceedings of PPopp 2013, pp. 135–146. ACM (2013)
17. Shvachko, K., Kuang, H., Radia, S., Chansler, R.: The hadoop distributed filesystem. In: IEEE MSST 2010, pp. 1–10 (2010)
18. Siek, J., Lee, L., Lumsdaine, A.: The boost graph library (BGL) (2000)
19. Team, T., et al.: Apache mahout project (2014). https://mahout.apace.org
20. Toledo, S.: A survey of out-of-core algorithms in numerical linear algebra. Extern. Mem. Algorithms Vis. **50**, 161–179 (1999)
21. Zaharia, M., Chowdhury, M., Franklin, M.J., Shenker, S., Stoica, I.: Spark:cluster computing with working sets. In: Proceedings of HotCloud 2010, vol. 10, p. 10 (2010)

Low-Overhead Fault-Tolerance Support Using DISC Programming Model

Mehmet Can Kurt[1]([✉]), Bin Ren[2], and Gagan Agrawal[1]

[1] Department of Computer Science and Engineering,
The Ohio State University, Columbus, OH, USA
{kurt,agrawal}@cse.ohio-state.edu
[2] Pacific Northwest National Laboratory, Richland, WA, USA
bin.ren@pnnl.gov

Abstract. DISC is a newly proposed parallel programming paradigm that models many classes of iterative scientific applications through specification of a domain and interactions among domain elements. Accompanied with an associated runtime, it hides the details of inter-process communication and work partitioning (including partitioning in the presence of heterogeneous processing elements) from the programmers. In this paper, we show how these abstractions, particularly the concepts of *compute-function* and *computation-space* objects, can be also used to leverage low-overhead fault-tolerance support. While *computation-space* objects enable automated application level checkpointing, replicated execution of *compute-functions* helps detect soft errors with low overheads. Experimental results show the effectiveness of the proposed solutions.

1 Introduction

High performance computing is undergoing a significant transformation in the sense that resilience is becoming as equally important as performance. Computing power is constantly being increased with more number of cores, hence with more parallelism. This trend results in a significant decrease in Mean Time To Failure (MTTF) rates in HPC systems due to the large number of components. At the same time, parallel machines are becoming more memory and I/O bound. These two trends together are implying that resilience is not only a major problem, but also the commonly used solutions for fault-tolerance, mostly based on system-level checkpointing, are becoming too expensive. The total cost of fault-tolerance support with checkpointing, which is the sum of the costs of taking checkpoints (which increases as checkpointing frequency increases), the net time spent on recomputation (which increases as checkpointing frequency decreases), and the time spent on restart after a failure, can dominate the actual execution time. An analysis of a 100,000 core job, where each node has a MTTF of 5 years, indicates that these three costs can add up to 65 % of the total execution time, i.e. only 35 % of the time will be productively used [10]. Technology trends indicate that this situation will only get worse in the near future in the sense that MTTF

© Springer International Publishing Switzerland 2016
X. Shen et al. (Eds.): LCPC 2015, LNCS 9519, pp. 20–36, 2016.
DOI: 10.1007/978-3-319-29778-1_2

values will become so small that the time required to complete a checkpoint can exceed the MTTF making the existing approach completely inapplicable [4].

Moreover, in recent years, there is a growing concern about a new class of failures, namely, soft errors. These errors involve bit flips in either processing cores, the memory, or the disk. Although radiation has been considered the main cause of such random bit flips [20], use of smaller and smaller transistors and efforts to improve power-efficiency in hardware are now attributed as the cause of these faults occurring more frequently [25]. Many recent publications have summarized the observed frequency of these faults [10], for example, double bit flips (which cannot be corrected by Error Correcting Codes) occur daily at a national lab's Cray XT5, and similarly, such errors were frequent in BG/L's unprotected L1 cache. Although the traditional solutions to deal with soft errors have been implemented at the hardware level, clearly there is a need for software solutions to this problem.

These developments are imposing new challenges for application programmers. On one hand, they need to be able to manually implement efficient application-level checkpointing and recovery. Even more challenging for them is to implement techniques for dealing with soft errors. One pressing question is whether programming models can help automate fault-tolerant solutions.

In this paper, we address this question in the context of the DISC programming model recently developed by the authors. DISC [15] is a programming model and associated runtime system based on *domain* and *domain element* interaction concepts and particularly targets iterative scientific applications with structured grids, unstructured grids and N-body simulation patterns. While these applications have different communication patterns, they are similar in an important way, i.e., they have an underlying domain, and most of the computation occurs due to the interactions among domain elements. Our programming model supports an API by which the domain, interaction among domain elements, and functions for updating any attributes of these domain elements can be explicitly specified. Starting from this model, inter-process partitioning of the work and the communication is handled automatically by the runtime system. Our previous work has shown how the system is almost as efficient as MPI for homogeneous clusters, while allowing repartitioning of work for dealing with heterogenous configurations.

In this paper, we examine another important application of this programming model. We extended DISC model so that it also leverages low-overhead fault-tolerance support. We show that the abstractions that DISC model provides to hide the details of process communication and work partitioning/re-partitioning help also identify the main execution state and the functions that are the most susceptible to soft errors. Exposure of such vital program state and instructions is utilized in order to implement two fault-tolerance mechanisms within the runtime. First, with the concept of *computation-space* objects, DISC API makes it feasible to support automated, yet efficient, application-level checkpointing. This as a result can reduce checkpointing overheads significantly. Second, with the concept of *compute-functions*, DISC runtime is capable of detecting soft errors using a partial replication strategy. Here, only the set of instructions most likely to corrupt the main execution state is executed with redundancy and the results are compared efficiently with computed checksums.

To show the effectiveness of our approach, we have developed two stencil computations, one unstructured grid based computation, and a molecular dynamics mini-application (MiniMD, a representative of a full-scale molecular dynamics application). We first compare the cost of checkpointing in our model, against system-level checkpointing in MPI (which is the only automated solution available today). Next, we compare the performance of DISC implementations with replication support to normal execution without any redundancy and show how further improvements in replication overheads can be achieved.

2   Related Work

Fault-tolerance for high performance computing against hard errors has been extensively studied. Much of this research specifically targets MPI [1,3,6,12,14, 17,26]. Recent efforts on optimizing the process include combination of coordinated and uncoordinated checkpointing [23] and compression for reducing the overheads of checkpointing [13]. Another approach is algorithm-level fault-tolerance [2,5,7,19], where properties of an algorithm are exploited (typically to build-in redundancy). While this approach can overcome many of the overheads of general checkpointing, it has two key limitations: (1) as the name suggests, the solution is very specific to a particular algorithm, and (2) the fault-tolerant algorithm needs to be implemented by the programmer manually while developing the application. As for soft errors, the general detection approach is through redundant execution. This redundancy can be achieved at various levels. For instance, in [18], each computing node in execution is paired with a buddy node that performs the same work. Paired nodes checkpoint and exchange their local state periodically and the resulting computations in paired nodes are cross compared through their respective checkpoints. [10] provides a new MPI implementation that creates replica MPI tasks and performs online verification during communication only on MPI messages. Studies in [22,24] execute all dynamic instructions in a program twice by redundant threads and compare the first and second result. If there is a mismatch, both threads restart execution from the faulty instruction. There have been some efforts to reduce the overheads associated with redundancy; [27] exploits high-level program information at compile time to minimize data communication between redundant threads, whereas [21] explores the partial redundant threading spectrum, in which only a dynamic subset of instructions is duplicated to near single threaded execution performance at the expense of limited fault coverage. [9] combines redundant threading with symptom-based detectors by quantifying the likelihood that a soft-error impacting an instruction creates a symptom such as branch mispredicts or cache misses. Resultingly, it only duplicates the instructions that can not generate any such symptoms. Although the proposed solutions achieve significant reductions in associated overheads, none of them attempts to implement redundancy at the programming model level. As we show in next sections, proper abstractions at programming model level can expose the most vital program state and instructions and can help automate redundant execution with small overheads.

3   DISC Programming Model

In this section, we present the key concepts of DISC programming model as a background for next section which explains how its abstractions leverage low-overhead fault-tolerance support.

3.1   Domain and Subdomain

DISC model treats the entire input space of an application as a multidimensional *domain*, which consists of *domain elements*. At the beginning of execution, programmers provide information about the domain. This information is used to initialize the runtime system and it includes (1) whether the domain represents a structured grid, an unstructured grid or a particle set, (2) number of dimensions and boundary values for each dimension and (3) the type of interaction among domain elements. Once this information is passed to the runtime, it decomposes the entire domain into non-overlapping rectilinear regions referred as *subdomains* and assigns each subdomain to a processing unit. Since subdomain decomposition and assignment is performed by the runtime, it is able to hold a high-level view of the domain.

As a concrete example, consider a molecular dynamics application such as MiniMD which simulates the motion of a large number of atoms in three-dimensional space throughout a predefined number of time-steps. When implemented using DISC model, the three-dimensional space is treated as an N-body simulation domain and each atom in the simulation corresponds to a domain element. DISC runtime for MiniMD is initialized with the following lines of code;

```
// provide domain information and initialize DISC runtime
DomainProps props;
props.set_ndims(3); // number of dimensions
props.set_min_bounds(0, 0, 0); // x, y, z min−bounds
props.set_max_bounds(XMAX, YMAX, ZMAX); // x, y, z max−bounds
NBodyDomain domain(props);
```

3.2   Attributes

Each domain element in a DISC domain has associated coordinate values. In some domain types such as structured grids, coordinate values of domain elements might stay fixed during the entire execution and can be inferred directly from the boundary values of assigned subdomains. However, for other domain types, they might be updated periodically and their initial values should be explicitly provided by programmers. In addition to coordinates, each domain element can also be associated with a set of *attributes*. For instance, each atom in MiniMD has three additional attributes that store velocity values of the corresponding atom on x, y and z axis. The key advantage of DISC model is its ability to perform data exchange operations based on the interaction pattern automatically and to re-partition the domain on the fly in presence of heterogeneity by migrating domain elements within the domain. To fulfill both of these promises, programmers register coordinates and attributes of domain elements within each subdomain via DISC API, so that the runtime is informed of the data structures that maintain associated information on each domain element. Using the same example, the code snippet below shows how attributes of domain elements in MiniMD are passed to the runtime through DISC objects called *DoubleAttribute*;

```
DoubleAttribute velocities[3]; // x, y, z velocities
/* fill in attribute object velocities with initial values of x, y, z velocities */
domain.register_attributes(&velocities);
```

3.3   Compute-Function and Computation-Space

In DISC model, each processing unit performs computations for the assigned portion of the domain. In other words, the domain elements that a processing unit processes lie within the boundaries of the subdomain that has been assigned to it by the runtime. DISC requires programmers to express underlying computation, which typically comprises of calculating new values for attributes associated with domain elements, in a single or a set of functions referred as *compute-functions*. Compute-functions generally host the portion of code on which most of the execution time is spent. Programmers specify these functions by passing function pointers to the runtime. At each iteration during a program's execution, the runtime invokes these functions in the order that they are specified.

For each compute-function, programmers explicitly declare one or more objects called *computation-space*. A computation-space object coupled with a compute-function stores the results of computation carried out by that function. It generally contains an entry for each domain element in the corresponding subdomain and programmers perform any updates related to the domain elements directly on the computation-space object itself. This way, the runtime is aware of what additional data structures along with coordinates and attributes describe the domain elements in a subdomain completely. This abstraction leverages automated migration of domain elements within the domain if needed. Note that mapping a value in computation-space to the corresponding domain element can be inferred from domain type in most cases. Otherwise, programmers can pass additional functions to the runtime that dictate this mapping.

In MiniMD, atoms interact with other atoms in a given radius and this interaction results in recomputation of coordinates and velocities of each atom at every time-step. The code snippet below reflects this by defining six computation-space objects (three for new coordinates and three for new velocities). These objects are coupled with the compute-function *minimd_kernel* and passed to the runtime via DISC API;

DoubleAttribute computation_space[6]; // new x, y, z coords and velocities
domain.add_compute_function(minimd_kernel, &computation_space);

3.4   Interaction Between Domain Elements

As indicated before, a key advantage of DISC model is that the runtime handles communication automatically based on the type of interaction between domain elements. Currently, DISC model supports three types of communication; based on nearest neighbor interactions in stencil kernels, based on radius-based interactions in molecular dynamics applications and based on a list provided explicitly by programmers that dictates pair-wise sinteractions. Further details for runtime communication generation can be found in [15].

4   Fault-Tolerance Support

We now describe two fault-tolerance approaches that have been implemented for the applications developed using DISC model.

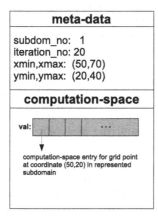

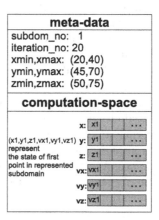

(a) Structured Grid   (b) Particle Set

Fig. 1. Sample checkpoint files for a 2D stencil (a) and 3D molecular dynamics application (b). Both files consist of two parts as meta-data and computation-space objects.

4.1   Checkpointing

DISC model automates application-level checkpointing, alleviating the need for expensive system-level checkpointing that is normally used for programming models like MPI. Like any checkpointing-based approach, we assume the existence of a persistent storage where the checkpoint files can be written into.

Two important questions for application-level checkpointing are: (1) when should checkpoints be taken, and (2) what data structures will be needed to restart the computation in case of a failure, and therefore, need to be check-pointed. It turns out that the DISC model simplifies these decisions. Particu-larly, the end of an iteration of the time-step loop (after data exchange and main computation have been completed by the runtime system) is a natural point for taking the checkpoint. Compared to system-level checkpointing, we get a coordinated checkpoint (in the sense that there is no need for message log-ging for recovery), while not requiring any time-consuming coordination between processes.

Now, let us return to the question of which data structures need to be check-pointed. DISC model encapsulates the computational progress made on each domain element in objects that we introduced in previous section; *attribute* and *computation-space* objects. At each iteration, attribute objects store the cur-rent information associated with domain elements, whereas computation-space objects capture the updates on them performed through compute-functions. As a concrete example, if we consider MiniMD, after each time-step, the attributes and the computation-space objects contain previous and updated coordinate and velocity values of each atom. The collection of attribute and computation-space objects represent the main execution state of applications at any given time. This collection along with the high-level information such as initial domain decompo-sition (boundaries of each subdomain) can be used to recover the state of DISC runtime and the underlying application completely.

If an application has multiple compute-functions, not all computation-space objects may be live at the end of an iteration of the time-step loop, i.e., cer-tain computation-space objects could have been consumed already. Moreover, some of the attribute objects might entirely depend on and be calculated from a small set of remaining attributes without incurring a significant recomputa-tion cost. This implies that during failure recovery not all of the attributes and computation-space objects are needed to recreate the execution state of domain elements. Some of them can be ignored by the checkpointing mechanism to save bandwidth, hence time, and also storage space. While compiler analysis can pro-vide this information, our model currently asks the programmers to explicitly annotate this information by passing additional arguments during instantiation of these objects. This way, programmers can explore the tradeoff space in check-pointing the entire domain state vs. recalculation of a small portion from saved data structures. Note that any other application state besides the ones associated directly with domain elements should be explicitly checkpointed by program-mers. However, considering the computation patterns that DISC model targets, such additional state is limited and recomputed efficiently from checkpointed attribute and computation-space objects.

Checkpointing frequency as well as other important information like the file path where the checkpoint files will reside can be set via DISC API. We insert some meta-data information to the head of checkpoint files including the current iteration number, and also the boundaries of the subdomain that attribute and computation-space objects represent. This meta-data is utilized to reconstruct the application state during recovery. Figures 1(a) and (b) illustrate the content of sample checkpoint files, which are taken at the 20th iteration of a 2D stencil grid computation and a 3D molecular dynamics application. In both (a) and (b), only the computation-space objects are saved.

Recovery. During recovery from a failure, DISC model is able to restart the computation both with the same or a fewer number of processes, unlike the current checkpointing approaches in MPI, which can only allow restart with the same number of processes. For instance, assuming that there are N processing units in the system before the failure, if the computation is restarted with a fewer number of nodes, say $N - 1$, the domain is decomposed into $N - 1$ subdomains.

Whether with the same or fewer number of nodes, the most critical operation for recovery is to recreate the computational state of a subdomain from existing checkpoint files. If a processing unit has been assigned the same subdomain as before, it will be sufficient to access that subdomain's checkpoint file and load its content into computation-space object in entirety. However, after decomposition, a change in subdomain boundaries is very likely. Therefore, each processing unit may need to read several checkpoint files. In such cases, the metadata information mentioned previously is utilized to filter down the checkpoint files either completely or at least partially, i.e. we check if there is an intersection between processing unit's newly assigned subdomain and the boundaries of the subdomain that the checkpointed computation-space object represents.

Once computation-space objects for the new domain have been reconstructed from the checkpoint files, application can restart from the iteration in which the last checkpoint was taken.

4.2   Replication

Soft error detection has drawn significant attention from community in recent years. Such error detection could be from a variety of sources including hardware or software error detection codes such as ECC, symptom-based error detectors [11] and application-level assertions. One approach to detect such errors is to create two or more independent threads of execution and compare the execution state of different threads. This work has been done at multiple levels – replication at process level [10] or replication at the instruction level [9]. However, trivial replication of the entire program execution and comparison of resulting computation might incur significant overheads. We claim that concepts of *compute-functions* and *computation-space* objects in DISC model can be used to implement a partial replication strategy to reduce associated overheads substantially.

As emphasized before, compute-functions contain the lines of code to which majority of program execution time is devoted. A soft error in combinatorial logic components including register values, ALUs and pipeline latches is most likely to occur when processing cores carry out the instructions expressed in compute-functions. Since computations, and hence updates on domain elements, defined in compute-functions are directly reflected on the computation-space objects coupled with them, a soft error occurring during the execution of these functions eventually corrupts the computation-space objects, either directly and transitively. This observation suggests that soft errors can be efficiently detected by replication of compute-functions only and cross-comparison of their associated computation-space objects after each iteration. Note that replication mechanism described next assumes that processor components other than the memory are susceptible to soft errors. A produced value is assumed to be resilient once it leaves the processor and is stored back in memory. Control flow variables and memory references are protected by other means such as invariant assertions against the possibility of causing fatal errors such as segmentation faults. Hence, we mainly protect execution against soft errors on calculated values that are used to update computation-space objects.

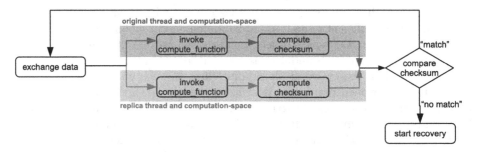

Fig. 2. Flow of execution at each iteration when replication strategy is in use.

Replication Mechanism. Figure 2 demonstrates the execution flow at each iteration when this partial replication strategy is implemented in the DISC runtime. After data exchange operations are performed, the runtime splits the main execution thread into two as *original* and *replica*. Each thread is associated with its own computation-space object, but they both invoke the same compute-function in parallel. During compute-function execution, both original and replica threads use the same set of input space, i.e. attributes of domain elements and any global data structures in application code. Sharing the same memory space, except the computation-space objects, leads to a significant reduction in overall memory footprint of replication strategy.

Currently, the replication strategy in DISC model makes the assumption that compute-functions provided by the programmer are side-effect free, meaning that they do not modify any global data structures. This is mainly to avoid possible race conditions. Note that one can synchronize original and replica threads by pragma directives with respect to the threading library used by the DISC runtime.

Checksum Calculation. After both threads finish executing the compute-function, they calculate a checksum value over their own computation-space object. We employ integer module operation as the checksum function. Regardless of their data type, we treat the bit representation of values in computation-space objects as an integer and accumulate them into a single sum [16]. After checksum calculation, the two threads merge and checksum values are compared by the main thread. If the values match, application advances to the next iteration. Otherwise, DISC runtime ceases the execution and informs the programmer that a soft error has been detected and a recovery procedure should be initiated.

Improvements for Cache Utilization. The initial replication scheme calculates checksums over computation-space objects once individual threads finish execution of compute-functions. Although checksum calculation can be performed quite efficiently, especially in architectures with vector units, accessing the entire computation-space objects once again leads to a large number of cache misses, and hence to high overheads, especially when computation-space objects are large. To remedy this, we present an improvement on top of the plain replication scheme presented previously. Instead of performing it in a separate step, we incorporate checksum calculation directly into compute-functions. Particularly, pure compute-functions provided by programmers are modified in a way that entries in a computation-space object contribute to the checksum on the fly, right after they are assigned a value. *On the fly checksum calculation* increases temporal locality of overall replication strategy and helps us avoid the data access costs incurred by an isolated checksum calculation phase.

Another source of overhead is the need to create a second copy of computation-space objects. Having additional computation-space objects for replica threads both increases the total memory footprint and at the same time diminishes overall cache utilization. Thus, as a second improvement, we avoid creating replica computation-space objects by modifying compute-functions further. Particularly, assignments to computation-space objects in replica thread are replaced by instructions that accumulate the assigned variables to the checksum values instead. Having *no replica computation-space object* in replica threads results in further improvements in data locality. In the next section, we demonstrate how these two optimizations affect performance of replication strategy, especially for applications with large output space.

5   Experiments

In this section, we present results from a number of experiments we conducted to evaluate the fault-tolerance solutions that we implemented within DISC model. Our evaluation is based on four applications. We chose one molecular dynamics application (MiniMD), one application involving an unstructured grid (Euler), and two smaller kernels involving stencil computations (Jacobi and Sobel).

5.1   Checkpointing

One of the key advantages of DISC model is the support for automated application-level checkpointing. We now show how the cost of checkpointing with our approach

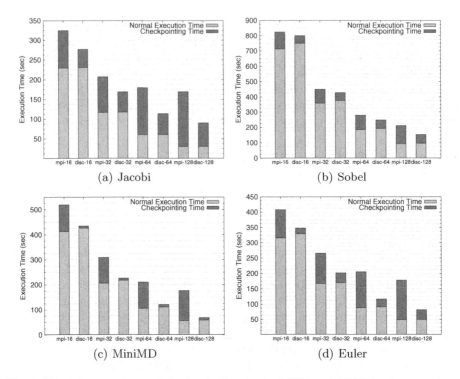

Fig. 3. Normal execution and checkpointing times of MPI and DISC implementations of four applications with varying number of nodes.

compares with the only automated solution currently available with MPI, which is system-level checkpointing. Moreover, we also examine how the total execution time of our system and MPI versions compare, when checkpointing overheads are included.

For checkpointing support in MPI implementations, we used MPICH2-BLCR, which is one of the most popular system-level checkpoint/restart libraries. MPI versions of all evaluated applications have been written by ourselves, except MiniMD which was obtained from the Mantevo suite[1]. Experiments in this section are performed on a cluster where each node has two quad-core 2.53 GHz Intel(R) Xeon(R) processors, with 12 GB RAM, executing RedHat Enterprise Linux Server release 6.1, and Gigabit ethernet as the interconnect. Our programming model is implemented in C++ language and uses MPICH2 (version 1.4.1p1) as the underlying communication library. The comparisons have been performed over a varying number of nodes ranging between 16 and 128 (with only one core at each node), consistent with our focus on distributed memory parallelism. Both in this and next section, we repeated each experiment 5 times and report the average results.

---

[1] Please see https://software.sandia.gov/mantevo.

Figure 3(a) and (b) demonstrate the execution times of Jacobi and Sobel, as we increase the number of nodes. Gray portions of the bars correspond to normal execution times, whereas red portion on top of each bar shows the additional time spent for checkpointing. For both applications, we use a grid structure with 400 million elements, execute them for 1000 iterations and trigger checkpoint mechanism every 250 iterations. Compared to the MPI versions, our model's implementations have average overheads less than 1 % for Jacobi and 4 % for Sobel in normal execution times. The size of each global checkpoint in Jacobi and Sobel is 6 GB for MPI and 3 GB for our model. Corresponding figures show that checkpointing operations in our model are completed approximately in half of the time than MPI.

Figure 3(c) and (d) report the same results for MiniMD and Euler. In MiniMD, we simulate the behavior of 4 million atoms, whereas we use 12 million nodes for Euler. We run each application for up to 1000 iterations and take checkpoints every 100 iterations. Results show that implementing MiniMD and Euler with DISC brings an average overhead less than 5 % in normal execution without checkpointing. In MiniMD, each global checkpoint of MPI version is nearly 2 GB in size, whereas with our programming model, the application-level checkpoint is only 192 MB. Consequently, on the average, checkpointing time of MPI is nearly 12 times higher. As the number of nodes increases, checkpointing times increase, due to the fact that more nodes are contending for pushing the data to file system at the same time. In Euler, the global snapshot size is again 2 GB for MPI, and 640 MB with our programming model. As a result, the time required for checkpointing in MPI is nearly 4 times higher.

It is also useful to note that in all cases, after adding the normal execution and checkpointing times, our model is faster. In some of the cases, particularly, execution of MiniMD and Euler on 128 nodes, our model reduces the total execution time at least by a factor of 2, when checkpointing overheads are included. Furthermore, we can see that with increasing number of nodes, as well as with increasing complexity of applications, the relative advantage of our model increases. The former is because of increasing contention for I/O related to checkpointing, whereas, the latter is because a full application has many more structures than those that need to be checkpointed at the application level. Because Jacobi and Sobel are small templates, the application-level checkpoint is nearly 50 % of the size of system-level checkpoint. In comparison, for a more complex application like MiniMD, the ratio is close to 10 %. Thus, we can see that for most applications, we can expect significant performance from our model.

5.2   Replication

Next, we present the results for DISC implementations of the previous applications, when we replicate compute-function execution in each process. We evaluate our partial replication approach on Intel Xeon Phi 7110P many-core coprocessor. The reason for choosing this architecture is that many-core systems are likely to

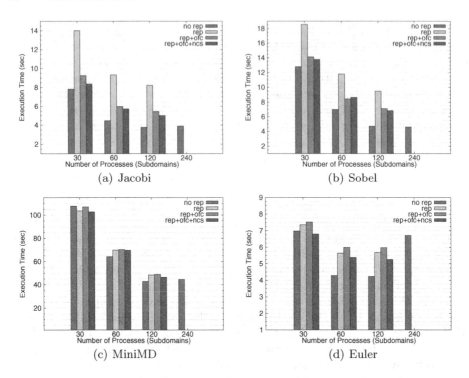

Fig. 4. Execution times of four applications without any replication (*no rep*), with plain replication (*rep*) and replication with improvements for cache utilization (*rep+ofc* and *rep+ofc+ncs*). Execution times for *no rep* with 1 process are 307.9, 398.9, 2686.2 and 213.2 s in Jacobi, Sobel, MiniMD and Euler, respectively. The same execution times for the best replication version *rep+ofc+ncs* are 316.2, 474.5, 2738.3 and 214.8 s.

be common in the exascale era, where soft errors will also be more likely. Specifically, the coprocessor we have used has 61 cores running at 1.1 GHz with 32KB L1 cache, 512 KB L2 cache per core and 8GB device memory for all cores, and is capable of running 244 hardware threads with hyperthreading support. All applications were compiled by Intel icpc-13.1.0 compiler with -O3 optimization with auto vectorization flag on. Each process replicates the compute-function execution step using OpenMP multi-threading library. We run all applications for 100 iterations. To mitigate the impact of system noise, we dedicate core0 of Xeon Phi to the OS and pin DISC processes to hardware threads between core1 and core60. Original and replica threads in each process are pinned to the same core, except configurations where we have 1 and 30 processes.

Figure 4(a) and (b) present the replication results for Jacobi and Sobel. For each application, we compare the performance of four DISC versions; (1) execution without any replication (*no rep*), (2) execution with plain replication (*rep*), (3) execution with replication and on the fly checksum calculation (*rep+ofc*), and finally (4) execution with replication, on the fly checksum calculation and no replica computation-space (*rep+ofc+ncs*). All DISC versions are run with 1,

30, 60, 120 processes. For 240 processes, we only report the results for no replication version, since the replication versions utilize all of the 240 hardware threads with 120 processes. The figure shows that for Jacobi at 120 processes DISC replication versions *rep*, *rep+ofc* and *rep+ofc+ncs* have 118 %, 44 % and 33 % overheads, respectively, over execution with no replication. Note that because the 240 thread *no rep* version does not have better performance over the 120 thread version, the results from 120 threads can be used to establish overheads of replication over the most efficient execution without replication. For Sobel, with the same number of processes, the overheads are 102 %, 51 % and 45 %. These results indicate that two improvements over the plain replication scheme lead to significant reductions in total overhead by reducing data access costs during checksum calculation and improving overall cache utilization.

Figure 4(c) and (d) present the results for MiniMD and Euler. At 120 processes, DISC replication strategy causes 13 %, 15 % and 9 % overheads in MiniMD, respectively for *rep*, *rep+ofc* and *rep+ofc+ncs* versions. In Euler, the same overheads are 34 %, 41 % and 24 %. Although the overheads with the plain replication version itself is quite small, we see that the suggested improvements do not lead to substantial benefits compared to Jacobi and Sobel. This is mainly due to the fact that computation-space objects in MiniMD and Euler have a smaller size and they fit in the L2 cache of Xeon Phi cores. Another potential reason is the following. Xeon Phi employs software and hardware-based data prefetching to reduce data access latencies. The prefetching mechanism works very aggressively for stencil kernels and accessing the same data within a core both by original and replica threads might lead to capacity and conflict misses. Furthermore, an existing analysis on Xeon Phi in [8] reports drops in bandwidth when different threads access the same memory space simultaneously due to the effects of contention at the interconnect level. Hence, we believe that any data locality optimization such as *on the fly checksum calculation* and *no replica computation-space object* for kernels such as stencils result in substantial improvements. On the other hand, due to the irregular data access patterns in MiniMD and Euler, the amount of data prefetching is limited. The overhead for plain replication is not too high to begin with and the improvements in *rep+ofc* and *rep+ofc+ncs* versions are less visible.

Table 1. Error detection rates for plain replication (*rep*) and replication with on the fly checksum and no replica computation-space object (*rep+ofc+ncs*) versions both without and with soft error injection.

	Normal execution		With error injection	
	rep	rep+ofc+ncs	rep	rep+ofc+ncs
Jacobi	0 %	0 %	100 %	100 %
Sobel	0 %	0 %	100 %	100 %
MiniMD	0 %	0 %	100 %	100 %
Euler	0 %	0 %	24 %	100 %

As the last experiment, we show how effective DISC partial replication strategy is in detecting soft errors. Table 1 reports error detection rates when the four applications are run both when there is no soft error occurrence during execution and when a single soft error is injected. Error injection is done manually by flipping a single bit of a random stack variable during the execution of compute-functions. We repeat the same experimental setup for two versions; plain replication (*rep*) and replication with on the fly checksum and no replica computation-space (*rep+ofc+ncs*). Each configuration is performed 50 times and error detection rates show how many times DISC detected an error in these runs as a percentage. Results show that when there is no soft error injection, error detection rate for both versions is 0 % meaning that DISC replication strategy does not produce any false positives. Moreover, in Jacobi, Sobel and MiniMD, both versions are able to detect injected soft errors and achieve 100 % error detection rate. As the only exception, in Euler, plain replication version detects only 24 % of injected errors, whereas *rep+ofc+ncs* again achieves a 100 % detection rate. This is due to the fact that in Euler each corrupted stack variable makes two contributions to the computation-space objects, one being positive and the other negative. When checksums are calculated in plain replication scheme, positive and negative contributions seem to cancel out each other reducing overall detection rate. In contrary, *rep+ofc+ncs* version is insusceptible to such cancellation, since checksums are calculated by using the corrupted assigned values directly and ignoring their sign.

6   Conclusion

In this paper, we presented how DISC, a parallel programming model for iterative scientific applications based on structured, unstructured grids and N-body simulations, is extended to leverage low-overhead fault-tolerance support. We showed that the existing abstractions in DISC model for automated inter-process communication and work partitioning/re-partitioning can be also used for automated application-level checkpointing and replicated execution to detect soft error occurrences. The experimental evaluation shows that checkpointing in DISC model provides significant improvements over system-level checkpointing scheme and soft errors can be detected by a partial replication strategy with low overheads.

Acknowledgments. This work was supported by National Science Foundation under the award CCF-1319420, and by the Department of Energy, Office of Science, under award DE-SC0014135.

References

1. Agbaria, A., Friedman, R.: Starfish: fault-tolerant dynamic MPI programs on clusters of workstations. In: 1999 Proceedings of the Eighth International Symposium on High Performance Distributed Computing, pp. 167–176 (1999)

2. Arnold, D., Miller, B.: Scalable failure recovery for high-performance data aggregation. In: 2010 IEEE International Symposium on Parallel Distributed Processing (IPDPS), pp. 1–11, April 2010
3. Bouteiller, A., Cappello, F., Herault, T., Krawezik, G., Lemarinier, P., Magniette, F.: MPICH-V project: a multiprotocol automatic fault tolerant MPI. Int. J. High Perform. Comput. Appl. **20**(3), 319–333 (2006)
4. Cappello, F.: Fault tolerance in petascale/ exascale systems: Current knowledge, challenges and research opportunities. Int. J. High Perform. Comput. Appl. **23**(3), 212–226 (2009)
5. Chen, Z.: Algorithm-based recovery for iterative methods without checkpointing. In: Proceedings of the 20th International Symposium on High Performance Distributed Computing, HPDC 2011, pp. 73–84. ACM, New York (2011)
6. Coti, C., Herault, T., Lemarinier, P., Pilard, L., Rezmerita, A., Rodriguez, E., Cappello, F.: Blocking vs. non-blocking coordinated checkpointing for large-scale fault tolerant MPI. In: Proceedings of the ACM/IEEE Conference on Supercomputing, SC 2006. ACM, New York (2006)
7. Davies, T., Karlsson, C., Liu, H., Ding, C., Chen, Z.: High performance linpack benchmark: A fault tolerant implementation without checkpointing. In: Proceedings of the International Conference on Supercomputing, ICS 2011, pp. 162–171. ACM, New York (2011)
8. Fang, J., Varbanescu, A.L., Sips, H., Zhang, L., Che, Y., Xu, C.: An Empirical Study of Intel Xeon Phi. ArXiv e-prints, October 2013
9. Feng, S., Gupta, S., Ansari, A., Mahlke, S.: Shoestring: Probabilistic soft error reliability on the cheap. SIGPLAN Not. **45**(3), 385–396 (2010)
10. Fiala, D., Mueller, F., Engelmann, C., Riesen, R., Ferreira, K., Brightwell, R.: Detection and correction of silent data corruption for large-scale high-performance computing. In: Proceedings of the International Conference on High Performance Computing, Networking, Storage and Analysis, SC 2012, pp. 78:1–78:12. IEEE Computer Society Press, Los Alamitos (2012)
11. Hari, S.K.S., Adve, S.V., Naeimi, H.: Low-cost program-level detectors for reducing silent data corruptions. In: DSN, pp. 1–12 (2012)
12. Hursey, J., Squyres, J., Mattox, T., Lumsdaine, A.: The design and implementation of checkpoint/restart process fault tolerance for open MPI. In: IEEE International Parallel and Distributed Processing Symposium, IPDPS 2007. pp. 1–8, March 2007
13. Islam, T.Z., Mohror, K., Bagchi, S., Moody, A., de Supinski, B.R., Eigenmann, R.: Mcrengine: A scalable checkpointing system using data-aware aggregation and compression. In: Proceedings of the International Conference on High Performance Computing, Networking, Storage and Analysis, SC 2012, pp. 17:1–17:11. IEEE Computer Society Press, Los Alamitos (2012)
14. Kranzlmüller, D., Kacsuk, P., Dongarra, J.: Recent advances in parallel virtual machine and message passing interface. Int. J. High Perform. Comput. Appl. **19**(2), 99–101 (2005)
15. Kurt, M.C., Agrawal, G.: Disc: A domain-interaction based programming model with support for heterogeneous execution. In: Proceedings of the International Conference for High Performance Computing, Networking, Storage and Analysis, SC 2014, pp. 869–880. IEEE Press, Piscataway (2014)
16. Maxino, T., Koopman, P.: The effectiveness of checksums for embedded control networks. IEEE Trans. Dependable Secure Comput. **6**(1), 59–72 (2009)

17. Moody, A., Bronevetsky, G., Mohror, K., de Supinski, B.R.: Design, modeling, and evaluation of a scalable multi-level checkpointing system. In: Proceedings of the 2010 ACM/IEEE International Conference for High Performance Computing, Networking, Storage and Analysis, SC 2010, pp. 1–11. IEEE Computer Society, Washington, DC (2010)

18. Ni, X., Meneses, E., Jain, N., Kalé, L.V.: ACR: Automatic checkpoint/restart for soft and hard error protection. In: Proceedings of the International Conference on High Performance Computing, Networking, Storage and Analysis, SC 2013, pp. 7:1–7:12. ACM, New York (2013)

19. Plank, J., Kim, Y., Dongarra, J.: Algorithm-based diskless checkpointing for fault tolerant matrix operations. In: Twenty-Fifth International Symposium on Fault-Tolerant Computing, 1995, FTCS-25. Digest of Papers, pp. 351–360, June 1995

20. Quinn, H., Graham, P.: Terrestrial-based radiation upsets: a cautionary tale. In: 13th Annual IEEE Symposium on Field-Programmable Custom Computing Machines, FCCM 2005, pp. 193–202, April 2005

21. Reddy, V.K., Rotenberg, E., Parthasarathy, S.: Understanding prediction-based partial redundant threading for low-overhead, high- coverage fault tolerance. SIGARCH Comput. Archit. News $34(5)$, 83–94 (2006)

22. Reinhardt, S.K., Mukherjee, S.S.: Transient fault detection via simultaneous multithreading. In: Proceedings of the 27th Annual International Symposium on Computer Architecture, ISCA 2000, pp. 25–36. ACM, New York (2000)

23. Riesen, R., Ferreira, K., Da Silva, D., Lemarinier, P., Arnold, D., Bridges, P.G.: Alleviating scalability issues of checkpointing protocols. In: Proceedings of the International Conference on High Performance Computing, Networking, Storage and Analysis, SC 2012, pp. 18:1–18:11. IEEE Computer Society Press, Los Alamitos (2012)

24. Rotenberg, E.: AR-SMT: a microarchitectural approach to fault tolerance in microprocessors. In: Twenty-Ninth Annual International Symposium on Fault-Tolerant Computing, Digest of Papers, pp. 84–91, June 1999

25. Schroeder, B., Pinheiro, E., Weber, W.-D.: DRAM errors in the wild: A large-scale field study. In: Proceedings of the Eleventh International Joint Conference on Measurement and Modeling of Computer Systems, SIGMETRICS 2009, pp. 193–204. ACM, New York (2009)

26. Stellner, G.: CoCheck: checkpointing and process migration for MPI. In: Proceedings of the 10th International Parallel Processing Symposium, IPPS 1996, pp. 526–531, April 1996

27. Wang, C., Kim, H.-S., Wu, Y., Ying, V.: Compiler-managed software-based redundant multi-threading for transient fault detection. In: Proceedings of the International Symposium on Code Generation and Optimization, CGO 2007, pp. 244–258. IEEE Computer Society, Washington, DC (2007)

Efficient Support for Range Queries and Range Updates Using Contention Adapting Search Trees

Konstantinos Sagonas and Kjell Winblad$^{(\boxtimes)}$

Department of Information Technology, Uppsala University, Uppsala, Sweden
kjell.winblad@it.uu.se

Abstract. We extend contention adapting trees (CA trees), a family of concurrent data structures for ordered sets, to support linearizable range queries, range updates, and operations that atomically operate on multiple keys such as bulk insertions and deletions. CA trees differ from related concurrent data structures by adapting themselves according to the contention level and the access patterns to scale well in a multitude of scenarios. Variants of CA trees with different performance characteristics can be derived by changing their sequential component. We experimentally compare CA trees to state-of-the-art concurrent data structures and show that CA trees beat the best data structures we compare against with up to 57 % in scenarios that contain basic set operations and range queries, and outperform them by more than 1200 % in scenarios that also contain range updates.

1 Introduction

Data intensive applications on multicores need efficient and scalable concurrent data structures. Many concurrent data structures for ordered sets have recently been proposed (e.g [2,4,8,11]) that scale well on workloads containing *single key operations*, e.g. insert, remove and get. However, most of these data structures lack efficient and scalable support for operations that atomically access multiple elements, such as range queries, range updates, bulk insert and remove, which are important for various applications such as in-memory databases. Operations that operate on a single element and those that operate on multiple ones have inherently conflicting requirements. The former achieve better scalability by using fine-grained synchronization, while the latter are better off performance-wise if they employ coarse-grained synchronization. The few data structures with scalable support for some multi-element operations [1,3] have to be parameterized with the granularity of synchronization. Setting this parameter is inherently difficult since the usage patterns and contention level are sometimes impossible

---

Research supported in part by the European Union grant IST-2011-287510 "RELEASE: A High-Level Paradigm for Reliable Large-scale Server Software" and the Linnaeus centre of excellence UPMARC (Uppsala Programming for Multicore Architectures Research Center).

X. Shen et al. (Eds.): LCPC 2015, LNCS 9519, pp. 37–53, 2016.
DOI: 10.1007/978-3-319-29778-1_3

to predict. This is especially true when the data structure is provided as a general purpose library.

Contention adapting trees (*CA trees*) [18] is a new family of concurrent data structures for ordered sets, that adapt their synchronization granularity according to the contention level and the access patterns even when these change dynamically. In this work, we extend CA trees with support for operations that atomically access multiple elements. As we will see, CA trees provide good scalability both in contended and uncontended situations. Moreover they are flexible: CA tree variants with different performance characteristics can be derived by selecting their underlying sequential data structure component. CA trees support the common interfaces of sets, maps and key-value stores as well as range queries, range updates, bulk inserts, bulk removes and other operations that atomically access multiple keys. Experiments on scenarios with a variety of mixes of these operations show that CA trees provide performance that is significantly better than that obtained by state-of-the-art data structures for ordered sets and range queries. All these make CA trees suitable for a multitude of applications, including in-memory databases, key-value stores and general purpose data structure libraries.

Definitions. A *range query* operation atomically takes a snapshot of all elements belonging to a range $[a, b]$ of keys. A *range update* atomically applies an update function to all values associated with keys in a specific key range. A *bulk insert* atomically inserts all elements in a list of keys or key-value pairs. (A *bulk remove* is defined similarly.) We call operations that operate on a range of elements *range operations* and use *multi-element operations* as a general term for operations that atomically access multiple elements.

Overview. We start by reviewing related work (Sect. 2) before we introduce the CA trees in detail (Sect. 3) and compare them experimentally to related data structures (Sect. 4). The paper ends with some discussion and concluding remarks (Sect. 5).

2   Related Work

In principle, concurrent ordered sets with linearizable range operations can be implemented by utilizing software transactional memory (TM): the programmer simply wraps the operations in transactions and lets the TM take care of the concurrency control to ensure that the transactions execute atomically. Even though some scalable data structures have been derived by carefully limiting the size of transactions (e.g. [1,7]), currently transactional memory does not offer a general solution with good scalability; cf. [1].

Brown and Helga have extended the *non-blocking k-ary search tree* [4] to provide lock-free range queries [3]. A k-ary search tree is a search tree where all nodes, both internal and leaves, contain up to k keys. The internal nodes are utilized for searching, and leaf nodes contain all the elements. Range queries are performed in k-ary search trees with immutable leaf nodes by using a scan and a validate step. The scan step scans all leaves containing keys in the range and the validate step checks a dirty bit that is set before a leaf node is replaced by a modifying operation. Range queries are retried if the validation step fails. Unfortunately, non-blocking k-ary search trees provide no efficient way to perform atomic range updates or multi-element modification operations. Additionally, k-ary search trees are not balanced, so pathological inputs can easily make them perform poorly. Robertson investigated the implementation of lock-free range queries in a skip list: range queries increment a version number and a fixed size history of changes is kept in every node [15]. This solution does not scale well because of the centralized version number counter. Also, it does not support range updates.

Functional data structures or copy-on-write is another approach to provide linearizable range queries. Unfortunately, this requires copying all nodes in a path to the root in a tree data structure which induces overhead and makes the root a contended hot spot.

The *Snap tree* data structure [2] provides a fast $\mathcal{O}(1)$ linearizable clone operation by letting subsequent write operations create a new version of the tree. Linearizable range queries can be performed in a Snap tree by first creating a clone and then performing the query in the clone. Snap's clone operation is performed by marking the root node as shared and letting subsequent update operations replace shared nodes while traversing the tree. To ensure that no existing update operation can modify the clone, an epoch object is used. The clone operation forces new updates to wait for a new epoch object by closing the current epoch and then waits for existing modifying operations (that have registered their ongoing operation in the epoch object) before a new epoch object is installed. The *Ctrie* data structure [13] also has a fast clone operation whose implementation and performance characteristics resembles Snap; see [3].

Range operations can be implemented in data structures that utilize fine-grained locking by acquiring all necessary locks. For example, in a tree data structure where all elements reside in leaf nodes, the atomicity of the range operation can be ensured by locking all leaves in the range. This requires locking at least n/k nodes, if the number of elements in the range is n and at most k elements can be stored in every node. When n is large or k is small the performance of this approach is limited by the locking overhead. On the other hand, when n is small or k is large the scalability is limited by coarse-grained locking. In contrast, as we will see, in CA trees k is dynamic and adapted at runtime to provide a good trade-off between scalability and locking overhead.

The *Leaplist* [1] is a concurrent ordered set implementation with native support for range operations. Leaplist is based on a skip list data structure with fat nodes that can contain up to k elements. The efficient implementation of the Leaplist uses transactional memory to acquire locks and to check if read data is valid. The authors of the Leaplist mention that they tried to derive a Leaplist version based purely on fine-grained locking but failed [1], so developing a Leaplist without dependence on STM seems to be difficult. As in trees with fine-grained locking, the size of the locked regions in Leaplists is fixed and does not adapt according to the contention as in CA trees. Furthermore, the performance of CA trees does not depend on the availability and performance of STM.

Operations that atomically operate on multiple keys can be implemented in any data structure by utilizing coarse-grained locking. By using a readers-writer lock, one can avoid acquiring an exclusive lock of the data structure for some operations. Unfortunately, locking the whole data structure is detrimental to scalability if the data structure is contended. The advantage of coarse-grained locking is that it provides the performance of the protected sequential data structure in the uncontended case. As we will soon see, CA trees provide the high performance of coarse-grained locking in the uncontended cases and the scalability of fine-grained synchronization in contended ones by adapting their granularity of synchronization according to the contention level.

3   Contention Adapting Search Trees

The structure and components of CA trees are as follows. The elements (key-value pairs or keys) contained in a CA tree are stored in sequential ordered set data structures (e.g., AVL trees, skip lists, etc.) which are rooted by *base nodes*. Each base node contains a *lock* that maintains statistics about the current level of the node's contention. The synchronization of accesses to a particular base node is handled independently of all other base nodes.

Base nodes are linked together by *routing nodes* as depicted in Fig. 1. The routing nodes do not contain elements; instead they contain keys which are only used to facilitate searching. As in ordinary binary search trees, all elements contained in the left branch of a routing node with key K have keys smaller than K and all elements contained in the right branch have keys greater than or equal to K. When it is detected that contention on a particular base node B is high, the subtree rooted by B is *split* to reduce the contention. Symmetrically, if contention on a base node B is detected to be low, B is *joined* with a neighbor base node to reduce the search path and to make atomic access of larger parts of the CA tree more efficient. An example of a split and a join operation is shown in Fig. 2.

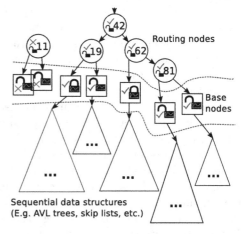

Fig. 1. The structure of a CA tree. Numbers denote keys, a node whose flag is valid is marked with a green hook; an invalid one with a red cross (Color figure online).

Contention detection is done by simply checking whether waiting for the lock of a base node was required or not, and increasing or decreasing the statistics counter (which is located in the base node lock) accordingly. Thresholds for this counter are used to decide when adaptation shall be performed. A good heuristic is to do adaptation for high contention eagerly and adaptation for low contention only when the contention has been low for many operations. This heuristics also avoids too frequent adaptations back and forth [18]. This mechanism for contention detection has low overhead and works well in practice. Still, other mechanisms can be used, e.g., based on the back-off time in an exponential back-off spin lock [12].

Searching in the routing node layer is done without acquiring any locks. However, as seen in Fig. 1, besides a key, routing nodes also have a valid flag (✓or ✗) and a lock. These are used to synchronize between concurrent join operations (i.e., adaptations for low contention). Since, as explained above, join operations happen relatively infrequently in CA trees, the locks in the routing nodes do not limit scalability in practice.

Single-key Modification Operations. Operations such as insert and remove start from the root of the CA tree and search for the base node B under which the element/key that is given as parameter to the operation will be inserted or removed. Recall that the traversal of the routing nodes does not acquire any locks. When B is reached, it is locked and then its valid flag is checked. If this flag is false (✗), the search needs to be retried. A base node becomes invalid when it is replaced by a split or a join. A search that ends up in an invalid base node thus needs to be retried until a valid base node is found. When this has happened, the operation is simply forwarded to the sequential data structure rooted by the base node. Before the base node is unlocked and the operation completes, we check if enough contention or lack of contention has been detected to justify an adaptation. If high contention is detected, the elements in the base node are split into two new base nodes that are linked together by a routing node. Figure 2a and b show CA trees before and after base node B_2 and the data structure Y is split (75 is the split key). In the reverse direction, if low contention is detected, the sequential data structure of the base node B is joined with that of a neighbor base node and the parent routing node of B is spliced out together with B. Figure 2a and c show CA tree structures before and after base node B_2 is spliced out from the tree and the elements of its Y structure are joined with those of X. We refer to [18] for pseudocode and a detailed description of the algorithms for splitting and joining base nodes and single key operations.

Single-key Read-only Operations. Read-only operations like get, contains, find-Max, etc. can work in a similar fashion as modification operations. However, on a multicore system, acquiring even a RW lock in read mode for read-only operations can cause bad scalability due to increased cache coherence traffic. Therefore, the performance and scalability of read-only operations can be improved if acquiring a lock can be avoided. By using a *sequence lock* [10] in the base nodes, read-only operations can attempt to perform the operation optimistically by checking the sequence number in the lock before and after the read-only operation has been performed on the base node. If the optimistic attempt fails, the base node lock can be acquired non-optimistically. This sequence lock optimization avoids writing to shared memory in the common case when the base node

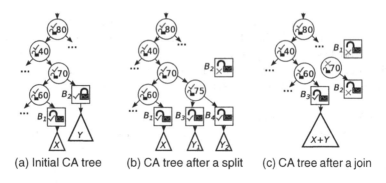

(a) Initial CA tree   (b) CA tree after a split   (c) CA tree after a join

Fig. 2. Effect of the split and join operations on the CA tree of Fig. 2a.

is not contended, which greatly improves performance in practice [18]. The concurrency in the data structure can be further improved by using a sequence lock with support for concurrent execution of read-only critical sections. By using such a lock, one can acquire the base node lock in read-only mode when the optimistic read attempt fails, and thus allowing concurrent reads to read from the base node at the same time. Note that an optimistic read does not change the statistics counter, because that would involve writing to shared memory and would defeat the purpose of having such operations. If the optimistic read fails and the lock is acquired in read mode, our implementation adds to the contention statistics to decrease the likelihood of optimistic read failures in the future[1].

Multi-element Operations. CA trees also support operations that atomically operate on several keys, such as bulk insert, bulk remove, and swap operations that swap the values associated with two keys. Generic pseudocode for such operations appears in Fig. 4a; its helper function manageCont appears in Fig. 3a. Such operations start by sorting the elements given as their parameter (line 7). Then all the base nodes needed for the operations are found (line 12) and locked (lines 15–16) in sorted order. Locking base nodes in a specific order prevents deadlocks. The method lockIsContended in the base node, locks the base node lock and return true if contention was detected while locking it and the method lockNoStats locks the base node lock without recording any contention. When multi-element operations are given keys that all reside in one base node, only this base node needs to be locked. One simply has to query the sequential data structure in the current base node for the maximum key (line 26) to see which of the given elements must belong to a base node. This can be compared to data structures that utilize non-adaptive fine-grained synchronization and thus either need to lock the whole data structure or all involved nodes individually.

---

[1] We perform the change to the contention statistics counter non-atomically. Thus, it is possible for a concurrent read operation to overwrite the change. Note that this does not effect the correctness of the data structure as it only affects the frequency of its adaptations.

Finally, multi-key operations end by adjusting the contention statistics, unlock all acquired locks, and split or join one of the base nodes (lines 35–46) if required.

Range Operations. We will now describe an algorithm for atomic range operations that locks all base nodes that can contain keys in the range $[a, b]$. Generic pseudocode for such operations can be seen in Fig. 4b and its helper function `manageCont` and `getNextBaseNodeAndPath` can be seen in Fig. 3. To prevent deadlocks, the base nodes are always locked in increasing order of the keys that they can contain. Therefore, the first base node to lock is the one that can contain the smallest key a in the range. This first base node can be found (line 5 in Fig. 4b) and locked (line 6) using the algorithm described for single-key operations [18]. Finding the next base node (line 21 in Fig. 4b) is not as simple as it might first seem, since routing nodes can be spliced out and base nodes can be split. The two problematic cases that may occur are illustrated in Fig. 2. Suppose that the base node marked B_1 has been found through the search path with routing nodes with keys $80, 40, 70, 60$ as depicted in Fig. 2a. If the tree stays as depicted in Fig. 2a, the base node B_2 would be the next base node. However,

```
1  void manageCont(BaseNode base, boolean contended) {
2    if (contended) base.lock.statistics += FAIL_CONTRIB;
3    else base.lock.statistics -= SUCC_CONTRIB;
4    if (base.lock.statistics > MAX_CONTENTION) {
5      if (size(base.root) < 2) base.lock.statistics = 0;
6      else highContentionSplit(tree, base, base.parent);
7    } else if (base.lock.statistics < MIN_CONTENTION) {
8      if (base.parent == null) base.lock.statistics = 0;
9      else lowContentionJoin(tree, base, base.parent);
10   }
11 }
```

(a) Manage contention

```
1  BaseNode, List<RouteNode>
2  getNextBaseNodeAndPath(BaseNode b, List<RouteNode> p) {
3    List<RouteNode> newPathPart;
4    BaseNode bRet;
5    if (p.isEmpty()) { // The parent of b is the root
6      return null, null;
7    } else {
8      List<RouteNode> rp = p.reverse();
9      if (rp.head().left == b) {
10       bRet, newPathPart =
11         leftmostBaseNodeAndPath(rp.head().right);
12       return bRet, p.append(newPathPart);
13     } else {
14       K pKey = rp.head().key; // pKey = key of parent
15       rp.removeFirst();
16       while (rp.notEmpty()) {
17         if (rp.head().isValid() && pKey < rp.head().key) {
18           bRet, newPathPart =
19             leftmostBaseNodeAndPath(rp.head().right);
20           return bRet, rp.reverse().append(newPathPart);
21         } else {
22           rp.removeFirst();
23         }
24       }
25     }
26     return null, null;
27   }
28 }
```

(b) Find next base node

Fig. 3. Helper functions for Fig. 4.

B_2 may have been spliced out while the range operation was traversing the routing nodes (Fig. 2c) or split (Fig. 2b). If one of these cases happens, we will detect this since we will end up in an invalid base node in which case the attempt to find the next base node will be retried. When we find the next base node we will *not* end up in the same invalid base node twice if the following algorithm is applied (also depicted in Fig. 3b):

1. If the last locked base node is the left child of its parent routing node P then find the leftmost base node in the right child of P (Fig. 3b, line 11).
2. Otherwise, follow the reverse search path from P until a *valid* routing node R with a key greater than the key of P is found (Fig. 3b, line 17). If such an R is not found, the current base node is the rightmost base node in the tree so all required base nodes are already locked (Fig. 3b, lines 6 and 26). Otherwise, find the leftmost base node in the right branch of R (Fig. 3b, line 19).

The argument why this algorithm is correct is briefly as follows. For case 1, note that the parent of a base node is guaranteed to stay the same while the base node is valid; cf. also [16]. For case 2, note that once we have locked a valid base node we know that no routing nodes can be added to the search path that was used to find the base node, since the base node in the top of the path must be locked for a new routing node to be linked in. Also, the above algorithm never ends up in the same invalid base node more than once since the effect of a split or a join is visible after the involved base nodes have been unlocked. Finally, if the algorithm ever finds a base node B_2 that is locked and valid and the previously locked base node is B_1, then there cannot be any other base node B' containing keys between the maximum key of B_1 and the minimum key of B_2. This is true because if a split or a join had created such a B', then B_2 would not be valid.

An Optimistic Read Optimization for Range Queries. For the same reasons, as discussed previously for single-key read-only operations, it can be advantageous to perform range queries without writing to shared memory. This can be done by first reading the sequence numbers (in the locks) and validating the base nodes containing the elements in the range. This optimistic attempt is aborted if a sequence number indicates that a write operation is currently changing the content of the base node. After acquiring sequence numbers for all involved base nodes, the range query is continued by reading all elements in the range, checking the sequence number again after the elements in a base node have been read. If the sequence numbers have not changed from the initial scan to after the elements have been read, then one can be sure that no write has interfered with the operation. Thus, the range query will appear to be atomic. As soon as a validation of a sequence number fails or inconsistent state is detected in the sequential data structure, the optimistic attempt will abort. Range queries for which the optimistic attempt failed are performed by acquiring the base node locks belonging to the range in read mode.

Contention Statistics in Multi-element Operations. A multi-element operation performed by non-optimistic locking that only requires one base node changes the contention statistics counter in the same way as single-element operations and also uses the same split and join thresholds as single-element operations. The pseudocode that handles contention in this case can be found in Fig. 3a and is called from line 36 in Fig. 4a and line 37 in Fig. 4b. When contention is detected, the contention statistics counter in that base node is increased (line 2) to make a base node split more likely and otherwise the contention statistics counter is decreased (line 3) to make a base node join more likely. Lines 4 to 10 check if one of the thresholds for adaptation has been reached and performs the appropriate adaptation in that case.

If a multi-element operation performed by non-optimistic locking requires more than one base node, the contention statistics counter is decreased (lines 42–43 in Fig. 4a and lines 44–45 in Fig. 4b) in all involved base nodes to reduce the chance that future multi-element operations will require more than one base node. Before unlocking the last base node, low-contention join or

```
 1  Object[] doBulkOp(CATree tree, Op op, K[] keys, Object[] es) {
 2    keys = keys.clone();
 3    es = es.clone();
 4    Object[] returnArray = new Object[keys.size];
 5    boolean first = true;
 6    boolean firstContended = true;
 7    sort(keys, es);
 8    Stack<BaseNode> lockedBaseNodes = new Stack<BaseNode>();
 9    int i = 0;
10    while (i < keys.size()) {
11    find_base_node_for_key:
12      BaseNode baseNode = getBaseNode(tree, keys[i]);
13      if (baseNode != lockedBaseNodes.top()) {
14        if (first) {
15          firstContended = baseNode.lockIsContended();
16        } else baseNode.lockNoStats();
17        if (!baseNode.isValid()) {
18          baseNode.unlock();
19          goto find_base_node_for_key; // Retry
20        }
21        lockedBaseNodes.push(baseNode);
22      }
23      first = false;
24      returnArray[i] = op.execute(baseNode.root, keys[i], es[i]);
25      i++;
26      K maxKey = baseNode.maxKey();
27      while (i < keys.size() && maxKey != null
28            && keys[i] <= maxKey) {
29        returnArray[i] = op.execute(baseNode.root,
30                           keys[i], es[i]);
31        i++;
32      }
33    }
34    BaseNode[] lockedBaseNodesArray = lockedBaseNodes.toArray();
35    if (lockedBaseNodes.size() == 1) {
36      manageCont(lockedBaseNodesArray[0], firstContended);
37      lockedBaseNodesArray[0].unlock();
38    } else {
39      for (int i = 0; i < lockedBaseNodes.size(); i++) {
40        baseNode = lockedBaseNodesArray[i];
41        if (i == (lockedBaseNodes.size()-1)) {
42          manageCont(baseNode, false);
43        } else baseNode.lock.statistics -= SUCC_CONTRIB;
44        baseNode.unlock();
45      }
46    }
47    return returnArray;
48  }
```

(a) Bulk operations

```
 1  Object[] rangeOp(CATree tree, Op op, K lo, K hi) {
 2    List<RouteNode> path; BaseNode baseNode;
 3    Stack<BaseNode> lockedBaseNodes = new Stack<BaseNode>();
 4  fetch_first_node:
 5    baseNode, path = getBaseNodeAndPath(lo);
 6    boolean firstContended = baseNode.lockIsContended();
 7    if (!baseNode.isValid()) {
 8      baseNode.unlock();
 9      goto fetch_first_node; // Retry
10    }
11    while (true) {
12      lockedBaseNodes.push(baseNode);
13      K baseNodeMaxKey = baseNode.maxKey();
14      if (baseNodeMaxKey != null && hi <= baseNodeMaxKey) {
15        break; // All needed base nodes are locked
16      }
17      BaseNode lastLockedBaseNode = baseNode;
18    search_next_base_node:
19      List<RouteNode> pathBackup = path.clone();
20      baseNode, path =
21        getNextBaseNodeAndPath(lastLockedBaseNode, path);
22      if (baseNode == null) {
23        break; // All needed base nodes are locked
24      }
25      baseNode.lockNoStats();
26      if (!baseNode.isValid()) {
27        baseNode.unlock();
28        path = pathBackup;
29        goto search_next_base_node; // Retry
30      }
31    }
32    Buffer<Object> retBuff = new Buffer<Object>();
33    BaseNode[] lockedBaseNodesArray = lockedBaseNodes.toArray();
34    if (lockedBaseNodesArray.size() == 1) {
35      baseNode = lockedBaseNodesArray[0];
36      retBuff.add(performOpToKeysInRange(baseNode, lo, hi, op));
37      manageCont(baseNode, firstContended);
38      baseNode.unlock();
39    } else {
40      for (int i = 0; i < lockedBaseNodes.size(); i++) {
41        baseNode = lockedBaseNodesArray[i];
42        retBuff.add(performOpToKeysInRange(baseNode, lo, hi, op));
43        if (i == (lockedBaseNodes.size()-1)) {
44          manageCont(baseNode, false);
45        } else baseNode.lock.statistics -= SUCC_CONTRIB;
46        baseNode.unlock();
47      }
48    }
49    return retBuff.toArray();
50  }
```

(b) Range operations

Fig. 4. Pseudocode for bulk operations and range operations.

high-contention split is performed on that base node if the thresholds are reached (line 42 in Fig. 4a and line 44 in Fig. 4b).

Range operations where the optimistic attempt succeeds do not change the contention statistics of any of the base nodes that they use. Doing so would defend the purpose of the optimistic attempt which is to avoid writing to shared state. However, if the optimistic attempt fails, the contention statistics is updated as described before.

Correctness. In a previous publication [18] we provided proofs for that the algorithm for single-key operations is deadlock free, livelock free as well as a proof sketch for its linearizability. Here, we will briefly repeat the outlines of the proofs for single-key operations and provide a proof sketch that the properties deadlock freedom, livelock freedom and linearizability are all provided by CA trees when extended with the range operations and bulk operations that we have described in detail in this paper. The interested reader can find more detailed proofs in a technical report available online [16].

Deadlock freedom can be shown by proving that all locks are acquired in a specific order. All single-key operations (except operations that perform a low-contention join) acquire a single lock; cf. [16]. Low-contention join can acquire base node locks in different orders but since this is done with a non-blocking try lock call and all locks that the operation is holding are released if the try lock call fails, this cannot cause a deadlock. The proof for deadlock freedom can easily be extended to also include bulk operations and range operations that we have described in this paper. As presented earlier, these operations acquire the base node locks in a specific order (increasing order of the keys that they can store), with the exception that they might also perform a low-contention join which cannot cause deadlocks as we have described above. Thus, a CA tree with multi-element operations is deadlock free since there is a specific order in which the locks are acquired. Whenever locks are acquired in a different order, this is done with a try lock call and all held locks are released if the try lock call fails.

Livelock freedom can be shown by proving that when an operation or part of an operation has to be retried due to interference from another thread, some other thread must have made progress. The two types of retries are the same for both multi-element operations and single-key operations. The first type of retry can happen in the function for low-contention join and is caused by a concurrent low-contention join that removes a routing node. This can not cause a livelock since, if a retry is triggered at this point, another thread must have successfully spliced out a routing node from the tree and this routing node will not be observed when we retry; cf. [16]. The second type of retry happens when an invalid base node is observed. An invalid base node is only observed if another thread has successfully performed a contention-adapting split or join which means that another thread has made progress. Single-key operations handle this case by retrying the whole operation, while operations involving multiple keys only need to retry the search for the next base node. When the search for a base node is retried the same invalid base node will not be found since the effect of the split or join that sets the base node to invalid will be visible after the base node(s) involved in the split or join has(have) been unlocked.

Linearizability. The linearization point of an operation that locks all base nodes that it reads from or writes to is at some point while holding the base node locks of all the base nodes that it operates on. The linearization point of an operation that is successfully performed with an optimistic read attempt is somewhere between the first and second sequence number scan. If the optimistic read attempt fails, the operation will instead acquire the locks non-optimistically and the linearization point will be at some point while holding all the base node locks. It can be proven [16] that CA trees maintain the following property: If a thread t has searched in a CA tree for a key K using the binary search tree property and ended up in base node B that it has locked and validated, then K must be in B and not in any other base node if it is in the abstract set represented by the CA tree. Using this property as well as the properties mentioned above in the arguments for the correctness of range operations it is easy to see that the CA tree operations appear to happen atomically at their linearization points, since they are either holding locks of all base nodes that can contain keys involved in the operation or ensuring that no other thread has changed any key involved in the operation while the operation is being performed by the final check of the sequence numbers in the sequence locks.

Flexibility of CA Trees. A split operation in an ordered set data structure splits the data structure into two data structures so that all elements in one are smaller than the elements in the other. The join operation merges two data structures where the greatest key in one of them is smaller than the smallest key in the other. Any sequential ordered set data structure that has efficient support for the split and join operations can be used to store elements under the base nodes of CA trees. This property makes CA trees highly flexible since the underlying sequential data structure can be changed without changing the CA tree structure itself. The sequential data structure component of a CA tree could be passed as a parameter by the user when creating a CA tree instance. One could even change the sequential ordered set data structure at run time depending on which type of operations are most frequent; however, it is beyond the scope of this paper to investigate the effect of this possibility.

Many ordered set data structures support efficient split and join operations including red-black trees and AVL trees that do these operations in $\mathcal{O}(log(N))$ time [9,19]. Skip lists are randomized data structures for ordered sets that also have efficient support for split[2] and join [14]. By using both back and forward pointers in the skip list, both split and join as well as maxKey have efficient implementations; in fact constant time in skip lists with a fixed number of levels. Skip lists also provide efficient support for range operations since all elements are connected in an ordered list at the top level of a skip list. Using a skip list with so called *fat nodes*, i.e., nodes that contain more than one element, we can further increase the performance of range operation due to improved locality. We will experiment with AVL trees and skip lists with fat nodes in the next section. Our skip list implementation can store up to k elements in its nodes. The nodes are split if an insert would cause a node to contain $k + 1$ elements, and nodes are spliced out if a remove operation would create an empty node. The keys in the skip list are kept in compact arrays to improve cache locality when searching and performing range operations.

4   Experiments

Let us now investigate the scalability of two CA tree variants: one with an AVL tree as sequential structure (CA-AVL) and one with a skip list with fat nodes (CA-SL) as sequential structure. We compare them against the lock-free k-ary search tree [3] (k-ary), the Snap tree [2] (Snap) and a lock-free skip list (SkipList). All implementations are those provided by the authors.

---

[2] The efficient skip list split operation splits the data structure so that on average half the keys will be in each resulting split.

SkipList is implemented by Doug Lea in the Java Foundation Classes as the class `ConcurrentSkipListMap`.[3]

SkipList marked with dashed gray lines in the graphs does not cater for linearizable range queries nor range updates. We include SkipList in the measurements only to show the kind of scalability one can expect from a lock-free skip list data structure if one is not concerned about consistency of results from range operations. Range operations are implemented in SkipList by calling the `subSet` method which returns an iterable view of the elements in the range. Since changes in SkipList are reflected in the view returned by `subSet` and vice versa, range operations are not atomic.

In contrast, the k-ary search tree supports linearizable range queries and the Snap tree supports linearizable range queries through the `clone` method. However, neither the k-ary nor the Snap tree provide support for linearizable range updates. In the scenarios where we measure range updates we implement them in these data structures by using a frequent read optimized readers-writer lock[4] with a read indicator that has one dedicated cache line per thread. Thus, all operations except range updates acquire the RW-lock in read mode. We have confirmed that this method has negligible overhead for all cases where range updates are not used, but use the implementations of the data structures without range update support in scenarios that do not have range updates.

We use $k = 32$ (maximum number of elements in nodes) both for CA-SL and k-ary trees. This value provides a good trade-off between performance of range operations and performance of single-key modification operations. For the CA trees, we initialize the contention statistics counters of the locks to 0 and add 250 to the counter to indicate contention; we decrease the counter by 1 to indicate low contention. The thresholds -1000 and 1000 are used for low contention and high contention adaptations.

The benchmark we use measures throughput of a mix of operations performed by N threads on the same data structure during T seconds. The keys and values for the operations get, insert and remove as well as the starting key for range operations are randomly generated from a range of size R. The data structure is pre-filled before the start of each benchmark run by performing $R/2$ insert operations. In all experiments presented in this paper $R = 1000000$, thus we create a data structure containing roughly 500000 elements. In all captions, benchmark scenarios are described by a strings of the form w:$A\%$ r:$B\%$ q:$C\%$-R_1 u:$D\%$-R_2, meaning that on the created data structure the benchmark performs $(A/2)\%$ insert, $(A/2)\%$ remove, $B\%$ get operations, $C\%$ range queries of maximum range size R_1, and $D\%$ range updates with maximum range size R_2.

---

[3] We do not compare experimentally against the Leaplist [1] whose main implementation is in C. Prototype implementations of the Liplist in Java were sent to us by its authors, but they ended up in deadlocks when running our benchmarks which prevented us from obtaining reliable measurements. Instead, we refer to Sect. 2 for an analytic comparison to the Leaplist.

[4] We use the write-preference algorithm [5] for coordination between readers and writers and the `StampedLock` from the Java library for mutual exclusion.

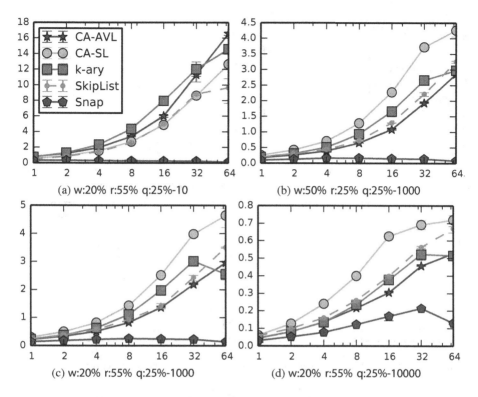

(a) w:20% r:55% q:25%-10

(b) w:50% r:25% q:25%-1000

(c) w:20% r:55% q:25%-1000

(d) w:20% r:55% q:25%-10000

Fig. 5. Scalability of throughput (ops/μs) on the y-axis and thread count on the x-axis.

The size of each range operation is randomly generated between 1 and the maximum range size. The benchmarks presented in this paper were run on a machine with four AMD Opteron 6276 (2.3 GHz, 16 cores, 16M L2/16M L3 Cache), giving a total of 64 physical cores and 128 GB or RAM, running Linux 3.10-amd64 and Oracle Hotspot JVM 1.8.0_31 (started with parameters -Xmx4g, -Xms4g, -server and -d64).[5] The experiments for each benchmark scenario were run in a separate JVM instance and we performed a warm up run of 10 seconds followed by three measurement runs, each running for 10 seconds. The average of the measurement runs as well as error bars for the minimum and maximum run are shown in the graphs, though often the error bars are very small and therefore not visible.

Benchmarks without Range Updates. Let us first discuss the performance results in Fig. 5, showing scenarios without range updates. Figure 5a, which shows throughput in a scenario with a moderate amount of modifications (20 %) and

---

[5] We also ran experiments on a machine with four Intel(R) Xeon(R) E5-4650 CPUs (2.70GHz each with eight cores and hyperthreading) both on a NUMA setting and on a single chip, showing similar performance patterns as on the AMD machine. Results are available online [6].

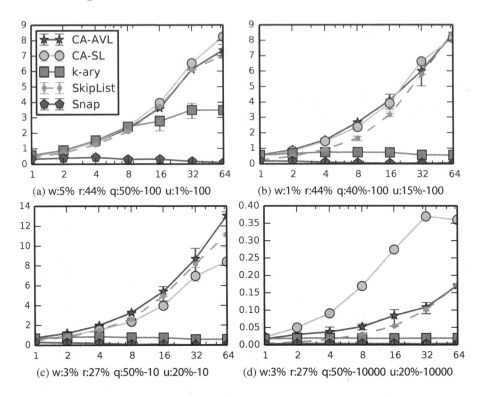

(a) w:5% r:44% q:50%-100 u:1%-100

(b) w:1% r:44% q:40%-100 u:15%-100

(c) w:3% r:27% q:50%-10 u:20%-10

(d) w:3% r:27% q:50%-10000 u:20%-10000

Fig. 6. Scalability of throughput (ops/μs) on the y-axis and thread count on the x-axis.

small range queries, shows that the k-ary and CA-AVL tree perform best in this scenario, tightly followed by the CA-SL and SkipList with the non-atomic range queries. We also note that the Snap tree does not scale well in this scenario, which is not surprising since a range query with a small range size will eventually cause the creation of a copy of every node in the tree. Let us now look at Fig. 5b showing throughputs in a scenario with many modifications (50 %) and larger range queries, and Fig. 5c corresponding to a scenario with the same maximum range query size and a more moderate modification rate (20 %). First of all, the better cache locality for range queries in CA-SL and k-ary trees is visible in these scenarios where the range sizes are larger. k-ary only beats CA-AVL with a small amount up to 32 threads and then k-ary's performance drops. This performance drop might be caused by its starvation issue in the range query operation that can cause a range query to be retried many times (possibly forever). This can be compared to the CA trees that acquire locks for reads if the first optimistic attempt fails and thus reducing the risk of retries. The scalability of the CA trees shown in Fig. 5b, i.e., in a scenario with 50 % modification operations, shows that the range queries in the CA trees tolerate high contention. Finally, the scenario of Fig. 5d with very wide range queries and moderate modification rate (20 %) shows both the promise and the limit in the scalability of

Table 1. Average base node counts (in k) at the end of running two sets of benchmarks: one using 64 threads but varying the range size R, and one varying the number of threads.

R	10	100	1000	10000
CA-SL	14.4	8.8	4.0	2.5
CA-AVL	15.6	8.7	3.6	2.2

(a) w:3% r:27% q:50%-R u:20%-R

threads	2	4	8	16	32	64
CA-SL	0.36	0.73	1.2	1.9	2.7	4.0
CA-AVL	0.34	0.68	1.1	1.6	2.4	3.6

(b) w:3% r:27% q:50%-1000 u:20%-1000

CA-SL. However, we note that SkipList, which does not even provide atomic range queries, does not beat CA-SL that outperforms the other data structures by at least 57 % at 16 threads.

Benchmarks with Range Updates. Let us now look at the scenarios that also contain range updates shown in Fig. 6. The first of them (Fig. 6a) shows that k-ary tree's scalability flattens out between 16 and 32 threads even with as little as 1 % range updates. Instead, the CA trees provide good scalability all the way. Remember that we wrap the k-ary operations in critical sections protected by an RW-lock to provide linearizable range updates in the k-ary tree. In the scenario of Fig. 6b, where the percentage of range updates is 15 %, we see that the k-ary tree does not scale at all while the CA trees and SkipList with the non-atomic range operations scale very well, outperforming the k-ary tree with more than 1200 % in this case. The two scenarios in Fig. 6c and d have the same rate of operations but different maximum size for range queries and range updates. Their results clearly show the difference in performance characteristics that can be obtained by changing the sequential data structure component of a CA tree. CA-SL is faster for wider range operations due to its fat nodes providing good cache locality, but CA-SL is generally slower than the CA-AVL in scenarios with small range sizes. In Fig. 6d, where the conflict rate between operations is high, CA-SL reaches its peak performance at 32 threads where it outperforms all other data structures by more than two times.

We also report average base node counts for the CA trees in the end of running two sets of scenarios. The numbers in Table 1a show node counts (in k) for running with 64 threads but varying the maximum range size R. Table 1b shows node counts (also in k) for scenarios with R fixed to 1000 but varying the number of threads. These numbers confirm that the CA trees' synchronization is adapting both to the contention level (increasing the number of threads results in more base nodes) and to the access patterns (increased range size results in fewer base nodes). We also confirmed by increasing the running time of the experiments that the number of base nodes stabilizes around a specific value for each scenario, which means that base nodes do not get split indefinitely.

5   Concluding Remarks

Given the diversity in sizes and heterogeneity of multicores, it seems rather obvious that current and future applications will benefit from, if not require, data structures that can adapt dynamically to the amount of concurrency and the usage patterns of applications.

This paper has advocated the use of CA trees, a new family of lock-based concurrent data structures for ordered sets of keys and key-value pair dictionaries. CA trees' salient feature is their ability to adapt their synchronization granularity according to the current contention level and access patterns. Furthermore, CA trees are flexible and efficiently support a wide variety of operations: single-key operations, multi-element operations, range queries and range updates. Our experimental evaluation has demonstrated the good scalability and superior performance of CA trees compared to state-of-the-art lock-free concurrent data structures in a variety of scenarios.

In other work [17], we have described the use of CA trees for speeding and scaling up single-key operations of the `ordered_set` component of the Erlang Term Storage, Erlang's in-memory key-value store. We intend to extend that work with support for atomic multi-element and range operations and evaluate the performance benefits of doing so in "real-world" applications. The experimental results in this paper strongly suggest that the performance gains will be substantial. In addition, we intend to investigate CA trees with more kinds of adaptations: for example, adaptations in the underlying sequential data structure component.

References

1. Avni, H., Shavit, N., Suissa, A.: Leaplist: Lessons learned in designing TM-supported range queries. In: Proceedings of the ACM Symposium on Principles of Distributed Computing, PODC 2013, pp. 299–308. ACM, New York, NY, USA (2013)
2. Bronson, N.G., Casper, J., Chafi, H., Olukotun, K.: A practical concurrent binary search tree. In: Proceedings of the 15th ACM SIGPLAN Symposium on Principles and Practice of Parallel Programming, PPOPP, pp. 257–268. ACM (2010)
3. Brown, T., Avni, H.: Range queries in Non-blocking k-ary search trees. In: Flocchini, P., Binoy, R., Baldoni, R. (eds.) OPODIS 2012. LNCS, vol. 7702, pp. 31–45. Springer, Heidelberg (2012)
4. Brown, T., Helga, J.: Non-blocking k-ary search trees. In: Fernàndez Anta, A., Lipari, G., Roy, M. (eds.) OPODIS 2011. LNCS, vol. 7109, pp. 207–221. Springer, Heidelberg (2011)
5. Calciu, I., Dice, D., Lev, Y., Luchangco, V., Marathe, V.J., Shavit, N.: NUMA-aware reader-writer locks. In: Proceedings of the 18th ACM SIGPLAN Symposium on Principles and Practice of Parallel Programming, PPOPP, pp. 157–166. ACM, New York, NY, USA (2013)
6. CA Trees. http://www.it.uu.se/research/group/languages/software/ca_tree
7. Crain, T., Gramoli, V., Raynal, M.: A speculation-friendly binary search tree. In: Proceedings of the 17th ACM SIGPLAN Symposium on Principles and Practice of Parallel Programming, PPOPP 2012, pp. 161–170. ACM, New York, NY, USA (2012)
8. Fraser, K.: Practical lock-freedom. Ph.D. thesis, University of Cambridge Computer Laboratory (2004)

9. Knuth, D.E.: The Art of Computer Programming: Sorting and Searching, 2nd edn. Addison-Wesley, Reading (1998)
10. Lameter, C.: Effective synchronization on Linux/NUMA systems. In: Proceedings of the Gelato Federation Meeting (2005)
11. Natarajan, A., Mittal, N.: Fast concurrent lock-free binary search trees. In: Proceedings of the 19th ACM SIGPLAN Symposium on Principles and Practice of Parallel Programming, PPOPP 2014, pp. 317–328. ACM, New York, NY, USA (2014)
12. Österlund, E., Löwe, W.: Concurrent transformation components using contention context sensors. In: Proceedings of the 29th ACM/IEEE International Conference on Automated Software Engineering, ASE 2014, pp. 223–234. ACM, New York, NY, USA (2014)
13. Prokopec, A., Bronson, N.G., Bagwell, P., Odersky, M.: Concurrent tries with efficient non-blocking snapshots. In: Proceedings of the 17th ACM SIGPLAN Symposium on Principles and Practice of Parallel Programming, PPopp 2012, pp. 151–160. ACM, NY, USA (2012)
14. Pugh, W.: A skip list cookbook. Technical report, College Park, MD, USA (1990)
15. Robertson, C.: Implementing contention-friendly range queries in non-blocking key-value stores. Bachelor thesis, The University of Sydney, November 2014
16. Sagonas, K., Winblad, K.: Contention adapting trees. Technical Report, available in[6] (2014)
17. Sagonas, K., Winblad, K.: More scalable ordered set for ETS using adaptation. In: ACM Erlang Workshop, pp. 3–11. ACM, September 2014
18. Sagonas, K., Winblad, K.: Contention adapting trees. In: 14th International Symposium on Parallel and Distributed Computing, pp. 215–224. IEEE, June 2015
19. Tarjan, R.E.: Data Structures and Network Algorithms, vol. 14. SIAM (1983)

Optimizing Framework

Polyhedral Optimizations for a Data-Flow Graph Language

Alina Sbîrlea[1]([⊠]), Jun Shirako[1], Louis-Noël Pouchet[2], and Vivek Sarkar[1]

[1] Rice University, Houston, USA
alina@rice.edu
[2] Ohio State University, Columbus, USA

Abstract. This paper proposes a novel optimization framework for the Data-Flow Graph Language (DFGL), a dependence-based notation for macro-dataflow model which can be used as an embedded domain-specific language. Our optimization framework follows a "dependence-first" approach in capturing the semantics of DFGL programs in polyhedral representations, as opposed to the standard polyhedral approach of deriving dependences from access functions and schedules. As a first step, our proposed framework performs two important legality checks on an input DFGL program — checking for potential violations of the single-assignment rule, and checking for potential deadlocks. After these legality checks are performed, the DFGL dependence information is used in lieu of standard polyhedral dependences to enable polyhedral transformations and code generation, which include automatic loop transformations, tiling, and code generation of parallel loops with coarse-grain (fork-join) and fine-grain (doacross) synchronizations. Our performance experiments with nine benchmarks on Intel Xeon and IBM Power7 multicore processors show that the DFGL versions optimized by our proposed framework can deliver up to 6.9× performance improvement relative to standard OpenMP versions of these benchmarks. To the best of our knowledge, this is the first system to encode explicit macro-dataflow parallelism in polyhedral representations so as to provide programmers with an easy-to-use DSL notation with legality checks, while taking full advantage of the optimization functionality in state-of-the-art polyhedral frameworks.

1 Introduction

Hardware design is evolving towards manycore processors that will be used in large clusters to achieve exascale computing, and at the rack level to achieve petascale computing [29], however, harnessing the full power of the architecture is a challenge that software must tackle to fully realize extreme-scale computing. This challenge is prompting the exploration of new approaches to programming and execution systems, and specifically, re-visiting of the dataflow model — but now at the software level.

In the early days of dataflow computing, it was believed that programming languages such as VAL [5], Sisal [27], and Id [7] were necessary to obtain the benefits of dataflow execution. However, there is now an increased realization that

© Springer International Publishing Switzerland 2016
X. Shen et al. (Eds.): LCPC 2015, LNCS 9519, pp. 57–72, 2016.
DOI: 10.1007/978-3-319-29778-1_4

"macro-dataflow" execution models [30] can be supported on standard multi-core processors by using data-driven runtime systems [3,4,36]. There are many benefits that follow from macro-dataflow approaches, including simplified programmability [12], increased asynchrony [15], support for heterogeneous parallelism [32], and scalable approaches to resilience [39]. As a result, a wide variety of programming systems are exploring the adoption of dataflow principles [21,28,31], and there is a growing need for compiler and runtime components to support macro-dataflow execution in these new programming systems.

At the other end of the spectrum, polyhedral and other compiler frameworks implicitly uncover dataflow relationships in sequential programs through dependence analysis and related techniques. Though this approach can result in good performance, it usually requires a sequential program as input, which often limits portability when compared to higher-level dataflow program specifications.

We argue that a combination of declarative dataflow programming and imperative programming can provide a practical approach both for migrating existing codes and for writing new codes for extreme-scale platforms. We propose the use of a Data-Flow Graph Language (DFGL) as an embedded domain-specific language (eDSL) for expressing the dataflow components in an application. The DFGL notation is based on the Data Flow Graph Representation (DFGR) introduced in [31]. It enables individual computations to be implemented as arbitrary sequential code that operates on a set of explicit inputs and outputs, and defers the packaging and coordination of inter-step parallelism to the compiler and the runtime system. We propose a novel optimization framework for DFGL which enables correctness analysis of the application as well as low level transformations using a polyhedral compiler. Our performance experiments with nine benchmarks on Intel Xeon and IBM Power7 multicore processors show that the DFGL versions optimized by our proposed framework can deliver up to 6.9× performance improvement relative to standard OpenMP versions of these benchmarks.

Section 2 provides the background for this work, Sect. 3 discusses the motivation for the DFGL approach, Sect. 4 gives an overview of the compiler flow for DFGL subprograms, Sect. 5 describes the key technical points in our approach, Sect. 6 presents our experimental results, Sect. 7 discusses related work and Sect. 8 contains our conclusions.

2   Background

This section briefly summarizes the underlying DFGL programming model and the polyhedral compilation framework, which together form the foundation for the approach introduced in this paper.

2.1   DFGL Model

The Data-Flow Graph Language (DFGL) model is a dependence based notation for dataflow parallelism, which is based on the Concurrent Collections (CnC) model [12,21] and the Data Flow Graph Representation (DFGR) [31].

DFGL describes computations using two main components: *steps*, that represent sequential subcomputations; and *items*, that represent data read and written by steps. The user describes an application by writing a graph that captures the relation among the items and steps.

As in the CnC model, steps are grouped into *step collections*, and represent all dynamic invocations of the same computational kernel. A unique identifier (*tag*) identifies a dynamic instance of a step S in a collection, (S: *tag*). A special env step handles communications with "outside", e.g., initialization and emitting final results. Items are grouped into *item collections* and model all data used as inputs and outputs to steps. Analogous to tags for steps, elements in item collection A are uniquely identified by a *key*: [A: *key*]. In general, keys are represented as functions of step tags, such as affine functions or pure functions evaluated at run time [31]. The relations among steps and items are described by the "->" and "::" operations. The operation -> describes data-flow as follows: [A: *key*] -> (S: *tag*) denotes item(s) read by a step[1], (S: *tag*) -> [A: *key*] denotes item(s) written by a step, and (S: *tag1*) -> (S: *tag2*) denotes a step-to-step ordering constraint. The operation :: describes step creation; i.e., (S: *tag1*) ::(T: *tag2*) denotes instance(s) of T created by an instance of S[2]. The detailed semantics are shown in past work [31].

DFGL guarantees determinism and data race freedom by enforcing a dynamic single assignment rule. This rule states that any item in any collection can only be written once during the whole execution of the program. The model can be implemented to rely on different underlying runtimes. The compiler also has a lot of freedom in packaging the parallelism through code transformations such as loop tiling and generation of fine-grained (doacross) parallelism.

2.2 Polyhedral Compilation Framework

The polyhedral model is a flexible representation for arbitrarily nested loops. Loop nests amenable to this algebraic representation are called *Static Control Parts* (SCoPs) and represented in the SCoP format, where each statement contains three elements, namely, iteration domain, access relations, and schedule. SCoPs require their loop bounds, branch conditions, and array subscripts to be affine functions of iterators and global parameters.

Iteration Domain, $\mathcal{D}^S$: A statement S enclosed by m loops is represented by an m-dimensional polytope, referred to as an iteration domain of the statement [19]. Each element in the iteration domain of the statement is regarded as a statement instance $i \in \mathcal{D}^S$.

Access Relation, $\mathcal{A}^S(i)$: Each array reference in a statement is expressed through an access relation, which maps a statement instance i to one or more array elements to be read/written [40]. This mapping is expressed in the affine form of loop iterators and global parameters; a scalar variable is considered as a degenerate case of an array.

---

[1] Step I/O may comprise a list of items, and item keys may include range expressions.
[2] A typical case is env step to create set of step instances where tag is a range.

Fig. 1. Computation and dependence for Smith-Waterman.

```
[int A];
(corner:i,j) -> [A:i,j];
(top:i,j) -> [A:i,j];      (left:i,j) -> [A:i,j];
[A:i-1,j-1], [A:i-1,j], [A:i,j-1] -> (main_center:i,j) -> [A:i,j];
env::(corner:0,0);
env::(top:0,{1 .. NW});   env::(left:{1 .. NH},0);
env::(main_center:{1 .. NH},{1 .. NW});
[A:NH,NW] -> env;
```

Fig. 2. Input: DFGL for Smith-Waterman.

```
corner(0, 0);
for (c3 = 1; c3 <= NW; c3++) top(0, c3);
for (c1 = 1; c1 <= NH; c1++) left(c1, 0);
#pragma omp parallel for private(c3, c5, c7) ordered(2)
for (c1 = 0; c1 <= NH/32; c1++) {
    for (c3 = 0; c3 <= NW/32; c3++) {
#pragma omp ordered depend(sink: c1-1, c3) depend(sink: c1, c3-1)
        for (c5 = max(1, 32*c1); c5 <= min(NH, 32*c1+31); c5++)
            for (c7 = max(1, 32*c3); c7 <= min(NW, 32*c3+31); c7++)
                main_center(c5, c7);
#pragma omp ordered depend(source: c1, c3)
} }
```

Fig. 3. Output: optimized OpenMP for Smith-Waterman (using our system).

Schedule, $\Theta^S(i)$: The sequential execution order of a program is captured by the schedule, which maps instance i to a logical time-stamp. In general, a schedule is expressed as a multidimensional vector, and statement instances are executed according to the increasing lexicographic order of their time-stamps.

Dependence Polyhedra, $\mathcal{D}^{S \to T}$: The dependences between statements S and T are captured by dependence polyhedra — i.e., the subset of pairs $(i, i') \in \mathcal{D}^S \times \mathcal{D}^T$ which are in dependence. We note n the dimensionality of $\mathcal{D}^{S \to T}$. Given two statement instances i and i', i' is said to depend on i if (1) they access the same array location, (2) at least one of them is a write and (3) i has lexicographically smaller time-stamp than i', that is $\Theta^S(i) \prec \Theta^T(i')$.

3   Motivating Example

The Smith-Waterman algorithm is used in evolutionary and molecular biology applications to find the optimal sequence alignment between two nucleotide or protein sequences, using dynamic programming to obtain the highest scoring solution. We show how this algorithm is encoded in our graph-based representation and then optimized by our polyhedral framework.

Figure 1 gives a visual representation of the Smith-Waterman algorithm, which contains 4 kind of steps: a single *corner* step (C) computing the top-left matrix corner and collections of steps computing the *top* row (T), *left* column (L) and the *main* body (M) of the matrix. The three-way arrows mark the flow of data between steps. As mentioned in Sect. 2.1, each instance of the same step collection is identified by a unique tag. Using a (NH+1)×(NW+1) integer matrix (which comprises item collection A), there are NH × NW main steps, each of which is identified by a tuple-tag (i,j), with $1 \leq i \leq$ NH and $1 \leq j \leq$ NW.

The data dependences (represented by arrows in Fig. 1) are modeled by using the tag (i,j) to identify a step instance and keys (affine functions of tag) to specify items; Note that all main steps read 3 items and write one item of collection A: [A:i-1,j-1], [A:i-1,j], [A:i,j-1] -> (M:i,j) -> [A:i,j].

The DFGL specification for Smith-Waterman is shown in Fig. 2. The first line of code declares an item collection, where each item is of type int. The next four lines of code specify, for each of the 4 steps, what items are read and written, as a function of the step instance's tag.

The final four lines specify what the environment needs to produce for the graph to start, and what it needs to emit after completion of the graph as output data. The environment starts all computation steps via :: operation, (e.g., main steps of {1 .. NH} × {1 .. NW}). It also reads one item resulting from the computation (the bottom right corner, which contains the optimal sequence alignment cost).

Although the dependences in this DFGL program expose a wavefront parallelism (e.g., step instances (M:1,10), (M:2,9), ... (M:10,1) can run in parallel), the computation granularity of each instance is too small to be implemented as a concurrent task on current computing systems. Furthermore, there are several choices on how to implement this wavefront parallelism, e.g., as a regular forall loop parallelism via loop restructuring (skewing) or using a special runtime that supports software pipelining. Figure 3 shows the optimized code in OpenMP, as generated by our framework. Loop tiling is applied to the kernel so as to improve both data locality and computation granularity. To implement the pipeline parallelism, we rely on an OpenMP-based fine-grained synchronization library [34], which will be supported in OpenMP 4.1 standard [28]. These transformations brought significant improvements as reported in Sect. 6.

4   Converting DFGL to Polyhedral Representation

In this section, we first introduce the programming flow using DFGL as an embedded domain-specific language (eDSL) for expressing the dataflow components in

```
void foo() {
    //C region
    int A[NH+1][NW+1];
    ...
    #pragma dfgl
    {
        //DFGL region
        [int A];
        ...
    }
    print(A[NH][NW]);
}
```

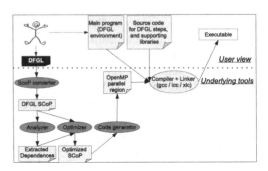

Fig. 4. DFGL as an embedded DSL

Fig. 5. Optimization and build flow for a DFGL parallel region.

an application. We also introduce the overview of our optimization framework, as well as the restrictions placed upon DFGL programs for compatibility with the polyhedral framework.

4.1 Embedded DFGL Programming Flow

As shown in Fig. 4, we use pragma dfgl to specify a DFGL program embedded in a regular C program. Each item collection in the DFGL program requires a corresponding array that is declared and in scope at the dfgl pragma. Users can initialize items and obtain computation results outside the DFGL program via the corresponding arrays. To enable legality check in Sect. 5.2, users need to describe which items are to be initialized/emitted as a form of write/read on the environment, e.g., env -> [A: key] or [A: key] -> env. The flow for compiling a DFGL parallel region is shown in Fig. 5. The user creates the DFGL description and provides the main program (DFGL environment) and codes for the compute steps. Then, they use our toolchain, which couples an extended translator [37] that we created for conversion to SCoP, and an extension to ROSE Compiler framework [2,33], to obtain an executable for running the application.

The first component of the toolchain is the *SCoP converter* that transforms the DFGL representation into a simplified SCoP format as described in Sect. 5.1. Next, we use the *Analyzer* to report errors in the input DFGL program and obtain the dependences. The dependences, along with the information from the DFGL SCoP, are then fed into the *Optimizer*. The final stage is the generation of the optimized OpenMP code, which is built together with the user-provided main program, kernels and libraries to obtain the executable.

4.2 DFGL Restrictions for Enabling Polyhedral Optimizations

To facilitate the conversion to a polyhedral representation, we focus on a restricted subset of DFGL that can be summarized as follows: (1) step tags are of the form

$i = (i_1, ..., i_k)$ with k the dimensionality of the associated step collection; (2) item keys are affine expressions of step tags; and (3) all steps are started by the environment such that the set of steps started can be described using only affine inequalities of the step tag. Note that a step-to-step dependence is converted into step-to-item and item-to-step dependences using a new item collection. Both rectangular regions (ranges [31]) and simple polyhedra shaped by affine inequalities of step tags are supported in DFGL. In practice, ranges and simple polyhedra are often enough to express the tag sets needed to model regular applications. They also come with the benefit of easy compilation to a loop-based language, which we will use to generate parallel OpenMP code.

The implementation we propose relies on generation of C code due to the benefits of high performance given by a low level language and the ease of programming provided by DFGL, which abstracts applications using a high-level representation. This approach is also appropriate for using DFGL as an embedded DSL, since the OpenMP code that our toolchain generates can be integrated into larger code bases (in effect, an OpenMP parallel region is generated for each DFGL parallel region), while the user steps, which the generated code calls, can themselves be optimized routines or library calls (possibly with non-affine data accesses, since only the DFGL program is processed by the polyhedral framework, not the internal step code).

5   Polyhedral Optimizations for DFGL

In this section, we present the details of our analysis and optimizations for an input DFGL program, in the context of a polyhedral compilation framework.

5.1   Polyhedral Representation of DFGL Program

This section introduces our approach for creating a polyhedral representation of a DFGL program. Each step is viewed as a polyhedral statement, for which an iteration domain is constructed by analyzing the creation of step instances by the environment and access functions are constructed by analyzing the dataflow expressions.

SCoP for DFGL Model. As shown in Sect. 2.2, the original SCoP format consists of three components: iteration domain, access relation, and schedule. The restricted DFGL model defined in Sect. 4.2 allows to seamlessly create the iteration domain to be represented as a polyhedron bounded by affine inequalities, and the I/O relations of each step instance to be modeled as affine read/write access relations. Examples of DFGL code fragments and their SCoP representations are shown below.

$$\texttt{[A:i-1,j+1]->(S:i,j)->[B:i,j]} \Leftrightarrow \mathcal{A}^{S_{R_1}}(i,j) = (A, i-1, j+1),\ \mathcal{A}^{S_{W_1}}(i,j) = (B, i, j)$$

$$\texttt{env::(S:\{1 .. N\},\{i .. M\})} \Leftrightarrow \mathcal{D}^S = \{(i,j) \in \mathbb{Z}^2 \mid 1 \leq i \leq \texttt{N} \wedge i \leq j < \texttt{M}\}$$

Instead of specifying the sequential execution order (total order) among all step instances, the DFGL model enforces ordering constraints via dataflow: a step instance is ready to execute only once all of its input items (data elements) are available. Therefore, the SCoP format specialized for DFGL contains iteration domains and access functions, but no explicit schedule.

Dependence Computations. To compute polyhedral dependences between any two step instances, we need to determine their *Happens-Before* (HB) relation — i.e., which instance must happen before another [24]. By definition of the dynamic single assignment form, only flow dependences can exist and any read to a memory location must necessarily happen after the write to that location. So we can define the HB relation between instance i of step S and i' of step T as:

$$\mathcal{HB}^{S \to T}(i, i') \equiv \mathcal{A}^{S_{W_l}}(i) = \mathcal{A}^{T_{R_m}}(i') \wedge (S \neq T \vee i \neq i')$$

This simply captures the ordering constraints of the DFGL model: step instance i' reading an item cannot start before step instance i writing that item completed, even if step instance i' of T appears lexically before instance i of step S in the DFGL program. According to the definition in Sect. 2.2, dependence polyhedra between steps S and T are simply expressed as:

$$\mathcal{D}^{S \to T} \equiv \{(i, i') \mid i \in \mathcal{D}^S \wedge i' \in \mathcal{D}^T \wedge \mathcal{HB}^{S \to T}(i, i')\}$$

which captures that i/i' is an instance of step S/T, i writes the item read by i' (access equation), and i happens before i' (HB relation). Because of the dynamic single assignment rule, the DFGL model disallows Write-After-Write dependence and Write-After-Read dependences. The next section outlines how polyhedral analysis can be used to check of these error cases.

5.2   Legality Analysis

This section introduces the compile-time analyses to verify the legality of a DFGL program. Enforcing the DFGL semantics, it detects the violation of the dynamic-single-assignment rule, plus three types of deadlock scenarios.

Violation of the single-assignment rule is equivalent to the existence of Write-After-Write dependences, and is represented by the following condition, which indicates that instances i and i' write an identical item (data element):

$$\exists i \in \mathcal{D}^S, \exists i' \in \mathcal{D}^T : \mathcal{A}^{S_{W_l}}(i) = \mathcal{A}^{T_{W_m}}(i') \wedge (S \neq T \vee i \neq i' \wedge l \neq m)$$

Self deadlock cycle is the simplest case of deadlock. An instance i needs to read an item which is written by i itself, thereby resulting in indefinite blocking.

$$\exists i \in \mathcal{D}^S : \mathcal{A}^{S_{W_l}}(i) = \mathcal{A}^{S_{R_m}}(i)$$

General deadlock cycle is the second of deadlock scenarios, where the dependence chain among multiple step instances creates a cycle. Any instance on the cycle waits for its predecessor to complete and transitively depends on itself. As discussed in Sect. 5.3, transformations in the polyhedral model are equivalent to a multidimensional affine schedule such that, for each pair of instances in dependence, the producer is scheduled before the consumer. The existence of such legal schedule [18] guarantees the absence of general deadlock cycle, and optimizers are built to produce only legal schedules.

Deadlock due to absence of producer instance is the third deadlock scenario. Even without a cycle in the dependence chain, it can be possible that a step instance i' needs to read an item that any other step instance does not write. Detecting this scenario is represented by the following condition, which means there is no step instance i that writes an item to be read by i'. Note that the items written/read by the environment env are also expressed as domains and access relations (Sect. 4.1)[3].

$$\exists i' \in \mathcal{D}^T \; : \; \neg \, (\exists i \in \mathcal{D}^S \; : \; \mathcal{A}^{S_{W_l}}(i) = \mathcal{A}^{T_{R_m}}(i'))$$

For instance, the following compile-time error message is shown if we remove the second line "(corner:i,j) -> [A:i,j];" in Fig. 2:
`Legality check: Deadlock due to no producer of (main_center:1,1)`

5.3 Transformations

Given a set of dependence polyhedra $\{\mathcal{D}^{*\to*}\}$ that captures all program dependences, the constraints on valid schedules are:

$$\Theta^S(i) \prec \Theta^T(i'), \; (i, i') \in \mathcal{D}^{S\to T}, \; \mathcal{D}^{S\to T} \in \{\mathcal{D}^{*\to*}\}$$

For any dependence source instance i of step S and target instance i' of step T, i is given a lexicographically smaller time-stamp than i'. Because of the translation of the DFGL program into a complete polyhedral description, off-the-shelf polyhedral optimizers can be used to generate imperative code (i.e., C code) performing the same computation as described in the DFGL program. This optimization phase selects a valid schedule for each step based on performance heuristics — maximizing objective functions. There have been a variety of polyhedral optimizers in past work with different strategies and objective functions e.g., [11,33]. The schedule is then implemented to scan the iteration domains in the specified order, and a syntactic loop-based code structure is produced using polyhedral code generation [8].

We used the PolyAST [33] framework to perform loop optimizations, where the dependence information provided by the proposed approach is passed as input. PolyAST employs a hybrid approach of polyhedral and AST-based compilations; it detects reduction and doacross parallelism [17] in addition to regular doall parallelism. In the code generation stage, doacross parallelism can be efficiently expressed using the proposed doacross pragmas in OpenMP 4.1 [28,34]. These pragmas allow for fine-grained synchronization in multidimensional loop nests, using an efficient synchronization library [38].

---

[3] In future work, we may consider the possibility of not treating this case as an error condition by assuming that each data item that is not performed in the DFGL region has a initializing write that is instead performed by the environment.

6   Experimental Results

This section reports the performance results of the proposed DFGL optimization framework obtained on two platforms: (1) an IBM POWER7: node with four eight-core POWER7 chips running at 3.86 GHz, and (2) an Intel Westmere: node with 12 processor cores per node (Intel Xeon X5660) running at 2.83 GHz. For benchmarks, we use Smith-Waterman, Cholesky Factorization, LULESH and six stencil kernels from PolyBench [25].

Smith-Waterman is used as our motivating example (Sect. 3). We run the alignment algorithm for 2 strings of size 100,000 each, with a tile size varying between 16 and 1024 in each dimension. As the baseline OpenMP implementation, we manually provided a wavefront doall version via loop skewing. Figure 6 shows the speedup results on our two test platforms, relative to the sequential implementation. We observe that the performance varies depending on the tile size chosen: for Westmere the best tile size is 1024, while for POWER7 the best tile size is 64. However our approach gives a big performance improvement compared with the skewed wavefront OpenMP implementation: up to 6.9× on Westmere and up to 2.3× on POWER7 for the maximum number of cores, due to cache locality enhancement via tiling and efficient doacross synchronizations.

Table 1. Overall and synchronization time (Smith-Waterman onPower7 with 32 cores)

	OpenMP	DFGL-16	DFGL-64	DFGL-256	DFGL-512	DFGL-1024
Overall	9.863 s	4.508 s	4.188 s	4.283 s	4.571 s	5.047 s
Synch.	1.720 s	0.482 s	0.163 s	0.128 s	0.129 s	0.143 s

To evaluate the efficiency of doacross (point-to-point synchronizations) and wavefront doall (barriers), we provided variants that removes all computations in the kerenel and only contains synchronizations. Table 1 shows the synchronization and overall execution times in second. When using 32 cores, the synchronization overheads for doacross with tile size = 64 and wavefront doall is 0.163[sec] and 1.72[sec], respectively. In addition to this synchronization efficiency, loop tiling by the optimization framework enhanced data locality; overall improvement over the OpenMP variant is 2.36× when using 32 cores and tile size = 64.

Cholesky Factorization is a linear algebra benchmark that decomposes a symmetric positive definite matrix into a lower triangular matrix and its transpose. The input matrix size is 2000 × 2000 and the generated code has 2D loop tiling with tile size varying between 4 and 32. In Fig. 7 that even though this approach does not yield a large speedup, it still gives improvement compared to the OpenMP implementation: 1.4× on Westmere and 3.0× on POWER7.

As reported in previous work [13], the combination of data tiling (layout transformation) and iteration tiling is a key technique for Cholesky Factorization while

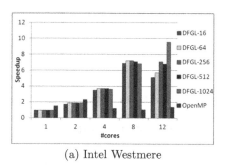
(a) Intel Westmere

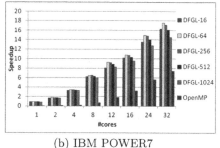
(b) IBM POWER7

Fig. 6. Smith-Waterman using 2 sequences of 100 k elements each. Results are for DFGL optimized code with loop tiling using tile sizes between 16 and 1024, and OpenMP baseline with parallelism obtained via loop skewing.

the current toolchain supports only iteration tiling. Alternatively, we manually implemented 50×50 iteration and data tiling within the user-provided steps and underlying data layout; the input DFGL is unchanged and our toolchain generated the same inter-step parallel code via doacross. This version brought significant improvements due to optimized cache locality, up to 15× on Westmere and up to 10.8× on POWER7 over standard OpenMP implementation. Furthermore, it gives on par performance with Parallel Intel MKL on 12 cores, on Westmere[4] and outperforms ATLAS on POWER7[5] on more than 4 cores.

These results further motivate our work, since the application tuning can be accomplished both by the polyhedral transformations and the user by replacing the steps with optimized versions. For example, in the case of cholesky, it is possible to call optimized MKL/ATLAS kernels inside the user steps. In our results, these steps are regular sequential steps and all parallelism comes from the OpenMP code generated by the polyhedral tools. Further, since DFGL can be used as an embedded DSL, the OpenMP code being generated can be incorporated in larger applications and coupled with optimized user steps.

LULESH is a benchmark needed for modeling hydrodynamics [1]. It approximates the hydrodynamics equations discretely by partitioning the spatial problem domain into a collection of volumetric elements defined by a mesh. In this implementation each element is defined as a cube, while each node on the mesh is a point where mesh lines intersect and a corner to 4 neighboring cubes. The mesh is modeled as a 3D space with N^3 elements and $(N+1)^3$ nodes. The benchmark uses an iterative approach to converge to a stable state. We pre-tested the application and saw a convergence after 47 iterations; thus in our results we use a fixed number of 50 iterations for simplicity.

Figure 8 gives the results for a 100^3 space domain and our toolchain tiled both the time loop and the 3D loop nest corresponding to the space. We see that even

---

[4] MKL is the best tuned library for Intel platforms. We compare against Sequential and Parallel MKL.

[5] On POWER7 we use ATLAS — the sequential library — as MKL cannot run on POWER7, and a parallel library was not available.

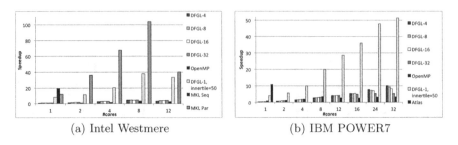

(a) Intel Westmere   (b) IBM POWER7

Fig. 7. Cholesky Factorization using 2000×2000 matrix. Results are for loop tiling using tile sizes between 4 and 32, OpenMP parallelism, data tiling resulting of the inner steps and reference MKL/Atlas implementations.

with a time tile size of 2, this leaves only 25 parallel iterations at the outermost doacross loop, which for the POWER7 in particular leads to a smaller speedup. The best results are obtained with no time tiling and a space tile of 8^3, on both Westmere and POWER7. We also observe a significant increase in performance compared with the reference C++ implementation which uses OpenMP [22].

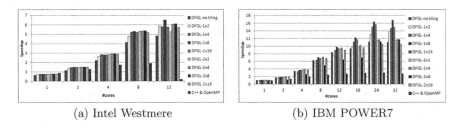

(a) Intel Westmere   (b) IBM POWER7

Fig. 8. LULESH for 50 time iterations and a 100^3 space domain. Results are for time loop tiling with tiles 1,2 and space loop tiles 2,4,8,16, and reference C++ OpenMP implementation.

Finally, we summarize results for the stencil benchmarks from the Polybench suite [25]: *Jacobi-2D*, *Jacobi-1D*, *Seidel-2D*, *FDTD* (Finite Different Time Domain), *FDTD-APML* (FDTD using Anisotropic Perfectly Matched Layer) and *ADI* (Alternating Direction Implicit solver) in Fig. 9 when using the maximum number of cores on each platform. We created the baseline OpenMP implementations in a standard manner: parallelism added at the outer most loop for fully parallel loops and after skewing for loops with loop-carried dependences. We did not add manual polyhedral optimizations.

The results show that the best tile sizes vary between platforms: on the Westmere the best results are generally for the larger time tile (4) and the largest space tile size (128), while for the POWER7 the best results are for the smaller time tile (2) and the smallest space tile (16). We also note that the results obtained using the DFGL toolchain outperform the OpenMP implementations for most cases, with up to 1.8× speedups.

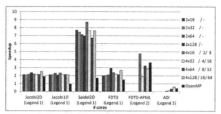

(a) Intel Westmere, 12 cores

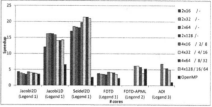

(b) IBM POWER7, 32 cores

Fig. 9. Stencil benchmarks from the Polybench suite. Results compare DFGL tiling with standard OpenMP parallel versions.

7   Related Work

DFGL has its roots in Intel's Concurrent Collections (CnC) programming model [12,21], a macro-dataflow model which provides a separation of concerns between the high level problem specification and the low level implementation. The original CnC implementation did not offer a means for definiting dependences at a high level, and an extended CnC model proposed for mapping onto heterogeneous processors [32] became the foundation for DFGL.

Compared to past work related to CnC, DFGL pushes the use of a high-level data-flow model as an embedded DSL for enabling robust compiler optimizations using a state-of-the-art polyhedral compilation framework that is capable of generating code for the new OpenMP 4.1 doacross construct. In addition, to the best of our knowledge, this work is the first to use polyhedral analyses to detect potential deadlocks and violations of the dynamic single assignment rule in a dataflow graph program specification. Other data-flow models also use a parallel underlying runtime to achieve performance, either a threading library, such as pthreads used in TFlux [35], or a task library, such as TBB used in Intel's CnC, or a parallel language such as Cilk used in Nabbit [6]. Legion [9] is another language which aims to increase programmability, however it requires an initial sequential specification of a program, similar to the input assumed by polyhedral compiler frameworks. DFGL eases programmability by separating the application description from its concrete implementation, and ensures that the optimized parallel code generated is not handled by the user. In addition, DFGL regions can be integrated in large scale applications as an embedded DSL, and can be coupled with optimized step code implementations or library calls.

Domain specific languages aim to give a high-level view of the applications and to ease programmability but are generally restricted to particular sets of problems, such as stencil computations [26] or graph processing problems [20]. In contrast, DFGL aims to combine the programmability benefits of DSLs with the optimizability of polyhedral regions, by using an approach that enables portable specifications of parallel kernels. Alpha [42] is a language which can be viewed as an eDSL for the polyhedral model. However the specification for Alpha is that of a full language, whereas DFGL can be composed with optimized step code defined in other languages, as long as these can be built together.

A number of papers addressed data-flow analysis of parallel programs using the polyhedral model, including extensions of array data-flow analysis to data-parallel and/or task-parallel programs [16,41]. These works concentrate on analysis whereas our main focus is on transformations of macro-dataflow programs. Kong et al. [23] applied polyhedral analysis and transformations for the Open-Stream language, a representative dataflow task-parallel language with explicit intertask dependences and a lightweight runtime. PolyGlot [10] was the first end-to-end polyhedral optimization framework for pure dataflow model such as LabVIEW, which describes streaming parallelism via wires (edges) among source, sink, and computation nodes. On the other hand, our framework aims at optimizing macro-dataflow model, where asynchronous tasks are coordinated via input/output variables in data-driven manner.

8   Conclusions

In this paper, we proposed an optimization framework that uses as input the DFGL model, a dataflow graph representation that results in high performance generated by polyhedral tools while still allowing the programmer to write general (non-affine) code within computation steps. We outlined the language features of DFGL and presented our implementation of the model, which provides a tool that reads in the DFGL specification and generates the SCoP format for polyhedral transformations. We then described the technical details for computing dependences based on the access functions and domain, as described in the SCoP format, using the dynamic single assignment property of DFGL. Further we described compile-time analyses to verify the legality of DFGL programs by checking for potential dynamic single assignment violations and potential deadlocks. We have shown experimental results for our implementation of the DFGL model, which offers good scalability for complex graphs, and can outperform standard OpenMP alternatives by up to 6.9×. The current restrictions on DFGL are inherited from the polyhedral model itself and should be also addressed in future work [14]. This work focuses on the C language; future work could consider C++ notational variants.

Acknowledgments. This work was supported in part by the National Science Foundation through awards 0926127 and 1321147.

References

1. Hydrodynamics Challenge Problem, Lawrence Livermore National Laboratory. Technical report LLNL-TR-490254
2. The PACE compiler project. http://pace.rice.edu
3. The Swarm Framework. http://swarmframework.org/
4. Building an open community runtime (OCR) framework for exascale systems, supercomputing 2012 Birds-of-a-feather session, November 2012

5. Ackerman, W., Dennis, J.: VAL - A Value Oriented Algorithmic Language. Technical report TR-218, MIT Laboratory for Computer Science, June 1979
6. Agrawal, K., et al.: Executing task graphs using work-stealing. In: IPDPS (2010)
7. Arvind., Dertouzos, M., Nikhil, R., Papadopoulos, G.: Project Dataflow: A parallel computing system based on the Monsoon architecture and the Id programming language. Technical report, MIT Lab for Computer Science, computation Structures Group Memo 285, March 1988
8. Bastoul, C.: Code generation in the polyhedral model is easier than you think. In: PACT, pp. 7–16 (2004)
9. Bauer, M., Treichler, S., Slaughter, E., Aiken, A.: Legion: expressing locality and independence with logical regions. In: SC (2012)
10. Bhaskaracharya, S.G., Bondhugula, U.: PolyGLoT: a polyhedral loop transformation framework for a graphical dataflow language. In: Jhala, R., De Bosschere, K. (eds.) Compiler Construction. LNCS, vol. 7791, pp. 123–143. Springer, Heidelberg (2013)
11. Bondhugula, U., Hartono, A., Ramanujam, J., Sadayappan, P.: A practical automatic polyhedral parallelizer and locality optimizer. In: PLDI (2008)
12. Budimlić, Z., Burke, M., Cavé, V., Knobe, K., Lowney, G., Newton, R., Palsberg, J., Peixotto, D., Sarkar, V., Schlimbach, F., Taşirlar, S.: Concurrent collections. Sci. Program. **18**, 203–217 (2010)
13. Chandramowlishwaran, A., Knobe, K., Vuduc, R.: Performance evaluation of concurrent collections on high-performance multicore computing systems. In: 2010 IEEE International Symposium on Parallel Distributed Processing (IPDPS), pp. 1–12, April 2010
14. Chatarasi, P., Shirako, J., Sarkar, V.: Polyhedral optimizations of explicitly parallel programs. In: Proceedings of PACT 2015 (2015)
15. Chatterjee, S., Tasrlar, S., Budimlic, Z., Cave, V., Chabbi, M., Grossman, M., Sarkar, V., Yan, Y.: Integrating asynchronous task parallelism with MPI. In: IPDPS (2013)
16. Collard, J.-F., Griebl, M.: Array dataflow analysis for explicitly parallel programs. In: Bougé, L., Fraigniaud, P., Mignotte, A., Robert, Y. (eds.) Euro-Par 1996. LNCS, vol. 1123, pp. 406–416. Springer, Heidelberg (1996)
17. Cytron, R.: Doacross: beyond vectorization for multiprocessors. In: ICPP 1986, pp. 836–844 (1986)
18. Feautrier, P.: Some efficient solutions to the affine scheduling problem, part II: multidimensional time. Int. J. Parallel Program. **21**(6), 389–420 (1992)
19. Feautrier, P., Lengauer, C.: The polyhedron model. In: Encyclopedia of Parallel Programming (2011)
20. Hong, S., Salihoglu, S., Widom, J., Olukotun, K.: Simplifying scalable graph processing with a domain-specific language. In: CGO (2014)
21. IntelCorporation: Intel (R) Concurrent Collections for C/C++. http://softwarecommunity.intel.com/articles/eng/3862.htm
22. Karlin, I., et al.: Lulesh programming model and performance ports overview. Techical report. LLNL-TR-608824, December 2012
23. Kong, M., Pop, A., Pouchet, L.N., Govindarajan, R., Cohen, A., Sadayappan, P.: Compiler/runtime framework for dynamic dataflow parallelization of tiled programs. ACM Trans. Archit. Code Optim. (TACO) **11**(4), 61 (2015)
24. Lamport, L.: Time, clocks, and the ordering of events in a distributed system. Commun. ACM **21**(7), 558–565 (1978). http://doi.acm.org/10.1145/359545.359563
25. Pouchet, L.-N.: The Polyhedral Benchmark Suite. http://polybench.sourceforge.net

26. Lu, Q., Bondhugula, U., Henretty, T., Krishnamoorthy, S., Ramanujam, J., Rountev, A., Sadayappan, P., Chen, Y., Lin, H., Fook Ngai, T.: Data layout transformation for enhancing data locality on NUCA chip multiprocessors. In: PACT (2009)

27. McGraw, J.: SISAL - Streams and Iteration in a Single-Assignment Language - Version 1.0. Lawrence Livermore National Laboratory, July 1983

28. OpenMP Technical Report 3 on OpenMP 4.0 enhancements. http://openmp.org/TR3.pdf

29. Sarkar, V., Harrod, W., Snavely, A.E.: Software Challenges in Extreme Scale Systems, special Issue on Advanced Computing: The Roadmap to Exascale, January 2010

30. Sarkar, V., Hennessy, J.: Partitioning parallel programs for macro-dataflow. In: ACM Conference on LISP and Functional Programming, pp. 202–211, August 1986

31. Sbirlea, A., Pouchet, L.N., Sarkar, V.: DFGR: an intermediate graph representation for macro-dataflow programs. In: Fourth International Workshop on Data-Flow Modelsfor Extreme Scale Computing (DFM 2014), August 2014

32. Sbîrlea, A., Zou, Y., Budimlić, Z., Cong, J., Sarkar, V.: Mapping a data-flow programming model onto heterogeneous platforms. In: LCTES (2012)

33. Shirako, J., Pouchet, L.N., Sarkar, V.: Oil and water can mix: an integration of polyhedral and AST-based transformations. In: Proceedings of the International Conference on High Performance Computing, Networking, Storage and Analysis, SC 2014 (2014)

34. Shirako, J., Unnikrishnan, P., Chatterjee, S., Li, K., Sarkar, V.: Expressing DOACROSS loop dependencies in OpenMP. In: 9th International Workshop on OpenMP (IWOMP) (2011)

35. Stavrou, K., Nikolaides, M., Pavlou, D., Arandi, S., Evripidou, P., Trancoso, P.: TFlux: a portable platform for data-driven multithreading on commodity multicore systems. In: ICPP (2008)

36. The STE—AR Group: HPX, a C++ runtime system for parallel and distributed applications of any scale. http://stellar.cct.lsu.edu/tag/hpx

37. UCLA, Rice, OSU, UCSB: Center for Domain-Specific Computing (CDSC). http://cdsc.ucla.edu

38. Unnikrishnan, P., Shirako, J., Barton, K., Chatterjee, S., Silvera, R., Sarkar, V.: A practical approach to DOACROSS parallelization. In: Kaklamanis, C., Papatheodorou, T., Spirakis, P.G. (eds.) Euro-Par 2012. LNCS, vol. 7484, pp. 219–231. Springer, Heidelberg (2012)

39. Vrvilo, N.: Asynchronous Checkpoint/Restart for the Concurrent Collections Model. MS thesis, Rice University (2014). https://habanero.rice.edu/vrvilo-ms

40. Wonnacott, D.G.: Constraint-based Array Dependence Analysis. Ph.D. thesis, College Park, MD, USA, uMI Order No. GAX96-22167 (1995)

41. Yuki, T., Feautrier, P., Rajopadhye, S., Saraswat, V.: Array dataflow analysis for polyhedral X10 programs. In: Proceedings of the 18th ACM SIGPLAN Symposium on Principles and Practice of Parallel Programming, PPoPP 2007 (2013)

42. Yuki, T., Gupta, G., Kim, D.G., Pathan, T., Rajopadhye, S.: AlphaZ: a system for design space exploration in the polyhedral model. In: Kasahara, H., Kimura, K. (eds.) LCPC 2012. LNCS, vol. 7760, pp. 17–31. Springer, Heidelberg (2013)

Concurrent Cilk: Lazy Promotion from Tasks to Threads in C/C++

Christopher S. Zakian[✉], Timothy A.K. Zakian, Abhishek Kulkarni,
Buddhika Chamith, and Ryan R. Newton

Indiana University Bloomington, Bloomington, USA
{czakian,tzakian,adkulkar,budkahaw,rrnewton}@indiana.edu

Abstract. Library and language support for scheduling non-blocking
tasks has greatly improved, as have lightweight (user) threading packages. However, there is a significant gap between the two developments.
In previous work—and in today's software packages—lightweight thread
creation incurs much larger overheads than tasking libraries, *even* on
tasks that end up never blocking. This limitation can be removed. To
that end, we describe an extension to the Intel Cilk Plus runtime system,
Concurrent Cilk, where tasks are *lazily* promoted to threads. Concurrent
Cilk removes the overhead of thread creation on threads which end up
calling no blocking operations, and is the first system to do so for C/C++
with legacy support (standard calling conventions and stack representations). We demonstrate that Concurrent Cilk adds negligible overhead
to existing Cilk programs, while its promoted threads remain more efficient than OS threads in terms of context-switch overhead and blocking
communication. Further, it enables development of blocking data structures that create non-fork-join dependence graphs—which can expose
more parallelism, and better supports data-driven computations waiting
on results from remote devices.

1 Introduction

Both **task-parallelism** [1,11,13,15] and **lightweight threading** [20] libraries
have become popular for different kinds of applications. The key difference
between a task and a thread is that threads may block—for example when
performing IO—and then resume again. Lightweight threading libraries usually require cooperative multitasking but can, in return, support over a million
threads, which is naturally useful for applications such as servers that involve
concurrent IO-driven computations. Tasks, in contrast, are of finite duration and
do not block. Indeed the non-blocking assumption is baked deeply into libraries
such as TBB (Threading Building Blocks [15]) and language extensions such as
Cilk [4]. Tasks are executed on shared worker threads where blocking such a
thread is a **violation of the contract** between programmer and library, which
can cause subtle deadlocks, as well as a loss of parallel efficiency.

If the no-blocking-guarantee can be met, then task-parallelism libraries
offer an order of magnitude lower overhead for creating parallel tasks ("many

© Springer International Publishing Switzerland 2016
X. Shen et al. (Eds.): LCPC 2015, LNCS 9519, pp. 73–90, 2016.
DOI: 10.1007/978-3-319-29778-1_5

tasking" rather than "multi-threading"). Cilk [4], in particular, is well known for its low-overhead *spawn* feature where the overhead of creating a parallel *fiber* with `cilk_spawn f(x)` is as little as 2–5 times the overhead of a regular function call, `f(x)`. The key to this low-overhead is that Cilk fibers are essentially *lazily parallel*: fibers execute sequentially, exposing the continuation of the parallel call with a minimum of overhead, and lazily promoting the continuation to a parallel continuation only when *work-stealing occurs*—and even then only using shared resources, not fiber-private stacks.

Because a traditional Cilk program must run even with *sequential semantics*—spawned fibers cannot serve the role of threads in the sense that they cannot be used for managing concurrent IO. That is, even continuations lazily promoted to *parallel* status, are not truly *concurrent*—they don't have their own stacks. It is this extra lazy promotion we add in Concurrent Cilk.

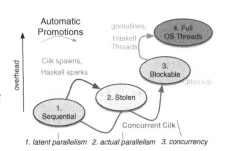

Fig. 1. State transitions possible for a fiber in each of several existing systems. At level (1), the fiber executes entirely within the stack of its caller. Work stealing transitions to (2) where a pre-existing system worker stack (allocated at startup) is used to execute the continuation of f in parallel. A blocked fiber requires additional storage for its state (3). Finally, blocking on underlying OS calls requires an OS thread (4).

To the programmer, a `cilk_spawn` and a thread spawn look very similar, but current limitations require knowing *at the point of the call*, which variant will be required: will the spawned computation need to suspend, and thus require its own stack? This decision point remains even in high-level languages designed with both parallelism and concurrency in mind, which support both tasks and threads using *separate* language mechanisms. For example, the Glasgow Haskell Compiler supports "sparks" (tasks) and language-level "IO threads" with different APIs [13].

Concurrent Cilk, on the other hand, extends the Cilk runtime interface with new primitives for *pausing* a fiber and returning a handle[1] that will allow other fibers (or Pthreads) to unpause the computation, and extends the states through which a fiber is promoted with a third, fully concurrent, state:

1. Executing sequentially, continuation uninstantiated
2. Executing in parallel with continuation, shares stacks
3. Fully concurrent, private stack, able to pause/resume

---

[1] This handle is similar to a [parallel] *one-shot continuation*. Continuations are well studied control constructs [9,17] and known to be sufficient to build cooperative threading (coroutines) [9] as well as blocking data structures that enable, for example, stream-processing with back-pressure.

That is, Concurrent Cilk initially executes fibers *sequentially*, lazily promoting them to "parallel work" during stealing, and lazily promoting them to "threads" only when necessary (Fig. 1). It then becomes possible to use the cilk_spawn feature for *all* parallelism and concurrency, even if it is not known (or even knowable) at the point of its creation whether the fiber will need to block—for example, for a computation on a server to wait on further communications with the client, or for a ray tracer to fetch remote data to compute a particular pixel.

Previous attempts to provide blocking, lightweight fibers in C have either required changing calling conventions and breaking legacy binary support [19], or create a full [linear] call-stack for each fiber [20]. Concurrent Cilk is the first system to enable lightweight threads in C, with legacy support, and memory-use (number of stacks) proportional to *blocked* fibers, not total spawned fibers.

On the other hand, for parallel languages with specialized compiler support, and no backwards compatibility concerns (linear stacks), lazy thread spawning *has* been explored, namely in the context of Id90 [7]. (Although Id90 used only states (1) and (3) above, not the full three-state algorithm.) And yet today, Concurrent Cilk is, to our knowledge, the only threading system that uses this algorithm, even including languages like Go, Haskell, and Erlang with good lightweight threading support. Nevertheless, with the prevalence of asynchronous workflows, especially in the web-services domain, we argue that this is an idea whose time has come. It provides a better abstraction to the programmer—with a single logical spawn construct replacing careful reasoning about non-blocking tasks, shared threads, and user threads—and it is implementable even in mature systems like Intel Cilk.

In this paper, we make the following contributions:

- We present the first system for unified lightweight tasking and threading that supports C/C++ code and existing binaries. We describe the changes that are necessary to add concurrency constructs (pause/resume a parallel fiber) to a mature, commercial parallelism framework, and we argue that other many-tasking frameworks could likewise adopt lazy-promotion of tasks to threads.
- We show how to build blocking data structures (e.g. IVars, channels) on top of the core Concurrent Cilk pause/resume primitives.
- We use Linux's epoll mechanism to build a *Cilk IO library* that provides variants of POSIX routines like read, write, and accept which block only the current Cilk fiber, and not the OS thread.
- We evaluate Concurrent Cilk in terms of (1) additional runtime-system overhead across a set of applications (Sect. 6.1); (2) opportunities for improved performance by *sync elision* (Sect. 6.3); (3) a study of injecting blocking IO in parallel applications, or, conversely, injecting parallel computation inside IO-driven server applications (Sect. 6.4).

2   Background and Motivation

Cilk itself dates from 1996 [4]; it is a simple language extension that adds parallel subroutine calls to C/C++. Only two constructs make up the core of Cilk:

cilk_spawn for launching parallel subroutine calls, and cilk_sync for waiting on outstanding calls (with an implicit cilk_sync at the end of each function body). For example, here is a common scheduler microbenchmark, parallel fibonacci:

Logically, each cilk_spawn creates a virtual thread, i.e. a fiber. Cilk then multiplexes these fibers on any number of OS *worker threads*, determined at runtime. Cilk only instantiates fibers in parallel when random work-stealing occurs.[2] Thus running parfib(42) does not create stack

```
long parfib(int n) {
  if (n<2) return 1;
  long x = cilk_spawn parfib(n-1);
  long y =              parfib(n-2);
  cilk_sync;
  return x+y;
}
```

space for half a billion fibers, rather it typically uses one worker thread for each processor or core.

Cilk is surprisingly successful as a language extension. This appears to be largely due to (1) Cilk's extreme simplicity, and (2) the legacy support in Intel Cilk Plus. That is, Cilk programs can be linked with previously compiled libraries and legacy code may even call Cilk functions through function pointers.

The work-stealing model supported by Cilk has been adopted by many other C/C++ libraries (Intel TBB, Microsoft TPL, and others). Unfortunately, so has its lack of support for blocking operations within parallel tasks. None of these C/C++ runtime systems can react to a task blocking—whether on a system call or an in-memory data structure. For example, TBB blocking data structures (e.g. queues) are not integrated with TBB task scheduling.

2.1   Blocking Deep in a Parallel Application

To illustrate the problem Concurrent Cilk solves, we begin by considering adding network IO to a plain Cilk application. Take, for example, software that renders movie frames via ray tracing.[3] A rendering process runs on each machine in a render farm, and may use all the processors/cores within that machine. Let us suppose the software evolved from a sequential application, but has been parallelized using Cilk constructs.

Somewhere in our rendering application we might expect to see a parallel loop that launches a ray for each pixel we are interested in. Contemporary Cilk implementations provide a cilk_for drop-in replacement for for, which is implemented in terms of cilk_spawn and cilk_sync.

---

[2] Cilk is a *work first* system, which means that the thread that executes **spawn f** will begin executing **f** immediately; it is the *continuation* of spawn that is exposed for stealing.

[3] Ray tracing follows an imaginary line from each pixel in the image into the scene to see what objects are encountered, rather than starting with the objects and drawing (rasterizing) them onto the screen.

Suppose now that in this context—deeply nested inside a series of parallel and sequential function calls—we encounter a situation where the ray has left the local virtual space, whose textures and geometry are loaded on the current machine, and entered an adjacent area stored elsewhere in networked storage. In this hypothetical rendering application, if every ray rendered had its own *Pthread* (which is impractical), then it would be fine to block that thread by directly making a network request as a system call.

```
sort(pix_groups);

cilk_for (i < start; i<end; i++){
    ... cast_ray(pix_groups[i]) ...
}
```

But if Cilk has been used to parallelize the application, the above is very dangerous indeed. First, because there is generally one Cilk worker thread per core, blocking a worker thread often *leaves a core idle*. Second, any attempts to hold locks or block on external events invalidates the traditional space and time bounds on Cilk executions [4].

```
// Deep in the stack,
// in the midst of rendering:
void handle_escaped(ray r, id rsrc){
    blob f = webapi.request(rsrc);
    // Block a while here,
    // waiting on the network...
    load_into_cache(f);
    resume_ray(r);
}
```

Finally, blocking calls can deadlock the system if there are enough such calls to stall all Cilk worker threads, starving other computations that might proceed—including, potentially, the one that would unblock the others!

Attempted Fix 1: Avoid Blocking. To *avoid* blocking within a parallel task, how can the application be refactored? If the need for IO operations is discovered dynamically (as in ray tracing), there are two options: (1) fork a Pthread at the point where IO needs to occur, passing an object bundling up the rest of the computation that needs to occur, *after* the IO completes;[4] or (2) return failure for the parallel task, wait until the parallel region is finished, then perform IO and try again (a trampoline). Because Cilk allows (strictly) nested parallelism, deferring actions until the end of a parallel region potentially requires restructuring the control-flow of the entire application—pulling all potential-IO in deeply nested contexts to the application's "outer loop".

Attempted Fix 2: Overprovision to Tolerate Blocked Workers. Of course, it is possible to provision additional Cilk workers, say, $2P$ or $4P$ (where P is the number of processors or cores). This would indeed hide some number of blocking operations, keeping processors from going idle, at the cost of additional memory usage and some inefficiency from over-subscription. Unfortunately, this puts the requirements on the user to understand the *global* pattern of blocking operations at a given point in program execution, which is especially difficult within a parallel region. Moreover, if blocked threads are interdependent on one another—for example using in-memory blocking data-structures for inter-fiber

---

[4] In other words, manually converting the application to *continuation passing style* (CPS).

communication—then the *maximum possible* simultaneously blocked computa-tions is key to deadlock avoidance. In general, violating the Cilk scheduler's contract (by blocking its workers) is a dangerous action that cannot be used composably or abstracted inside libraries.

Thus we argue that, if Cilk fibers must block their host threads, then it is better to create replacement worker threads on demand (as Cilk instantiates fibers on demand, upon stealing) as an integral part of the runtime system. Hence Concurrent Cilk.

3   Programming Model

Concurrent Cilk follows the Cilk tradition of using a small set of powerful, com-posable primitives, which can then form the basis for higher-level abstractions or syntactic sugar. The core primitives for Concurrent Cilk are pause and resume on fibers, and while library implementers directly use these primitives, most end users will prefer to use higher-level data structures. Thus we begin our exposition of the programming model using one such high-level structure—the *IVar*—as an example, and then we return to the lower level API later on in this section.

An IVar is a single-assignment data structure that exists in either an empty or full state. The basic interface is:

```
void ivar_clear(ivar*);
ivar_payload_t ivar_get(ivar*);
void ivar_put(ivar*, ivar_payload_t);
```

New IVars are stack- or heap-allocated and then set to the empty state with `ivar_clear`.[5] Get operations on an empty IVar are *blocking*—they pause the current fiber until the IVar becomes full. Once an IVar has transitioned to a full state, readers are woken so they can read and return the IVar's contents. IVars do not allow emptying an already full IVar.

Further, IVars are only one representative example of a synchronization structure built with pausable fibers—*MVars* would allow synchronized empty-ing and refilling of the location, or a bounded queue with blocking enqueues and dequeues.

Pausing the Fiber. In fact, all these data structures make use of the underlying Concurrent Cilk API in the same way. Here we show a simplified API, which will be optimized shortly, but which demonstrates *two phase* pausing, as follows.

1. `pause_fiber()` – capture the current context (`setjmp`), and begin the process of shelving the current fiber.
2. `commit_pause()` – jump to the scheduler to find other work.

---

[5] Here, and in the rest of this paper, we omit the prefix `__cilkrts_` which is found in most of the symbols in CilkPlus, and our fork, Concurrent Cilk https://github. com/iu-parfunc/concurrent_cilk.

In between these two operations, the fiber that is about to go to sleep has time to store a reference to itself inside a data structure. Without this step, it would not be possible for other computations to know that the fiber is asleep, and wake it. In the case of IVars, each empty IVar with blocked readers stores a pointer to a *waitlist*, which will be discussed in the next section. Further, as an implementation note, the `pause_fiber` routine must be implemented as an inline function or preprocessor macro—so that it calls `setjmp` from within the correct stack frame.

Waking the Fiber. The job for the `ivar_put` operation is simpler: attempt a compare and swap to fill the IVar, and retrieve the `waitlist` at the same time. If it finds the IVar already full, it errors. When put processes the `waitlist`, it uses a third Concurrent Cilk API call, which we introduce here, that has the effect of enqueuing the paused fiber in a ready-queue local to the core on which it was paused.

3. `wakeup_fiber(w)` – take the worker structure, and enqueue it in the readylist.

Naturally, thread wakeup and migration policies are a trade-off: depending on the size and reuse distance of the working set for the blocked computation, relative to the amount data communicated to it through the IVar. It could be best to wake the fiber either where it paused or where it was woken, respectively. We chose the former as our default.

4   Another High-Level Interface: I/O Library

Before delving deeper into the low-level Concurrent Cilk API and scheduler implementation, we first describe another abstraction layered on top of Concurrent Cilk, one which provides a programmer-facing abstraction that is key to the goal of Concurrent Cilk: blocking I/O calls intermingled with parallel tasks.

The Cilk I/O library we implemented provides a way for fibers to block—not just on application-internal events like another fiber writing an IVar—but on external events such as network communication. The programmer-visible API matches the normal POSIX API with functions prefixed with `cilk_`. Except, of course, blocking semantics are achieved, not by blocking the entire OS thread, but rather the Concurrent Cilk fiber. Our current implementation uses the Libevent library, which provides an abstraction over OS mechanisms like Linux's `epoll`. Libevent provides a programming interface for registering events with associated callbacks. It raises the abstraction level from raw `epoll` by, for example, handling the *event loop(s)* internally.

An initialization routine, `cilk_io_init`, needs to be called before calling any IO methods. This launches a new daemon thread to run the event loop. The `cilk_accept`, `cilk_read`, `cilk_write`, and `cilk_sleep` procedures register corresponding events to the event loop before yielding the control to a different fiber by blocking on an IVar read. In this, their implementations are *all* similar to the `ivar_get` implementation. Accordingly, `ivar_put` is performed by the event callback, running on the daemon thread containing the event loop. Note, however, that we do not need to worry about running computation *on* the event loop thread (which would delay it from processing events)—`ivar_puts` are cheap and constant time, only calling `wakeup_fiber()` to resume computation. As we saw before `wakeup_fiber()` *always* resumes the fiber on the worker thread where it went to sleep, which can never be the event loop thread.

In Sect. 6, we will return to the topic of the IO library as a foundation for server applications. Finally, note that it would be possible to use `LD_PRELOAD` or related methods to patch in Cilk IO calls instead of standard system calls, but this is beyond the scope of this paper; it could be built separately and on top of what we provide.

5   Low-Level Implementation and Scheduler

Cilk *workers* live in a global array which is accessed during the work-stealing process. When a worker becomes starved for work, another worker is then chosen, at random, from the global array and if there is any work available, the *thief* steals from the currently busy worker (victim) and computes on its behalf. There have been several implementations of Cilk, and other papers describe their implementation and interfaces in detail, from the early MIT versions of Cilk [6], to the binary ABI specification of Intel Cilk Plus [2]. Thus we do not go into detail here.

5.1   Adding the Concurrent Cilk Extensions

The idea of Concurrent Cilk is simple; however, the Cilk Plus runtime system is a complex and comparatively difficult to modify artifact, so implementation must proceed with care. Our basic approach is that if a Cilk worker becomes blocked, detach the worker from its OS thread[6] and substitute a *replacement worker* that then steals computation from any of the workers in the global worker array. When the blocking operation has finished, the worker is restored to an OS thread at the next opportunity and the replacement worker is cached for future use. In this way, all OS

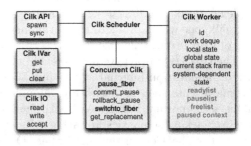

Fig. 2. The architecture of the modified Concurrent Cilk runtime system. Also pictured is the included, but optional, Cilk IO library. The bold red entries in the worker structure represent Concurrent Cilk extensions (Color figure online).

threads managed by the Cilk runtime are kept active. This strategy is similar

---

[6] A Cilk worker represents a thread local state which sits on top of an OS level thread.

to other lightweight threading systems [8, 13, 20], except in that Concurrent Cilk "threads" (fibers) start out *without* stacks of their own.

As pictured in Fig. 2, most Cilk worker state is thread-local—including a stack of stealable Cilk stack frames, a linear C stack, and many book-keeping and synchronization related fields. A cache of stacks is kept both at the global and thread-local levels, with local caches "filling" and spilling over into the shared pool. Concurrent Cilk adds three main additional fields:

1. Paused list – workers that cannot currently run
2. Ready list – workers that have unblocked and are ready for execution
3. Free list – an additional cache of workers that previously were paused and now can be used as replacements for newly paused fibers

Each of the lists above is currently implemented as a lock-free Michael and Scott queue [14]. This gives a standard round-robin execution order to ready-threads. When the current fiber pauses, work-stealing only occurs if there are not already local fibers on the ready list.

5.2   Scheduler Modifications

The additional Concurrent Cilk data structures described above are primarily touched by the pause, commit pause, and wakeup routines, and so they do not interfere with traditional Cilk programs that never block. However, there *must* be some modification of the core scheduler loop so as to be able to run work in the ready list.

The core scheduler algorithm picks random victims and attempts to steal in a loop, eventually going to sleep temporarily if there is no work available. We inject checks for the extra workers in two places:

- In the stealing routine – if a first steal attempt fails, rather than moving on from a victim, we attempt to steal work from any blocked workers on the same core (which may also have exposed stealable continuations before being blocked).
- At the top of the scheduler loop – we do *not* engage in work stealing if there are already threads in the ready list prepared to run. In this way, cooperative multi-tasking is possible in which no work-stealing is performed, and control transfers directly from thread to thread as in other lightweight threading systems. To make this maximally efficient, however, in the next Section we will have to extend the pause/wakeup API from the simplified form we have seen. Preferentially handling ready (local) threads over stealable work has precedent in existing (multi-paradigm) parallel language runtimes [13] that prioritize user-created, explicit concurrency over exploiting latent parallelism.

The above modifications change how we find victims, while at the same time we retain the global (static) array of workers as it is in Intel Cilk Plus—as the starting point for all work-stealing. In Concurrent Cilk the global array

represents the *active* workers, of which there are the same number in Concurrent
Cilk and Cilk. To maintain this invariant, we must necessarily rotate out which
workers reside in the global array. Whenever one worker pauses and activates
another, that replacement becomes "on top".

In Concurrent Cilk, paused or ready fibers may *also* have exposed stealable
continuations, that can be executed in parallel by a thief.[7] In terms of prioritizing
different work sources, we conjecture that it remains best to **steal from active
workers first**. Their working sets are more likely to be in a shared level of
cache. For that reason we only check paused fibers when the active one yields
no work.

From a software engineering perspective, leaving the global array of workers
in place and fixed size enables us to avoid breaking a system wide invariant in the
Cilk Plus runtime system, which would require substantial re-engineering. At the
same time, by modifying work-stealing to look deeper inside the list of paused
and ready workers, we retain a liveness guarantee for parallel continuations: *If
a physical worker thread is idle, all logically parallel work items are reachable
by stealing.* Any violation of this guarantee could greatly reduce the parallel
efficiency of an application in worst-case scenarios.

5.3   Optimized Pause/Resume Interface

Before proceeding to evaluation, there
is one more implementation issue
to address that can significantly
improve performance. The two-phase
pausing process described above
(`pause_fiber()`, `commit_pause(w)`) does
not specify *where* the current thread
yields control to upon `commit_pause` for
the simple reason that it always jumps
to the scheduler. When we round-robin
threads through a given core, it is more
efficient if one thread can long-jump
directly to the next one.

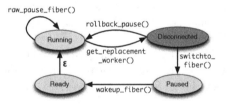

Fig. 3. Transitions in the state of a worker.
Disconnected is a temporary invalid state,
which requires either rollback or switching
to a replacement to restore to a good state.

Like other library interfaces (e.g., Boost smart/intrusive pointers) we provide
both a convenient interface, and a more "intrusive" but performant interface,
which requires that the API client assume more of the responsibility. This takes
two forms.

First, as promised, we enable direct `longjmp` between threads, but at the
expense of replacing `commit_pause` with a multiple calls in a finer grained
interface.

---

[7] The original proof of Cilk's space and time bounds relies on the critical path of the
computation remaining always accessible in this way. Non-uniform probabilities in
work-stealing are a concern to some authors of Cilk.

A `get_replacement` function returns a pointer to the replacement rather than jumping to the scheduler. This replacement *may* enter the scheduler but it could also go directly to another thread. It becomes the client's *responsibility* to dispatch to the replacement with `switchto_fiber`:

The protocol is that calling (1) by itself is fine, but after calling (2), one of the options in (3) *must* be called to restore the worker to a good state (Fig. 3). If the latter (`rollback_pause`) is chosen, that

1. `raw_pause_fiber(jmp_buf*)`
2. `get_replacement(worker*, jmp_buf*)`
3. `switchto_fiber(worker*, worker*)`
   OR
   `rollback_pause(worker*, worker*)`

simply rolls back the state of the current thread and current worker to before the call sequence began at (1).

In this API we can also see the second way in which we place additional obligations on the client: `raw_pause_fiber` also takes a `jmp_buf*` argument. The principle here is the same as with the IVar's waitlist—each blocked worker has a full stack, so it is possible to avoid dynamic memory allocation by making good use of this stack space, including, in this case, stack-allocating the `jmp_buf` that will enable the fiber to later resume. Thus all paused stacks store their own register context for later reenabling them after `wakeup_fiber` is called. This optimized, fine-grained version of the pausing API is what we use to implement our current IVar and Cilk IO libraries which we evaluate in the next section.

6 Evaluation

Because Concurrent Cilk proposes a new API, it is not sufficient to run an existing suite of Cilk benchmarks. Thus to evaluate Concurrent Cilk we examine each of its (potential) pros and cons, and design an experiment to test that feature.

- Possible Con: overhead on applications that don't use Concurrent Cilk.
- Possible Pro: lower fork overhead than eager lightweight threading packages.
- Possible Pro: sync elision – express non-fork-join dependence structures
- Possible Pro: better utilization of cores; no idleness on blocking
- Possible Pro: simpler programming model with uniform construct for spawning tasks and threads.

In this section, we characterize the overhead of Concurrent Cilk's extensions to the Cilk runtime through several scheduling microbenchmarks. We further compare the performance and scalability of Concurrent Cilk's blocking, context-switching and unblocking mechanisms through a performance shootout with other task runtime systems. The plots include min/max error bars with three trials.

The overhead tests in Sect. 6.1 and the scheduling microbenchmarks in Sect. 6.2 were run on a Dell PowerEdge R720 node equipped with two 8-core 2.6 GHz Intel Xeon E5-2670 processors (16 cores in total, and hyperthreading enabled) and 32 GB memory was used. The operating system used was Ubuntu

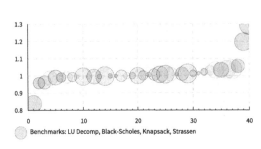

Benchmarks: LU Decomp, Black-Scholes, Knapsack, Strassen

Fig. 4. The overhead of adding Concurrent Cilk to the Cilk scheduler. The Y axis is the speedup/slowdown factor (higher better), and the X axis is the count of benchmarks. Each color represents one of the benchmarks from the set of regression tests, and for each benchmark there is a different bubble for each thread setting, where larger bubbles imply more threads (Color figure online).

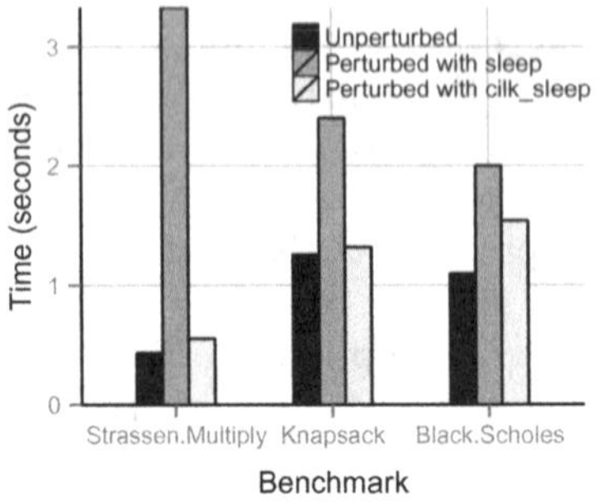

Fig. 5. The effect of perturbing existing computational kernels with simulated network dependencies. We sleep on a timer (either the OS thread or using epoll through the Cilk IO library) to simulate these network dependencies. Perturbations are random, and calibrated to happen for 50 % of total *CPU* time.

Linux 12.04.5 with kernel version 3.2.0. The tests in Sect. 6.3 were run on a quad socket system with Westmere Intel Xeon (E7-4830, 24M Cache) processors, each with 8 cores running at 2.13 GHz, hyperthreading disabled. The compiler used was ICC version 13.0.0 on optimize level 3, on Redhat 4.4.7-3 with kernel version 2.6.32-358.0.1.

6.1 Overhead of Concurrent Cilk Modifications

In modifying the Cilk runtime, the first principle is "do no harm"—have we incurred overhead for existing Cilk programs that do not pause fibers? In order to measure this overhead, we ran a series of existing Cilk benchmarks both with and without the Concurrent Cilk code in the runtime, scheduler loop, and work-stealing code path.

- LU Decomp: LU decomposition of a 2048 × 2048 matrix.
- Strassen: Strassen's algorithm for matrix multiplication on 2048 × 2048 matrices.
- Black-Scholes: Computes the financial, option-pricing algorithm.
- Knapsack: Solve the 0–1 knapsack problem on 30 items using branch and bound.

The results of these benchmarks, as summarized in Fig. 4, show that the slow-down to regular Cilk programs due to the added functionality of Concurrent

Cilk is a geometric mean of 1.1 %, with all but two benchmark configurations of knapsack showing no overhead throughout – and even then the overhead only happening while using hyperthreading. Note that in this plot, each different thread setting is considered a different benchmark instance.

Further, as a variation on these traditional benchmarks, in Fig. 5, we inject simulated network IO into the middle of parallel regions in each program. This models the situation described at the outset of this paper (e.g., a ray-tracer that has to fetch network data or do RPCs). The version using the Cilk IO library can hide the latency of "network" operations, keeping cores busy. Here, cilk_sleep is provided by the Cilk IO library to block only the fiber, while keeping the core busy, just as with cilk_read.

What is surprising is that, in the Strassen benchmark, the version that perturbs Cilk by knocking out a Pthread (true sleep rather than cilk_sleep), slows down the total runtime by *more* than would be predicted based on the total volume of blocked time and compute time. The problem is that with random injection of these "network" dependencies, sometimes the blocked region increases the critical path of the program in a way parallelism does not compensate for.

6.2 Scheduling Microbenchmarks

The parallel Fibonacci algorithm (Sect. 1) is a widely used microbenchmark for testing scheduler overhead, because it does very little work per spawned function. Cilk is known for its low-overhead spawns, with good constant factors and speedups on parallel Fibonacci in spite of the spawn density. Here we use this microbenchmark in two ways, to perform a shootout with or without using *first class synchronization variables*.

Shootout with First-Class Sync Variables. More general than Cilk's strictly-nested, fork-join model is the class of parallel programming models with arbitrary task dependence DAGs and first-class synchronization variables (e.g., IVars, MVars, channels). After adding IVars, Concurrent Cilk joins that more general family. In this subsection—before comparing against restricted many-tasking libraries—we first examine this more expressive class of schedulers by itself. That is, we compare implementations of parfib in which data is returned only via first-class synchronization variables, and which every spawned computation is at least *potentially* a blockable thread. Figure 6 shows this comparison.

Shootout with Task Runtimes. Again, the best-in-class performance for low-overhead parallel function calls goes to languages and runtimes like traditional Cilk. Figure 7 shows common task-parallel libraries compared against two different implementations running on the Concurrent Cilk runtime: the first is a traditional fork-join parfib running on Concurrent Cilk using cilk_spawn and return results simply with return/cilk_sync rather than through IVars. The second is the same implementation of parfib but using IVars—instead of syncs–to enforce data-dependencies.

Note that this graph runs a much larger input size (40 rather than 30), which is due to the fact that the multi-threading rather than multi-tasking runtimes cannot scale to nearly the same size of inputs. (In fact, they can exceed

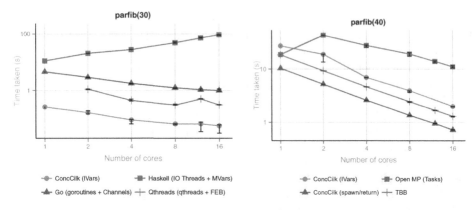

Fig. 6. A comparison of lightweight threaded runtimes with parallel fibonacci implemented by blocking on a **first-class synchronization object**. Concurrent Cilk does well, because of lazy thread creation. Each synchronization on an IVar *could* block, but not all do. Thus, initialization overhead is only incurred when needed.

Fig. 7. Restricted task-only libraries' performance on parallel fibonacci, with Concurrent Cilk (IVars) included for comparison. The IVar-based version does quite well here in spite of blocking threads on reads—it scales as well as TBB and raw Cilk (spawn/return), and outperforms Open MP.

maximum-thread limits and crash!) In this plot we see that while the Concurrent Cilk/IVar implementation cannot keep up with TBB or traditional Cilk, the gap is *much* smaller than it would be with Qthreads, Go, or Haskell threads.

6.3 "Sync elision" and Exposing Parallelism

In this set of benchmarks we examine the potential effects on performance of enabling *unrestricted* program schedules not normally possible in a strictly fork-join model. The most clear-cut example of a place where scheduling is over-constrained by Cilk is when we have a `producer` and a `consumer` separated by a sync. The `producer` and `consumer` may or may not contain enough parallelism to fill the machine, but because of the `cilk_sync`, there is no possibility of pipeline parallelism between producer and consumer.[8] We examine a simple case of this pipeline parallelism opportunity: a sequential producer that fills and then reads an array of 10,000 IVars for 1000 iterations. It takes Cilk 0.6356 s, whereas Concurrent Cilk in this case—which allows simply *deleting* the `cilk_sync` statement—takes 0.3981 s making the program 37 % faster by

---

[8] However, the specific, narrow case of linear, synchronous dataflow graphs is addressed by recent work on extending Cilk with pipeline parallelism via a new looping construct [10].

introducing a benevolent producer/consumer race condition; if the consumer gets ahead, it blocks on an unavailable IVar, allowing the producer to catch up.

It is in this way that the Concurrent Cilk version of the producer-consumer allows overlapping producing and consuming phases thus improving performance. This sort of example could be generalized to more traditional stream processing by replacing the array of IVars with a bounded queue.

Exposing More Parallelism: Wavefront. The topic of removing syncs to increase performance has received some previous attention, and in particular the Nabbit project [3] built an explicit task-DAG scheduler on top of Cilk, demonstrating its benefits on a *wavefront* benchmark. Concurrent Cilk is a different tool than Nabbit in that it allows true continuation capture rather than explicit registration

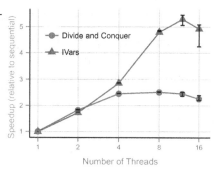

Fig. 8. A wavefront algorithm ran in two modes: first, in a divide-and-conquer recursive structure that divides the matrix into quadrants, executing the NW sequentially, and the NE and SW in parallel. The second mode is to simply fork a computation for each tile, and let IVars track the inter-tile data dependencies.

of callbacks (i.e., a manual form of *continuation passing style* which is a frequent source of complaints in, e.g., JavaScript web programming). In Fig. 8, we can see the speedup enabled on a relatively *coarse* grained wavefront computation (16×16 matrix of inner data structures of size 512×512). Because the granularity is fairly coarse, there is a shortage of parallelism in this example (which causes us to not speed up at 16 cores). The fork-join model "wastes" parallelism by adding unnecessary scheduling dependencies via syncs, whereas the IVar-based version retains all the application-level parallelism.

6.4   Servers with Per-Client Parallel Compute

A server that performs computations on behalf of a client can be an instance of *nested parallelism*: (1) Parallelism between clients ("outer loop"), and (2) Parallelism within the requested work for one client ("inner loop").

To be robust against both extremes—a single client with a large work item, and many small client requests—the Cilk approach to nested data parallelism would seem ideal. However, there's a drawback. In the server case, the outer loop includes blocking communication: to accept client connections, and then to send data to and receive data from each client.

The simplest way to program such a server is to use the same mechanism for parallelism at both levels: either `pthread_create` or `cilk_spawn`. Yet both of these implementations expose a problem. Forking too many pthreads can slow down or crash the application, whereas traditional Cilk spawns do not prevent underutilization when blocking calls are made (and blocking calls underneath a cilk_spawn can even be seen as a semantically incorrect contract violation).

In this experiment, we use an arbitrary parallel workload as the per-client request: compute parallel fibonacci of 40 or 30, bottoming out to a sequential implementation below $fib(10)$, and taking about 600 ms and 4 ms, respectively, when executed on one core. The important thing is that there is enough work to keep all cores busy, *even* with a single concurrent client.

We consider different strategies corresponding to how the outer/inner loop is handled. Thus "Conc cilk/cilk" uses Concurrent Cilk spawns at both levels, with cilk_accept, cilk_recv, and cilk_send in

Table 1. Throughput for different numbers of clients for alternate server implementation strategies at differing server workloads.

variant	# conc clients	work-per request	throughput (requests/s)
pthread/seq	1	fib(40)	2.53
	4	fib(40)	9
	8	fib(40)	18
cilk/cilk	1	fib(40)	33
	4	fib(40)	33
	8	fib(40)	35
conc cilk/cilk	1	fib(40)	35
	4	fib(40)	35
	8	fib(40)	35
pthread/seq	8	fib(30)	1891
cilk/cilk	8	fib(30)	1690
conc cilk/cilk	8	fib(30)	1656
pthread/pthread	1	fib(30)	0.48
	4	fib(30)	0.12
	8	fib(30)	died

place of the regular system calls. In contrast, "cilk/cilk" uses spawn at both levels, but regular system calls (i.e. it makes no use of Concurrent Cilk). Likewise "pthread/seq" spawns one pthread per client, but runs the inner computation sequentially. As we see in Table 1, pthread/seq is a perfectly reasonable strategy when there are enough clients. But when there is only a single client at a time, Cilk variants perform much better because they can utilize all cores even for one client. Likewise, Concurrent Cilk narrowly beats Cilk (35 vs. 32 requests per second), based on keeping all cores utilized. Of course, "pthread/pthread" cannot scale far due to limitations in OS thread scaling.

7   Related Work

In this section we consider Concurrent Cilk in the context of recent languages designed with concurrency/parallelism in mind: *e.g.* Go [8], Manticore [5], Concurrent ML [16], and Haskell. Haskell IO threads, for example, share one or more OS threads *unless* a blocking foreign function call is encountered [12], in which case more OS threads are recruited on demand. Likewise, "goroutines" in Go will share a fixed number of OS threads unless a thread makes a blocking call. Like the classic Stein and Shaw 1992 system, these systems *eagerly* create thread contexts upon spawning.

They specialize the stack representation, however. For example Go uses a segmented stack representation, heap-allocating a small stack to start and growing as needed [8]. Thus, Go and Haskell (and Manticore, CML, etc.) can spawn hundreds of thousands or millions of threads. Specifically, Go or Haskell can execute `parfib(30)`—using a forked thread in place of `cilk_spawn`, and a channel to communicate results back—in 4.7 s and 3.1 s respectively on a typical desktop.[9] This represents 1.3 million forked threads. But the programs also take 2.6 Gb and 1.43 Gb of memory, respectively! Also, as seen in Fig. 6, Concurrent Cilk supports the same program with the same semantics (first class sync vars and suspendable threads) at much higher performance.

MultiMLton—a whole program compiler for a parallel dialect of SML—is a recent system which employs a lazy thread creation technique called *parasitic threads* [18]. These leverage relocatable stack frames to execute forked threads immediately inside the callers stack, moving them lazily only if necessary. This technique is effective, but not applicable to C/C++ where stack frames are non-relocatable.

8 Conclusions and Future Work

We have shown how, even with the constraint of legacy language support (C/C++ with linear stacks) and the complications of a mature parallel runtime system (Cilk Plus), lazy thread creation can still be an appealing prospect. Implementing it for Cilk Plus required only a couple points of contact with the existing scheduler code. Most of the complexity falls in higher level libraries, such as our IVar and Cilk IO libraries.

In future work, we plan to continue building high-level concurrent data structures and control constructs on top of the simple pause/resume fiber interface. As we saw in Sect. 6, IVars are already sufficient to speed up some programs with data-driven control-flow in a non-fork-join topology, and the Cilk IO library is sufficient to build server applications that mix concurrency and implicit parallelism.

Acknowledgements. This material is based in part upon work supported by the Department of Energy under Award Number DE-SC0008809, and by the National Science Foundation under Grant No. 1337242.

References

1. Intel Cilk Plus. http://software.intel.com/en-us/articles/intel-cilk-plus/
2. Intel Cilk Plus Application Binary Interface Specification. https://www.cilkplus. org/sites/default/files/open_specifications/CilkPlusABI_1.1.pdf
3. Agrawal, K., Leiserson, C., Sukha, J.: Executing task graphs using work-stealing. In: IPDPS, pp. 1–12, April 2010
4. Blumofe, R.D., Joerg, C.F., Kuszmaul, B.C., Leiserson, C.E., Randall, K.H., Zhou, Y.: Cilk: an efficient multithreaded runtime system. SIGPLAN Not. **30**, 207–216 (1995)

---

[9] Using all four cores of an Intel Westmere processor (i5-2400 at 3.10 GHz), 4 Gb memory, Linux 2.6.32, GHC 7.4.2 and Go 1.0.3.

5. Fluet, M., Rainey, M., Reppy, J., Shaw, A., Xiao, Y.: Manticore: a heterogeneous parallel language. In: 2007 Workshop on Declarative Aspects of Multicore Programming, DAMP 2007, pp. 37–44. ACM, New York (2007)
6. Frigo, M., Leiserson, C.E., Randall, K.H.: The implementation of the cilk-5 multithreaded language. SIGPLAN Not. **33**(5), 212–223 (1998)
7. Goldstein, S.C., Schauser, K.E., Culler, D.E.: Lazy threads: implementing a fast parallel call. J. Parallel Distrib. Comput. **37**(1), 5–20 (1996)
8. Google. The Go Programming Language. https://golang.org
9. Haynes, C.T., Friedman, D.P., Wand, M.: Obtaining coroutines with continuations. Comput. Lang. **11**(3.4), 143–153 (1986)
10. Lee, I., Angelina, T., Leiserson, C.E., Schardl, T.B., Sukha, J., Zhang, Z.: On-the-fly pipeline parallelism. In: Proceedings of the 25th ACM Symposium on Parallelism in Algorithms and Architectures, pp. 140–151. ACM (2013)
11. Leijen, D., Schulte, W., Burckhardt, S.: The design of a task parallel library. SIGPLAN Not. **44**, 227–242 (2009)
12. Marlow, S., Jones, S.P., Thaller, W.: Extending the haskell foreign function interface with concurrency. In: Proceedings of the ACM SIGPLAN Workshop on Haskell, pp. 22–32. ACM (2004)
13. Marlow, S., Peyton Jones, S., Singh, S.: Runtime support for multicore haskell. In: International Conference on Functional Programming, ICFP 2009, pp. 65–78. ACM, New York (2009)
14. Michael, M.M., Scott, M.L.: Simple, fast, and practical non-blocking and blocking concurrent queue algorithms. In: Proceedings of the Fifteenth Annual ACM Symposium on Principles of Distributed Computing, PODC 1996, pp. 267–275. ACM, New York (1996)
15. Reinders, J.: Intel Threading Building Blocks: Outfitting C++ for Multi-core Processor Parallelism. O'Reilly Media, Sebastopol (2007)
16. Reppy, J.H.: Concurrent ML: design, application and semantics. In: Lauer, P.E. (ed.) Functional Programming, Concurrency, Simulation and Automated Reasoning. LNCS, vol. 693, pp. 165–198. Springer, Heidelberg (1993)
17. Rompf, T., Maier, I., Odersky, M.: Implementing first-class polymorphic delimited continuations by a type-directed selective cps-transform. SIGPLAN Not. **44**, 317–328 (2009)
18. Sivaramakrishnan, K., Ziarek, L., Prasad, R., Jagannathan, S.: Lightweight asynchrony using parasitic threads. In: Workshop on Declarative Aspects of Multicore Programming, DAMP 2010, pp. 63–72. ACM, New York (2010)
19. von Behren, R., Condit, J., Zhou, F., Necula, G.C., Brewer, E.: Capriccio: scalable threads for internet services. SIGOPS Oper. Syst. Rev. **37**(5), 268–281 (2003)
20. Wheeler, K.B., Murphy, R.C., Thain, D.: Qthreads: an api for programming with millions of lightweight threads. In: IPDPS, pp. 1–8. IEEE (2008)

Interactive Composition of Compiler Optimizations

Brandon Nesterenko[✉], Wenwen Wang, and Qing Yi

University of Colorado Colorado Springs, Colorado Springs, USA
{bnestere,wwang2,qyi}@uccs.edu

Abstract. Conventional compilers provide limited external control over the optimizations they automatically apply to attain high performance. Consequently, these optimizations have become increasingly ineffective due to the difficulty of understanding the higher-level semantics of the user applications. This paper presents a framework that provides interactive fine-grained control of compiler optimizations to external users as part of an integrated program development environment. Through a source-level optimization specification language and a Graphical User Interface (GUI), users can interactively select regions within their source code as targets of optimization and then explicitly compose and configure how each optimization should be applied to maximize performance. The optimization specifications can then be downloaded and fed into a backend transformation engine, which empirically tunes the optimization configurations on varying architectures. When used to optimize a collection of matrix and stencil kernels, our framework was able to attain 1.84X/3.83X speedup on average compared with using icc/gcc alone.

1 Introduction

As software applications continue to become more complex and difficult to analyze, compilers have to be increasingly conservative and refrain from many optimization opportunities, due to the lack of sufficient understanding of their input code. While developers are allowed some control over various strategies adopted by compilers through command line options, these controls are limited to very high level instructions, e.g., whether to attempt $-O1$, $-O2$, or $-O3$ optimizations. The internal decisions within the compiler are kept entirely away from developers. Although pragmas may be inserted into source code to guide optimizations of specific code regions, they are not always respected, as the compiler makes the correctness guarantee of the compiled code a top priority.

It is well known that compiler optimizations are generally over-conservative, not only because of the difficulty of understanding the higher-level semantics of an input code via static program analysis, but also because of the unpredictable interactions among the optimizations as the compiler tries to manage

This research is funded by NSF through award CCF1261811, CCF1421443, and CCF1261778, and DOE through award DE-SC0001770.

X. Shen et al. (Eds.): LCPC 2015, LNCS 9519, pp. 91–105, 2016.
DOI: 10.1007/978-3-319-29778-1_6

the increasingly large collection of machine resources, e.g., registers, caches, and shared memories, of the evolving modern architectures. In short, compilers need to allow developers to help more, especially when they are experts of high performance computing. By allowing developers to exert more deliberate and fine-grained control over compiler optimizations, their code may be more intelligently optimized without compromising program correctness.

This paper presents an integrated program development environment that provides compiler optimizations as an interactive toolset for developers to conveniently improve the efficiency of their applications. Our environment supports extensive parameterization for a set of available optimizations, fine-grained coordination among the optimizations once selected to optimize a piece of source code, and the empirical tuning of optimization configurations based on runtime feedback of differently optimized code. The objective is to provide a convenient interface for developers to control the optimization decisions without compromising the correctness or readability of their code.

Figure 1 shows the overall workflow of our interactive environment, which includes three main components. The first component is a web-based *Graphical User Interface (GUI)*, which a developer can use to select regions of their source code to optimize, potentially profitable optimizations for each selected region, and the configuration of each optimization. Annotations are then inserted into the source code to tag the selected regions as optimization targets, and the optimization decisions are encoded in a very high level (VHL) specification language and passed to an *Optimization Synthesis* component, which converts the VHL specification into a lower-level implementation encoded using the POET program transformation language [18]; The *POET Transformation Engine* component then interprets

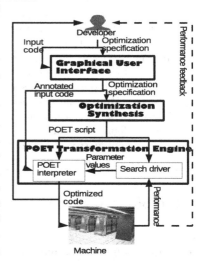

Fig. 1. The optimization workflow

the lower-level POET script to generate an optimized variant of the annotated input source code. The developer may then test the performance gain of the optimizations and repeat the process until satisfactory performance is attained. The POET optimization script can be ported to different machines together with an annotated input program generated by the GUI. The *POET transformation engine*, easily installed on each machine, can then provide empirical tuning support by automatically interpreting the POET scripts with different optimization configurations until satisfactory performance is achieved.

Our environment currently supports a number of source-level loop and data layout optimizations, including OpenMP parallelization, loop distribution, fusion, interchange, skewing, blocking, unroll&jam, unrolling, array copying, and scalar replacement, which are known to be machine sensitive and to interact with one another in unpredictable ways. The key technical challenges addressed by our environment while interactively integrating these optimizations include:

- Extensive parameterization of optimizations: each optimization can be independently toggled on/off for each code region and associated with an arbitrarily large configuration space, e.g., cache/parallelization/register blocking factors. Fine-grained coordination among the optimizations is inherently supported through careful ordering of the selected optimizations and tracing of the code regions being modified.
- Programmable composition of extensively parameterized optimizations: the automatically generated POET output serves as an optimization script that intelligently composes the user-selected optimizations one after another while eliminating potential risks of unpredictable interactions among them.

Auto-tuning of the optimized code is supported using the extension of a previously developed transformation-aware search algorithm [19]. On two machines, we have used the environment to optimize six scientific kernels and have attained 1.84X/3.83X speedup compared to using a vendor compiler alone.

The rest of the paper is organized as follows. Section 2 introduces our GUI for supporting interactive optimization selection and configuration. Section 3 introduces the POET transformation engine and how it can be used support the programmable control and flexible composition of the optimizations. Section 4 presents our optimization synthesis component, which automatically converts VHL specifications into a POET optimization script tailored for the user application. Experimental evaluation is presented in Sect. 5. Section 6 discusses related work. Finally, conclusions are drawn in Sect. 7

2   The Graphical User Interface

Developed to allow interactive selection and customization of compiler optimizations, our web-based GUI is implemented in JavaScript and HTML, with an Apache and PHP backend. The interface allows a user to upload an arbitrary number of files either as the source code of an application, optionally with previously selected regions of code annotated as optimization targets, or as an existing VHL specification saved from previous runs of the GUI to optimize some selected regions of the source code. For each uploaded source code, a user can select desired regions of code as targets of optimization, and customize the desired optimizations for each selected target. Then, the GUI automatically inserts code annotations that tag the selected optimization targets into the source and then generates a VHL specification from the user's customization. Both the annotated source code and VHL specifications can be downloaded and saved by the user for future use. At any time, the user can instruct the GUI to pass the active source code and its VHL specification to the backend components to generate optimized source code on the fly to be examined and experimented with by the user. Both the optimized source code and the auto-generated POET scripts can also be downloaded at any time as desired by the user.

Figure 3(a) shows the VHL specification that the GUI automatically generated for the matrix-multiplication kernel shown in Fig. 4(a). The sequence of interactions between the user and the GUI to generate the VHL specifications is shown in Fig. 2. The process starts with the user uploading a source code file (e.g. Figure 4(a)) to optimize. The uploaded file is then automatically parsed and analyzed by the GUI, which displays the code back to the user on the main panel of the web-page with potential optimization targets, e.g., nested loops and array references, highlighted. If an existing VHL specification is uploaded, each pre-specified optimization is validated, and the valid optimizations are added into the optimization configuration panel. The user can select highlighted code regions by clicking on the highlighted text and then providing a name to tag the selected optimization target. Once the targets have been identified, optimizations may be constructed. The user can interact with two HTML pick-lists to create each optimization: the first pick-list is comprised of all user-defined optimization targets, and the second holds all sup-

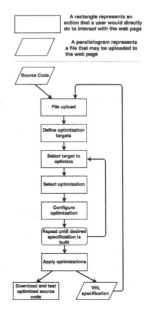

Fig. 2. Interacting with the user

ported optimizations. Once the target and optimization have been selected, a new optimization automatically appears in the optimization configuration panel, with a set of additional parameters to be further customized when the user clicks the optimization's "Edit" button. A majority of parameters are initially set to default values and can be automatically tuned later to suit the needs of user applications. If a user specifies out-of-range values for any parameters, the GUI will immediately display an error message on the screen.

Our framework allows developers to experiment with an assortment of optimizations as a toolbox without requiring detailed knowledge of the optimizations. When a set of optimizations is ready for testing, an "Apply Optimizations" button is clicked to start the automated process. The GUI first encodes the selected optimizations into the VHL specification language. It then passes the specification and source code to the *Optimization Synthesis* and *POET Translation Engine* components, with a logging panel displaying their working status. If the optimizations are successfully applied, the optimized source code is displayed on the main panel of the GUI. At this point the optimized source code and its VHL specifications are immediately available for download, allowing the users to save, examine, and test them for correctness or profitability. In the event that the optimized source code is unsatisfactory, the user can move back to the original source code and VHL specification to start over. Multiple files are supported by the GUI, with an HTML pick-list holding the names of all uploaded source files. As each file is selected in this pick-list, its content is displayed on the main panel, along with its previously configured optimizations in the optimization configuration panel.

```
                          1: include opt.pi
                          2: <parameter N2_blk_sz default=(32 32 32) />
                          3: <parameter N2_par_blk_sz default=(256) />
                          4: <trace inputCode,N1,N2,N4,N3 />
                          5: <input from="mm.c" syntax="Cfront.code" to=inputCode/>
Nests: N1, N2, N3, N4     6: <trace N2_cleanup=(N2) /> <trace N2p=(N2_cleanup) />
PermuteLoops:inner_loop=N3 target=N2    7: <trace N2_private = (("j" "k" "i")) />
           order="3,1,2"  8:......
FuseLoops: loop_to_fuse=N1 target=N2    9:<eval EraseTraceHandle[repl=N2p](N2,inputCode);
FuseLoops: loop_to_fuse=N1 target=N4   10:   PermuteLoops[order=(3 1 2)](N3[N.body],N2);
ParallelizeLoop: target=N2             11:   FuseLoops(N1,N2);
           private=j,k,i               12:   FuseLoops(N1,N4);
BlockLoops: inner_loop=N3 target=N2    13:   BlockLoops[factor=N2_par_blk_sz](N2[Nest.body],N2p);
           factor=32,32,32             14:   ParallelizeLoop[private=N2_private](N2p);
                                       15:   TraceNestedLoops(N2_cleanup,N2p[Nest.body]);
                                       16:   BlockLoops[factor=N2_blk_sz;
                                                       trace_ivars=N2_private](N3,N2);
                                       17:   CleanupBlockedNests(N2_cleanup); />
                                       18: <output syntax="Cfront.code" from=inputCode />
```

(a) VHL specification   (b) auto-generated POET script

Fig. 3. Applying loop optimizations to a matrix-multiplication kernel

3   The POET Transformation Engine

POET is a scripting language [18,20] designed to support programmable control and flexible composition of heavily parameterized compiler optimizations. As shown in Fig. 1, the transformation engine includes two components: the POET language interpreter, and an empirical search engine. The POET interpreter takes three inputs: the POET script describing what optimizations to apply, an annotated source code of the input program to optimize, and configurations of the optimization parameters. It then applies the desired optimizations and generates an optimized code. The empirical search engine [19], on the other hand, automatically explores the configuration space of the optimizing transformations and iteratively experiments with differently optimized code until satisfactory performance is attained. This empirical tuning support allows the optimized code to be automatically ported to different platforms without requiring the user to set the best optimization configurations. Both the language interpreter (together with its optimization libraries in POET) and the search engine are lightweight and can be easily ported to different machines, thereby supporting the performance portability of applications optimized through our interactive GUI.

Figure 3(b) illustrates the auto-generated POET optimization script from the VHL specification in (a). The inclusion of file *opt.pi* at line 1 in the script ensures that the POET *opt* library, which supports a large number of compiler optimizations, can be invoked by the given script. Lines 2–3 declare configuration parameters (blocking factors) of the optimizations to be empirically tuned by the search engine. Line 4 declares 5 special global variables (input-Code, N1 - N4) called *coordination handles* [21], which have been used to tag various fragments of the input code, as these code fragments are used either as the targets or additional configuration parameters of the selected optimizations. These coordination handles are embedded inside the input code, illustrated in Fig. 4(a)–(e), to automatically keep track of modifications to their content as the input code goes through each of the optimizations in the VHL specification. Line 5 parses the matrix multiplication code using C syntax descriptions specified in file *Cfront.code* and then stores the resulting AST to the coordination handle *inputCode*. Lines 6–7 declare two additional coordination handles, similarly embedded in the input code illustrated in Fig. 4(a)–(e). Lines 9–17 serve to apply the 5 optimizations specified in the VHL specification one after another, by using the 7 coordination handles (declared at lines 4, 6, and 7) and the tuning parameters (declared at lines 2–3) as parameters to invoke the underlying optimization implementations from the POET *opt* library. Each optimization modifies these handles to coordinate their transformations of the input code. Finally, the *output* command at line 18 unparses the optimized AST to standard output.

4   Optimization Synthesis

The optimization synthesis component automatically translates a VHL specification obtained from the GUI, e.g., Fig. 3(a), into a POET script that the *POET Transformation Engine* can use to systematically optimize the selected targets embedded inside the user application by the GUI. Our algorithm in Fig. 5 shows the steps taken for this process. As illustrated in Fig. 3(b), the resulting POET script needs to correctly perform the following tasks.

1. Parameterization of the optimizations: due to the difficulty of predicting the potential interactions among the optimizations and the characteristics of the machines that the input application may be ported to, all machine-sensitive optimizations need to be parameterized, so that their configurations can be empirically tuned later by the POET transformation engine.
2. Collective customization of the optimizations: since the user can select many optimizations for each region of code, the individually configured optimizations must be collectively customized to maximize their overall effectiveness.
3. Fine-grained coordination among optimizations: since the optimizations in the VHL specification must be applied one after another in the POET script, an earlier optimization may modify the input to such a point that a later one can no longer be applied correctly, unless all optimizations carefully coordinate with one another at every step.

To address the above challenges in a fully extensible fashion so that it can be easily made to include more optimizations in the future, our algorithm uses five configuration tables, summarized in the following, to save all information about the optimizations currently supported.

4.1   Configuration Tables

As shown at the beginning of Fig. 5, our *GenOptScript* algorithm requires six input parameters, including the VHL specification (*spec*), alongside the following

```
inputCode:{
void gemm(double *a,double
1: *b,double *c,double t,int n)
2: {
3: int i,j,k;
4: {N1:{for (j=0; j<n; j ++)
5:  for (i = 0; i < n; i ++)
6:   c[j*n+i] = t*c[j*n+i];}
7: N2p:{N2_cleanup:{N2:{
    for (k=0; k<n; k++)
8:  N4:{for (j=0; j<n; j++)
9:   N3:{for (i=0; i<n; i++)
10:   c[j*n+i] +=
       a[k*n+i] * b[j*n+k]; }}}
11:}}
        (a) original code
```

```
inputCode:{
void gemm(double *a,double
1: *b,double *c,double t,int n)
2: {
3: int i,j,k;
4: N1:{for (j = 0; j < n; j ++)
5:  for (i = 0; i < n; i ++)
6:   c[j*n+i] = t*c[j*n+i];}
7: N2p:{N2_cleanup:N2:{
    for (j=0;j<n;j++)
8:  N4:{for (i = 0; i < n; i ++)
9:   N3:{for (k=0; k<n; k++)
10:   c[j*n+i] +=
       a[k*n+i] * b[j*n+k]; }}}}
11:}}
      (b) after loop permutation
```

```
inputCode:{
void gemm(double *a,double
1: *b,double *c,double t,int n)
2: {
3: int i,j,k;
4: N2p:{N2_cleanup:N2:{
    for (j=0;j<n;j++)
5: N4:{for (i=0; i<n; i++) {
6:  N1:{c[j*n+i]=t*c[j*n+i];}
7:  N3:{for (k=0; k<n; k++)
8:   c[j*n+i] +=
      a[k*n+i] * b[j*n+k]; }
9:  }}}}
10:}}
      (c) after loop fusion
```

```
inputCode:{
void gemm(double *a,double
1: *b,double *c,double t,int n)
2: {
3: int i,j,k,i1,j1,k1;
4: N2p:{#pragma omp for private(j1,j,i,k)
5: for (j1 = 0; j < n; j +=256)
6:  N2_cleanup:{
7:  N2:{for (j=0; j<min(256,n-j1); j++)
8:  N4:{ for (i = 0; i<n; i ++) {
9:   N1:{c[j*n+i]=t*c[j*n+i];}
10:   N3:{for (k=0; k<n; k++)
11:   c[j*n+i] +=
       a[k*n+i] * b[j*n+k]; }
12:  }}}}
13:}}
      (d) after loop parallelization
```

```
inputCode:{
void gemm(double *a,double
1: *b,double *c,double t,int n)
2: {
3: int i,j,k,j1,k1,j2,i1;
4: N2p:{#pragma omp for private(j1,j,i,k,j2,i1,k1)
5: for (j1 = 0; j < n; j +=256)
7: N2_cleanup:{
8: N2:{for (j2=0; j2<min(256,n-j1); j2+=32)
9: N4:{for (i1 = 0; i1<n; i1+=32)
10: N3:{for (k1=0; k1<n; k1+=32)
11: for (j=0; j<min(32,n-j1-j2); j++)
12: for (i=0; i<min(32,n-i1); i++) {
13:  if (k1 == 0)
14:   N1:{ c[(j1+j2+j)*n+(i1+i)] =
        t*c[(j1+j2+j)*n+(i1+i)]; }
15:  for (k = k1; k<min(k1+32,n); k ++)
16:   c[(j1+j2+j)*n+(i1+i)] +=
       a[(k1+k)*n+(i1+i)] * b[(j1+j2+j)*n+(k1+k)];
17:  } }}}}
18:}}
      (e) after loop blocking
```

Fig. 4. Optimized code from optimization specifications

five extensible configuration tables, which save all the relevant information about the optimizations currently supported by our environment.

The Optimization Table (named *opt_table* in Fig. 5): indexed by the optimization names, this table stores the interface of each optimization and categorizes its parameters into three groups: the required input parameters, whose values must be supplied by the VHL specification; the optional parameters, each of which has a default value if not part of the VHL specification; and tuning parameters, which represent machine-sensitive configurations of the optimization and need to be empirically tuned.

The Parameter Table (named *param_table* in Fig. 5): indexed by the name of each parameter that may be used to configure an optimization, this table saves the semantics of the parameter irrespective of where it is used, including the range of acceptable values, its default value if unspecified in the VHL, and whether grouping is required if the parameter needs to be coordinated when multiple optimizations are applied to a single code region.

```
GenOptScript(spec, opt_table, param_table, cleanup_table, group_table, interfere_table)
1:  if not verify_correctness(spec,opt_table,param_table) then report_error endif
2:  /* coordination handles */handles=lookup_optimization_targets(spec);
    /*tuning parameters*/ tuning=∅; /* opt invocations*/ xforms = ∅; cleanup = ∅;
3:  for each f = (opt_name, opt_target, opt_config) ∈ spec do
3.0:   opt_table_spec = lookup_opt_params(opt_table, opt_name);
3.1:   /* collect tuning parameters of the opt */
       for each (p_name, p_type) ∈ opt_table_spec where p_type is a tuning parameter do
       tune_name=concat(p_name, opt_target); tune_info = lookup_param_info(param_table,p_name);
       tuning = tuning ∪ { gen_tuning_decl(tune_name, tune_info)};
       opt_config = opt_config ∪ { gen_opt_config(p_name, tune_name)}};
3.2:   /* collect any cleanup invocation required */
       for each clnup_opt ∈ lookup_cleanup_spec(cleanup_table, opt_name) do
       append_opt(cleanup, instantiate(clnup_opt, opt_config), group_table);
3.3:   /* categorize loop handles into groups */
       grp_idx = lookup_group_index(group_table, opt_name);
       for each (p_name, p_type) ∈ opt_table_spec where p_type requires a coordination handle do
       p_val = lookup_value(opt_config, p_name)
       if p_val != null then
         new_val = gen_group_handle(p_val, grp_idx); modify_value(opt_config, p_name, new_val);
         handles = append_handles(handles, new_val, grp_idx);
3.4:   /* generate fix-up invocations to accommodate interferences*/
       insert_before = insert_after = ∅;
       for each unprocessed opt g = (opt_name_2, opt_target, opt_config_2) ∈ spec ∪ cleanup do
       (new_params, opt_before, opt_after) = lookup_fixup(interfere_table, opt_name, opt_name2);
       opt_config = opt_config ∪ { instantiate(new_params, opt_config, opt_config_2) } ;
       append_opt(insert_before, instantiate(opt_before, opt_config, opt_config_2), group_table);
       append_opt(insert_after, instantiate(opt_after,opt_config,opt_config_2), group_table);
       cur_opt = concat(insert_before, gen_opt_invoke(opt_name,opt_target, opt_config), insert_after);
3.5:   append_opt(xforms, cur_opt, group_table);
4:  return gen_POET_script(tuning, handles, xforms, cleanup);
```

Fig. 5. Optimization synthesis algorithm

The Cleanup Table (named *cleanup_table* in Fig. 5): indexed by the optimization names, this table defines any additional followup operations that are required at the end of the POET script for each optimization, if the optimization is in the VHL specification. For example, if either loop blocking or unroll&jam are to be applied, the *cleanup_table* specifies additional loop splitting operations to clean up expensive conditionals inside of the optimized loops.

The Grouping Table (named *group_table* in Fig. 5): indexed by the optimization names, this table assigns each optimization to a group uniquely identified by an integer (*group_idx*), which combines with the values of an optimization configuration parameter to uniquely identify a coordination handle to create and be used by the optimization. To elaborate, each configuration parameter of an optimization requires a coordination handle to keep track of interferences from other optimizations. Optimizations of the same group can have their parameters share the same handle, if the parameters have the same value in the VHL. The group indices are further used as ordering constraints of the optimizations when they are appended to the final POET output at Steps 3.2 and 3.4 of Fig. 5. In particular, optimizations targeting the same handle are ordered by the *containment* relationship of their optimized code: OpenMP parallelization is done first, whose optimized code contains those of additional cache reuse optimizations, which generate code that in turn is used as input to CPU-level optimizations.

The Interference Table (named *interfere_table* in Fig. 5): indexed by pairs of optimization names, this table specifies how to resolve interferences between each pair of optimizations through two remedies: by directly modifying the configuration of the interfering optimization (e.g., by modifying the private variables of OpenMP parallelization after new local variables are created), and by inserting additional POET instructions to adjust the coordination handles, before or after the interfering optimization.

4.2   The Algorithm

Using the five configuration tables described above, our optimization synthesis algorithm translates a VHL specification into a lower-level implementation using the inherit support of optimization parameterization and fine-grained coordination supported by the POET language [17] through the following steps.

Input Validation (Steps 1 and 2 of Fig. 5). The algorithm starts by verifying the consistency of the input VHL specification against information obtained from the *opt_table* and the *param_table* (Step 1). Specifically, the algorithm verifies that all the required parameters for each optimization have been given a valid value, and all constraints between values of different parameters are satisfied. Then (Step 2), it initializes the four components of the final POET output: the declarations of all tuning parameters (*tuning*), the declarations of all coordination handles (*handles*), the list of POET invocations to be translated from the VHL specification (*xforms*), and the list of follow-up POET operations required to clean up the optimizations (*cleanup*). The validation provided by our GUI is purposefully limited to allow the developer to circumvent any over conservativeness by a conventional compiler as long as the manually specified optimizations can be carried out in a meaningful fashion, as enforced by the checking of optimization parameters.

Parameterization of the Optimizations (Steps 3.0 and 3.1). For each optimization in the VHL specification, Step 3.0 obtains its parameter specifications from the *opt_table*. Step 3.1 then identifies all the parameters that need to be empirically tuned, adds a new global variable declaration for each found tuning parameter, and then uses these tuning variables to customize (through the *opt_config* variable) the optimization from the VHL specification. These tuning variables are declared at line 2–3 of the example POET output in Fig. 3(b) and are used to customize the later optimizations at lines 10–17. If a value is given to the tuning parameter in the VHL specification, the specified value is used; otherwise, a default value obtained from the *param_table* is used.

Collective Customization of the Optimizations (Steps 3.2 and 3.5). The customization of the optimizations includes two aspects: the addition of any followup operations to be included in the final POET output, obtained from the *cleanup_table* for each optimization specified in the VHL at Step 3.2; and the adoption of predefined ordering of the optimizations, obtained from the *group_table* and enforced by the *append_opt* invocation at steps 3.2 and 3.5. Optimizations that belong to the same group are ordered as they appear in the original VHL specification. For example, the final POET output in Fig. 3(b) contains the additional optimization *CleanupBlockedNests* to cleanup after the *BlockLoops* optimization in the VHL specification, and all the optimizations are ordered so that loop parallelization is applied first, followed by cache-level optimizations (e.g., loop permutation and blocking), which are in turn followed by CPU-level optimizations (e.g., loop unroll&jam and unrolling).

Fine-Grained Coordination (Steps 3.3 and 3.4). As the optimizations must be applied one after another in the POET script, each optimization must carefully coordinate with the others in the POET output. Our algorithm automatically supports such coordinations through two steps. First, in Step 3.3, it creates a coordination handle for each configuration parameter that may be affected by other optimizations. Then, in Step 3.4, it inserts POET operations to adjust the values of all the affected coordination handles as each optimization is applied.

Since multiple optimization parameters may refer to the same piece of input code, their coordination handles need to be carefully managed so that their nesting relationships will not change irrespective of how many optimizations have been applied. In particular, our *group_table* organizes all the optimizations into distinct groups, with each group identified by a unique integer index, based on two constraints: (1) the parameters of all optimizations in the same group can share a single coordination handle if the parameters refer to the same piece of input code in the VHL specification, because their values will always remain the same; and (2), if two optimizations belong to distinct groups (e.g., loop blocking and loop unroll&jam), and some of their parameters refer to the same piece of input code in the VHL specification (e.g., both operating on the same target), then the optimization with the larger group index will always have a coordination handle that contains that of the smaller group index. This handle composition process is enforced by the *append_handles* operation in Step 3.3.

Figure 3(b) shows the handle grouping and composition results for the VHL specification in Fig. 3(a). Here two additional coordination handles, $N2\_cleanup$ and $N2p$, are created at lines 6 to be nested outside of the original optimization target $N2$ from the VHL. ParallelizeLoop has the highest group index and therefore is configured with the outermost coordination handle, $N2p$. Next, the cleanup optimization required for loop blocking causes yet another coordination handle, $N2\_cleanup$, to be created and nested inside $N2p$, but outside of $N2$. PermuteLoops, FuseLoops, and BlockLoops belong to a single group that has the lowest group index, therefore sharing the handle created to trace the original optimization target. Figures 4(b)–(e) illustrate how these coordination handles adjust as the input code is modified by each optimization specified.

The actual adjustment of the coordination handles are implemented by POET operations inserted by Step 3.4 of the algorithm, which looks in the interference table to identify what coordination is required for each pair of optimizations from the VHL specification or the cleanup operations to be inserted. Then, the coordination is applied either through direct modification of the optimization configurations or through POET operations inserted before or after the interfering optimization to adjust affected coordination handles.

Two interferences exist in the VHL specification from Fig. 3(a). The first occurs between ParallelizeLoop and BlockLoops and is accommodated by inserting the *trace_ivars* configuration for BlockLoops at line 16 of Fig. 3(b), so that new local variables created by BlockLoops are included as private variables of the OpenMP pragma. The second interference occurs between the ParallelizeLoop and the auto-generated CleanupBlockedNests and entails line 13 to be inserted before ParallelizeLoop to stripmine the loop being parallelized into two nested ones, so that the inner one can be used as target for additional single-thread optimizations, by moving the *N2_cleanup* handle to the inner loop at line 15.

Outputting the Result (Step 4). After obtaining all the necessary components, the final POET script is generated by simply putting everything together.

5   Experimental Evaluation

While our environment currently supports only a limited number of loop and array optimizations, shown in Table 1, our hypothesis is that when explicitly specified, the impact of these optimizations can be enhanced significantly through collective customization, fine-grained coordination, and empirical performance tuning, especially when a compiler fails to automatically recognize opportunities of applying some of them due to insufficient understanding of the input code.

To validate our hypotheses, we used our environment to interactively specify optimizations for six matrix and stencil computation kernels, shown in Table 1. All kernels are implemented in C/C++ in a form that is easy to analyze, as illustrated in Fig. 4(a). For each kernel, we selected the optimizations that can be safely applied to potentially improve its performance and relied on the empirical tuning support by the backend POET transformation engine to determine the best configurations. Three implementations are generated for each kernel: an *ICC/GCC* version, generated by using the vendor compiler (icc or gcc) to optimize the original code (with the −O3 flag); a *GUI-Default* version, generated by additionally applying optimizations interactively specified through our environment, using a default configuration for each optimization; and a *GUI-Tune* version, which further employs empirical tuning to find the best GUI-specified optimization configurations.

All kernels are evaluated on two platforms shown in Table 2, with the machines kept otherwise idle while running the experiment. Each evaluation is repeated 10 times, and the average elapsed time of running each kernel implementation is used to compute its GFLOPS (billion floating point operations per second). The variation among different runs is less than 10 %.

Figure 6(a) compares the performance of the differently optimized versions on the Intel platform. Even without empirical tuning, the additional optimizations applied by our environment were able attain 1.43X speedup on average for the kernels, and empirical tuning is able to further boost the average speedup to a factor of 1.84. An interesting observation is that without empirical tuning, the performance of the *GUI-Default-ICC* version for the kernel *jacobi7* did not improve the performance of the original version, while with tuning we were able

Table 1. Kernels used for experiments

Kernel	Description	Data size	Interactive optimizations
dger	Rank one update	10240^2	*ParallelizeLoop, BlockLoops, UnrollJam, ScalarRepl, UnrollLoop*
dgemm	dense matrix-matrix multiplication	1280^2	*PermuteLoops, FuseLoops, ParallelizeLoop, BlockLoops, UnrollJam, ScalarRepl*
dgemvN	dense matrix-vector multiplication	10240^2	*ParallelizeLoop, BlockLoops, UnrollJam, UnrollLoop*
dgemvT	dense matrix-vector multiplication with transpose	10240^2	*ParallelizeLoop, BlockLoops, UnrollJam, UnrollLoop*
jacobi7	3D 7-point Stencil	128^3	*ParallelizeLoop, BlockLoops, SkewLoops*
vmult	Sparse matrix-vector multiplication	5120^2	*ParallelizeLoop*

Table 2. Machine configuration

CPU		Intel(R) Xeon(R) CPU E5-2420 1.90 GHz, 12 Cores	AMD Opteron(tm) Processor 6128 2.00 GHz, 24 Cores
Cache	L1-Data	32 KBytes	64 KBytes
	L1-Instruction	32 KBytes	64 KBytes
	L2-Private	256 KBytes	512 KBytes
	L3-Shared	15360 KBytes	5118 KBytes
Main memory		16 GiB	64 GiB
Operating system		CentOS 6.6, Linux 2.6.32	Ubuntu 14.04.2, Linux 3.13.0
Compiler		icc 15.0.0 with $-$O3 flag	gcc 4.8.2 with $-$O3 flag

to attain 2.48X better performance. Since many of the optimizations we currently support are heavily machine sensitive, it is important to use the proper configurations to attain the desired performance improvement. The best speedup of 3.5X for the *GUI-Tune-ICC* version is attained for the *dgemm* kernel, which performs an order of N^3 computations on N^2 data. Here *BlockLoops* can significantly improve the performance by reusing the data already brought in cache, thereby changing the kernel's behavior from memory-bound to CPU-bound. For the other kernels, e.g., *dger* and *vmult*, which are fundamentally memory bound due to the lack of data reuse, our optimizations are not very effective and are able to attain only 1.05X speedup for *dger* and 1.17X speedup for *vmult*.

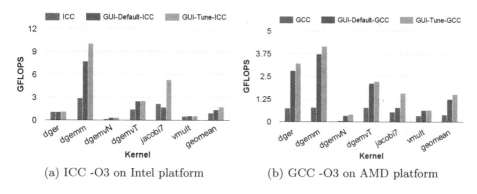

(a) ICC -O3 on Intel platform   (b) GCC -O3 on AMD platform

Fig. 6. Evaluation results of GUI

Figure 6(b) shows our evaluation results on the AMD platform. Here, every kernel, when optimized using our interactive environment, was able to attain significantly better performance when compared to using the *gcc* compiler alone. On average, our environment was able to attain 3.14X performance improvement over the original version with the default configurations of the optimizations, and empirical tuning was able to attain 3.83X additional speedup. Specifically, it attained an extra performance improvement of up to 8.67X and 5.28X for the dense matrix computation kernels *dgemvN* and *dgemm* respectively and a 1.9X improvement for the *vmult* kernel with the *GUI-Tune-GCC* version.

6   Related Work

Existing research has developed a large collection of compiler optimizations to automatically improve the performance of scientific applications [1,3,6,7,16]. Many of these optimizations can be naturally parameterized, e.g., loop blocking [10], fusion [11], unrolling [12], and software pipelining [8]. Cohen, *et al.* [3] used the polyhedral model to parameterize the composition of loop optimizations. Our framework supports many of these optimizations, with parameterized configurations, and aims to make them available as a toolset for interactive use by developers to attain portable high performance.

The importance of facilitating effective communication between optimizing compilers and developers has been well-recognized. Hall *et al.* [5] allows developers to provide a sequence of *loop transformation recipes* to guide optimizations by their compiler. The *X* language [4] uses C/C++ pragmas to guide the application of a collection of loop- and statement-level optimizations. Our work similarly provides direct access of compiler optimizations to the developers. Our framework provides additional support for interactive selection, extensive parameterization, and automated coordination of the optimizations.

Our work uses the POET language [18,20] to provide the underlying support for the interactive composition of parameterized compiler optimizations. Existing work has demonstrated that through fine-grained coordination and collective customization, POET can be used to specialize compiler optimizations to attain a highest level of portable performance for dense linear algebra kernels [15,21,22].

Yi [17] has used a source-to-source optimizing compiler to automatically produce parameterized POET scripts so that the optimization composition can be revised by developers if desired, and the optimization configurations can be empirically tuned. As a complimentary framework for this work, our GUI can be used to provide an interactive interface for developers to conveniently revise optimization decisions by their compilers. Our auto-generated POET scripts can be easily integrated with existing empirical tuning research [2,9,13,14,23] to automatically find desirable optimization configurations.

7   Conclusions and Future Work

We have presented a framework to enable compiler optimizations being used as an interactive toolset by developers. Our framework addresses the key technical challenge of interactive selection and composition of extensively parameterized compiler optimizations, while using the POET transformation engine [18,20] to support the programmable customization and empirical tuning of differently optimized code. We have demonstrated the practicality of this framework by using it to optimize six commonly used scientific computing kernels and have shown that significantly better performance can be achieved by the interactive optimization framework than using the conventional optimizing compilers alone.

Our approach exposes compiler optimizations to be interactively controlled and customized by developers by providing each optimization an explicit well-defined parameter space, far beyond the optimization flags supported by conventional compilers. We currently support only a subset of the optimizations applied manually by high performance computing specialists, consequently our attained performance still lag far behind those of hand optimized kernels. We expect to significantly increase the collection of optimizations in the future while efficiently exploring their configuration spaces to enhance application performance.

References

1. Carr, S., Kennedy, K.: Improving the ratio of memory operations to floating-point operations in loops. ACM Trans. Program. Lang. Syst. **16**(6), 1768–1810 (1994)
2. Chen, C., Chame, J., Hall, M.: Combining models and guided empirical search to optimize for multiple levels of the memory hierarchy. In: International Symposium on Code Generation and Optimization, March 2005
3. Cohen, A., Sigler, M., Girbal, S., Temam, O., Parello, D., Vasilache, N.: Facilitating the search for compositions of program transformations. In: ICS 2005: Proceedings of the 19th Annual International Conference on Supercomputing, pp. 151–160. ACM, New York, NY, USA (2005)
4. Donadio, S., Brodman, J., Roeder, T., Yotov, K., Barthou, D., Cohen, A., Garzarán, M.J., Padua, D., Pingali, K.: A language for the compact representationof multiple program versions. In: LCPC, October 2005
5. Hall, M., Chame, J., Chen, C., Shin, J., Rudy, G., Khan, M.M.: Loop transformation recipes for code generation and auto-tuning. In: Gao, G.R., Pollock, L.L., Cavazos, J., Li, X. (eds.) LCPC 2009. LNCS, vol. 5898, pp. 50–64. Springer, Heidelberg (2010)

6. Lam, M., Rothberg, E., Wolf, M.E.: The cache performance and optimizations of blocked algorithms. In: Proceedings of the Fourth International Conference on Architectural Support for Programming Languages and Operating Systems, Santa Clara, April 1991

7. McKinley, K., Carr, S., Tseng, C.: Improving data locality with loop transformations. ACM Trans. Program. Lang. Syst. **18**(4), 424–453 (1996)

8. O'Boyle, M., Motogelwa, N., Knijnenburg, P.: Feedback assisted iterative compilation. In: Languages and Compilers for Parallel Computing (2000)

9. Pan, Z., Eigenmann, R.: Fast automatic procedure-level performance tuning. In: Proceedings of Parallel Architectures and Compilation Techniques (2006)

10. Pike, G., Hilfinger, P.: Better tiling and array contraction for compiling scientific programs. In: Conference on SC, Baltimore, MD, USA (2002)

11. Qasem, A., Kennedy, K., Mellor-Crummey, J.: Automatic tuning of whole applications using direct search and a performance-based transformation system. J. Supercomput. **36**(2), 183–196 (2006)

12. Stephenson, M., Amarasinghe, S.: Predicting unroll factors using supervised classification. In: CGO, San Jose, CA, USA (2005)

13. Voss, M.J., Eigenmann, R.: High-level adaptive program optimization with ADAPT. In: ACM SIGPLAN Symposium on Principles and Practice of Parallel Programming (2001)

14. Vuduc, R., Demmel, J., Yelick, K.: OSKI: An interface for a self-optimizing library of sparse matrix kernels (2005)

15. Wang, Q., Zhang, X., Zhang, Y., Yi, Q.: Augem: Automatically generate high performance dense linear algebra kernels on x86 cpus. In: Proceedings of SC13: International Conference for High Performance Computing, Networking, Storage and Analysis, SC 2013, pp. 25:1–25:12, New York, NY, USA (2013)

16. Wolfe, M.J.: More iteration space tiling. In: Proceedings of Supercomputing, Reno, November 1989

17. Yi, Q.: Automated programmable control and parameterization of compiler optimizations. In: CGO 2011: ACM/IEEE International Symposium on Code Generation and Optimization, April 2011

18. Yi, Q.: POET: A scripting language for applying parameterized source-to-source program transformations. Softw. Pract. Exp. **42**, 675–706 (2012)

19. Yi, Q., Guo, J.: Extensive parameterization and tuning of architecture-sensitive optimizations. In: iWapt 2011: The Sixth International Workshop on Automatic Performance Tuning, June 2011

20. Yi, Q., Seymour, K., You, H., Vuduc, R., Quinlan, D.: POET: Parameterized optimizations for empirical tuning. In: POHLL 2007: Workshop on Performance Optimization for High-Level Languages and Libraries, March 2007

21. Yi, Q., Wang, Q., Cui, H.: Specializing compiler optimizations through programmable composition for dense matrix computations. In: Proceedings of the 47th Annual IEEE/ACM International Symposium on Microarchitecture, MICRO-47, pp. 596–608. IEEE Computer Society, Washington, DC, USA (2014)

22. Yi, Q., Whaley, C.: Automated transformation for performance-critical kernels. In: LCSD 2007: ACM SIGPLAN Symposium on Library-Centric Software Design, Montreal, Canada, October 2007

23. Yotov, K., Li, X., Ren, G., Garzaran, M., Padua, D., Pingali, K., Stodghill, P.: A comparison of empirical and model-driven optimization. In: IEEE special issue on Program Generation Optimization, and Adaptation (2005)

Asynchronous Nested Parallelism for Dynamic Applications in Distributed Memory

Ioannis Papadopoulos$^{(\boxtimes)}$, Nathan Thomas, Adam Fidel, Dielli Hoxha,
Nancy M. Amato, and Lawrence Rauchwerger

Parasol Laboratory, Department of Computer Science and Engineering,
Texas A&M University, College Station, TX, USA
ipapadop@cse.tamu.edu

Abstract. Nested parallelism is of increasing interest for both expressivity and performance. Many problems are naturally expressed with this divide-and-conquer software design approach. In addition, programmers with target architecture knowledge employ nested parallelism for performance, imposing a hierarchy in the application to increase locality and resource utilization, often at the cost of implementation complexity.

While dynamic applications are a natural fit for the approach, support for nested parallelism in distributed systems is generally limited to well-structured applications engineered with distinct phases of intra-node computation and inter-node communication. This model makes expressing irregular applications difficult and also hurts performance by introducing unnecessary latency and synchronizations. In this paper we describe an approach to asynchronous nested parallelism which provides uniform treatment of nested computation across distributed memory. This approach allows efficient execution while supporting dynamic applications which cannot be mapped onto the machine in the rigid manner of regular applications. We use several graph algorithms as examples to demonstrate our library's expressivity, flexibility, and performance.

Keywords: Nested parallelism · Asynchronous · Isolation · Graph · Dynamic applications

1 Introduction

Writing parallel applications is difficult, and many programming idioms taken for granted in sequential computing are often unavailable. One of these tools, program composition via *nested function invocation*, is not present in many parallel programming models, at least not in a general form that is abstracted from the target architecture. Indeed, while *nested parallelism* is a natural way to express many applications, employing it is often constrained by the deep memory hierarchies and multiple communication models of modern HPC platforms.

While the efficient mapping of the application's hierarchy of algorithms onto the machine's hierarchy is important for performance, we believe requiring developers to explicitly coordinate this effort is overly burdensome. Furthermore,

X. Shen et al. (Eds.): LCPC 2015, LNCS 9519, pp. 106–121, 2016.
DOI: 10.1007/978-3-319-29778-1_7

direct management leads to ad-hoc solutions that significantly decrease *software reuse*, which is key to addressing the difficulties of parallel programming.

This work describes the support for nested parallelism in the runtime system of STAPL [8], a generic library of components for parallel program composition. The STAPL-RTS [29] serves the higher levels of the library, providing a uniform interface for computation and communication across distributed systems, while internally using shared memory optimizations where possible.

In this paper, we show how this uniform interface extends to the creation of nested parallel sections that execute STAPL algorithms. These nested SPMD (Single Program Multiple Data) sections provide an isolated environment from which algorithms, represented as task dependence graphs, execute and can spawn further nested computation. Each of these sections can be instantiated on an arbitrary subgroup of processing elements across distributed memory.

While the STAPL-RTS supports collective creation of nested parallel sections, in this work we focus on the *one-sided* interface. The one-sided interface allows a local activity (e.g., visiting a vertex in a distributed graph) on a given location to *spawn* a nested activity (e.g., following all edges in parallel to visit neighbors). As we will show, both the creation and execution of this nested activity are asynchronous: calls to the STAPL-RTS are non-blocking and allow local activities to proceed immediately. Hence, the one-sided, asynchronous mechanism is particularly suitable for dynamic applications.

Nested sections are also used to implement *composed data structures* with data distributed on arbitrary portions of the machine. Together, this support for nested algorithms and composed, distributed containers provides an increased level of support for irregular applications over previous work. In the experimental section, we demonstrate how the algorithms and data interact in a STAPL program, initially with finding the minimum element on composed containers created such that computation is imbalanced. We also use a distributed graph with vertex adjacency lists being stored in various distributed configurations. Without any changes to the graph algorithm, we are able to test a variety of configurations and gain substantial performance improvements (2.25x at 4 K cores) over the common baseline configuration (i.e., sequential storage of edge lists).

Our contributions include:

Uniform Nested Parallelism with Controlled Isolation. Support for arbitrary subgroups of processing elements (i.e., locations) across distributed memory. The sections are logically isolated, maintaining the hierarchical structure of algorithms defined by the user. For instance, message ordering and traffic quiescence is maintained separately for each nested section.

Asynchronous, One-sided Creation of Parallel Sections. The ability to asynchronously create nested parallel sections provides latency hiding which is important for scalability. We combine one-sided and asynchronous parallel section creation, presenting a simple and scalable nested parallel paradigm.

Use of STAPL-RTS to Implement Dynamic, Nested Algorithms. We use our primitives to implement several fundamental graph algorithms, and demonstrate how various distribution strategies from previous work can be generalized under a common infrastructure using our approach to nested parallelism.

2   Related Work

When introduced, nested parallelism was used primarily for expressiveness, as in NESL [4]. The NESL compiler applies flattening, transforming all nested algorithms to a flat data parallel version, a technique with performance limitations.

OpenMP [27] has had nested parallelism capabilities since its inception. There is some work on nested parallelism for performance [15]. However, the `collapse` keyword in OpenMP 3.0 that flattens nested parallel sections attests to the difficulty of gaining performance from nested parallelism in OpenMP.

Other parallel programming systems employ nested parallelism for performance. Users express algorithms using nested sections for the sole purpose of exploiting locality. Restrictions are often imposed to achieve performance, limiting expressiveness. MPI [25] allows creating new MPI communicators by partitioning existing ones or by spawning additional processes. This functionality can be used to map nested parallel algorithms to the machine, however it mostly suits static applications, as each process must know through which MPI communicator it should communicate at any given point in the program.

Several systems enhance the MPI approach, while simplifying the programming model. Neststep [23] is a language that extends the BSP (bulk synchronous parallel) model and allows the partitioning of the processing elements of a superstep to smaller subsets or subgroups that can call any parallel algorithm. These subgroups need to finish prior to the parent group continuing with the next superstep. UPC [14] and Co-Array Fortran [24] have similar restrictions.

Another common approach is to use MPI for the first level parallelism (distributed memory) and OpenMP for the shared memory parallelism [10,33], leading to ad-hoc solutions with manual data and computation placement.

Titanium [22] and UPC++ [38] introduce the Recursive SPMD (RSPMD) model and provide subgrouping capabilities, allowing programmers to call parallel algorithms from within nested parallel sections that are subsets of the parent section. Similarly to Neststep, they also require that the nested sections finish before resuming work in the parent section.

The Sequoia [16] parallel programming language provides a hierarchical view of the machine, enforcing locality through the nested parallelism and thread-safety with total task isolation: tasks cannot communicate with other tasks and can only access the memory address space passed to them. This strong isolation, in conjunction with execution restrictions to allow compile-time scheduling of task scheduling and task movement, limits its usefulness in dynamic applications.

Several systems support task-based parallelism, allowing the user to spawn tasks from other tasks. The programmer can thus express nested parallelism with the system responsible for placement. These include Intel Thread Building Blocks [32] and Cilk [5]. Since task placement is done in absence of knowledge about locality, one of the benefits of nested parallelism is lost.

X10 [12], Habanero-Java [11], HPX [20], and Fortress [21] all offer task-based parallelism, going a step further and allowing control over task placement. However, they suffer from loss of structure of the execution of the algorithms, as tasks are independent of each other. Building on top of Habanero, Otello [37] addresses the issue of isolation in nested parallelism. While maintaining a task parallel system, Otello protects shared data structures through analysis of which object each task operates on and the spawning hierarchy of tasks.

Chapel [9] is a multi-paradigm parallel programming language and supports nested parallelism. While it supports data and task placement, users are given only two parallel algorithms (parallel for, reduce). Other parallel algorithms have to be implemented explicitly using task parallelism.

Legion [3] retains Sequoia's strong machine mapping capabilities while relaxing many of the assumptions of Sequoia, making it a good fit for dynamic applications. It follows a task parallel model in which tasks can spawn subtasks with controlled affinity. However, this process leads to loss of information about the structure of the parallel sections, as with other task parallel systems.

From Trilinos [2], Kokkos supports nested parallelism by allowing the division of threads in teams recursively. While threads in the same team are concurrent, teams cannot execute concurrently, and only three algorithms (parallel for, reduce and scan) are available to be invoked from within a nested parallel section.

Phalanx [19] can asynchronously spawn SPMD tasks that execute on multiple threads. Programmers allocate memory explicitly on supported devices (CPU, GPU, etc.) and invoke tasks on them, creating parallel sections. Phalanx has a versatile programming model and is the most similar related work to the STAPL-RTS. Its main difference from the STAPL-RTS is that Phalanx requires explicit control of resources. Data and task placement needs to be statically specialized with the target (e.g., GPU, thread, process), transferring the responsibility of resource management to the user and creating the need for multi-versioned code.

3   STAPL Overview

The *Standard Template Adaptive Parallel Library* (STAPL) [8] is a framework developed in C++ for parallel programming. It follows the generic design of the Standard Template Library (STL) [26], with extensions and modifications for parallelism. STAPL is a library, requiring only a C++ compiler (e.g., gcc) and established communication libraries such as MPI. An overview of its major components are presented in Fig. 1.

STAPL provides *parallel algorithms* and *distributed data structures* [18,34] with interfaces similar to the STL. Instead of iterators, algorithms are written with *views* [7] that decouple the container interfaces from the underlying storage. The *skeletons framework* [36] allows the user to express an application as a composition of simpler parallel patterns (e.g., map, reduce, scan and others).

Algorithmic skeletons are instantiated at runtime as task dependence graphs by the PARAGRAPH, STAPL's data flow engine. It enforces task dependencies and is responsible for the transmission of intermediate values between tasks.

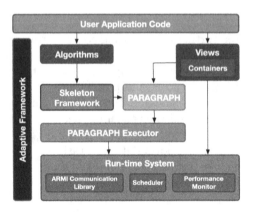

Fig. 1. STAPL components

The runtime system (STAPL-RTS) [29,35] provides portable performance by abstracting the underlying platform with the concept of *locations*. A *location* is a component of a parallel machine that has a contiguous memory address space and has associated execution capabilities (e.g., threads). Locations only have access to their own address space and communicate with other locations using *Remote Method Invocations* (RMIs) on distributed objects (p_objects).

Containers and PARAGRAPHs are both distributed objects (i.e., p_objects). RMIs are used in the containers to read and write elements. RMIs are used in the PARAGRAPH to place tasks, resolve dependencies, and flow values between tasks that are not on the same location.

Each p_object has an associated set of locations on which it is distributed. The STAPL-RTS abstracts the platform and its resources, providing a uniform interface for all communication in the library and applications built with it. This abstraction of a virtual distributed, parallel machine helps STAPL support general nested parallelism.

4   Asynchronous Nested Parallelism in STAPL

As with STL programs, a typical STAPL application begins with the instantiation of the necessary data structures. Each container has its own distribution and thus defines the affinity of its elements. Container composition is supported, as well as complete control over the distribution of each container (e.g., balanced, block cyclic, arbitrary). For example, the graph algorithms presented in Sect. 5.2 execute on composed instances of the STAPL **array** for vertex and edge storage, with various distribution strategies considered for each nested edge list. Users write applications with the help of skeletons [36] and views, that abstract the computation and data access, respectively. The views provide element locality information, projecting it from the underlying container.

An algorithm's execution is performed by a PARAGRAPH, a distributed task dependence graph responsible for managing task dependencies and declaring

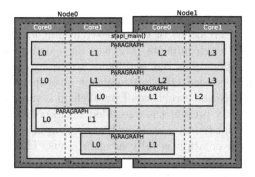

Fig. 2. Execution model

which tasks are runnable. Each PARAGRAPH executes in an isolated environment, with data access provided by the views. Each task may itself be a parallel algorithm, for which a new nested parallel section is created. A default policy *places* a PARAGRAPH for execution based on the locality of the data it accesses, and custom policies can be passed to the PARAGRAPH at creation. Figure 2 shows an example execution instance of an application that has a number of PARAGRAPH invocations in isolated parallel sections over the same set of hardware resources.

4.1   STAPL Design Considerations

In order to take advantage of nested parallelism and realize its full potential, we have made several design decisions that influence our implementation including:

Expressiveness. STAPL users express algorithms as a composition of simpler parallel algorithms using algorithmic skeletons [36]. This specification is independent of any target architecture. The responsibility for mapping it onto the machine is left to the library, though it can be customized by more experienced users at an appropriate level of abstraction.

Preserving Algorithm Structure. We maintain the hierarchy of tasks defined by the application when mapping it to the machine. Hence, each nested section's tasks remain associated with it and are subject to its scheduling policy. Each algorithm invocation is run within an SPMD section, from which both point-to-point and collective operations are accounted for independent of other sections. The SPMD programming model has been chosen since scaling on distributed machines has favored this programming model (e.g., MPI [25]) more than fork-join or task parallel models.

Parallel Section Isolation. STAPL parallel sections exhibit controlled isolation for safety and correctness. The uncontrolled exchange of data between parallel sections is potentially unsafe due to data races. Performance can be impacted, as isolation means that collective operations and data exchanges are in a controlled environment. We discuss techniques to mitigate these overheads in [29]. Users provide views to define the data available for access in each section.

Asynchronous, One-sided Parallel Section Creation. We support both *partitioning* (collective creation) of existing environments and *spawning* (one-sided creation) of new environments. Partitioning existing parallel sections is beneficial for static applications but is difficult to use in dynamic applications. On the other hand, one-sided creation may not give optimal performance for static applications where the structure of parallelism is more readily known.

In this paper, we only present the one-sided world creation, as the collective implementation is similar to other systems for subgrouping (e.g., Titanium, MPI and others). One-sided creation is fully asynchronous. This allows us to effectively hide latency and supports our always distributed memory model. Table 1 summarizes the main differences between our model and similar approaches.

Table 1. Nested Parallelism (NP) capabilities comparison

Name	SPMD NP sections	Asynchronous	Locality aware	Any algorithm allowed in NP section
MPI	Yes	No	Manual	Yes
UPC++, Co-Array Fortran, Titanium	Yes	No	Manual	Yes
Sequoia	Yes	No	Compile-time	Yes
Habanero, X10	No	Yes	Yes	Yes
Chapel	No	Yes	Yes	No
Charm++	No	Yes	Yes	Yes
Legion	No	Yes	Yes	Yes
Phalanx	Yes	Yes	Manual	Yes
STAPL	Yes	Yes	Yes	Yes

4.2   Execution Model

The STAPL-RTS presents a *unified interface* for both intra-node and inter-node communication to support performance portability. Internally the *mixed-mode* implementation uses both standard shared and distributed memory communication protocols when appropriate. For scalability and correctness, we employ a *distributed Remote Method Invocation* (RMI) model.

Each processing element together with a logical address space forms an isolated computational unit called a *location*. Each location has an isolated, virtual address space which is not directly accessible by other locations. When a location wishes to modify or read a remote location's memory, this action must be expressed via RMIs on distributed objects, called p_objects.

Gangs represent STAPL-RTS subgroup support. Each gang is a set of N locations with identifiers in the range $[0, \ldots, N-1]$ in which an SPMD task executes.

It has the necessary information for mapping its locations to processing elements and describing a topology for performing collective operations. While the locations of a gang execute a single SPMD task, they communicate asynchronously independently of each other, making them a more loosely knit group than for example MPI groups or Titanium/UPC teams. To create a new gang, one either:

- *Partitions* an existing gang with *collective gang creation* over the locations that participate in the new gang.
- *Spawns* a gang, whereby one location creates a new gang in an asynchronous and one-sided manner, using a subset of locations in an existing gang.

p_objects can be created within a gang, and as such, each p_object is associated with exactly one gang and is distributed across its locations. A gang can have any number of p_objects. Each p_object can be referenced either with a regular C++ reference inside the gang it was created or through handles.

4.3   One Sided Gang Creation

The STAPL-RTS provides primitives for the one-sided creation of gangs via allocating p_objects on a set of pre-existing locations. An example is shown in Fig. 3. The first construct call creates a new parallel section over the locations $\{0, 2, 4, 5, 6\}$ of the current section and creates an instance of T. The second construct call creates an object of type U in a new gang that is co-located with the gang of the previous object.

Multiple variations are supported, such as creating gangs on arbitrary ranges of locations (or all) of either the current parallel section or that of another p_object. The STAPL-RTS is responsible for translating location IDs to processing element (PE) IDs and for building a suitable multicast tree on the PEs which it uses to construct the gang and the associated p_object. We plan on extending this support to define gangs over specific parts of an hierarchical or heterogeneous machine, such as over a specific socket or accelerator.

A gang's lifetime is tied to that of the p_objects present in it (see Fig. 4).

```
1  using namespace stapl;
2
3  // Create a p_object of type T by passing args to the constructor, in a
       new gang over the given locations and return a future to its handle
4  future<rmi_handle::reference> f1 =
5     construct<T>(location_range, {0, 2, 4, 5, 6}, args...);
6
7  // Get object handle
8  auto h = f1.get();
9
10 // Create a new p_object of type U on a new gang co-located with the
       gang of the first object
11 future<rmi_handle::reference> f2 =
12    construct<U>(h, all_locations, args...);
```

Fig. 3. Construct example usage.

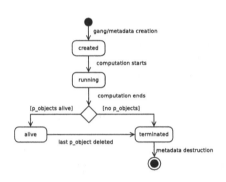

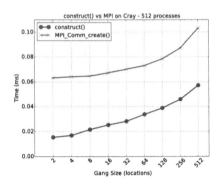

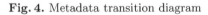

Fig. 4. Metadata transition diagram

Fig. 5. Construct vs MPI on 512 processes on Cray XK7m-200

- Upon construction, the gang is *created*. The necessary metadata is generated and everything is set up to execute the SPMD task.
- When the task executes, the gang is declared *running*. While the task executes, p_objects can be created and they are automatically associated with the gang. The scope of the automatic p_objects (stack allocated) is the scope of the SPMD task, however heap-allocated p_objects can outlive it.
- If the task finishes and there are no associated p_objects, the gang is *terminated* and its metadata is deleted.
- If there are still p_objects associated with the gang, then it is declared *alive* and its metadata preserved. The gang remains alive until the last p_object is deleted. RMIs can still be invoked on the p_objects.

Figure 5 presents a micro benchmark of the **construct** primitive on a Cray XK7m-200 (described in Sect. 5). It compares our range-based **construct** against **MPI_Comm_create** over the same number of processes, when the global parallel section is 512 processes. The combined effect of asynchronous creation and deletion, as well as the fact that the MPI primitive is collective over the set of processing elements (our primitive is one-sided), result in competitive performance against MPI and shows that it is a scalable approach.

5   Experimental Evaluation

We performed our experiments on two different systems. The code was compiled with maximum optimization levels (-DNDEBUG -O3).

Cray is a Cray XK7m-200 with twenty-four compute nodes of 2.1GHz AMD Opteron Interlagos 16-core processors. Twelve nodes are single socket with 32 GB RAM, and twelve are dual socket with 64 GB RAM. The compiler was gcc 4.9.2.

BG/Q is an IBM BG/Q system at Lawrence Livermore National Laboratory. It has 24, 576 nodes, each with a 16-core IBM PowerPC A2 processor at 1.6 GHz and 16 GB of RAM. The compiler used was gcc 4.7.2.

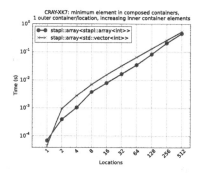

Fig. 6. min_element on array<array<int>> (log-log graph)

5.1 Minimum Element on Composed Containers

In this section, we make the case that nested parallelism can be a solution to work imbalance. We compare a nested parallel implementation of finding the minimum element over a composed container (stapl::array<stapl::array<int>>) against a flat parallel implementation with a distributed container of non-distributed containers (stapl::array<std::vector<int>>).

For the stapl::array<std::vector<int>> version we find the minimum element by invoking a parallel stapl::min_element algorithm over the results of std::min_element calls over the inner std::vector<int> containers whereas for the container composition version (stapl::array<stapl::array<int>>) we recursively call stapl::min_element over the outer and the inner containers.

We intentionally create imbalance, by setting the number of elements of each inner container c_i to $10000 + 400000 * i$ ints, where i is the index of c in the outer container C ($c_i = C[i]$). For example when C has 512 inner containers, c_0 has 10000 ints and c_{511} has 204810000 ints. In Fig. 6 we compare the two versions in which the outer container, C, is a stapl::array with n elements, where n is the total number of locations that the experiment is run on. The inner containers c are either std::vector<int> for the flat implementation of minimum element or stapl::array<int> for the nested parallel implementation.

In the case of stapl::array<stapl::array<int>> the inner containers are distributed across all n locations. While we over-distribute the inner containers, in turn increasing the number of concurrent nested parallel sections that find the minimum element in the inner containers, invoking nested parallel algorithms, presents the benefit of more efficiently distributing the work across the system. This results in better performance, up to $2.64x$ at 4 locations and $1.16x$ at 512 locations. As the number of location increases, the cost of creating and scheduling nested parallel sections over all the locations diminishes the benefits; this suggests that the nested containers should be distributed across subsets of locations in the application, something we intend to explore.

5.2   Graph Algorithms

Processing large-scale graphs has become a critical component in a variety of fields, from scientific computing to social analytics. An important class of graphs are *scale-free* networks, where the vertex degree distribution follows a power-law. These graphs are known for the presence of *hub vertices* that have extremely high degrees and present challenges for parallel computations.

In the presence of hub vertices, simple 1D partitioning (i.e., vertices distributed, edges colocated with corresponding vertex) of scale-free networks presents challenges to balancing per processor resource utilization, as the placement of a hub could overload a processor. More sophisticated types of partitioning have been proposed, including checkerboard 2D adjacency matrix partitioning [6], edge list partitioning [30] and specialized techniques for distributing hub vertices [17,31]. However, these strategies often change both the data representation as well as the algorithm, making it difficult to unify them in a common framework.

We represent the graph as a distributed array of vertices, with each vertex having a (possibly) distributed array of edges. Using construct, we define several strategies for distributing the edges of hub vertices, that can be interchanged without changing the graph algorithm itself. The first distribution strategy (EVERYWHERE) places a hub's adjacency list on all locations of the graph's gang. The second (NEIGHBORS) places the edges only on locations where the hub has neighbors. This strategy is especially dynamic as the distribution of each hub edge list is dependent on the input data. Thus, we rely heavily on the arbitrary subgroup support of STAPL-RTS. The last strategy (STRIPED) distributes the adjacency list on one location per shared-memory node in a strided fashion to ensure that no two hubs have edges on the same location.

Even though the distribution strategy of the edges changes, the edge visit algorithm remains unchanged; the PARAGRAPH executing the algorithm queries the edge view about the locality of the underlying container and transparently spawns the nested section onto the processing elements where locations in the container's gang are present. This one-sided, locality driven computational mapping is a natural fit for the application and allows easily experimentation with novel and arbitrary mappings of the edges to locations, without the overhead of rewriting and hand-tuning the algorithm to support these changes.

We implemented the Graph 500 benchmark [1], which performs a parallel breadth-first search (BFS) on a scale-free network. Figure 7(a) shows the BFS algorithm on the Graph 500 input graph. As shown, all three edge distribution strategies fare well over the baseline of non-distributed adjacency lists for modest number of hubs, and then degrade in performance as more vertices are distributed. The EVERYWHERE and NEIGHBORS strategies behave similarly, as the set of locations that contain any neighbor is likely to be all locations for high-degree hub vertices. The EVERYWHERE and NEIGHBORS strategies are 49 % and 51 % faster than the baseline, respectively. The STRIPED strategy performs up to 75 % faster than the baseline, which is a further improvement over the other strategies. On Cray, cores exhibit high performance relative to the interconnect, and thus modest amounts of communication can bring about large performance degradation.

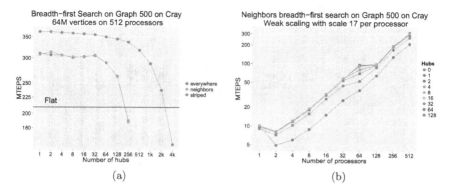

Fig. 7. Graph 500 breadth-first search on Cray varying (a) the number of hubs on 512 processors and (b) the number of processors for a weak scaling experiment.

The STRIPED strategy reduces the amount of off-node communication to create the parallel section from the source vertex location, bringing the performance of the algorithm above the other two strategies. We are investigating this phenomenon to derive a rigorous model for distributing edge lists.

Figure 7(b) shows a weak scaling study of the neighbor distribution strategy on Cray. As shown, the flat BFS scales poorly from 1 to 2 processors due to an increase in the amount of communication. By distributing the edges for hubs, we reduce this communication and provide better performance than the flat algorithm. The number of distributed hubs must be carefully chosen: too few hubs will not provide sufficient benefit in disseminating edge traversals, whereas too many hubs could overload the communication subsystem.

In order to evaluate our technique at a larger scale, we evaluated BFS on the Graph 500 graph on BG/Q in Fig. 8(a). We found that although faster than the flat version, all three distribution strategies performed comparably with each other. At 4,096 processors, the distributed adjacency list versions of BFS are 2.25x faster than the flat baseline. Hence, the distribution strategy is machine-dependent, further reinforcing the need for a modular and algorithm-agnostic mechanism to explore the possible configuration space for nested parallelism in parallel graph algorithms.

Finally, to show the generality of our approach we implement two other popular graph analytics algorithms: Hash-Min connected components (CC) [13] and PageRank [28] (PR). In Fig. 8(b) we present the *oracle speedup* of the nested parallel versions over the flat version, where speedup is measured as the ratio between the best configuration and hub count for the nested parallel version and the flat version. All three algorithms show marked improvement for all core counts except for 1, where the nested section creation overhead is measured. The nested parallel version is able to achieve upwards of 3x speedup, such as on connected components at 32 cores.

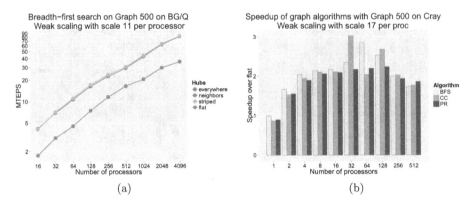

Fig. 8. Graph 500 (a) breadth-first search with various adjacency distributions on BG/Q and (b) various graph analytics algorithms on Cray.

6 Conclusion

In this paper we presented support for one-sided, asynchronous nested parallelism in STAPL-RTS. It is utilized in STAPL for the implementation of composed containers and the PARAGRAPH which manages algorithm execution. These components provide flexible support for nested parallelism, with intelligent placement of parallel sections based on the abstract locality information provided by our runtime. We demonstrated the benefit of the approach wth both container composition and graph algorithms, where significant gains were attained by tuning the locality of the data structure *independent of the algorithm specification*.

For future work, we want to implement other dynamic programs using the one-sided nested parallel constructs. We also plan to use our graph framework to explore other possible computation and data distribution strategies with the aim of performance portability. We think these nested parallelism constructs are applicable to a broad range applications, allowing STAPL to provide a high level of expressiveness, while still mapping efficiently onto large, distributed systems.

Acknowledgments. This research is supported in part by NSF awards CNS-0551685, CCF-0702765, CCF-0833199, CCF-1439145, CCF-1423111, CCF-0830753, IIS-0916053, IIS-0917266, EFRI–1240483, RI-1217991, by NIH NCI R25 CA090301-11, by DOE awards DE-AC02-06CH11357, DE-NA0002376, B575363, by Samsung, IBM, Intel, and by Award KUS-C1-016-04, made by King Abdullah University of Science and Technology (KAUST). This research used resources of the National Energy Research Scientific Computing Center, which is supported by the Office of Science of the U.S. Department of Energy under Contract No. DE-AC02-05CH11231.

References

1. The grapph 500 list. (2011). http://www.graph500.org
2. Baker, C.G., Heroux, M.A.: Tpetra, and the use of generic programming in scientific computing. Sci. Program. **20**(2), 115–128 (2012)
3. Bauer, M., Treichler, S., Slaughter, E., Aiken, A.: Legion: expressing locality and independence with logical regions. In: 2012 International Conference for High Performance Computing, Networking, Storage and Analysis (SC), pp. 1–11, November 2012
4. Blelloch, G.: NESL: A Nested Data-Parallel Language. Technical report CMU-CS-93-129, Carnegie Mellon University (1993)
5. Blumofe, R.D., et al.: Cilk: An efficient multithreaded runtime system. In: Proceedings of the Fifth ACM SIGPLAN Symposium on Principles and Practice of Parallel Programme (PPoPP), vol. 30, pp. 207–216. ACM, New York, July 1995
6. Buluç, A., Madduri, K.: Parallel breadth-first search on distributed memory systems. In: Proceedings of 2011 International Conference for High Performance Computing, Networking, Storage and Analysis, SC 2011, pp. 65:1–65:12. ACM, New York (2011)
7. Buss, A., et al.: The STAPL pView. In: Cooper, K., Mellor-Crummey, J., Sarkar, V. (eds.) LCPC 2010. LNCS, vol. 6548, pp. 261–275. Springer, Heidelberg (2011)
8. Buss, A., Harshvardhan, Papadopoulos, I., Pearce, O., Smith, T., Tanase, G., Thomas, N., Xu, X., Bianco, M., Amato, N.M., Rauchwerger, L.: STAPL: Standard template adaptive parallel library. In: Proceedings of Annual Haifa Experimental Systems Conference (SYSTOR), pp. 1–10. ACM, New York (2010)
9. Callahan, D., Chamberlain, B.L., Zima, H.P.: The cascade high productivity language. In: The Ninth International Workshop on High-Level Parallel Programming Models and Supportive Environments, vol. 26, pp. 52–60, Los Alamitos (2004)
10. Cappello, F., Etiemble, D.: MPI versus MPI+OpenMp on IBM SP for the NAS benchmarks. In: Proceedings of the ACM/IEEE Conference on Supercomputing, SC 2000. IEEE Computer Society, Washington, DC (2000)
11. Cavé, V., Zhao, J., Shirako, J., Sarkar, V.: Habanero-Java: The new adventures of old X10. In: Proceedings of the 9th International Conference on Principles and Practice of Programming in Java, PPPJ 2011, pp. 51–61. ACM, New York (2011)
12. Charles, P., Grothoff, C., Saraswat, V., Donawa, C., Kielstra, A., Ebcioglu, K., von Praun, C., Sarkar, V.: X10: an object-oriented approach to non-uniform cluster computing. In: Annual ACM SIGPLAN Conference on Object-Oriented Programming, Systems, Languages, and Applications, pp. 519–538. ACM Press, New York (2005)
13. Chitnis, L., et al.: Finding connected components in map-reduce in logarithmic rounds. In: Proceedings of the 2013 IEEE International Conference on Data Engineering, ICDE 2013, pp. 50–61. IEEE Computer Society, Washington, DC (2013)
14. Consortium, U.: UPC Language Specifications V1.2, (2005). http://www.gwu.edu/~upc/publications/LBNL-59208.pdf
15. Duran, A., Silvera, R., Corbalán, J., Labarta, J.: Runtime adjustment of parallel nested loops. In: Chapman, B.M. (ed.) WOMPAT 2004. LNCS, vol. 3349, pp. 137–147. Springer, Heidelberg (2005)
16. Fatahalian, K., et al.: Sequoia: programming the memory hierarchy. In: Proceedings of the ACM/IEEE Conference on Supercomputing, SC 2006. ACM, New York (2006)

17. Gonzalez, J.E., et al.: Powergraph: distributed graph-parallel computation on natural graphs. In: Proceedings of the 10th USENIX Conference on Operating Systems Design and Implementation, OSDI 2012, pp. 17–30. USENIX Association, Berkeley (2012)
18. Harshvardhan, A.F., Amato, N.M., Rauchwerger, L.: The STAPL parallel graph library. In: Kasahara, H., Kimura, K. (eds.) LCPC 2012. LNCS, vol. 7760, pp. 46–60. Springer, Heidelberg (2013)
19. Hartley, T.D.R., et al.: Improving performance of adaptive component-based dataflow middleware. Parallel Comput. **38**(6–7), 289–309 (2012)
20. Heller, T., et al.: Using HPX and LibGeoDecomp for scaling HPC applications on heterogeneous supercomputers. In: Proceedings of the Workshop on Latest Advances in Scalable Algorithms for Large-Scale System, ScalA 2013, pp. 1:1–1:8. ACM, New York (2013)
21. Steele Jr., G.L., et al.: Fortress (Sun HPCS Language). In: Padua, D.A. (ed.) Encyclopedia of Parallel Computing, pp. 718–735. Springer, Heidelberg (2011)
22. Kamil, A., Yelick, K.: Hierarchical computation in the SPMD programming model. In: Caşcaval, C., Montesinos-Ortego, P. (eds.) LCPC 2013 - Testing. LNCS, vol. 8664, pp. 3–19. Springer, Heidelberg (2014)
23. Keßler, C.W.: NestStep: nested parallelism and virtual shared memory for the BSP model. J. Supercomput. **17**(3), 245–262 (2000)
24. Mellor-Crummey, J., et al.: A new vision for coarray Fortran. In: Proceedings of the Third Conference on Partitioned Global Address Space Programing Models, PGAS 2009, pp. 5:1–5:9. ACM, New York (2009)
25. MPI forum. MPI: A Message-Passing Interface Standard Version 3.1 (2015). http://mpi-forum.org/docs/mpi-3.1/mpi31-report.pdf
26. Musser, D., Derge, G., Saini, A.: STL Tutorial and Reference Guide, 2nd edn. Addison-Wesley, Boston (2001)
27. OpenMP Architecture Review Board. OpenMP Application Program Interface Specification (2011)
28. Page, L., et al.: The pagerank citation ranking: bringing order to the web (1998)
29. Papadopoulos, I., et al.: STAPL-RTS: An application driven runtime system. In: Proceedings of the 29th ACM on International Conference on Supercomputing, ICS 2015, Newport Beach/Irvine, CA, USA, pp. 425–434, June 2015
30. Pearce, R., Gokhale, M., Amato, N.M.: Scaling techniques for massive scale-free graphs in distributed (external) memory. In: Proceedings of the 2013 IEEE 27th International Symposium on Parallel and Distributed Processing, IPDPS 2013, pp. 825–836. IEEE Computer Society, Washington (2013)
31. Pearce, R., Gokhale, M., Amato, N.M.: Faster parallel traversal of scale free graphs at extreme scale with vertex delegates. In: Proceedings of the International Conference for High Performance Computing, Networking, Storage and Analysis, SC 2014, pp. 549–559. IEEE Press, Piscataway (2014)
32. Reinders, J.: Intel Threading Building Blocks. O'Reilly & Associates Inc., Sebastopol (2007)
33. Sillero, J., Borrell, G., Jiménez, J., Moser, R.D.: Hybrid OpenMP-MPI turbulent boundary layer code over 32k cores. In: Cotronis, Y., Danalis, A., Nikolopoulos, D.S., Dongarra, J. (eds.) EuroMPI 2011. LNCS, vol. 6960, pp. 218–227. Springer, Heidelberg (2011)
34. Tanase, G., Buss, A., Fidel, A., Harshvardhan, Papadopoulos, I., Pearce, O., Smith, T., Thomas, N., Xu, X., Mourad, N., Vu, J., Bianco, M., Amato, N.M., Rauchwerger, L.: The STAPL parallel container framework. In: Proceedings of ACM

SIGPLAN Symposium Principles and Practice Parallel Programming (PPoPP), San Antonio, pp. 235–246 (2011)

35. Thomas, N., et al.: ARMI: a high level communication library for STAPL. Parallel Process. Lett. **16**(2), 261–280 (2006)

36. Zandifar, M., Abdul Jabbar, M., Majidi, A., Keyes, D., Amato, N.M., Rauchwerger, L.: Composing algorithmic skeletons to express high-performance scientific applications. In: Proceedings of the 29th ACM International Conference on Supercomputing, ICS 2015, pp. 415–424. ACM, New York (2015)

37. Zhao, J., et al.: Isolation for nested task parallelism. In: Proceedings of the 2013 ACM SIGPLAN International Conference on Object Oriented Programming Systems Languages & Applications, OOPSLA 2013, pp. 571–588. ACM, New York (2013)

38. Zheng, Y., et al.: UPC++: A PGAS extension for C++. In: 2014 IEEE 28th International Parallel and Distributed Processing Symposium, pp. 1105–1114, May 2014

Parallelizing Compiler

Multigrain Parallelization for Model-Based Design Applications Using the OSCAR Compiler

Dan Umeda$^{(\boxtimes)}$, Takahiro Suzuki, Hiroki Mikami, Keiji Kimura, and Hironori Kasahara

Green Computing Systems Research Center, Waseda University, Tokyo, Japan
{umedan,taka,hiroki}@kasahara.cs.waseda.ac.jp,
{keiji,kasahara}@waseda.jp
http://www.kasahara.cs.waseda.ac.jp/

Abstract. Model-based design is a very popular software development method for developing a wide variety of embedded applications such as automotive systems, aircraft systems, and medical systems. Model-based design tools like MATLAB/Simulink typically allow engineers to graphically build models consisting of connected blocks for the purpose of reducing development time. These tools also support automatic C code generation from models with a special tool such as Embedded Coder to map models onto various kinds of embedded CPUs. Since embedded systems require real-time processing, the use of multi-core CPUs poses more opportunities for accelerating program execution to satisfy the real-time constraints. While prior approaches exploit parallelism among blocks by inspecting MATLAB/Simulink models, this may lose an opportunity for fully exploiting parallelism of the whole program because models potentially have parallelism within a block. To unlock this limitation, this paper presents an automatic parallelization technique for auto-generated C code developed by MATLAB/Simulink with Embedded Coder. Specifically, this work (1) exploits multi-level parallelism including inter-block and intra-block parallelism by analyzing the auto-generated C code, and (2) performs static scheduling to reduce dynamic overheads as much as possible. Also, this paper proposes an automatic profiling framework for the auto-generated code for enhancing static scheduling, which leads to improving the performance of MATLAB/Simulink applications. Performance evaluation shows 4.21 times speedup with six processor cores on Intel Xeon X5670 and 3.38 times speedup with four processor cores on ARM Cortex-A15 compared with uniprocessor execution for a road tracking application.

Keywords: Automatic parallelization · Multi-core · Model-based design · MATLAB/Simulink · Automatic code generation

1 Introduction

The Model-based design like MATLAB/Simulink [1] has been widely used since it enables high software productivity in reduced turn-around times for embedded

© Springer International Publishing Switzerland 2016
X. Shen et al. (Eds.): LCPC 2015, LNCS 9519, pp. 125–139, 2016.
DOI: 10.1007/978-3-319-29778-1_8

systems [2]. Commercial model-based design tools support auto-code generation from a model that is represented by a block diagram [3,4]. MATLAB/Simulink is one of the most popular tools for the model-based design of automotive systems, aircraft systems, and medical systems. This tool can generate C/C++ code for embedded systems with Embedded Coder [5] (formerly known as Real-Time Workshop). The automatic code generation feature saves programmers from developing embedded applications in error-prone programming languages, however, this code generator does not optimize the application for target systems. Of course, it does not parallelize the application, even though a target system has a multi-core processor.

Several approaches have been proposed to utilize multi-cores for the application developed in MATLAB/Simulink. Some products have supported semi-automatic parallelization techniques for a multi-core processor using task partitioning by an application developer [6,7]. These technique can achieve a functional distribution of MATLAB/Simulink application, but cannot reduce load balancing which is most important for embedded real-time application. In addition, these tools support parallel processing in limited environments for simulation using Simulink. For an automatic parallelization of MATLAB/Simulink applications, Arquimedes et al. proposed an automatic equation-level parallelization technique of a Simulink model [8]. Their approach exploited parallelism among Mealy blocks such as integrators, derivatives, unit delays and so on. However, their method is only applicable to applications for simulation including mealy blocks. This approach does not focus on embedded systems. As an automatic parallelization technique for embedded applications, Kumura et al. proposed a model based parallelization by analyzing of dependencies from block connections among Simulink blocks [9]. This technique makes it possible to perform a parallel processing by exploiting block level parallelism from a model. However, exploiting this parallelism does not always allow us to exploit the full capability of multi-cores since a granularity of task depends on how the MATLAB/Simulink users define a block. A model information is too abstract to represent multi-grain parallelism including parallelism intra-blocks such as library Simulink blocks and users customized blocks. Therefore, this may lose an opportunity for optimizations, for example, by causing unequal workload on each core.

Unlike these prior approaches, this paper proposes an automatic parallelization method using an automatic multigrain parallelizing compiler, or the OSCAR compiler [10] from auto-generated C code developed by MATLAB/Simulink. While this approach successfully analyzes the C code because it is easy for the compiler to exploit parallelism using pattern matching and the code does not require a sophisticated pointer analysis for readability and MISRA-C, it is possible that future versions of Embedded Coder could limit the analysis of parallelism. The compiler exploits both of coarse grain parallelism inter-block and loop level parallelism intra-block from the auto-generated C code. Then, the compiler adjusts a task granularity with the minimum overhead by performing inline expansion and task fusion for conditional branches to improve the utilization of each core. After optimization, the compiler assigns parallel task onto processor cores using a static task scheduling considering profiling information on MATLAB/Simulink. Then, the compiler finally generates parallelized C code regardless of target processors. Although this paper focuses on the application developed by MATLAB/Simulink, the proposed method has a potential to apply to other model-based design tools since it exploits parallelism from the auto-generated C code regardless of a grammar of the tools. The features of the proposed method include:

- Fully automatic parallelization technique of the C code generated by a model-based design tool for embedded systems without dependence on a grammar of this tool.
- Construction of automatic profiling framework for a MATLAB/Simulink model to improve performance of the statically scheduled parallel code.
- Multigrain parallelization technique of model-based design applications that enables to overcome the limitation of the block level parallelization technique that is common in the field of model-based design.

The rest of this paper is organized as follows: Sect. 2 provides a framework for parallelization of model-based design applications. Section 3 introduces how to exploit parallelism from MATLAB/Simulink application using the OSCAR compiler. Section 4 describes multi-grain parallel processing method for the applications. Section 5 shows performance evaluation for the applications using the proposed method. Finally, Sect. 6 represents some conclusions.

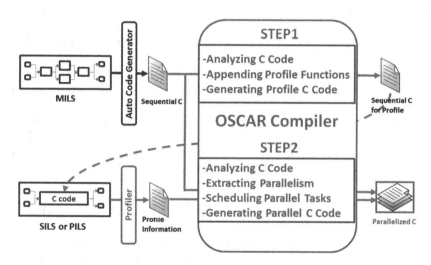

Fig. 1. Overview of the proposed framework for parallelization of model-based design applications

2   Framework for Parallelization of Model-based Design Applications

This section describes a framework for parallelization of model-based design applications. The model-based design tools with an automatic code generator like

MATLAB/Simulink are widely used since it enables high software productivity for embedded systems. However, the code generator like Embedded Coder does not optimize the application for target multi-cores. Therefore, several researchers have proposed the parallelization technique for the application on multi-cores. The previous works [8,9] analyzed a model file *model.mdl* to exploit parallelism among blocks in the model. This may lose an opportunity to exploit the whole parallelism in the model. For example, their approaches lose to exploit hierarchical multigrain parallelism, even though a model has parallelism inner Simulink blocks. It may cause unequal workload on each core. Additionally, they depend on a grammar of the model-based design tool. Indeed, the model file *model.mdl* have changed to a new model file *model.slx* from MATLAB R2012a.

In contrast, our proposed method analyzes auto-generated C code developed by MATLAB/Simulink with Embedded Coder to exploit hierarchical multigrain parallelism which is not represented in the model file. This approach does not depend on the grammar of model-based design tools since it analyzes the code to extract parallelism. Additionally, the proposed framework uses profiling information including execution counts and time to handle dynamic features of programs such as conditional branches and fluctuations in the number of iterations of loops.

Figure 1 shows an overview of the proposed framework. At the step1, the OSCAR compiler analyzes C code that is generated by Embedded Coder from a model. Then, the compiler instruments a sequence of C code inserting profile functions and the MATLAB/Simulink interface (MEX function [11]). This code is used to gather profiling information about a program execution on MATLAB/Simulink. Thereby, this framework can gather the profiling information in software-in-the-loop simulation (SILS) or processor-in-the-loop simulation (PILS) on the model-based design tool. Then, the profiler generates the profiling information during executing a model including the profile C code. At the step2, the compiler analyzes the auto-generated C code and exploits hierarchical multigrain parallelism in the whole program. After exploiting parallelism, the compiler schedules parallel tasks onto processor cores and finally generates parallelized C code using the profiling information.

3 Exploiting Parallelism Using the OSCAR Compiler

This section explains a method to exploit multigrain parallelism from auto-generated C code developed by MATLAB/Simulink using the OSCAR compiler.

3.1 Example of MATLAB/Simulink Application

This paper takes an example of MATLAB/Simulink application to describe the parallelism in it. The example is simple to explain parallelism of the model, however, real applications are too sophisticated to extract all parallelism because there are many of block connections and feedback loops. Therefore, it is difficult to achieve efficient performance on multi-cores using manual parallelization.

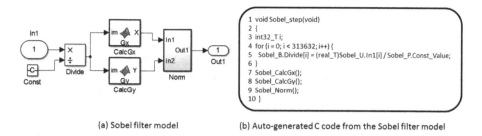

(a) Sobel filter model   (b) Auto-generated C code from the Sobel filter model

Fig. 2. Sample Simulink model and auto-generated C code from the model using the Embedded Coder

Figure 2(a) shows a model of Sobel filter that performs edge detection of a binary image. It consists of a `Const` block, a `Divide` block, `MATLAB Function` blocks (user's library functions) named as `CalcGx` and `CalcGy`, and a `Subsystem` block named as `Norm`. Evidently, the model has parallelism among `CalcGx` and `CalcGy` because there is no connection among them.

Figure 2(b) shows auto-generated C code from the model in Fig. 2(a) by Embedded Coder. A loop as shown in line 4–6 corresponds to the `Divide` block in Fig. 2(a). Each of functions of `Sobel_CalcGx` and `Sobel_CalcGy` corresponds each of the `MATLAB Function` blocks named as `CalcGx` and `CalcGy` in Fig. 2(a). A function of `Sobel_Norm` corresponds to the `Subsystem` block named as `Norm` in Fig. 2(a).

3.2   Coarse Grain Task Parallel Processing

Coarse grain task parallel processing uses parallelism among three kinds of coarse grain tasks, namely macro-tasks (MTs). Parallelism is expressed graphically as a macro-task graph (MTG) including data dependencies and control dependencies among MTs. The MTs on the MTG are assigned to processor cores by a static or a dynamic task scheduling method. As a result of the assignment, the OSCAR compiler generates parallelized C code while preserving the original semantics of the program.

Generation of Macro-Tasks. In the coarse grain task parallelization of the OSCAR compiler, auto-generated C code from a MATLAB/Simulink model is decomposed into the MTs. The MTs include basic blocks (BBs), repetition blocks or loops (RBs), and subroutine blocks (SBs). The MTs can be hierarchically defined inside each sequential loop or a function [10]. Moreover, the RB is transformed LOOP, which means the compiler analyzes this loop as a sequential loop, or DOALL which means the compiler analyzes this loop as a parallelizable loop.

Exploiting of Coarse Grain Task Parallelism. After generation of MTs, data dependencies, and control flow among MTs are analyzed. The compiler generates a hierarchical macro-flow graph (MFG) which represents control flow and data dependencies among MTs [10].

Then, the Earliest Executable Condition Analysis [10] is applied to the MFG to exploit coarse grain task parallelism among MTs by taking into account both the control dependencies and the data dependencies. This analysis generates a hierarchical macro-task graph (MTG). The MTG represents coarse grain task parallelism among MTs. If SB or RB has nested inner layer, MTGs are generated hierarchically. Figure 3 shows a hierarchical MTG of the C code in Fig. 2(b). Nodes represent MTs. Small circles inside a node represents conditional branches, for example, bb1 and bb4 in MTG2-1. Solid edges represent data dependencies. Dotted edges in MTG2-1, MTG3-1, and MTG4-1 represent extended control dependencies. The extended control dependency means ordinary control dependency and the condition on which a data dependence predecessor of an MT is not executed. Solid and dotted arcs, connecting solid and dotted edges have two different meanings. The solid arc represents that edges connected by the arc are in AND relationship. The dotted arc represents that edges connected by the arc are in OR relationship. In an MTG, edges having arrows represents original control flow edges or branch direction.

sb2 and sb3 in MTG0 are in parallel. Therefore, block level parallelism among CalcGx and CalcGy in Fig. 2 (a) are exploited from the auto-generated C code. Additionally, loop level parallelism which is not represented in Fig. 2(a) is exploited from the auto-generated C code since the compiler analyzes doall in Fig. 3 as parallelizable loops. Therefore, coarse grain task parallel processing using the compiler allows us to exploit hierarchical multigrain parallelism of MATLAB/Simulink applications from the auto-generated C code.

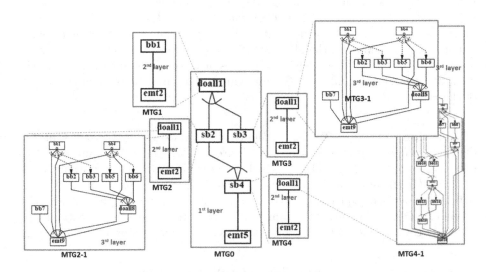

Fig. 3. Hierarchical MTG

Scheduling of Coarse Grain Task onto Multi-cores. After exploit of hierarchical multigrain parallelism, a static task scheduling or a dynamic task scheduling is chosen for each MTG to assign MTs onto multi-cores. If an MTG has only data dependencies and is deterministic, a static task scheduling at compilation time is applied to it by the OSCAR compiler. In the static task scheduling, the compiler uses four heuristic scheduling algorithms including CP/ETF/MISF, ETF/CP/MISF, DT/CP/MISF and CP/DT/MISF [12]. The compiler chooses the best schedule from those scheduling. If an MTG is non-deterministic by conditional branches or runtime fluctuations among MTs, the dynamic task scheduling at runtime is applied to it to handle the runtime uncertainties. The compiler generates dynamic task scheduling routines for non-deterministic MTGs and inserts it into a parallelized code. The static task scheduling is generally more effective than the dynamic task scheduling since it can minimize data transfer and synchronization an overhead without a runtime scheduling overhead.

Parallelized C Code Generation Using the OSCAR API. The OSCAR compiler generates parallelized C code with the OSCAR API [13] that is designed on a subset of OpenMP for preserving portability over a wide range of multi-core architectures. If data is shared on threads, the compiler inserts synchronizing instructions using spin locks. Additionally, MEX functions are inserted as necessary to execute parallelized C code in the SILS or PILS on MATLAB/Simulink.

4 Multigrain Parallel Processing Method for MATLAB/Simulink Applications

This section describes a proposed multigrain parallel processing method for MATLAB/Simulink applications. Embedded applications are generally executed repeatedly within a short period. Therefore, reducing overhead as much as possible is important for efficient parallel processing on multi-cores. The proposed method enables us to parallelize the application using hierarchical multigrain parallelism with a minimum overhead for embedded systems. The kernel technique is to generate the statically scheduled parallel code using multigrain parallelism. The proposal method consists of the following steps.

Step1. Automatic profiling in SILS or PILS on MATLAB/Simulink to handle dynamic features of programs.
Step2. Inline expansion to exploit more parallelism over hierarchies or program structure.
Step3. Macro task fusion for conditional branches to generate statically scheduled parallel code.
Step4. Converting loop level parallelism into task level parallelism to perform efficient parallel processing among loops and other MTs without an overhead of loop level parallelization.

The following provides details of the proposed method.

4.1   Automatic Profiling in Model-based Development

Profiling is an important technique for improving the preciseness of static task
scheduling by a parallelizing compiler. Moreover, it is particularly effective for
handling dynamic features of programs such as conditional branches and the
fluctuations in the number of loop iterations. For this purpose, the compiler
generates a sequence of code to collect profiling information. Additionally, MEX
functions as the interface between C code and MATLAB/Simulink are inserted
into this code to obtain the profiling information in the SILS or the PILS on
the model-based tool. Two types of profile functions are inserted immediately
before and after each MT. The one is a function to measure execution counts of
each MT. This information is utilized for estimating branch probability and the
number of loop iterations. The other is a function to measure the execution time
of each MT. This information is utilized for optimization and the static task
scheduling in the compiler. In the other words, execution counts and time in the
level of MT are attained with executing the code. The profiler finally generates
the profiling information including longest path, shortest path, and average path
in repeated executions during executing a model including the profile C code.

4.2   Inline Expansion

The OSCAR compiler generates a hierarchical MTG to perform hierarchical parallelization [10]. It is effective to perform parallel processing for applications having large execution time, for example, simulation of scientific computation. However, real embedded applications are generally executed repeatedly within a short
period. Therefore, it is not enough parallelism to parallelize efficiently in each
hierarchy. Thus, the proposed method uses an inline expansion technique [14]

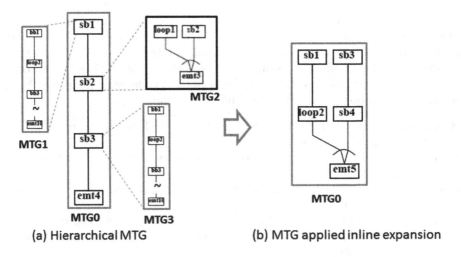

(a) Hierarchical MTG   (b) MTG applied inline expansion

Fig. 4. Overview of the inline expansion technique

to exploit multigrain parallelism from programs over hierarchies or nested levels. This technique analyzes parallelism after each SB is inline expanded. After the analysis, the compiler selects SBs to improve parallelism and expands them. Figure 4 shows an overview of the inline expansion technique. In Fig. 4(a), it is not enough parallelism to parallelize hierarchically in MTG0, MTG1, and MTG3. The inline expansion applies sb2 in MTG0 including parallelism inner the block to improve parallelism. As a result, the compiler generates an MTG in Fig. 4(b). As shown in Fig. 4(b), more coarse grain parallelism is exploited than that of the MTG in Fig. 4(a).

4.3   Macro Task Fusion

The OSCAR compiler has two types of task scheduling as mentioned in Sect. 3.2. The one is the dynamic task scheduling that is applied to an MTG including conditional branches. The other is the static task scheduling that is applied to an MTG including no conditional branches. The static task scheduling is preferable for parallelization of the embedded applications because of its few runtime overhead. However, most of MATLAB/Simulink applications have Switch, Saturation and Trigger blocks that are converted into if-statements by Embedded Coder. It introduces to choose the dynamic task scheduling including the runtime overhead. Since these conditional branches cannot be handled by the static task scheduling, the proposed scheme applies macro task fusion to MFG to hide conditional branches inside MTs. The method is described as follows.

Step 1. Search MFG nodes having a conditional branch.
Step 2. For each conditional branch node found in step 1, apply step 3–6.
Step 3. Search a set of MFG nodes that is post-dominated by the conditional branch node.
Step 4. Define a post-dominator node having a minimum number of the MT with the exception of the conditional branch node as an exit node.
Step 5. Merge a group from the conditional branch node and the exit node into a single MT.
Step 6. Generate a fused MT including conditional branches inner the MT.

This process eliminates all conditional branches from an MFG. After the technique, if the fused MT has enough parallelism inner the MT, duplications of if-statements [15] is applied to it for an improvement of parallelism.

Figure 5 shows an overview of the macro task fusion technique. At the step 1, the compiler searches MFG nodes having a conditional branch from an MFG. At the step 2, the compiler applies step 3–6 to each conditional branch node found step 1. At the step 3, the compiler searches a post-dominator of the conditional branch node. At the step 4, the compiler chooses a node having a minimum number in the post-dominators with the exception of the conditional branch node. Then, the node is defined as an exit node of the conditional branch node. At the step 5, the compiler merges a group from the conditional branch node and the exit node into a single MT. As a result, the compiler generates a fused MT including conditional branches inner the MT at the step 6.

In this example, the compiler chooses bb1 and bb7 having a small circle inside a node that represents a conditional branch in Fig. 5(a). In Fig. 5(a), bb1 dominates bb1, bb5, sb6, bb7, bb10 and emt11. Additionally, bb7 dominates bb7, bb10 and emt11. Therefore, the compiler chooses bb5 and bb10 as the exit node for each of the conditional branch nodes. Merging bb1--5 and bb7--10, the compiler generates an MFG as shown in Fig. 5(b). In this figure, block shows the merged MT by the technique. Exploiting parallelism using the Earliest Executable Condition Analysis, the compiler generates an MTG as shown in Fig. 5(c). Then, the duplication of if-statements applies to inner block3 not to eliminate parallelism. bb1 including if-statements is duplicated, and block3 is divided into two nodes. As a result, the compiler generates an MTG having duplicated MTs such as block3 and block4 as shown in Fig. 5(d). Thus, a compiler coarsens MTs without losing parallelism and can apply static task scheduling without runtime overhead to an MTG having conditional branches.

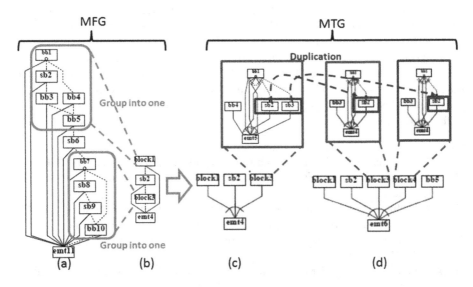

Fig. 5. Overview of the macro task fusion technique

4.4   Converting Loop Level Parallelism into Task Level Parallelism

Kumura et al. [9] has proposed the block level parallelization technique from the data flow graph of the block diagram of a model. This method enables us to exploit parallelism among blocks in the model. However, it is difficult to exploit parallelism in a block using only information of the block diagram. In contrast, this paper proposes the multigrain parallelization technique from auto-generated C code. The code level analysis in this method enables us to exploit loop level parallelism in addition to task level parallelism. In this paper, parallelizable loops shown as Doall are decomposed into n small Doalls (or MTs) statically to perform parallel processing efficiently without a runtime overhead of loop level parallelization. In this method, the n is a number decided by less than a number of processor cores and T_{min}. T_{min} is defined as a minimum task cost for loop level parallelization considering overheads of parallel thread fork/join and task scheduling on each target multi-core [10].

These decomposed small Doalls can be executed in parallel among other MTs. After parallelizable loop decomposition, the static task scheduler in Sect. 3.2 assigns all MTs including decomposed Doalls onto processor cores.

5   Performance Evaluation of MATLAB/Simulink Applications on Multi-cores

This section describes performance evaluation of the proposed multigrain parallelization technique for MATLAB/Simulink applications on several multi-core platforms.

5.1   Target MATLAB/Simulink Applications

This section evaluates the performance on Intel and ARM multi-cores using three important applications such as road tracking for self-driving cars, vessel detection for medical image recognition, and anomaly detection for pattern recognition really used an industry. These applications have both parallelism among Simulink blocks and inner a block. Therefore, they are suitable to be parallelized by the automatic multigrain parallelization technique. Each application is described in the following.

Road Tracking. Road tracking in a model of [16] is an image processing to detect and track edges set in primarily residential settings where lane markings may not be present. The model has over one hundred Simulink blocks and block level parallelism among Simulink blocks in the left road and right road. The size of an input image is 320×240 pixels. In this evaluation, `For Iterator` blocks are expanded and S-Function blocks of parallel Hough transformation [17] are used instead of library `Hough Transformation` block to be close real embedded applications.

Vessel Detection. Vessel detection model implemented from [18] is an image processing to detect vessels from retinal images for a diagnosis of various eye diseases. The model is simplest in the three applications and includes one `Data Type Conversion`, one `MinMax`, one `Switch` and eight `MATLAB Function` blocks using the Kirsch's edge operator blocks. The operator blocks are in parallel. The size of an input image is 200×170 pixels.

Anomaly Detection. Anomaly detection model is a real product application in A&D CO., LTD. and an image processing to detect anomaly from
an input image. The model is most complex and has longest execution time
in the three applications. It includes morphological opening, morphological
dilation, blob analysis blocks and so on. There is parallelism among some
image processing block. The size of the input image is 600 × 600 pixels.

5.2   Evaluation Environment

This evaluation uses the Intel Xeon X5670 and the ARM Cortex-A15. The Xeon
X5670 processor has six processor cores with each processor core running at
2.93 GHz. Each processor core has 32 KB L1-cache and 256 KB L2-cache. 12 MB
L3 cache is shared on six processor cores. The Cortex-A15 processor has four
1.60 GHz processor cores. Each processor core has 32 KB L1-cache, and four
processor cores has a shared 2 MB L2-cache.

5.3   Performance Evaluation on Multi-cores

Figure 6(a) and (b) shows average speedup obtained by using only the task
level parallelization technique that is similar to the single level parallelization
technique in [9] and the multigrain parallelization technique corresponds to proposed method on Intel Xeon X5670 and ARM Cortex-A15. The speedups in
Fig. 6(a) and (b) are relative to sequential execution using only one core of each
application. 1.92 times speedup for the road tracking application, 2.65 times
speedup for vessel detection application and 2.50 times speedup for the anomaly
detection application can be achieved using the task level parallelization technique on Intel Xeon X5670 with six processor cores. On ARM cortex-A15 with
four processor cores, 1.94 times speedup for the road tracking application, 2.74
times speedup for the vessel detection application and 2.29 times speedup for the
anomaly detection application can be achieved using the task level parallelization
technique.

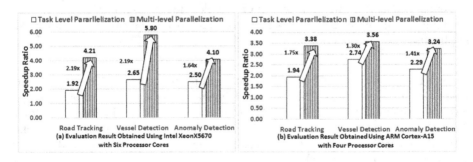

Fig. 6. Speedup ratio for MATLAB/Simulink applications on Intel and ARM
multi-cores

In speedup of the proposed method, 4.21 times speedup for the road tracking application, 5.80 times speedup for the vessel detection application and 4.10 times speedup for the anomaly detection application can be achieved using the multigrain parallelization technique on Intel Xeon X5670 with six processor cores. On ARM cortex-A15 with four processor cores, 3.38 times speedup for the road tracking application, 3.56 times speedup for the vessel detection application and 3.24 times speedup for the anomaly detection application can be achieved using the multigrain parallelization technique. Therefore, the proposed method attains 2.19 times speedup for the road tracking application, 2.19 times speedup for the vessel detection application and 1.64 times speedup for the anomaly detection application compared with the execution using the task level parallelization technique on Intel Xeon X5670 using six processor cores. On ARM Cortex-A15 with four processor cores, 1.75 times speedup for the road tracking application, 1.30 times speedup for the vessel detection application and 1.41 times speedup for the anomaly detection application compared with the execution using the task level parallelization technique.

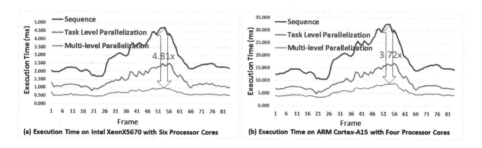

Fig. 7. Execution time per a frame for the road tracking application on Intel and ARM multi-cores

Further, this paper describes execution time per a frame for the road tracking application with a scatter per an input image. Figure 7(a) and (b) shows execution time per a frame on Intel Xeon X5670 and ARM Cortex-A15 for the road tracking application. The upper lines in Fig. 7(a) and (b) show execution time of ordinary execution. Each of the execution fluctuates from 1.705 ms to 4.728 ms on Intel Xeon X5670 and from 10.58 ms to 32.36 ms on ARM Cortex-A15. The middle lines in Fig. 7(a) and (b) show execution time using the task level parallelization technique. Each of the execution fluctuates from 0.815 ms to 2.510 ms on Intel Xeon X5670 with six processor cores and from 4.88 ms to 17.02 ms on ARM Cortex-A15 with four processor cores. The lower lines in Fig. 7(a) and (b) show the execution time using the multigrain parallelization technique. Each of the execution fluctuates from 0.459 ms to 0.983 ms on Intel Xeon X5670 with six processor cores and from 3.38 ms to 9.04 ms on ARM Cortex-A15 with four processor cores. Clearly, each variance of the execution time of the multigrain parallelized program is much lower than that of each sequential program on each processor. Therefore, the proposed method allows us to perform stable execution regardless of on input image. In worst case of sequential execution time on each processor, proposed method gives us 4.81 times speedup on Intel Xeon X5670 with six processor cores, and 3.72 times speedup on ARM Cortex-A15 with four processor cores using the multigrain parallelization technique compared with the sequential execution on each processor.

6 Conclusions

This paper has proposed the automatic multigrain parallelization scheme using the OSCAR compiler for embedded applications developed by MATLAB/ Simulink. This scheme exploits multigrain parallelism from auto-generated C code by Embedded Coder and optimizes this code. The proposed method includes three techniques of the inline expansion, the macro task fusion of conditional branches and the converting loop level parallelism into task level parallelism. The inline expansion is used to exploit more parallelism over hierarchies or nested levels. The macro task fusion is used to generate the statically scheduled parallel code without the runtime overhead. The converting loop level parallelism into task level parallelism is used to improve parallelism without the overhead of loop level parallelization. Additionally, the proposed method also includes the automatic profiling framework to improve performance of the statically scheduled parallel code.

Using the proposed method, this paper parallelized three important applications such as road tracking for self-driving cars, vessel detection for medical image recognition, and anomaly detection for pattern recognition really used an industry. In the performance evaluation, the OSCAR compiler with proposed method gave us 4.21 times speedup for the road tracking application, 5.80 times speedup for the vessel detection application and 4.10 times speedup for the anomaly detection application on Intel Xeon X5670 with six processor cores. Moreover, 3.38 times speedup for road tracking, 3.56 times speedup for the vessel detection application and 3.24 times speedup for the anomaly detection application on ARM Cortex-A15 with four processor cores. Comparing with the execution using the task level parallelization technique that is similar to the previous method for MATLAB/Simulink applications, the proposed method attained from 1.30 to 2.19 times speedup on different multi-cores such as Intel or ARM. The proposed method has successfully improved performance applications developed by MATLAB/Simulink on multi-core processors.

Acknowledgment. This work has been partly supported by A&D CO., LTD. for providing the anomaly detection model. We would like to express appreciation to A&D CO., LTD..

References

1. MATLAB/Simulink. http://www.mathworks.com/products/simulink/
2. Kamma, D., Sasi, G.: Effect of model based software development on productivity of enhancement tasks - an industrial study. In: Software Engineering Conference (2014)
3. Hanselmann, H., Kiffmeier, U., Köster, L., Meyer, M., Rükgauer, A.: Production quality code generation from sirnulink block diagrams. In: Proceedings of the International Symposium on Computer Aided Control System Design (1999)
4. Gluch, D., Kornecki, A.: Automated code generation for safety related applications: a case study. In: Proceedings of the International Multiconference on Computer Science and Information Technology (2006)
5. Embedded Coder. http://www.mathworks.com/products/embedded-coder/
6. Parallel Computing Toolbox. http://www.mathworks.com/products/parallel-computing/
7. RTI-MP. http://www.dspace.com/en/inc/home/products/sw/impsw/rtimpblo.cfm
8. Canedo, A., Yoshizawa, T., Komatsu, H.: Automatic parallelization of simulink applications. In: Proceedings of the International Symposium on Code Generation and Optimization (2010)
9. Kumura, T., Nakamura, Y., Ishiura, N., Takeuchi, Y., Imai, M.: Model based parallelization from the simulink models and their sequential C Code. In: SASIMI (2012)
10. Obata, M., Shirako, J., Kaminaga, H., Ishizaka, K., Kasahara, H.: Hierarchical parallelism control for multigrain parallel processing. In: Pugh, B., Tseng, C.-W. (eds.) LCPC 2002. LNCS, vol. 2481, pp. 31–44. Springer, Heidelberg (2005)
11. MEX Function. http://www.mathworks.com/help/matlab/apiref/mexfunction.html
12. Kasahara, H.: Parallel Processing Technology. CORONA PUBLISHING CO., LTD(1991)
13. Kimura, K., Mase, M., Mikami, H., Miyamoto, T., Shirako, J., Kasahara, H.: OSCAR API for real-time low-power multicores and its performance on multicores and SMP servers. In: Gao, G.R., Pollock, L.L., Cavazos, J., Li, X. (eds.) LCPC 2009. LNCS, vol. 5898, pp. 188–202. Springer, Heidelberg (2010)
14. Shirako, J., Nagasawa, K., Ishizaka, K., Obata, M., Kasahara, H.: Selective inline expansion for improvement of multi grain parallelism. In: The IASTED International Conference on Parallel and Distributed Computing and Networks (2004)
15. Umeda, D., Kanehagi, Y., Mikami, H., Hayashi, A,. Kimura, K., Kasahara, H.: Automatic parallelization of hand written automotive engine control codes using OSCAR compiler. In: CPC (2013)
16. Road Tracking. http://www.mathworks.com/help/vision/examples.html
17. Yen-Kuang C., Li, E., Jianguo L., Tao, W.: Novel parallel hough transform on multi-core processors. In: Acoustics, Speech and Signal Processing (2008)
18. Bhadauria, H., Bisht, S., Singh, A.: Vessels extraction from retinal images. IOSR J. Electron. Commun. Eng. 6(3), 79–82 (2013)

HYDRA : Extending Shared Address Programming for Accelerator Clusters

Putt Sakdhnagool[✉], Amit Sabne, and Rudolf Eigenmann

School of Electrical and Computer Engineering,
Purdue University, West Lafayette, USA
{psakdhna,asabne,eigenman}@purdue.edu

Abstract. This work extends shared address programming to accelerator clusters by pursuing a simple form of shared-address programming, named HYDRA, where the programmer only specifies the parallel regions in the program. We present a fully automatic translation system that generates an MPI + accelerator program from a HYDRA program. Our mechanism ensures scalability of the generated program by optimizing data placement and transfer to and from the limited, discrete memories of accelerator devices. We also present a compiler design built on a high-level IR to support multiple accelerator architectures. Evaluation results demonstrate the scalability of the translated programs on five well-known benchmarks. On average, HYDRA gains a 24.54x speedup over single-accelerator performance when running on a 64-node Intel Xeon Phi cluster and a 27.56x speedup when running on a 64-node NVIDIA GPU cluster.

1 Introduction

The past decade has seen a steady rise in the use of accelerators towards high-performance computing. Many supercomputers rely on devices such as NVIDIA or AMD GPUs and Intel Xeon Phis to accelerate compute-intensive workloads. Various programming models and frameworks [8,14] have so far been proposed to effectively use accelerators on individual compute nodes. As the productivity of these frameworks has risen over the years, there is growing interest in programming systems that can efficiently use accelerators on *all* nodes of a cluster.

Writing a program to exploit CPU clusters in itself is a tedious and error-prone task. The need for accelerator programming adds further to this difficulty, as the involved programming models differ substantially from those of common CPUs. To achieve greater productivity, high-level programming models for accelerator clusters are needed.

In response to such requirements, this paper presents compiler and runtime techniques required for a shared address programming model for accelerator clusters. In our research, we pursue a simple model, called *HYDRA*, where programmers only specify parallel regions and shared data in the program. From our observation, most parallel applications in well-known benchmark suites, such as Rodinia [4], can be implemented using only this construct. To demonstrate

© Springer International Publishing Switzerland 2016
X. Shen et al. (Eds.): LCPC 2015, LNCS 9519, pp. 140–155, 2016.
DOI: 10.1007/978-3-319-29778-1_9

the effectiveness of our techniques, we developed a source-to-source translation system that converts a HYDRA program into an MPI + accelerator program (referred to as accelerated MPI program hereafter).

There are two important performance factors for accelerator cluster programs: single-accelerator speed and scalability across nodes. Researchers have previously proposed advanced techniques for generating optimized single-accelerator code from shared address programs [8, 14]. By contrast, this paper focuses on the scalability aspect, which is crucial, as large clusters are expected to efficiently process increasingly large problem sizes. Optimization techniques for single accelerators are insufficient. Realizing shared address programming with high scalability on accelerator clusters poses the following three challenges. These challenges do not exist on CPU clusters. Their solutions represent the specific contributions of this paper.

1. The first challenge comes from the fact that, unliked CPUs, current accelerators have discrete and limited memories. Full data allocation of today's typical problem sizes on accelerator memories could exceed available capacities. This limitation would result in failure of single-accelerator execution and an inability to scale to multiple nodes. Programmers of accelerated MPI code avoid this problem by allocating only the part of the data accessed by each process of a distributed program. By contrast, shared address programming hides the access distribution from programmers and, instead, relies on the compiler or runtime support to extract such information. The distribution of the data accesses is related to the partitioning of the program computation. The system must be aware of such partitioning to precisely allocate memory on accelerators. Without advanced analysis, a compiler may allocate the entire shared data on the accelerator memory, which could result in the said failure. Our first contribution overcomes this issue by introducing a precise compile-time memory allocation method.

2. A second critical issue is related to the data transfer between accelerator and host memory. Minimizing this transfer is critical for scalability. The challenge lies in the single machine image of the shared address space, where programmers do not specify data movements between CPU and accelerator memories. The compiler, having to derive such transfer from the program, might send entire shared data structures to/from accelerator memory, introducing excessive overhead. Our second contribution introduces a compile-time solution to minimize such transfers.

3. Both proposed techniques are architecture-agnostic. We show results on two common accelerators: NVIDIA's GPUs and Intel Xeon Phis (referred to as MIC hereafter). Our compiler design includes support for multiple architectures. Our third contribution lies in this design, which separates passes that are common across architectures and specialized passes for the target architectures. The compiler takes HYDRA programs as input, and translates them into accelerated MPI programs, using CUDA or OpenCL, depending upon the underlying architecture.

We demonstrate the efficacy of the proposed techniques by experimenting with five common applications on two clusters of 64 nodes each; one has NVIDIA GPUs, the other has Intel MICs. The speedup against optimized single-accelerator performance is as high as 43.81x on a 64-node GPU cluster and 45.18x on a MIC cluster.

The remainder of this paper is organized as follows. Section 2 describes the baseline system on which HYDRA is built. Section 3 discusses the requirements for the translation and our solutions. Section 4 describes the implementation of the HYDRA translation system. Section 5 presents experimental results on five benchmarks. We discuss related work in Sect. 6 and present conclusions in Sect. 7.

2   Background

2.1   OMPD Baseline System

Our work builds on the OMPD [10] hybrid compiler-runtime system, which enables OpenMP programs to utilize nodes of a distributed system.

The compiler is responsible to partition the program computation and to perform the static part of the communication analysis. The compilation process of OMPD consists of two phases: (1) program partitioning and (2) static communication analysis. In program partitioning, the compiler divides the program into sections, referred to as *program blocks*, each containing either serial code or a parallel loop. The serial program blocks are replicated across processes while the parallel blocks are work-shared. The parallel loop's iterations are partitioned and distributed across MPI processes. A barrier is placed at the end of each program block, representing a potential communication point. The static communication analysis performs array data flow analysis, described in Sect. 2.2, determining local uses and local definitions of each program block. The compiler transfers this information to the runtime system for complete communication analysis.

All inter-node communication is generated and executed at runtime. At each barrier, the runtime system analyzes *global uses*, which determines future read accesses of all data at any needed communication point. The communication messages are determined by intersecting local definitions and global uses. The runtime system uses this information to schedule communication and generate MPI messages.

2.2   Array Data Flow Analysis

Array data flow analysis [11] enables the compiler to analyze the precise producer and consumer relationships between program blocks. The result of the analysis is a set of local uses and local definitions of each program block, at each barrier in the program. Every process will have its own local definitions and local uses. For shared array A at barrier i, the local use is denoted by $LUSE_i^A$ and local definition by $LDEF_i^A$, defined as

$$LUSE_i^A = \{use_{(i,j)}^A | 1 \leq j \leq n\} \qquad (1)$$

$$LDEF_i^A = \{def_{(i,k)}^A | 1 \leq k \leq m\} \qquad (2)$$

where each *use* represents a read access of array A in the program block after barrier i and each *def* represents a write access of array A in the program block before barrier i. n and m are the number of read accesses in the program block after barrier i and the number of write accesses in the program block before barrier i of array A, respectively. For a p-dimensional array A, each *use* and *def* is defined as a pair of lower bound and upper bound accesses in each dimension of the array. For dimension d, the lower and upper bound are represented as $[lb_d : ub_d]$. An example of *use* and *def* for a p-dimensional array is as follows

$$use_{(i,j)}^A = [lb_{p-1} : ub_{p-1}]...[lb_1 : ub_1][lb_0 : ub_0]$$

$$def_{(i,j)}^A = [lb_{p-1} : ub_{p-1}]...[lb_1 : ub_1][lb_0 : ub_0]$$

We extend this array data flow analysis framework for the new optimizations described in Sect. 3.

3 Extending Shared Address Programming Beyond CPU Clusters

Extending CPU-based shared address programming to support accelerator clusters poses a number of challenges. While the model is convenient for users, the programs abstraction hides information that is relevant for the translator. Thus, the compiler needs sophisticated techniques to extract this information. The need for such techniques is critical in our HYDRA programming model, as programmers only specify parallel regions and do not include such information as data transfer and communication. Section 3.1 describes the model in more detail.

Our techniques deal with the fact that accelerators are independent computational components with separate address spaces, reduced memory capacities, and diverse architectures. Section 3.2 explains these threee challenges in more detail and presents our solutions.

3.1 HYDRA Programming Model

HYDRA is a directive-based shared address programming model offering a single parallel loop construct

```
#pragma hydra parallel for [clauses]
```

The clauses are syntactically optional but might be needed for program semantics. Table 1 lists all available clauses for the HYDRA parallel loop directive. The **shared**, **private**, and **firstprivate** clauses specify characteristics of variables. Variables not listed explicitly are **shared** by default. The **reduction** clause indicates that the annotated loop performs a reduction operation on variables in **varlist** using operator **op**.

Table 1. Parallel loop directive clauses

Clause	Format	Description
shared	shared(varlist)	List of shared variables.
private	private(varlist)	List of private variables.
firstprivate	firstprivate(varlist)	List of private variables, whose value must be initiated before the start of the parallel loop
reduction	reduction(op:varlist)	List of variables to perform reduction with operator op

Despite HYDRA's simplicity, many parallel applications can be implemented using only this single HYDRA construct. All of our evaluation benchmarks were available in the form of OpenMP programs. We generated HYDRA versions by a simple, syntactic translation. We chose HYDRA instead of available models, such as OpenACC and OpenMP, for research purposes, which are to explore the concepts of the translation and the generic characteristic of shared-address models.

3.2   Compiler Analyses for Accelerator Data Management

In distributed programming, the computation is partitioned and distributed across processes. The programmer is responsible for doing so. HYDRA instead holds the underlying compiler and runtime responsible for these tasks. Programmers do not need to express any information about access ranges of shared data.

The lack of such information may require the compiler to assume that each process is accessing the entire data, although in reality, only a portion of the data is being accessed. This problem is not critical in CPU clusters because of large physical memory space and virtual address systems; however, accelerator memory is much smaller and does not have virtual memory support. As the typical problem sizes used on clusters are much larger than a single accelerator's memory, allocating the entire data required by the computation on each accelerator would result in program failure due to insufficient memory. Even if the data fits in the accelerator memory, another issue would arise: accelerator memory is discrete and input data must be transferred to it before being used. Transferring the entire data would introduce excessive overhead. Therefore, data access information is crucial to the scalability of accelerator cluster programs.

Data Transfer Analysis. To minimize data transfers, a compiler analysis must precisely identify the data accessed by each program block. The precise access information can be identified by the union of read and write sections of live data. The details of the analysis are as follows: The first part of our data transfer analysis identifies the shared data that are live-in and live-out of a given program block executing on the accelerators, B_i. This information can be derived from the $LUSE$ information, generated by the array data flow analysis described in Sect. 2.2.

Let Br_i denote the barrier before B_i, Br_f denote the future barriers that the program will reach after B_i, and $ShareVar(B_i)$ denote the set of shared variables accessed in the program block B_i. Let $A \in ShareVar(B_i)$. If there exists $LUSE^A_{Br_i}$, array A will be used in B_i and a data transfer from host to accelerator is required. On the other hand, if there exists $LUSE^A_{Br_f}$ array A will be used in the future, requiring a data transfer from accelerator to host.

If the analysis determines that a data transfer is required for an array A at barrier Br_i, the next step is to identify the section of array A that will be transferred. The required section of an array A on each dimension can be obtained as $[lb_{min,Br_i} : ub_{max,Br_i}]$ where lb_{min,Br_i} is the minimum lower bound of all local accesses of array A and ub_{max,Br_i} is the maximum upper bound of all local accesses of array A at barrier Br_i in that dimension. Note that the upper and lower bounds can be symbolic expressions. The analysis obtains lb_{min,Br_i} and ub_{max,Br_i} by using the symbolic analysis capabilities of Cetus [1].

Memory Allocation Optimization. Memory allocation/deallocation could be done at the beginning/end of each kernel, based on the data size computed for the transfer. However, as the same array may be accessed in multiple kernels, one can do better. Our method performs global analysis to summarize all accesses of the shared array in the program and allocates/deallocates only once, saving costs and improving re-use of the allocated memory. There is a small sacrifice in precision, in terms of the memory size allocated, which however is always conservatively larger. Such sacrifice does not affect the correctness of the program and is outweighed by the saved costs of repeated allocation and possible re-transfer of data.

The optimization is based upon global array dataflow analysis for precise array sections. The implementation also makes use of the advanced array dataflow framework and symbolic analysis capabilities available in the Cetus compiler infrastructure. The memory space requirement of an array A is extracted from the union of $LDEF^A$ and $LUSE^A$, where $LUSE^A$ represents all read accesses and $LDEF^A$ represents all write accesses of an array A in the program. $LDEF^A$ is the union of all $LUSE^A_{Br_i}$ and $LDEF^A$ is the union of all $LDEF^A_{Br_i}$ in the program. Thus, $LUSE^A \cup LDEF^a$ represents all accesses of array A in the program. The memory requirement for each dimension of the array can be defined as $[lb_{min} : ub_{max}]$ where $lb_{min} \in (LUSE^A \cup LDEF^A)$ is the minimum lower bound of all accesses of array A and $ub_{max} \in (LUSE^A \cup LDEF^A)$ is the maximum upper bound of all accesses of array A. $[lb_{min} : ub_{max}]$ indicates the bounds of any access to array A in the local process. Thus, it also defines the memory allocation for array A. The size of the new array is different from the original. The compiler must incorporate this change into all accesses of the new array by subtracting lb_{min} from all indices. The size and offset information is also utilized while generating the data transfers.

The analysis does not require array sections to be contiguous and can support arrays with any number of dimensions. In our current implementation, if the analysis results in multiple array sections, the algorithm will conservatively merge them together. Further analysis can be done to determine whether the sections should be merged or not, which we leave to future work.

4 Translation System Implementation

The HYDRA translation system consists of a compiler and a runtime system. The compiler performs source-to-source translation to generate accelerated MPI code from input HYDRA programs. Section 4.1 explains the compiler design to support multiple accelerator architectures. Section 4.2 presents the overall translation process of the HYDRA compiler. The HYDRA runtime system is responsible for remote accelerator-to-accelerator communication in the compiler-translated, accelerated MPI programs. The implementation of the runtime system is described in Sect. 4.3.

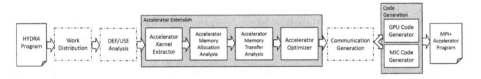

Fig. 1. HYDRA compiler translation process: grey boxes represent the new passes in the HYDRA compiler.

4.1 Supporting Multiple Accelerator Architectures

To support a wide-range of accelerator clusters, the compiler must be able to target different accelerator architectures. This requirement poses a challenge to the compiler design as different architectures have different features, some of which are common while others are unique to the specific architecture.

In the HYDRA compiler, most compilation passes are architecture agnostic with no specialization needed. The design defers specialization to as late as possible in the translation process. In this way, only the last compilation pass of code generation is architecture specific. The key to realizing such design is the internal representation (IR).

From our observation the following four operations are sufficient to express any accelerator program : (1) Memory Allocation, (2) Data Transfer, (3) Accelerator Kernel Execution, and (4) Memory Deallocation. By using these operations as IR constructs, the compiler can represent programs in an architecture-independent form. To generate architecture-specific code, the compiler converts architecture-independent constructs to their architecture-specific equivalents during the code generation pass.

4.2 HYDRA Translation Process

Figure 1 shows the overall translation process from the input HYDRA program to the accelerated MPI program. Accelerator extensions are highlighted using grey boxes. The dashed boxes represent existing CPU passes.

The compilation process starts with the CPU passes, which perform work partitioning and array dataflow analysis. The partitioned program is then passed to HYDRA's accelerator extension. The passes in the extension perform accelerator kernel generation, memory transfer analysis, memory allocation optimization and further architecture-independent optimization (e.g. hoisting memory transfers, prefetching, etc.). After the accelerator code is added, the compiler analyzes and adds communication code to the program. The compilation process completes with the code generation pass, which produces the accelerated MPI program with accelerator kernels specific to the target architecture.

The current implementation of the HYDRA compiler supports two accelerator types: NVIDIA CUDA GPUs and Intel MIC. As target languages, we choose CUDA for NVIDIA GPUs and OpenCL for Intel MICs. One might argue that different architectures could be supported by using OpenCL as the target language for all accelerator architectures; the compiler just needs to generate OpenCL + MPI programs, allowing the generated code to run on any accelerator cluster. However, OpenCL does not support accelerator-specific features, e.g. using warp-level functions in CUDA. Thus, the translated code cannot fully utilize the accelerator capabilities. Further, some architectures have limited support for OpenCL features [6].

The HYDRA compiler faces similar limitations as the baseline OMPD system: irregular programs are handled inefficiently for lack of compile-time information about data accesses. Such accesses may lead to conservative memory allocations and data transfers.

4.3 HYDRA Runtime System

The HYDRA runtime system is responsible for remote accelerator communication. In contrast to CPUs, accelerators cannot directly perform remote communication. The communication must be handled by the host CPU. Thus, additional data transfer between host and accelerator memories is required before and after the communication. We refer to such data transfer as *message relay*.

We designed a new runtime extension (ACC-RT), whose interaction with the host-side runtime system (HOST-RT) enables remote accelerator communication. The HOST-RT system is responsible for generating communication messages and executing host-to-host communication, while the ACC-RT system is responsible for managing host-accelerator data mapping and message relays. The ACC-RT system uses communication information from the HOST-RT system to generate message relays. The transfers are computed from the communication messages generated by the HOST-RT system, and the mapping information provided by the HYDRA compiler. A runtime interface is designed for the compiler to provide mapping information between host and accelerator data. The mapping information includes the host address, accelerator address, accelerator data size, and accelerator data offset. The accelerator offset is necessary in order to align accelerator and host data. The overhead of the ACC-RT system is negligible. In our experiments, we found this overhead to be less than 0.1 % of the total execution time on 64-node accelerator clusters.

5   Evaluation

This section evaluates the effectiveness of the proposed techniques on two accelerator clusters, one with NVIDIA GPUs and another with Intel MICs.

5.1   Experimental Setup

We used the Keeneland cluster [20] to evaluate the GPU versions of the HYDRA programs. Keeneland consists of 264 compute nodes, connected by an FDR Infiniband network. Each node has two 8-core Xeon E5-2670 running at 2.6 Ghz, 32 GB of main memory, and three NVIDIA Tesla M2090 GPUs. Each GPU has 6 GB of device memory available for computation. We evaluated the MIC program versions on a community cluster, where each node contains two 8-core Xeon E5-2670 CPUs, 64 GB of main memory, and two Intel Xeon Phi P5110 accelerators. Each Xeon Phi has 6 GB of device memory available for computation. The nodes are connected by an FDR-10 Infiniband network. Our evaluation uses up to 64 nodes with one MPI process and one accelerator per node.

We present the results for five representative benchmarks: Bilateral Filter, Blackscholes, Filterbank, Jacobi, and Heat3D. Bilateral Filter and Blackscholes are from the NVIDIA CUDA SDK. The benchmarks are implemented in HYDRA by converting their OpenMP counterparts. Bilateral Filter is a non-linear and edge-preserving filter used for noise reduction and image recovery. It uses a weighted average of intensity values from nearby pixels to update the intensity value of each individual image pixel. Blackscholes is a financial formula to compute the fair call and put prices for options. Filterbank is from StreamIt [19] benchmark suite. The benchmark creates a filter bank to perform multi-rate signal processing. Jacobi is a two-dimensional 5-point stencil computation that solves Laplace equations using Jacobi iterations. Heat3D is a three-dimensional 7-point stencil computation that solves a heat equation. Both Jacobi and Heat3D are common computations in scientific applications. These benchmarks represent a class of applications and computations that perform well on single-accelerator systems, and thus can be expected to take advantage of accelerator clusters.

5.2   Scalability

Strong Scaling. In the strong-scaling test, the problem size is kept fixed and the number of processes is varied. We use two problem sizes for each benchmark: *class-A* and *class-B*. A class-A problem is small enough to fit the entire computation data in a single accelerator's memory. A class-B problem requires more than one accelerator to execute, since the memory requirement exceeds the capacity of a single accelerator. Table 2 shows the setting of each problem class.

Table 2. Experimental setup for strong scaling

Benchmark	class-A problem size	class-B problem size	Number of iterations
Jacobi	20000 × 20000	24000 × 24000	1000
Heat3D	768 × 768 × 768	800 × 800 × 800	1000
Blackscholes	67,000,000 options	400,000,000 options	1000
Bilateral filter	12280 × 12280	20000 × 20000	1
Filterbank	67,000,000	134,000,000	32

Figure 2 shows the results for both MIC and GPU clusters. HYDRA programs with class-A problems achieve an average of 24.54x speedup on the 64-nodes MIC cluster and 27.56x speedup on the GPU cluster. The maximum speedup is 45.18x on the MIC cluster and 43.81x on the GPU cluster. The speedup is calculated against a single accelerator execution time. We show the average speedup only on class-A problems because they can correctly execute on a single node. For class-B problems, the performance is compared against the performance of a configuration with the smallest number of accelerators that allow the program to be executed successfully. Our result shows that Jacobi, Heat3D, and Blackscholes have good scalability on both MIC and GPU clusters.

Table 3. Experimental setup for weak scaling

Benchmark	MIC problem size	GPU problem size	Number of iterations
Jacobi	8192 × 8192	8192 × 8192	100
Heat3D	512 × 512 × 512	450 × 450 × 450	100
Blackscholes	67,000,000 options	32,000,000 options	100
Bilateral filter	5500 × 5500	5500 × 5500	1
Filterbank	4,000,000	4,000,000	32

Bilateral Filter shows limited scalability on both MIC and GPU clusters. The lack of coalesced memory accesses inside the accelerator kernel leads to inefficient execution, limiting performance gained by node-level parallelism. With 64 nodes, the speedup is 5.49x on MICs and 18.24x on GPUs. More advanced compiler analysis may enable coalesced memory accesses, thus improving the scalability of the generated program. Filterbank also exhibits scalability limitation on both MIC and GPU clusters. In contrast to Bilateral Filter, the cause of the limitation is the conservative methods of the array data flow analysis. The analysis summarizes memory accesses by all paths of conditional branches inside the parallel loops, resulting in extra broadcast communications.

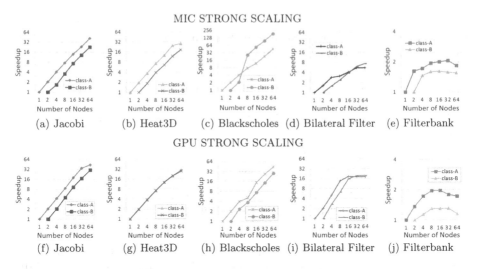

Fig. 2. Strong scaling experimental results of five benchmarks on MIC cluster(a–e) and GPU cluster (f–j). The speedup of the class-A problem is relative to a single-node performance. The speedup of class-B problem is relative to the performance of a configuration with the smallest number of accelerators that allow the program to be executed successfully.

On the MIC cluster, Blackscholes with class-B problem size shows super-linear speedup when the number of nodes increases from 4 to 8. The reason lies in the data transfers inside the iteration loop. The transfer on 4 nodes is 22.14x slower than on 8 nodes due to a MIC driver issue. This difference in data transfer time contributes to the super-linear speedup. This transfer could have been hoisted out of the iteration loop, however, automatic compiler hoisting did not take place in this case due to implementation limitations. We tried hoisting this transfer out of the loop manually, and observed that the achieved performance showed linear scaling, as in the class-A problem.

Weak Scaling. In the weak scaling test, the problem size is increased as the number of processes increases. The problem size per process is fixed. Table 3 shows the problem sizes per compute node used in the weak-scaling experiment on the GPU and MIC clusters. We performed this experiment using up to 32 accelerators. Figure 3 shows the weak-scaling results of both MIC and GPU clusters. The speedup is calculated over the execution time of a single node with one accelerator.

Jacobi, Heat3D, Bilateral Filter, and Blackscholes achieve high scalability in the weak scaling test. Filterbank performs the worst in terms of scalability due to excessive broadcast communication caused by the conservative array data flow analysis. Note that the achieved scalability is better on the MIC cluster than on the GPU one. This is because, on average, the accelerator execution time is greater on MICs than that for GPUs. Therefore, the communication overhead has a bigger impact on the scalability in the GPU cluster.

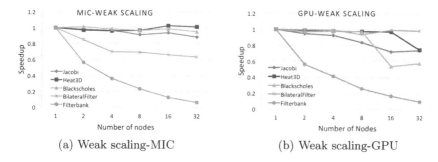

(a) Weak scaling-MIC   (b) Weak scaling-GPU

Fig. 3. Weak scaling results of five benchmarks on MIC cluster(a) and GPU cluster(b). The speedup shown is against the execution of a single-accelerator single-node setup.

5.3   Memory Allocation

In this experiment, we show only weak-scaling results on the MIC cluster. The other tests exhibited similar trends. Figure 4 shows the memory allocation requirement for each benchmark in the weak scaling experiment on the MIC cluster. Each chart shows the total amount of memory required by the entire problem and the amount of memory actually allocated on the accelerator for each benchmark. For all benchmarks, except Filterbank, the size of allocated memory on the accelerator memory is fixed as the number of nodes increases. The dotted line indicates the single accelerator memory limitation. It shows the scaling limit if the memory allocation optimization is not implemented. Without memory allocation optimization, Jacobi cannot exploit more than 8 nodes, while Heat3D, Blackscholes, and Bilateral Filter benchmarks cannot run beyond 4 nodes.

Unlike other benchmarks, the accelerator memories allocated by each process are different for Filterbank. We report the minimum memory (required by process 0) and the maximum memory (required by process N-1) in Fig. 4e. For process 0, the accelerator memory requirement remains the same for any problem size. For other processes (1 to N-1), however, the memory requirement grows with the problem size. This behavior is explained by the conservative array data flow analysis employed by HYDRA that results in over-allocation in the presence of conditional branches.

6   Related Work

Programming Models for Accelerator Clusters. Several previous efforts proposed programming models for accelerator clusters. OmpSs [2,3] considers a directive-based shared address programming model. This model requires the users to provide extra information to the compiler about computation offloading and data transfers. Programmers use data region to specify accessed regions of shared data; the underlying runtime system then manages the allocations and transfers of these regions. Several other approaches [13,16] extend a PGAS

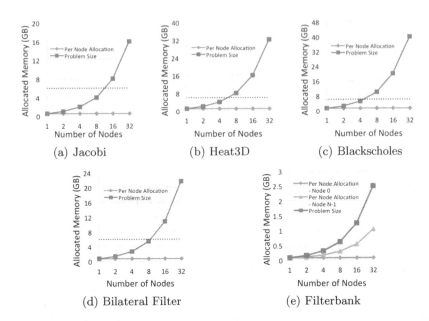

Fig. 4. Accelerator memory allocation in weak-scaling experiments on MIC cluster.

(Partitioned Global Address Space) language to support GPU clusters. PGAS languages require programmers to specify thread and data affinity explicitly. In contrast to this work, the HYDRA compiler derives the required information automatically from HYDRA programs, which are easier to write than PGAS programs. SnuCL [9] extends an OpenCL framework to run on CPU/GPU clusters. The SnuCL runtime system provides a single machine image, which allows single-node OpenCL programs to run on the cluster. In contrast to our work, SnuCL programmers still face the programming complexity of accelerator programming. Moreover, as we discussed earlier, OpenCL is not fully portable. Programmers need to customize OpenCL programs for each architecture to fully utilize CPUs and accelerators.

Memory Management and Communication. Memory management and communication are innate to any shared address programming model. Several previous efforts proposed shared address programming models for CPU clusters. There are two major approaches for memory allocation management in these contributions. The first approach is to rely on the underlying operating system or runtime system. For example, in OMPD [10], each process allocates the entire shared data in every process and lets the virtual memory system allocate the required physical memory when the data is accessed. This solution is not feasible on accelerators because of the lack of virtual address space on GPUs and the lack of swap space on MICs. Another example is Software Distributed Shared Memory (SDSM) [7]. The SDSM runtime system provides a shared address abstraction of the distributed system. The performance of this approach has remained far below that of MPI programming. Another approach relies on information provided by the programmers. In High Performance Fortran (HPF) [18], programmers explicitly provide data partitioning information through directives. In PGAS languages, such as UPC [5], Co-array Fortran [15], and Titanium [21], the programmers explicitly specify the affinity between processes and data. In contrast to these systems, HYDRA neither requires additional directives nor relies on the operating system. On the GPU side, another approach [17] proposed a hybrid compiler-runtime analysis, based upon the polyhedral model, to automate data allocation on multi-GPU machines. In contrast to this work, HYDRA uses symbolic analysis to perform compile-time memory allocation and transfer analyses targeting accelerator clusters and provides a complete translation system for multiple accelerator types. NVIDIA introduced Unified Memory Access to simplify memory management on GPUs; however, this system incurs high overhead [12].

7   Conclusion

We have introduced compile-time and runtime techniques for extending shared address programs for execution on accelerator clusters of multiple types.

The paper presented two novel, architecture-agnostic compile-time analyses, which ensure scalability of the translated program. We also presented a runtime system to support accelerator communication. To show the effectiveness of these analyses, we developed a source-to-source translation system that generated an accelerated MPI program from a simple shared address programming model called HYDRA. To support the architecture-agnostic nature of the proposed technique, a compiler design was presented. We demonstrate this design for two common accelerators: NVIDIA GPUs and Intel Xeon Phi. With the proposed techniques, we showed that the simple form of shared address programming can be extended to accelerator clusters without additional involvement of programmers.

HYDRA can achieve an average speedup of 24.54x against a single-accelerator performance when running on a 64-node cluster with Intel Xeon Phis and a 27.56x speedup when running on 64 nodes with NVIDIA GPUs. We also showed that our single-node performance is comparable to, or better than, a state-of-the-art OpenMP-to-CUDA translation system. There are additional opportunities for performance enhancements in our system for both computation and communication. Ongoing work is exploring these opportunities.

Acknowledgments. This work was supported, in part, by the National Science Foundation under grants No. 0916817-CCF and 1449258-ACI. This research used resources of the Keeneland Computing Facility at the Georgia Institute of Technology and the Extreme Sciene and Engineering Discovery Environment (XSEDE), which are supported by the National Science Foundation under awards OCI-0910735 and ACI-1053575, respectively.

References

1. Bae, H., Mustafa, D., Lee, J.W., Aurangzeb, B., Lin, H., Dave, C., Eigenmann, R., Midkiff, S.: The Cetus source-to-source compiler infrastructure: Overview and evaluation. Int. J. Parallel Program. **41**, 1–15 (2012)
2. Bueno, J., Planas, J., Duran, A., Badia, R., Martorell, X., Ayguade, E., Labarta, J.: Productive programming of GPU clusters with OmpSs. In: IEEE 26th International Parallel Distributed Processing Symposium, IPDPS 2012, pp. 557–568, May 2012
3. Bueno, J., Martorell, X., Badia, R.M., Ayguadé, E., Labarta, J.: Implementing OmpSs support for regions of data in architectures with multiple address spaces. In: Proceedings of the 27th International ACM Conference on International Conference on Supercomputing, pp. 359–368. ACM, NY, USA, New York (2013)
4. Che, S., Boyer, M., Meng, J., Tarjan, D., Sheaffer, J.W., Lee, S.H., Skadron, K.: Rodinia: A benchmark suite for heterogeneous computing. In: Proceedings of the 2009 IEEE International Symposium on Workload Characterization, IISWC 2009, pp. 44–54. IEEE Computer Society, Washington, DC (2009)
5. UPC Consortium: UPC language specifications, v1.2. Technical report LBNL-59208, Lawrence Berkeley National Lab (2005)
6. Corporation, I.: Intel® SDK for OpenCL applications XE R3. (2013). https://software.intel.com/sites/products/documentation/ioclsdk/2013XE/UG/index.htm
7. Dwarkadas, S., Cox, A.L., Zwaenepoel, W.: An integrated compile-time/run-time software distributed shared memory system. In: Proceedings of the Seventh International Conference on Architectural Support for Programming Languages and Operating Systems, ASPLOS VII, pp. 186–197. ACM, NY, USA, New York (1996)
8. Han, T.D., Abdelrahman, T.S.: hiCUDA: High-level GPGPU programming. IEEE Trans. Parallel Distrib. Syst. **22**, 78–90 (2011)
9. Kim, J., Seo, S., Lee, J., Nah, J., Jo, G., Lee, J.: SnuCL: An OpenCL framework for heterogeneous CPU/GPU clusters. In: Proceedings of the 26th ACM International Conference on Supercomputing, ICS 2012, pp. 341–352. ACM, NY, USA, New York (2012)
10. Kwon, O., Jubair, F., Eigenmann, R., Midkiff, S.: A hybrid approach of OpenMP for clusters. In: Proceedings of the 17th ACM SIGPLAN Symposium on Principles and Practice of Parallel Programming, pp. 75–84 (2012)
11. Kwon, O., Jubair, F., Min, S.-J., Bae, H., Eigenmann, R., Midkiff, S.P.: Automatic scaling of OpenMP beyond shared memory. In: Rajopadhye, S., Mills Strout, M. (eds.) LCPC 2011. LNCS, vol. 7146, pp. 1–15. Springer, Heidelberg (2013)
12. Landaverde, R., Zhang, T., Coskun, A.K., Herbordt, M.: An investigation of unified memory access performance in cuda. In: Proceedings of the IEEE High Performance Extreme Computing Conference (2014)
13. Lee, J., Tran, M.T., Odajima, T., Boku, T., Sato, M.: An extension of XcalableMP PGAS lanaguage for multi-node GPU clusters. In: Alexander, M., et al. (eds.) Euro-Par 2011, Part I. LNCS, vol. 7155, pp. 429–439. Springer, Heidelberg (2012)
14. Lee, S., Eigenmann, R.: OpenMPC: Extended OpenMP programming and tuning for GPUs. In: Proceedings of the 2010 ACM/IEEE International Conference for High Performance Computing, Networking, Storage and Analysis, pp. 1–11 (2010)
15. Numrich, R.W., Reid, J.: Co-array fortran for parallel programming. SIGPLAN Fortran Forum **17**(2), 1–31 (1998)
16. Potluri, S., Bureddy, D., Wang, H., Subramoni, H., Panda, D.: Extending Open-SHMEM for GPU computing. In: 2013 IEEE 27th International Symposium on Parallel Distributed Processing (IPDPS), pp. 1001–1012, May 2013

17. Ramashekar, T., Bondhugula, U.: Automatic data allocation and buffer management for multi-GPU machines. ACM Trans. Archit. Code Optim. **10**(4), 60: 1–60: 26 (2013)
18. Forum, High Performance Fortran: High performance fortran language specification. SIGPLAN Fortran Forum, vol. 12 (4), 1–86, December 1993
19. Thies, W., Karczmarek, M., Gordon, M.I., Maze, D.Z., Wong, J., Hoffman, H., Brown, M., Amarasinghe, S.: Streamit: A compiler for streaming applications. Technical report MIT/LCS Technical Memo LCS-TM-622, Massachusetts Institute of Technology, Cambridge, MA, December 2001
20. Vetter, J., Glassbrook, R., Dongarra, J., Schwan, K., Loftis, B., McNally, S., Meredith, J., Rogers, J., Roth, P., Spafford, K., Yalamanchili, S.: Keeneland: Bringing heterogeneous GPU computing to the computational science community. Comput. Sci. Eng. **13**(5), 90–95 (2011)
21. Yelick, K., Semenzato, L., Pike, G., Miyamoto, C., Liblit, B., Krishnamurthy, A., Hilfinger, P., Graham, S., Gay, D., Colella, P., Aiken, A.: Titanium: A high-performance Java dialect. In: ACM, pp. 10–11 (1998)

Petal Tool for Analyzing and Transforming Legacy MPI Applications

Hadia Ahmed[1]([⊠]), Anthony Skjellum[2], and Peter Pirkelbauer[1]

[1] University of Alabama at Birmingham, Birmingham, AL 35294, USA
{hadia,pirkelbauer}@uab.edu
[2] Auburn University, Auburn, AL 36830, USA
skjellum@auburn.edu

Abstract. Legacy MPI applications are an important and economically valuable category of parallel software that rely on the MPI-1, MPI-2 (and, more recently, MPI-3) standards to achieve performance and portability. Many of these applications have been developed or ported to MPI over the past two decades, with the implicit (dual) goal of achieving acceptably high performance and scalability, and a high level of portability between diverse parallel architectures. However they were often created implicitly using MPI in ways that exploited how a particular underlying MPI behaved at the time (such as those with polling progress and poor implementation of some operations). Thus, they did not necessarily take advantage of the full potential for describing latent concurrency or for loosening the coupling of the application thread from the message scheduling and transfer.

This paper presents a first transformation tool, Petal, that identifies calls to legacy MPI primitives. Petal is implemented on top of the ROSE source-to-source infrastructure and automates the analysis and transformation of existing codes to utilize non-blocking MPI and persistent MPI primitives. We use control flow and pointer alias analysis to overlap communication and computation. The transformed code is capable of supporting better application bypass, yielding better overlapping of communication, computation, and I/O. We present the design of the tool and its evaluation on available benchmarks.

1   Introduction

The Message Passing Interface (MPI) describes a library that enables the development of portable parallel software for large-scale systems. The first MPI standard [12] focused on providing a basic framework for point-to-point and collective communication. MPI-2 [8] introduced one-sided communication, added support for parallel file access, and dynamic process management, and extended the usefulness of two-group (inter-communicator) operations. MPI offers a small set of core functions that are sufficient for the development of many applications, and also offers functionality that helps experts optimize applications [10].

© Springer International Publishing Switzerland 2016
X. Shen et al. (Eds.): LCPC 2015, LNCS 9519, pp. 156–170, 2016.
DOI: 10.1007/978-3-319-29778-1_10

MPI bindings exist for C++, Fortran, and many other languages, making MPI one of the most prevalent programming models for high-performance computing. MPI is supported on many platforms, which makes applications developed with MPI portable to many large-scale systems. Building high-performance computing systems constitutes a large investment in human resources. As the communication infrastructure advances and the MPI standards and library implementations follow suite, legacy codes becomes a potential liability. Code that does not utilize more recent MPI primitives will not scale well on newer architectures. This effect will become more marked over time.

With Exascale systems on the horizon, the cost of communication is becoming a major concern. Compared to older architectures, communication incurs relatively more overhead. Legacy software written for older architectures often utilizes `MPI_Send` and `MPI_Recv` for the communication of point-to-point messages. These two primitives block until the data exchange completes (or at least till the send buffer can be reused by the calling thread). While this makes it easy for programmers to reason about communication, such methods fail to utilize computing resources efficiently. On next generation hardware, the implied cost of sending data using a polling and/or blocking mode of communication significantly rises and it is expected that software relying on blocking communication will have too much overhead. In order to take advantage of the architectural changes in Exascale, existing code needs to be transformed to use better primitives, some of which are only available in MPI-3 or higher. Non-blocking primitives allow overlap of communication with local computation[1]. A paired, non-blocking communication uses two MPI routines, one to start (`MPI_Isend`, `MPI_Irecv`) and one to complete (`MPI_wait`). After a communication has been initiated, code can compute, and only waits at the `MPI_wait` to synchronize with the communication operation. In addition to the benefits of non-blocking, applications that exhibit fixed point-to-point communication patterns can further utilize persistent operations introduced in MPI-1 and being extended in MPI-3.x. Persistent MPI primitives reduce communication overhead in applications that exhibit fixed patterns. Persistent MPI operations minimize the overhead incurred from redundant message setup.

Rewriting legacy MPI programs by hand is both tedious and error prone. To relieve programmers of the task of manually rewriting applications, the authors have developed tool support to replace uses of MPI primitives that are known to perform slowly on modern hardware (or may have better alternatives, especially on next-generation architectures) with better alternatives in the MPI standard. We have implemented a source code rejuvenation tool [16] called Petal using the ROSE source-to-source infrastructure [3,17]. We chose ROSE for its support of many languages relevant for high-performance computing. Petal analyzes existing source code and finds calls to `MPI_Send` and `MPI_Recv`. It replaces these primitives with their non-blocking counterparts and uses data-dependency

---

[1] Provided the underlying MPI does not poll excessively to make progress or for message completion, the messages are long enough, and there is sufficient memory bandwidth for both communication and computation.

and control-flow information to find code locations where corresponding calls to
MPI_Wait need to be inserted. If Petal can determine that the communication
partners, message buffer, and message length do not change, persistent communication primitives will be used in lieu of non-persistent functions.

Overall, this paper offers the following contributions:

- program analysis and transformation to replace blocking MPI calls with non-
  blocking calls;
- program analysis and transformation to introduce persistent MPI calls; and,
- analysis of persistent MPI implementations.

The remainder of this paper is organized as follows. Section 2 presents more
detailed information on MPI and ROSE. Section 3 describes our implementations
and Sect. 4 discusses our evaluation and findings. Section 5 gives an overview
of related work on MPI transformations, and Sect. 6 offers conclusions and an
outlook on possible future work.

2   Background

This section provides background information on MPI and the ROSE compiler
infrastructure.

2.1   MPI Primitives

MPI offers several modes of operation for point-to-point communication. Many
programs employ MPI_Send and MPI_Recv, two blocking MPI primitives. MPI_Send
takes the following arguments: base pointer to message data, the number of
elements to send, a type descriptor, the destination, and a communicator. The
base pointer to data typically points to a send buffer, but it could also point
to data described by a type descriptor. Blocking means that the MPI primitive
waits until the message buffer containing the data being sent/received is safe to
be used again by the calling process. Only then is control returned to the caller.
On send, actual implementations of MPI_Send may either block until all data has
been transmitted or copy the data to an intermediate internal buffer. The use of
blocking primitives may be prone to deadlocks, if programmers do not carefully
consider send and receive order [13]

MPI_Isend and MPI_Irecv are non-blocking versions for point-to-point message
communication. Compared to MPI_Send's arguments, MPI_Isend adds an additional argument for a request handle. The handle is used in calls to MPI_Wait
to identify which send to wait for. Non-blocking calls return immediately after
initiating the communication and the user thread can execute more operations,
eventually followed by a completion operation (a wait or test) on the request.
The communication is considered complete after a successful call to MPI_Wait (or
MPI_Test, etc.). Non-blocking is used to help promote overlap communication
and computation, resulting in communicating cost hiding and yielding overall

better performance on systems that support it. To avoid tampering with the data, programmers must ensure that the message data is not modified before the communication is completed.

Another mode is offered by persistent communication primitives. If a program exhibits regular communication patterns (static arguments), where the same communication partners exchange fixed size messages, utilization of persistent MPI enables exploitation of faster communication paths. Provided MPI implementations efficiently implement these operations, persistence supports reduced overhead by eliminating cost associated with repeated operations and streamlined processing of derived datatypes. Persistence also can reduce jitter and allow for preplanned choice of algorithms, such as for MPI collectives. Since persistence in MPI offers many benefits (potential and long observed), it is likely that future MPI standards will enhance support for persistent primitives, for example by supporting variable length messages between the same communication partners.

Note that all three modes can be used interchangeably. It is possible that one side uses persistent MPI, while the other side does not. That is why the functions are sometimes referred to as providing half-channels.

Figure 1 shows the use of blocking, non-blocking, and persistent operations for a simple 1D heat transfer code. The basic design of the heat-transfer code is depicted in Fig. 1d. The code uses two arrays, containing cells with temperature information. The initial temperatures are located in the even array. In odd numbered timesteps the odd array is computed from the even array and in even numbered timesteps vice versa. Red cells are computed by neighbors and dark blue cells are needed by neighbors for the next iteration. Figure 1a shows a blocking implementation. The order of sends and receives is important to avoid deadlock. Even-numbered MPI processes send first, odd numbered processes receive first. D stands for MPI_DOUBLE, and n is the rank of this node. For simplicity, the codes assume that each process has two neighbors and ignores send and receive status. Figure 1b demonstrates the overlap of communication and computation in non-blocking mode. The key idea is that the inner (light blue) cells can be computed before the data from neighbors are received. The code starts two receive operations to receive both neighbor's data from the last iteration. Then it starts two send operations to communicate its values from the previous iteration to its neighbors. While the communication is ongoing, the inner cells are computed. Before cells depending on neighbors' data can be computed, the code waits until the data have been received (Line 10). After computing the outer cells, the wait in Line 13 blocks until the data have been sent. This is necessary in order not to overwrite the data in the next iteration. Figure 1c shows the persistent version of the code. Since the communication patterns, buffer, and buffer size do not change, we can set up the communication for sends and receives at the beginning of the program, and reuse this pattern in every iteration.

```
1   double b[4]; // send/receive buffer

3   for (int i = 0; i<MAX; ++i) {
        data_to_buf(prev, b+2);
5
    if (n%2 == 0) {
7       MPI_Recv(b+0, 1, D, n−1, 0, com);
        MPI_Recv(b+1, 1, D, n+1, 0, com);
9   }
        MPI_Send(b+2, 1, D, n−1, 0, com);
11      MPI_Send(b+3, 1, D, n+1, 0, com);
        if (n%2 == 1) {
13          MPI_Recv(b+0, 1, D, n−1, 0, com);
            MPI_Recv(b+1, 1, D, n+1, 0, com);
15      }

17      buf_to_data(b, prev);
        compute_all(prev, curr);
19      swap(curr, prev);
    }
```

(a) Blocking operations

```
    MPI_request r[4]; // request handler
2   double b[4]; // send/receive buffer

4   for (int i = 0; i<MAX; ++i) {
        data_to_buf(prev, b+2);
6       MPI_Irecv(b+0, 1, D, n−1, 0, com, r+0);
        MPI_Irecv(b+1, 1, D, n+1, 0, com, r+1);
8       MPI_Isend(b+2, 1, D, n−1, 0, com, r+2);
        MPI_Isend(b+3, 1, D, n+1, 0, com, r+3);
10      compute_inner(prev, curr);
        MPI_Wait(2, req+0, IGNORE);
12      buf_to_data(b, prev);
        compute_outer(prev, curr);
14      MPI_Wait(2, req+2, IGNORE);
        swap(curr, prev);
16  }
```

(b) Non-blocking operations

```
    MPI_request r[4]; // request handler
2   double b[4]; // send/receive buffer

4   MPI_Recv_init(b+0, 1, D, n−1, 0, com, r+0);
    MPI_Recv_init(b+1, 1, D, n+1, 0, com, r+1);
6   MPI_Send_init(b+2, 1, D, n−1, 0, com, r+2);
    MPI_Send_init(b+3, 1, D, n+1, 0, com, r+3);
8   for (int i = 0; i<MAX; ++i) {
        data_to_buf(prev, b+2);
10      for (int j = 0; j < 4; ++j)
            MPI_Start(r+j);
12
        compute_inner(prev, curr);
14      MPI_Wait(2, r+0, IGNORE);
        buf_to_data(b, prev);
16      compute_outer(prev, curr);
        MPI_Wait(2, r+2, IGNORE);
18      swap(curr, prev);
    }
```

(c) Persistent operations

(d) Design Overview

Fig. 1. 1D heat transfer

2.2 The ROSE Compiler Infrastructure

The ROSE source-to-source translation infrastructure is under active development currently at the Lawrence Livermore National Laboratory (LLNL). ROSE provides front ends for many languages, including C/C++, Fortran 77/95/2003, Java, and UPC. ROSE also supports several parallel extensions, such as OpenMP and CUDA. ROSE generates an Abstract Syntax Tree (AST) for the source code. The ASTs are uniformly built for all input languages. ROSE offers many specific analyses (e.g., pointer alias analysis) and makes these available through an API. Users can write their own analyses by utilizing frameworks that ROSE provides. These include attribute evaluation traversals, call graph analysis, control flow graphs, class hierarchies, SSA representation, and dataflow analysis. The Fuse framework [4], is an object-oriented dataflow analysis framework that affords users with the ability to create their own inter- and intra-procedural dataflow analyses by implementing standard dataflow components. ROSE has been used for building custom tools for static analysis, program optimization, arbitrary program transformation, domain-specific optimizations, performance analysis, and cyber-security. With the representation of the code as an AST and using the static analysis provided from the ROSE libraries, one can explore the code and determine how to improve it by looking for certain code style, inserting new code, changing and/or removing old code, hence generating modified source code while preserving the semantics of the original code.

3   Implementation

In this section, we describe Petal's implementation of a mechanism to transform applications from using blocking MPI point-to-point routines to using non-blocking versions. We also describe the analysis and transformations to introduce persistent routines.

3.1   Design

Petal transforms code to use non-blocking MPI operations to reveal a better potential overlap of computation and communication and adds persistent operations, whenever possible, to eliminate much of the overhead of repeatedly communicating with a partner node.

Figure 2 shows an overview of our transformation framework. The tool takes MPI source files, for which ROSE compiles and generates the Abstract Syntax Tree (AST), then function calls are inlined if the function implementation should be available. Once inlined, ROSE's query and builder libraries are used to find and replace blocking with non-blocking calls and to identify where to insert corresponding calls to MPI_Wait. If some or all of these non-blocking calls are used repeatedly with the same arguments, they are replaced with persistent communication operations. At the end, Petal generates a new transformed source file as its output, using either non-blocking or persistent communications (which are always non-blocking).

The idea of following this approach is based on trying to maximize the overlap between communication and computation without compromising the semantics of the original application. Inlining eliminates the need to use inter-procedural analysis and simplifies moving MPI_Wait downward, crossing its original function boundaries if no unsafe access to the message buffer is found across the function calls. MPI uses pointers to the message buffers that they use in their communication. This fact allowed us to simplify the analysis used by the tool and focus only on using pointer alias analysis. ROSE's pointer alias analysis implements Steensgaard's algorithm, which has linear time complexity [19]. This allows our tool to scale well with large applications.

3.2   Blocking to Non-blocking Transformation

Petal allows changing the blocking function call MPI_Send/MPI_Recv to the corresponding MPI_Isend/MPI_Irecv while ensuring proper access to the message

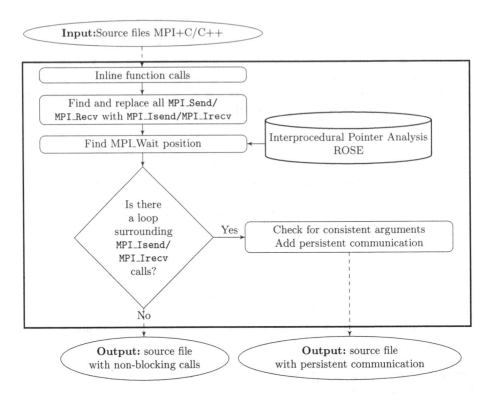

Fig. 2. Transformation framework

buffers, and once an operation that access the message buffer is encountered, MPI_Wait is inserted before it to ensure the safety of the data.

Calling MPI_Send/MPI_Recv is in effect the same as calling MPI_Isend/MPI_Irecv immediately followed by MPI_Wait. Our tool moves calls to MPI_Wait downward along forward control flow edges as long as the operations are safe with respect to the MPI operation and buffer access. Any write to a message buffer that is used in a send operation, and any access to a message buffer that is used in a receive operation is considered an unsafe access and MPI_Wait must be called before that to maintain the correctness of the code.

For each blocking call, to be replaced by the corresponding non-blocking, three variables are created, two of which are handlers for MPI_Request and MPI_Status plus a flag introduced to ensure the execution of MPI_Wait if and only if its corresponding non-blocking call is executed. Each blocking call is replaced with the corresponding MPI_Isend/MPI_Irecv. After finding and replacing blocking calls, control flow analysis is used to find subsequent statements, extract the variables used in these statements and use pointer analysis to test for aliasing between the message buffer used and the variables in hand. For the send operation, we identify potential update operations, such as a variable occurring on the left hand side of an assignment. We use pointer alias analysis to check whether an update could modify some data. For the receive operation, all expressions that read values from a variable are tested. Variable extraction includes subscripts of an array, arguments in non-inlined function calls, variables used in conditions of control statements, initial and increment statements of for loop, and operands of binary and unary operations. Our tool uses ROSE's pointer alias analysis to test whether the extracted variables and the communication buffer could alias. If there could be an alias, the tool inserts the corresponding MPI_Wait before the statement using this variable.

Because of inlining, Petal is able to bypass the end of the function and keep searching for potential usage of the message buffer outside the function containing the original MPI calls. If no alias is found in all the statements following the block call, the tool identifies where this statement is located. If it is in main(), that means that no alias is found and the MPI_Wait is inserted before the MPI_Finalize. Because of the complexity of loop-carried data dependencies, currently the tool does not support moving MPI_Wait outside the loop body. Hence, if it is in a loop statement (for, while, do-while) MPI_Wait is inserted as the last statement in the loop. Otherwise the statement following the block that has the blocking call is examined for alias analysis. To ensure that the MPI_Wait in its new position gets executed only if its corresponding non-blocking call is executed, a flag is set to true with each non-blocking call and then based on its value, the corresponding MPI_Wait is executed.

Figure 3 shows an example of a snippet of code before and after transformation. Figure 3a shows the original blocking code and Fig. 3b shows how the code looks after the transformation. Lines 3–5 shows the declaration of the MPI_Request. MPI_Status and the flag variables. Line 10 sets the flag to 1 where Line 21 tests for the flag's value before executing the MPI_Wait on Line 22. Since this is a send call, the printf function call is a safe read access and the wait call is inserted after it.

3.3   Non-persistent to Persistent Transformation

If a program exhibits regular communication patterns, where the same communication partners exchange fixed size messages, utilization of persistent MPI enables exploitation of faster communication paths[2]. In Shao et al. [18] work to identify communication patterns for MPI programs, they discovered that many programs that are considered dynamic can use persistent communication. This means that changing these programs to use persistence will result in better performance. The difficulty of persistent communications is that possible uses in real world codes are hard to determine statically. To overcome this limitation, we use dynamic analysis. Petal transforms code to persistent mode and inserts guards that test that the arguments did not change. Persistent communication is a four-step process. First, a persistent request is created. Then, data transmission is initiated. After that, wait routines must be called to ensure proper completion. Lastly, the persistent request handlers must be explicitly deallocated.

---

[2] At least on high quality implementations of MPI.

```
1   int *buffer;
    int x;
3   ... //code for main,initialization,...
5   for(int i=0;i<1000;i++)
7   {
9     if (myid == source) {
        *buffer = 123;
11      MPI_Send(buffer,count,MPI_INT,
            dest,tag,MPI_COMM_WORLD);
13      x = 0;
      }
15    else {
17      *buffer = 456;
        x = 1;
19    }
21    printf("%d\n",*buffer);
    }
```

(a) Before

```
    int *buffer;
2   int x;
    MPI_Request reqs[1];
4   MPI_Status stats[1];
    int flags[1];
6   ... //code for main,initialization,...
    for(int i=0;i<1000;i++)
8   {
      if (myid == source) {
10      flags[0]=1;
        *buffer = 123;
12      MPI_Isend(buffer,count,MPI_INT,
            dest,tag,MPI_COMM_WORLD,&reqs[0]);
14      x = 0;
      }
16    else {
        *buffer = 456;
18      x = 1;
      }
20    printf("%d\n",*buffer);
      if (flags[0] == 1)
22      MPI_Wait(&reqs[0],&stats[0]);
    }
```

(b) After

Fig. 3. Non-blocking transformation example

Changing to persistent mode is best suited for non-blocking calls in a loop. Petal does such transformations from non-blocking non-persistent to persistent automatically. A structure is created to hold initial values for non-blocking call arguments as its members. Using ROSE queries, the tool identifies MPI_Isend/ MPI_Irecv and checks to see which one is enclosed in a loop. If no call is in a loop, no transformations are performed. If one or more are found inside a loop, the tool initiates a persistent request with the same arguments as the corresponding non-blocking call and places this initiation process before the loop (MPI_Send/Recv_Init). In addition, it stores the values of the MPI_Isend/MPI_Irecv arguments in a struct variable for comparing the values across iterations. Then inside the loop, it inserts an if statement to check if the current values are the same as the persistent request argument values, if the outcome is yes, it uses this persistent request using MPI_Start(&request), otherwise it uses the normal MPI_Isend/MPI_Irecv call. After the loop, all the created persistent requests are freed.

Following the output from Figs. 3b and 4 shows the result of applying the persistence transformation. On the left side, line 6 shows the persistent request handler and line 7–16 shows the struct definition and its instance declaration. Line 20 initiates the persistent communication passing it all the non-blocking arguments and lines 23–29 represents the copying of the arguments values to the struct instance. On the right side, line 6–11 represents the test against the current values with the values stored in the persistent request. If they are the same MPI_Start on line 13 is executed, otherwise the original MPI_Isend is executed on line 16–17. Line 29 shows the deallocation of the persistent request.

```
 1   int *buffer;
     int x;
 3   MPI_Request reqs[1];
     MPI_Status stats[1];
 5   int flags[1];
     MPI_Request preqs[1];
 7   struct buf_data
     {
 9     void *buf;
       int count;
11     MPI_Datatype datatype;
       int dest;
13     int tag;
       MPI_Comm comm;
15   }
     struct buf_data temp_data[1];
17   ... //code for main,initialization,...

19   MPI_Send_init(buffer,count,MPI_INT,
21   dest,tag,MPI_COMM_WORLD,&preqs[0]);

23            temp_data[0] . buf = buffer;
            temp_data[0] . count = count;
25            temp_data[0] . datatype = MPI_INT;
            temp_data[0] . dest = dest;
27            temp_data[0] . tag = tag;
            temp_data[0] . comm =
29                  MPI_COMM_WORLD;
```

(a) Persistent

```
 1   for(int i=0;i<1000;i++)
     {
 3   if (myid == source) {
       flags[0]=1;
 5     *buffer = 123;
       if (temp_data[0] . buf == buffer
 7            && temp_data[0] . count == count
            && temp_data[0] . datatype == MPI_INT
 9            && temp_data[0] . dest == dest
            && temp_data[0] . tag == tag
11            && temp_data[0] . comm == MPI_COMM_WORLD
     {
13     MPI_Start(&preqs[0]);
     }
15     else {
       MPI_Isend(buffer,count,MPI_INT,
17     dest,tag,MPI_COMM_WORLD,&reqs[0]);
     }
19     x = 0;
     }
21     else {
       *buffer = 456;
23     x = 1;
     }
25     printf("%d\n",*buffer);
     if (flags[0] == 1)
27     MPI_Wait(&reqs[0],&stats[0]);
     }
29   MPI_Request_free(&preqs[0]);
```

(b) contd

Fig. 4. Persistent transformation example

3.4   Discussion

Even though the tool can detect any unsafe access to the message buffers correctly, the applied analysis has limitations in two cases. First, it treats any access to a part of the array as an access to the whole array. For example if MPI sends the first 10 elements of a 100-element array, an assignment to the 20th element will be considered unsafe even though it is in a different place and can be safely used. The second case is that Steensgaard algorithm treats a struct member access as an access to the whole struct [19]. These two cases might lead to placing the MPI_Wait in overly conservative positions in some applications. We plan to improve our tool to handles these cases better, since identifying these cases could result into achieving better communication-computation overlap.

Currently, Petal cannot combine multiple consecutive calls to MPI_Wait, if found together, into a single MPI_Waitall call. This is because different calls to MPI_Isend/MPI_Irecv may originate in alternative blocks. For example, two calls are part of the then and else branch of an if statement. We hope to find a better solution instead of using flags and if-statement, to ensure the semantics of the code and being able to take advantage of using MPI_Waitall.

4   Evaluation

In this section, we present the preliminary evaluation of using Petal and the effect of its transformations on overall application performance. The experiments were performed on the TACC Stampede system. Stampede is a 10 Petaflop (PF) Dell Linux Cluster with 6400+ Dell PowerEdge server nodes each with 32 GB memory, 2 Intel Xeon E5 (8-core Sandy Bridge) processors and an additional Intel Xeon Phi Coprocessor (61-core Knights Corner) (MIC Architecture) [20]. We used the mvapich2 MPI library. Petal was tested with the 1D heat decomposition described earlier, 2D heat [7] and DT from the NAS NPB 3.3 benchmark [1].

We tested the performance of the application while varying the number of MPI processes. For 1D heat, we varied the number of MPI processes in each case ranging from 6 to 200 tasks. For 2D heat and DT with classes W and A, the number of MPI processors varied between 16 and 256. Figure 5 shows the execution time speedup ($S = T_{\text{original}}/T_{\text{transformed}}$) after applying non-blocking transformation, and adding persistent communication. Figure 5a shows the effect when running applications with only 16 MPI processes, while Fig. 5b shows the effect on applications with 200 and more processes. As shown in the figures, we experienced good improvement with larger number of processes while flat to minor slowdown was observed with fewer numbers of processes. However, in both cases we experienced minor slowdown when adding persistence[3].

4.1 Discussion of Results

Petal was able successfully to transform applications from blocking to non-blocking while pushing MPI_Wait as far as possible, while also preserving the correctness of the code output. The results shows that with smaller programs and few tasks, the non-blocking improvement is negligible and sometimes hurts

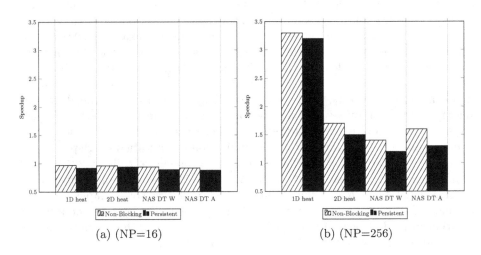

Fig. 5. Execution time speedup

---

[3] This indicates that mvapich may not optimize the code path for persistent send and/or receive.

the application performance. However, with increasing problem size and number of MPI tasks, non-blocking enhanced the performance by up to 30 %.

Unfortunately, even though Petal was able to transform code to persistent mode, the results of persistent performance showed a flat improvement and sometimes a slowdown.

To gain more insight into the usage of persistent communications, we applied the persistent transformation on the LULESH code from LLNL [11] on Stampede and on a Debian 7.6 amd64 computer with 1 Xeon E5410 @ 2.33 GHz using the Open MPI 1.6.5 library. LULESH already exploits non-blocking operations. Since it has some communications that are fixed for most of the program's execution time, persistent communication should be beneficial. However, upon transforming to persistent no gain was seen and with increasing number of tasks we saw a minor slowdown. Since Open MPI is open source, we investigated how it implements its non-blocking and persistent communications. We found that they optimize the code by creating persistent requests and using them whenever possible. Hence, changing the applications' code to persistent will not give a speedup as Open MPI already uses similar optimization techniques internally. The slowdown might be because of the overhead of checking the arguments on each iteration.

According to the MPI Forum [2], persistent requests are considered to be half-channels, which makes the connection faster by reducing the overhead of communication processing within each of the sender and receiver. Our results suggest that the performance improvement is dependent not only on the standard definition of how code should work but it also depends on the actual MPI implementation and architecture. While the tested systems did not show any performance improvements, the transformation may be beneficial on other systems.

5 Related Work

The idea of overlapping communication and computation code is of interest to many researchers because of the promising results in better performance it can give when applied efficiently. In this section, we describe previous research work done to produce overlapped communication and computation in MPI.

Several methods were studied and implemented to handle the communication computation overlap approach. Das et al. [6] represents the closest work to our tool in which they developed an algorithm for pushing wait downward in a segment of code. However, they use Static Single Assignment (SSA) use-def analysis to determine the statements that access the message buffer. Even though they describe a method for moving a MPI_Wait out of its current scope interval possibility of going to the parent, they did not implement their method and currently their compiler tool only detects MPI calls and finds MPI_Wait's final position; however, insertion is done by hand. Haque et al. [9] developed a similar tool for transforming blocking to non-blocking; however, it does not use any compiler analysis techniques and relies heavily on the programmer annotation to identify where to move the corresponding non-blocking call and its corresponding wait.

Another work is presented by Nguyen et al. in [14] in which they developed Bamboo, a transformation system that transforms MPI C code into a data-driven application that overlaps computation and communication. It was implemented with the ROSE compiler framework and runtime support using the Tarragon runtime library. Their approach is to determine task precedence. It relies on programmer annotations to mark parallel loops and data packing/unpacking plus calls to communication routines. Other approaches were developed using different techniques to achieve the same goal of maximizing communication and computation overlap. Danalis et al. developed the ASPhALT tool [5] within Open64. Their idea is based on automatically detecting where data is available and applying the pre-pushing transformation to send data as soon as possible. They focused on specific a type of applications that does its communication in two parts where at first, it computes the data in a loop with minimum dependencies across iterations, and then uses communication call(s) after the loop to exchange the data generated by the loop. Pellegrini et al. [15] offer a different approach in which they use the polyhedral model to determine exact dependencies and automatically detect potential overlap on a finer grain. To simplify the analysis, they normalize the code by changing non-blocking to blocking. Their work is limited by polyhedral model requirements of using only affine expressions.

Even though MPI included persistent communication since MPI-1 and these calls emphasize the benefits of using persistent, to our knowledge, no available work offers a tool that automatically transforms non-persistent to persistent communication, when such patterns can be identified.

6   Conclusions and Future Work

In this paper, we described our development of Petal, a tool that supports transforming a blocking MPI code to non-blocking version and introduces persistent communication if possible. We have described the approach used in order to push MPI_Wait as far as possible from the corresponding communication call in order to improve the potential for overlap of communication and computation code and also to use persistent communication whenever two points communicate the same type and amount of data over multiple iterations. Petal is based on the ROSE framework and uses ROSE's alias analysis to apply transformation required and to preserve correctness of the code. Preliminary results showed that we can improve performance by using non-blocking. In some cases we found that persistent communication does not improve performance even with code that is proved to have fixed communication for most of the execution time. It does not only depend on having fixed arguments but the MPI library used has an effect too. Further detailed analyses of persistent performance on different architectures with different libraries will be explored.

In addition to analyzing data dependency within loop iterations and moving MPI_Wait outside the loop body, if no dependency found, techniques to eliminate loop-carried dependencies on send and receive buffers and perhaps unrolling the loops will also be explored. This will provide another opportunity to move MPI_Wait(s) outside loops boundaries. Another future step is to work on cases where we have 3-D data models and to explore how they can be safely overlapped in communication.

We are also extending the Petal tool to do other automatic translation and/or refactoring that will allow a smooth transition for legacy MPI systems to Exascale systems, such as the use of one-sided communications and changing further to use non-blocking and persistent collective operations (being proposed at present in MPI-3.x).

Acknowledgements. This work used the Extreme Science and Engineering Discovery Environment (XSEDE), which is supported by National Science Foundation grant number ACI-1053575.

References

1. The NAS parallel benchmarks. https://www.nas.nasa.gov/publications/npb.html
2. Persistent MPI communication. http://www.mpi-forum.org/docs/mpi-1.1/mpi-11-html/node51.html. Accessed on 28 June 2015
3. The ROSE source-to-source compiler. http://rosecompiler.org
4. Aananthakrishnan, S., Bronevetsky, G., Gopalakrishnan, G.: Hybrid approach for data-flow analysis of mpi programs. In: Proceedings of the 27th International ACM Conference on International Conference on Supercomputing, ICS 2013, pp. 455–456. ACM, New York (2013)
5. Danalis, A., Pollock, L., Swany, M.: Automatic MPI application transformation with asphalt. In: Parallel and Distributed Processing Symposium, IPDpPS 2007, pp. 1–8, IEEE International, March 2007
6. Das, D., Gupta, M., Ravindran, R., Shivani, W., Sivakeshava, P., Uppal, R.: Compiler-controlled extraction of computation-communication overlap in MPI applications. In: IEEE International Symposium on Parallel and Distributed Processing, IPDpPS 2008, pp. 1–8, April 2008
7. Frexus: mpi-2d-plate (2013). http://project.github.com. Accessed on 1 September 2015
8. Gropp, W., Lusk, E., Thakur, R.: Using MPI-2: Advanced Features of the Message-Passing Interface. MIT Press, Cambridge (1999)
9. Haque, M., Yi, Q., Dinan, J., Balaji, P.: Enhancing performance portability of MPI applications through annotation-based transformations. In: 2013 42nd International Conference on Parallel Processing (ICPP), pp. 631–640, October 2013
10. Hoefler, T.: New and old features in MPI-3.0: The past, the standard, and the future, April 2012
11. Karlin, I., Keasler, J., Neely, R.: Lulesh 2.0 updates and changes. Technical report LLNL-TR-641973, August 2013
12. Forum, Message Passing Interface: MPI: A message-passing interface standard. Technical report, Knoxville (1994)
13. Message Passing Interface Forum: MPI: A message-passing interface standard version 3.1, June 2015

14. Nguyen, T., Cicotti, P., Bylaska, E., Quinlan, D., Baden, S.B.: Bamboo: translating MPI applications to a latency-tolerant, data-driven form. In: Proceedings of the International Conference on High Performance Computing, Networking, Storage and Analysis, SC 2012, pp. 39:1–39:11. IEEE Computer Society Press, Los Alamitos (2012)
15. Pellegrini, S., Hoefler, T., Fahringer, T.: Exact dependence analysis for increased communication overlap. In: Träff, J.L., Benkner, S., Dongarra, J.J. (eds.) EuroMPI 2012. LNCS, vol. 7490, pp. 89–99. Springer, Heidelberg (2012)
16. Pirkelbauer, P., Dechev, D., Stroustrup, B.: Source code rejuvenation is not refactoring. In: van Leeuwen, J., Muscholl, A., Peleg, D., Pokorný, J., Rumpe, B. (eds.) SOFSEM 2010. LNCS, vol. 5901, pp. 639–650. Springer, Heidelberg (2010)
17. Schordan, M., Quinlan, D.: A source-to-source architecture for user-defined optimizations. In: Böszörményi, L., Schojer, P. (eds.) JMLC 2003. LNCS, vol. 2789, pp. 214–223. Springer, Heidelberg (2003)
18. Shao, S., Jones, A., Melhem, R.: A compiler-based communication analysis approach for multiprocessor systems. In: 20th International Parallel and Distributed Processing Symposium, IPDpPS 2006, p. 10, April 2006
19. Steensgaard, B.: Points-to analysis in almost linear time. In: Proceedings of the 23rd ACM SIGPLAN-SIGACT Symposium on Principles of Programming Languages, POPL 1996, pp. 32–41. ACM, New York (1996)
20. Towns, J., Cockerill, T., Dahan, M., Foster, I., Gaither, K., Grimshaw, A., Hazlewood, V., Lathrop, S., Lifka, D., Peterson, G., Roskies, R., Scott, J., Wilkins-Diehr, N.: XSEDE: accelerating scientific discovery. Comput. Sci. Eng. **16**(5), 62–74 (2014)

Communication and Locality

Automatic and Efficient Data Host-Device Communication for Many-Core Coprocessors

Bin Ren[1], Nishkam Ravi[2,3], Yi Yang[3(✉)], Min Feng[3],
Gagan Agrawal[4], and Srimat Chakradhar[3]

[1] Pacific Northwest National Laboratories, Richland, USA
bin.ren@pnnl.gov
[2] Cloudera, Palo Alto, USA
nravi@cloudera.com
[3] NEC Laboratories America, Princeton, USA
{nravi,yyang,mfeng,chak}@nec-labs.com
[4] Department of Computer Science and Engineering,
The Ohio State University, Columbus, USA
agrawal@cse.ohio-state.edu

Abstract. Orchestrating data transfers between CPU and a coprocessor manually is cumbersome, particularly for multi-dimensional arrays and other data structures with multi-level pointers common in scientific computations. This paper describes a system that includes both compile-time and runtime solutions for this problem, with the overarching goal of improving programmer productivity while maintaining performance.

We find that the standard linearization method performs poorly for non-uniform dimensions on the coprocessor due to redundant data transfers and suppression of important compiler optimizations such as vectorization. The key contribution of this paper is a novel approach for heap linearization that avoids modifying memory accesses to enable vectorization, referred to as *partial linearization* with *pointer reset*.

We implement *partial linearization* with *pointer reset* as the compile time solution, whereas runtime solution is implemented as an enhancement to MYO library. We evaluate our approach with respect to multiple C benchmarks. Experimental results demonstrate that our best compile-time solution can perform 2.5x-5x faster than original runtime solution, and the CPU-MIC code with it can achieve 1.5x-2.5x speedup over the 16-thread CPU version.

1   Introduction

Many-core coprocessors can provide orders of magnitude better performance and efficiency for parallel workloads as compared to multi-core CPUs, and are being widely adopted as accelerators for high performance computing. The x86-compatible Intel Xeon Phi (MIC) coprocessor is a relatively recent member in the many-core coprocessor family. It is designed to leverage existing x86 experience and leverages popular parallelization tools, libraries, and programming models, including OpenMP [7], MPI [12], CilkPlus [3] and TBB [28]. Even with the

X. Shen et al. (Eds.): LCPC 2015, LNCS 9519, pp. 173–190, 2016.
DOI: 10.1007/978-3-319-29778-1_11

support of these programming models, there are many challenging technical issues that need to be solved to allow accelerators to become mainstream.

Accelerating parallel computing using many-core coprocessors requires specification of code regions (and corresponding data variables) that can be profitably offloaded to the coprocessor. Orchestrating data transfers between CPU and coprocessor gets challenging as the complexity of the data structures increases.

With the goal of improving developer productivity and maximizing application performance, we focus on compile time and runtime solutions for automating data transfers. While static arrays can be automatically handled by ICC compiler[1] today, and solutions proposed in the literature [13,16,20,24,27] handle dynamically allocated one-dimensional arrays, *handling of dynamically allocated multi-dimensional arrays and other structures with multi-level pointers is an open problem.*

It turns out that the problem is quite complex, particularly because the choice of the mechanism used for automatically inserting data transfer clauses impacts memory layouts and access functions (subscripts) on the coprocessor. Because of the nature of the accelerators, the performance can be impacted in multiple ways. Overall, in order for a solution to perform well:

- Redundant data transfers between the CPU and the accelerator should be eliminated or minimized due to the significant data transfer time and the limited device memory,
- Data transfer time should be reduced by utilizing Direct Memory Accesses (DMA) since it can be as significant as kernel runtime,
- Memory allocation overheads on the accelerator (or even the host) should be kept low since memory allocation is expensive on the accelerator, and
- Memory layout and access should allow for aggressive memory-related compiler optimizations (e.g., vectorization and prefetching) from the native compiler, as they are critical for obtaining performance from accelerators.

We observe that the prior solutions [15,20,27] do not consider these factors together, as they focus primarily on data transfer reduction. In particular, the effect of memory layout [6,34] on DMA, cache, and compiler optimizations have been largely overlooked.

This paper describes an automated framework that uses both compile-time and runtime solutions to address this problem. This system includes a simple but effective compile-time solution, where we linearize the heap without having to modify the memory accesses (subscripts), by using a *pointer reset* approach. The idea is to identify and parse all the malloc statements for a given multi-dimensional array and generate code for obtaining the total memory size (say s) for that multi-dimensional array. The malloc statements for the given array are then replaced by a single malloc statement that allocates a memory chunk of size s. Code is generated to correctly reset all the pointers of the array into this large chunk of memory. This allows the memory accesses to stay unmodified.

---

[1] Intel C++ Compiler. http://www.intel.com/Compilers.

This method scores well on all the four metrics mentioned above and maintains code readability.

For the cases where our compile-time approach cannot apply, we also explore runtime solutions. We investigate and optimize the performance of the runtime memory management approach, by providing certain improvements to the existing coherence protocol. The best compile-time solution consistently outperforms the optimized runtime scheme, but is not as generally applicable. In order to combine performance with generality, we describe a mechanism for integrating the two disjoint approaches using a simple source-to-source transformation. The idea is to simultaneously and selectively insert implicit and explicit data transfer clauses in the application at compile time.[2]

We have implemented our compile-time solution as a transformation using the Apricot framework [27], and evaluated it within the context of application execution on Xeon Phi coprocessor. We use a test suite comprising benchmarks from different sources, which involve dynamically allocated multi-level pointers. We show that our proposed compile-time solution can perform 2.5x-5x faster than original runtime solution, and the CPU-MIC code with our compile-time solution can achieve 1.5x-2.5x speedup comparing to the 16-thread CPU version.

Table 1. Key directives in common directive-based languages for accelerator programming

	Offload	Synchronization	Data transfer
LEO	`#pragma offload`	`<signal,wait>`	`<in,out,inout>`
OpenAcc	`#pragma acc kernels`	`<async,wait>`	`<copy,copyin,copyout>`
OpenHMPP	`#pragma hmpp codelet`	`<asynchronous,synchronize>`	`args[item].io=<in,out,inout>`
OmpSs	`#pragma omp task`	`<input,output,taskwait>`	`<copy_in,copy_out>`
OpenMPC	`#pragma cuda gpurun`	OpenMP `<nowait>`	`<c2gmemtr,g2cmemtr>`

2   Motivation and Problem Definition

Table 1 summarizes popular directive-based languages, which allow the developer to mark code regions in the application from which offloadable tasks can be generated by the compiler. These APIs are intended to improve developer productivity and simplify code maintenance, by hiding the details of data transfers and allocation on the accelerators. In this paper we work with LEO (Language Extension for Offload), which supports the *coprocessor offload interface* (COI), and is the primary annotation language for Xeon Phi. LEO provides `#pragma offload` directive for marking offloadable code regions. This is similar to OpenAcc's `#pragma acc kernels`[3]. Execution on the CPU is suspended when

---

[2] Due to the page limitation, we omit some details of the runtime optimization and the source-to-source transformation to integrate two approaches, and all of our code examples in this version. Please refer to our LCPC'15 conference version for more details: http://www.csc2.ncsu.edu/workshops/lcpc2015/lcpc15proc.pdf.

[3] OpenACC: Directives for Accelerators. http://www.openacc-standard.org/.

#pragma offload is encountered, continued on the coprocessor and then resumed on the CPU after the offloaded code region has executed to completion. Special synchronization primitives (e.g., `signal/wait`) can be used for enabling asynchronous offload.

2.1 Challenges in CPU-to-coprocessor Data Transfers

In order to orchestrate data transfers between CPU and coprocessor, the developer has to specify in/out/inout clauses along with `size` for each data variable. In the case of a single-dimensional array, only one contiguous memory region needs to be transferred. For multi-dimensional arrays, on the other hand, numerous array components scattered over memory have to be handled. This can be complex, cumbersome and non-performant. Note that this complexity arises because of the way C versions of most existing scientific applications allocate memory– an N dimensional array is allocated by allocating one-dimensional arrays inside an $N-1$ dimensional loop. In benchmarks such as Multi-Grid (MG) arrays are non-rectangular, which adds to the complexity.

Recall that in the previous section, we had stated four requirements while addressing the problem, which included needs for fully utilizing DMA, and reducing memory allocation overheads. To motivate their impact, we present certain experimental observations. Consider a dynamic two-dimensional array case. Each of the memory regions is allocated and transferred independently, using a separate offload statement (in a `for` loop). Automating this is not hard, once the malloc statements, memory accesses and offload code regions have been tracked. This is similar to what CGCM [15] does, which is the state-of-the-art compiler-based communication management system for GPUs. However, this approach leads to high memory allocation overheads as well as DMA suppression (since multiple small memory regions are transferred separately). Figure 1(a) compares the performance of this approach with one where data is linearized and transferred by a single offload statement, for a matrix addition micro-benchmark. Figure 1(b) shows the impact of number of offload statements on data transfer time. The results are shown for various array sizes. For a fixed array size, using

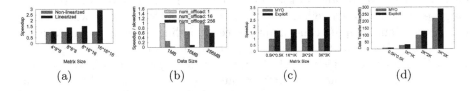

(a)   (b)   (c)   (d)

Fig. 1. (a) Performance of matrix addition with Non-linearized vs. Linearized data transfers, (b) Relationship between number of offload statements (for different array components) and data transfer time. (For a fixed data size, using fewer offload statements is beneficial, due to better DMA utilization and smaller memory allocation and offload overhead.) (c) Performance comparison between MYO and explicit data transfers using linearization for dgemm, (d) Total data transfer size for both. (MYO transfers less data but performs worse.)

fewer offload statements results in better DMA utilization and lower offload and memory allocation overhead.

In addition to the explicit data specification model, LEO also supports an implicit data transfer model and corresponding runtime mechanism (called MYO [30]) to automate data transfers between CPU and coprocessor. Any data element marked with the _Cilk_shared clause is automatically synced between the two processors. In the implicit model, offloadable code regions are marked with _Cilk_offload. MYO resembles state-of-the-art memory management solutions for GPU (Dymand [14] and AMM [26]), which all implement runtime data coherence mechanisms and create the illusion of virtual shared memory between the CPU and coprocessor.

We evaluate MYO with respect to a number of benchmarks and find that explicit data transfer specification using in/out clauses outperforms MYO by up to 3x (Fig. 1(c) and (d) show an example for matrix multiplication). To understand the performance difference, we investigate bottlenecks of the runtime memory management scheme and find that the mechanism that keeps track of dirty pages for minimizing redundant data transfers ends up imposing huge overheads. After disabling tracking of dirty pages, we are able to significantly improve performance of the runtime management scheme.

3 Background: Complete Linearization

Array linearization is commonly used to minimize the number of pointer indirections (and load instructions) for static arrays. For example, a two-dimensional array $A[i][j]$ would be accessed as $A[i * N + j]$ instead of $(A[i])[j]$, where N is the stride for i. The memory layout is not changed, only the memory accesses are linearized. This approach can be extended to facilitate efficient transfer of dynamically allocated multi-dimensional arrays between CPU and coprocessor, by linearizing the memory layout in addition to the memory accesses for dynamically. We refer to this approach as *complete linearization*. Next, we will describe this approach and point out its limitations.

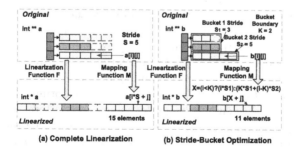

(a) Complete Linearization   (b) Stride-Bucket Optimization

Fig. 2. Different linearization schemes for handling data transfers for dynamically allocated multi-dimensional arrays

In *complete linearization*, all malloc statements for a given multi-dimensional array are replaced by a single malloc statement in the application source code. Instead of allocating multiple small chunks of memory for different array components, a single contiguous chunk of memory is allocated. Accordingly, the memory accesses are linearized as well. In essence, the complete linearization transforms a dynamically allocated multi-dimensional array into a one-dimensional array, as shown in Fig. 2(a).

Algorithm. To formally state the underlying compile-time transformation: let D_m be the data layout for a multi-dimensional array in the original code, let A_m be a memory access, let D_s be the data layout for the array in the transformed code and let A_s be a memory access, our goal is to implement two functions: (i) $F : D_m \rightarrow D_s$ and (ii) $M : A_m \rightarrow A_s$.

Let sz_0, sz_1,..,sz_k be the size of the elements in a given dimension. The malloc statement corresponding to element i in the original source code would be $malloc(sz_i * sizeof(datatype))$. For a dimension with equal-sized elements the stride value would be $s = sz_0 = sz_1,.., = sz_k$. For a dimension with variable-size elements (as in Fig. 2(a)), the stride value would be chosen as $s = max(sz_0, .., sz_k)$. For dimension d_i let the stride be s_i and the number of elements of the first dimension be m. For an n-dimensional array, the total memory size would be $total = m * s_1 * s_2.. * s_{n-1}$ and the corresponding malloc statement in the transformed source code would be $malloc(total * sizeof(datatype))$. Let A be an n-dimensional array. Memory access $A[m_1][m_2]..[m_n]$ in the original source code is transformed into $A[m_1 * s_1 * s_2..s_{n-1} + m_2 * s_2 * s_3..s_{n-1}.. + m_n]$.

Pros and Cons. As compared to allocating each row and column of the multi-dimensional structure separately, there are four distinct benefits of this approach: (i) since multiple malloc statements are replaced by a single statement, memory allocation overhead is reduced on both the CPU and coprocessor side, (ii) the overall data locality is improved because of contiguity, (iii) DMA utilization is maximized, since one large chunk of memory is transferred instead of multiple small chunks, and (iv) only one offload statement is required for data transfer.

This method has three main drawbacks. First, all memory accesses have to be identified, analyzed and modified using function M. Strong alias analysis is required. The mapping can potentially be complex and thus a source of bugs in the generated code, not to mention the loss of readability.

Second, since the subscripts are made complex, important compiler optimizations get suppressed in many cases. Optimizations like auto-vectorization and prefetching are sensitive to compiler's ability to recognize the memory access pattern. As we show later, losing important compiler optimizations (especially vectorization) can lead to significant performance loss on Intel MIC.

Third, for multi-dimensional arrays that have variable sized rows or columns, there is a trade-off between the linearized data size and the complexity of functions F and M. If we use uniform (maximum) length for each row or column, functions F and M are simplified, but redundant data transfers are introduced, as shown in Fig. 2(a). If variable stride values are used for each row/column, no redundant data transfers take place, but the complexity of F and M increases substantially. The stride values need to be stored in a table, transferred to the coprocessor and looked up during memory access. For example, instead of mapping $A[i][j]$ to $A[i * s_1 + j]$, it has to be mapped to $A[i * stride\_lookup(i) + j]$. This results in increased data transfer overheads and suppression of compiler optimizations. The use of uniform (maximum) stride typically performs better than a stride-lookup approach.

3.1 Stride-Bucket Optimization

To address the multi-dimensional arrays that have variable sized rows or columns, we design an optimization to reduce the amount of redundant data transfers, without significantly increasing the complexity of functions F and M. This optimization strives for a balance between the complexity of linearization and the amount of data transfer. The basic idea is to partition the multi-dimensional array into a finite number of *buckets* along the *first* dimension. Across these buckets, different stride values are used, whereas within each bucket, only one stride value is used. The current design uses *two* buckets, as described next.

Let sz_0, $sz_1, ..., sz_l$ be the size of elements in the first dimension. It is partitioned into two buckets P_1 and P_2, containing $m + 1$ and $l - m$ elements respectively. For P_1, the stride value $s_{P1} = max(sz_0, sz_1, .., sz_m)$. Similarly for P_2, the stride value $s_{P2} = max(sz_{m+1}, sz_{m+2}, .., sz_l)$. The element m serves as the bucket boundary. The size of the final array would be $size = s_{P1} * (m + 1) + s_{P2} * (l - m)$. Element m is picked as the bucket boundary, such that $size$ is minimized for m. For a given array, we first search for an optimal partitioning by trying different bucket boundaries. Interestingly, with the help of two assistant arrays recording the max stride values starting from the beginning and the end to the current position, our algorithm for picking the optimal partitioning runs in $O(l)$ time. Once the optimal partitioning is obtained, we calculate the total size of the final array and insert the new malloc statement. We then parse the code to replace each array access with the mapping function M. Finally, we generate code for data transfer and code offload.

Figure 2(b) shows an example for a two-dimensional array– the bucket boundary is 2, the two stride values are 3 and 5 respectively. As compared to the memory layout in Fig. 2(a), the new memory layout in Fig. 2(b) is around two-thirds of the size. The mapping function M now contains a branch operation–the stride is determined based on which of the two buckets the element belongs to. If the bucket boundary is k, the stride for the first bucket is s_1 and the stride for the second bucket is s_2, element $A[i][j]$ would be accessed as $A[index + j]$, where $index = (i < k)?(i * s_1) : (k * s_1 + (i - k) * s_2)$.

4   Compile-Time Automation of Data Transfers

In this section, we propose a novel linearization technique to handle the limitations of *complete linearization* (with and without *Stride-bucket* optimization). This is the main contribution of the paper.

4.1   Partial Linearization with Pointer Reset

Basic Idea. Complete linearization method suffers from three main drawbacks, as mentioned earlier. The first and second drawbacks arise from modification of memory accesses (i.e., function M). The third drawback arises from the use of uniform strides during memory allocation (i.e., function F), which allows simplification of M but imposes data transfer overheads, since holes are included in the memory layout.

We note that all three drawbacks can be eliminated if: (i) memory accesses do not have to be modified, and (ii) a single contiguous chunk of memory can be allocated for the entire multi-dimensional array without any holes in it. Our partial linearization approach achieves these two goals, using the following simple observations. First, only the last dimension of a multi-dimensional array contains the actual data, all the other dimensions only contain pointer addresses to get to this data. Now, if the data in the last dimension is linearized (i.e. we address the goal (ii)), the memory allocation and setting up of pointers can be done separately on both the CPU and the coprocessor. More specifically, the pointer structure of the multi-dimensional array can be reconstructed on the coprocessor side by simply *replicating the CPU-side code*. The pointer sizes do not have to be transferred. There is no mapping function M in this approach, since memory accesses are not modified (and we accomplish the goal (i)).

Algorithm. The details of partial linearization are given in Algorithm 1. The linearization procedure comprises three main steps. In the first step (i.e., function F_{data}), malloc statements for a given multi-dimensional array A are parsed and code is generated for computing the total data size ($total\_sz$) of the array by adding up the size of each element in the last dimension. A malloc statement is generated to allocate a memory chunk $data_A$ of $total\_sz$.

In the second step (i.e., function $F_{pointer}$), malloc statements for the last dimension are replaced by assignment statements, in order to set up the pointers into the contiguous chunk of memory allocated in the first step. For example, for each malloc of an integer array A, the statement $A[i] = (int*)malloc(size_i * sizeof(int))$ is replaced by $A[i] = pda$, $pda = pda + size_i$, where $size_i$ is the size of the ith element and pda is a moving pointer. Pointer pda is initialized to the starting address of the allocated memory chunk (i.e., $data_A$) and incremented with every pointer assignment.

In the third step, offload statements and data transfer clauses are generated for transferring the memory chunk $data_A$ to the coprocessor and back. The code for pointer allocation and construction (i.e., $F_{pointer}$) is replicated on the coprocessor side. Therefore, no stride information needs to be transferred.

As another note, placement of memory allocation statements and data transfer clauses in the code is important for performance. In our implementation, we hoist malloc statements, offload statements and data transfer clauses as far up the call graph as possible. By hoisting statements outside loops and up the call graph, redundant execution is minimized and memory reuse (across multiple offloads) is enabled.

Algorithm 1. PartialLinearizationPointerReset(Mul_dim_var_set D)

1: **for** each multi-dim var $A \in D$ **do**
2:     **if** A used by an offload region **and** satisfies legality checks **then**
3:         D_{sub}.append(A)
4:     **end if**
5: **end for**
6: **for** each multi-dim var $A \in D_{sub}$ **do**
7:     /***Linearization Function $F_{\mathbf{data}}()$***/
8:     ▷ Parse malloc stmts of A
9:     /*---*Calculate total data size*---*/
10:    ▷ Replicate the malloc stmts for last dimension
11:    $total\_sz = 0$
12:    **for** each replicated malloc stmt:
           $A[m_1]..[m_n] = $ malloc($size_i*$sizeof($type$)) **do**
13:        ▷ Replace it by: $total\_sz \mathrel{+}= size_i$
14:    **end for**
15:    ▷ Insert linear-alloc: $data_A = $ malloc($total\_sz$ * sizeof($type$))
16:    /***Pointer-Reset Function $F_{\mathbf{pointer}}()$***/
17:    /*---*Allocate and reset pointers*---*/
18:    $pda = data_A$
19:    **for** each original malloc-site for last dimension:
           $A[m_1]..[m_n] = $ malloc($size_i*$sizeof($type$)) **do**
20:        ▷ Replace it by:
              $A[m_1][m_2]..[m_n] = pda$, $pda \mathrel{+}= size_i$
21:    **end for**
22:    /*---*Generate offload code for coprocessor*---*/
23:    ▷ Generate $data_A$ malloc clause on coprocessor
24:    ▷ Replicate $F_{pointer}()$ code on coprocessor
25:    **for** each offload region R **do**
26:        **if** A is used by R **then**
27:            ▷ Generate data transfer and offload clauses for coprocessor
28:        **end if**
29:    **end for**
30:    ▷ Apply data reuse and hoisting opt for $data_A$
31: **end for**

Legality Checks: Because partial linearization modifies the values of pointers, a compiler should perform the code transformation in a very conservative way to ensure the correctness. In our case, our compiler applies partial linearization with pointer reset only if certain conditions are met. We summarize these conditions as follows. The first condition is that all elements in the multi-dimensional array must be of the same size. For example, if the code is in $C + +$, we may have the *polymorphism* issue. An existing data flow analysis reported in the literature [29] is used for this purpose. The second condition is that a pointer must have only one malloc statement associated. The goal is to ensure that there is no memory reallocation or conditional memory allocation, which may make our transformation unsafe (if at all applicable), and we prefer not to apply them in our implementation. For performing this check, malloc statements and memory accesses are tracked using *use-def* chains for arrays/pointers that are used in offloadable code regions, as identified by liveness analysis module within Apricot [27]. We collect all malloc sites for a specific multi-dimensional array, and check whether any pointer is represented multiple times. The third condition is that the value of a pointer must be unchanged during the computation. If the value of a pointer is changed, we may either miss copying data or read data from a wrong place on the accelerator.

These legality conditions are checked by our source-to-source compiler for each array. If an array fails to satisfy one or more conditions, it is annotated as such and handled by the runtime memory management system, as described in Sect. 5. For most scientific computing benchmarks, these legality conditions hold and our proposed approach can be applied.

4.2   Interaction with Compiler Optimizations

Our source-to-source translator (or another comparable system) depends upon the native compiler (ICC in the case of Xeon Phi) for accelerator for obtaining performance. Our experiments have shown that the various optimizations performed by the native compiler have a far more significant impact on the overall performance than the overheads of data transfer and other operations associated with the offload. As we mentioned, one of the critical considerations in automating handling of data transfers is preserving optimizations that would normally be performed by the compiler.

In Intel MIC (Xeon Phi), the SIMD width of each core is 512-bit, which means up to 16 floating point operations can be executed in one cycle on each of its 60 cores. This makes vectorization crucial for performance. Also, with increasing parallelism, memory accesses can become the bottleneck, and therefore, software prefetching is very important. Loop optimizations such as distribution, tiling, and interchange can also significantly impact performance, especially when they enable additional vectorization or prefetching. A key advantage of partial linearization is that original subscripts are not modified, whereas, complete linearization introduces more complex subscripts. While theoretically a compiler should be able to handle complex linearized subscripts, in practice, product compilers often fall short, due to aliasing, pointer arithmetic and complex interactions between the different optimizations [22]. We have verified this for the latest version of ICC as of writing this paper.

We evaluated on an example that involves a structure and a non-unit stride. From the optimization reports, we see that for the version with non-linearized subscripts, data dependencies are correctly resolved and the innermost loop is vectorized. While for the linearized version, auto-vectorization is not enabled by the compiler, which is likely because the compiler cannot conclude that there are no dependencies. In another example involving a three-dimensional arrays addition inside an OpenMP loop (not shown due to space constraints), we observed that software prefetching is not facilitated by the compiler. For the corresponding version with non-linearized subscripts, 4 cache lines are prefetched for the outer-most loop and 24 lines are prefetched for the inner-most loop. We continue this discussion in Sect. 5.

5   Evaluation

In this section, we evaluate our compile-time and runtime solutions in detail, and compare our CPU-MIC solution with multi-core CPU solution.

5.1   Implementation

We have implemented the compile-time solution for automatic insertion of data transfer clauses using *partial linearization with pointer reset* approach described in Sect. 4.1. It has been implemented as a source-to-source transformation on top of the Apricot [27] framework. Apricot provides modules for liveness analysis, handling of one-dimensional arrays and identification of offloadable code regions. We have also modified the coherence mechanism in MYO[4]. The solution architecture is shown in Fig. 3.

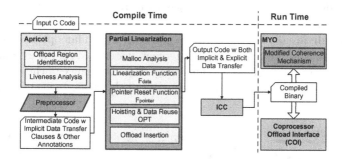

Fig. 3. Overall solution architecture

5.2   Experimental Methodology

The test suite consists of seven C benchmarks from different sources (shown in Table 2). These benchmarks contain dynamically allocated multi-dimensional arrays/multi-level pointers and OpenMP parallel regions. We particularly note that the first three benchmarks, MG, FT, and 330.art, are all more than 1,500 lines each (330.art is more than 2000), and are used to demonstrate the applicability of our approach (and the current implementation) on full-scale applications. All experiments were conducted on a Xeon E5-2609 server equipped with an Intel MIC (Xeon Phi) card and the necessary software. Xeon E5-2609 has 8 cores, each running at 2.40 GHz with 2 threads per core. Xeon Phi has 61 cores each running at 1.05 GHz with four threads per core, a total of 32 MB L2 cache and 8 GB GDDR5 memory. Our source-to-source compiler is invoked on each benchmark and the transformed source code is compiled with ICC at -O3 with additional compiler flags (-openmp -parallel [-ansi-alias] [-fno-alias]).

---

[4] As described in http://www.csc2.ncsu.edu/workshops/lcpc2015/lcpc15proc.pdf.

Table 2. Benchmarks

Benchmark	Source	Description
MG	NAS Parallel in C	Multi-Grid on meshes
FT	NAS Parallel in C	3D fast Fourier Transform
330.art	SPEC OMP	Image recognition by neural network
Heat3D	Heat 3D	Heat transfer simulation
27stencil	EPCC	3-d stencil kernel
convolution	CAPS OpenACC	2-d stencil kernel
dgemm	LINPACK	Double general matrix multiplication

There are several objectives in our evaluation. We evaluate the overall performance of our partial linearization with pointer reset solution, and compare it with the runtime method through MYO, as well as the complete linearization (optimized with stride-bucket, where applicable). Besides comparing the execution times, the amount of data transferred over PCIe is also measured and reported. To demonstrate the benefits of using the accelerator after applying our solution, we also evaluate the performance of our best multi-core CPU+MIC version over the multi-core CPU version.

We also individually evaluate the benefits of particular optimizations. Performance of the runtime memory management system (MYO) is evaluated with and without our optimization, and similarly, the performance of the complete linearization approach is evaluated with and without the stride-bucket optimization.

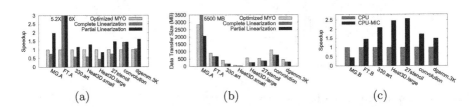

Fig. 4. Performance comparisons for all benchmarks: optimized MYO, complete linearization with stride-bucket, and partial linearization compared with respect to (a) Execution time and (b) Total data transfer sizes; (c) Execution time comparison between multi-core CPU, and multi-core CPU+MIC for large input data sizes. The CPU-MIC versions are obtained with our partial linearization

5.3   Results and Analysis

Overall Performance Evaluation. The overall performance comparison is shown as Fig. 4. Figure 4(a) compares the performance of complete linearization (further optimizes using the stride-bucket method) with our partial linearization approach. 1.6x-2.6x speedup is obtained with the partial linearization approach for five out of the seven benchmarks, whereas nearly 1.25x speedup is observed

Table 3. Impact of the two linearization approaches on key compiler optimizations

Benchmark	Vectorization		Prefetching		LoopDist	
	Comple Linear	Partial Linear	Comple Linear	Partial Linear	Comple Linear	Partial Linear
MG	10	10	131	542	0	3
FT	15	16	70	74	0	3
330.art	1	12	50	98	2	0
Heat3D	2	3	32	72	0	0
27stencil	2	3	40	48	0	12
convolution	1	1	10	10	0	0
dgemm	1	1	14	17	0	0

for the other two. While the approach benefits all benchmarks, the reasons for performance gains differ considerably. We now explain these, referring also to data transfer volumes (Fig. 4(b)), and details of compiler optimizations enabled for different versions (Table 3).

For MG, majority of the speedup comes from reduction in the total amount of data transferred as shown in Fig. 4(b), since it is a data-intensive benchmark with variable-size rows. We also notice more aggressive prefetching for the partial linearization version: total number of cache lines prefetched goes up from 131 to 542 (Table 3). For Heat3D and 27stencil, the main loop gets vectorized for the partial linearization version, resulting in a 2x speedup. Number of prefetched cache lines goes up from 32 to 72 for Heat3D. We also notice a significant increase in loop distribution for 27stencil: with the pointer reset version 12 loops are distributed as opposed to none for complete linearization. Both these benchmarks contain three-dimensional arrays. For 330.art a total of 12 loops are vectorized with partial linearization, as opposed to 1 for complete linearization. Prefetched cache lines go up from 50 to 98. This benchmark contains a two-dimensional struct array. For dgemm the outer loop gets vectorized for the pointer reset version, while the inner loop is vectorized for the complete linearization version. With outer loop vectorization the performance goes up by 1.5x.

Figure 4(a) also compares the performance of optimized MYO with both complete linearization (using stride-bucket) and pointer reset approach. Optimized MYO frequently outperforms complete linearization. However, partial linearization with pointer reset comes out on top. It performs 1.5x-2.5x faster than optimized MYO for most benchmarks and around 6x faster for FT.A.

Next, data transfer volumes are shown in Fig. 4(b). Except for MG, pointer reset and complete linearization have identical data transfers. Optimized MYO transfers around 1.5x more data on average for most benchmarks.

Finally, Fig. 4(c) shows the performance of the best CPU-MIC version for each benchmark (obtained with the partial linearization approach) and compares it with the original CPU version. The original CPU version uses 16 threads, while the CPU-MIC version uses 16 threads on the CPU and around 240 threads on Intel MIC. The CPU-MIC version runs 1.5x-2.5x faster for six out of the seven benchmarks. No gains are obtained for MG, which is a highly data intensive benchmark. Considering the benefits of using partial linearization that we reported earlier, it can be seen that most performance gains from the use of the coprocessor will not be possible without optimizing data transfers.

Optimizations Evaluation. In our overall evaluation above, we use the optimized version of runtime MYO solution and complete linearization (with stride-bucket) solution. We evaluate these optimizations as following to validate their efficacy.

Optimized MYO: Fig. 5(a) compares the performance of MYO with optimized MYO. Figure 5(b) shows the total amount of data transferred for the two MYO versions. With the modified MYO, the amount of data transfer increases by 1.5x on average (most of it comes from the increase in communication from coprocessor to CPU). This is because dirty pages are not tracked in the modified coherence mechanism. Despite an increase in data transfer, significant performance gains (1.5x-3.2x) are observed with modified MYO. There is a noticeable drop in the execution time of coprocessor side code with the modified coherence mechanism. Also, we notice a very small increase in the time spent on data transfers, which can be attributed to DMA.

Complete Linearization: Fig. 5(c) compares the performance of the complete linearization approach with the optimized one using stride-bucket, for varying input data sizes (class=W,A,B). MG is the only benchmark in our test-suite containing arrays with variable-size elements in the first dimension. Optimized linearization approach yields more than 1.5x speedup for classes A and B. There is no difference in the array data size between classes A and B, hence similar speedup is observed. Xeon Phi coprocessor runs out of memory for class C and above when using complete linearization. Data transfers are shown in Fig. 5(d). Stride-bucket linearization results in around 1.8x reduction in data size.

6   Related Work

In the last few years, numerous compilation systems have been built for accelerators. OpenMPC [20] compiler automatically converts OpenMP code to GPU kernels and in the process inserts data transfer clauses. Baskaran *et al.* [1] achieve the same in a system where the primary focus is on using a polyhedral framework for memory management. The PGI [13] compiler also automatically inserts data transfer clauses for OpenAcc applications. JCUDA [33] based on Java can automatically transfer GPU function arguments between CPU and GPU memories, however, it requires annotations indicating the live-in/out information for arguments. More recently, Sidelnik *et al.* [32] handle data movement problem within

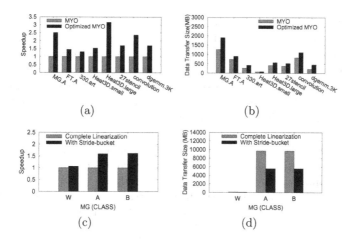

Fig. 5. Optimized MYO vs. MYO: (a) Execution time, (b) Total data transfer size; performance of complete linearization with and without stride-bucket optimization for varying input data sizes: (c) Execution time, (d) Total data transfer size

the scope of supporting Chapel, a high level parallel programming language, on GPUs, and provide both implicit and explicit data transfer mechanisms. Because these, as well as other comparable systems, generate the accelerator (CUDA) code also, interaction of the offload mechanism with optimizations inside the native compiler are not a concern for these systems.

Apricot [27] automatically inserts LEO offload and data transfer clauses in OpenMP applications for the Intel MIC coprocessor, using liveness analysis to determine data variables that need to be copied into and out of the coprocessor. It does not handle pointer arithmetic, aliasing or pointer indirection for dynamically allocated data. Similarly, statically allocated arrays can be automatically handled by ICC for Intel MIC without additional support. The challenge we have addressed here is to handle dynamically allocated multi-dimensional arrays and other structures with multi-level pointers.

Our work is closest to CGCM [15], which is a state-of-the-art compiler-based data management and optimization system for GPUs. CGCM incorporates a runtime library that tracks memory allocation at runtime and replicates allocation units on the GPU. It supports two key optimizations– *map promotion* and *alloca promotion*, to hoist runtime library calls and local variables up the call graph. However, CGCM does not linearize the heap. As a result, all the memory regions allocated for a multi-dimensional array or multi-level pointer are allocated and transferred separately. This would suffer from high memory allocation overheads and DMA suppression, as confirmed by our experiments for Intel MIC. More recently, Margiolas and O'Boyle [23] propose a portable and transparent data communication optimization, which involves analyzing the memory allocations for the data used in both CPU and GPU. Optimized memory allocation policies are then used for such memory segments. Their work focuses on optimization of OpenCL code which already has (possibly non-optimal) data transfer code, while our work focuses on generating the data transfer code automatically.

Moreover, some recent efforts with programming models like OmpSs [4] and libWater [11] handle data transfers on heterogeneous clusters by using optimized runtime methods. Dubach *et al.* [8] also adapt an optimized runtime method to handle data transfer, while they compile *Lime*, a high level language targeting heterogeneous systems. In addition, DyMand [14], AMM [26], and ADSM/G-MAC [10] are all runtime systems for automatic memory management for GPUs. Each of them implements runtime coherence mechanisms for supporting a virtual shared memory abstraction for the CPU and the GPU. They bear strong resemblance to MYO [30] and inherit the properties of software DSMs [2,21] and, to an extent, the PGAS [5,9,25,31] languages. AMM uses compiler analysis to optimize placement of coherence checks, but tracks read and write operations in order to monitor coherence status of Rails, similar to MYO's Arenas. We have implemented our optimizations on top of MYO, and a novel component of our effort is integrated static and runtime optimizations.

Our work applies the ideas in data layout optimizations [6,17–19,34] to automation of data transfers between CPU and coprocessor. By modifying the malloc sites and allocating one large chunk of memory instead of numerous small chunks for the array components distributed over memory space, we minimize memory allocation overheads (for both CPU and coprocessor), maximize DMA utilization for fast and asynchronous data transfer over PCIe and improve cache performance for both CPU and coprocessor. By retaining original memory accesses in the code, we allow ICC to be able to apply optimizations for multi-dimensional arrays.

7   Conclusions

This paper addresses the problem of automating and optimizing data transfers for coprocessors, with emphasis on dynamically allocated multi-dimensional arrays and other data structures with multi-level pointers. Our work includes a novel compiler-based approach, *partial linearization* with *pointer-reset*. The benefits of this approach include reduced data transfer volumes, use of DMA, reduced overheads of memory allocations, and most importantly, no modification to the memory access subscripts, which turns out to be crucial for preserving key compiler optimizations. This approach outperforms complete linearization by 1.6x-2.5x on average. We also devise a *stride-bucket* approach for optimizing the performance of the linearization method.

Acknowledgements. We would like to thank Ravindra Ganapathi from Intel for guiding us through the MYO library.

References

1. Baskaran, M.M., Bondhugula, U., Krishnamoorthy, S., Ramanujam, J., Rountev, A., Sadayappan, P.: Automatic data movement and computation mapping for multi-level parallel architectures with explicitly managed memories. In: PPoPP (2008)
2. Bennett, J.K., Carter, J.B., Zwaenepoel, W.: Munin: distributed shared memory based on type-specific memory coherence. In: PPoPP (1990)
3. Blumofe, R.D., Joerg, C.F., Kuszmaul, B.C., Leiserson, C.E., Randall, K.H., Zhou, Y.: Cilk: an efficient multithreaded runtime system. In: PPoPP (1995)
4. Bueno, J., Martorell, X., Badia, R.M., Ayguadé, E., Labarta, J.: Implementing OmpSs support for regions of data in architectures with multiple address spaces. In: ICS, pp. 359–368. ACM (2013)
5. Chamberlain, B., Callahan, D., Zima, H.: Parallel programmability and the chapel language. Int. J. High Perf. Comput. Appl. **21**, 291–312 (2007)
6. Chatterjee, S., Jain, V.V., Lebeck, A.R., Mundhra, S., Thottethodi, M.: Nonlinear array layouts for hierarchical memory systems. In: ICS (1999)
7. Dagum, L., Menon, R.: OpenMP: an industry standard API for shared-memory programming. IEEE Comput. Sci. Eng. **5**, 46–55 (1998)
8. Dubach, C., Cheng, P., Rabbah, R., Bacon, D.F., Fink, S.J.: Compiling a high-level language for GPUs: (via language support for architectures and compilers). In: PLDI. ACM (2012)
9. El-Ghazawi, T., Smith, L.: UPC: unified parallel C. In: SC. ACM (2006)
10. Gelado, I., Stone, J.E., Cabezas, J., Patel, S., Navarro, N., Hwu, W.-M.W.: An asymmetric distributed shared memory model for heterogeneous parallel systems. In: ASPLOS (2010)
11. Grasso, I., Pellegrini, S., Cosenza, B., Fahringer, T.: libWater: heterogeneous distributed computing made easy. In: ICS, pp. 161–172. ACM (2013)
12. Gropp, W.D., Lusk, E.L., Skjellum, A.: Using MPI: Portable Parallel Programming with the Message-Passing Interface. The MIT Press, Cambridge (1999)
13. T.P. Group. PGI Accelerator Compilers OpenACC Getting Started Guide (2013)
14. Jablin, T.B., Jablin, J.A., Prabhu, P., Liu, F., August, D.I.: Dynamically managed data for CPU-GPU architectures. In: CGO (2012)
15. Jablin, T.B., Prabhu, P., Jablin, J.A., Johnson, N.P., Beard, S.R., August, D.I.: Automatic CPU-GPU communication management and optimization. In: PLDI (2011)
16. Jeffers, J., Reinders, J.: Intel Xeon Phi Coprocessor High Performance Programming. Newnes (2013)
17. Ju, Y.-L., Dietz, H.G.: Reduction of cache coherence overhead by compiler data layout and loop transformation. In: LCPC (1992)
18. Ladelsky, R.: Matrix flattening and transposing in GCC. In: GCC Summit Proceedings, vol. 2007 (2006)
19. Lattner, C., Adve, V.S.: Automatic pool allocation: improving performance by controlling data structure layout in the heap. In: PLDI. ACM (2005)
20. Lee, S., Eigenmann, R.: OpenMPC: extended OpenMP programming and tuning for GPUs. In: SC (2010)
21. Li, K., Hudak, P.: Memory coherence in shared virtual memory systems. ACM Trans. Comput. Syst. **7**(4), 321–359 (1989)
22. Maleki, S., Gao, Y., Garzaran, M.J., Wong, T., Padua, D.A.: An evaluation of vectorizing compilers. In: PACT. IEEE (2011)

23. Margiolas, C., O'Boyle, M.F.: Portable and transparent host-device communication optimization for GPGPU environments. In: CGO. ACM (2014)
24. Newburn, C.J., Deodhar, R., Dmitriev, S., Murty, R., Narayanaswamy, R., Wiegert, J., Chinchilla, F., McGuire, R.: Offload Compiler Runtime for the Intel® Xeon PhiTM Coprocessor. In: Supercomputing. Springer (2013)
25. Numrich, R.W., Reid, J.: Co-array fortran for parallel programming. In: ACM Sigplan Fortran Forum. ACM (1998)
26. Pai, S., Govindarajan, R., Thazhuthaveetil, M.J.: Fast and efficient automatic memory management for GPUs using compiler-assisted runtime coherence scheme. In: PACT (2012)
27. Ravi, N., Yang, Y., Bao, T., Chakradhar, S.: Apricot: an optimizing compiler and productivity tool for x86-Compatible many-core coprocessors. In: ICS (2012)
28. Reinders, J.: Intel Threading Building Blocks: Outfitting C++ for Multi-Core Processor Parallelism. O'Reilly Media Inc., Sebastopol (2010)
29. Ren, B., Agrawal, G.: Compiling dynamic data structures in python to enable the use of multi-core and many-core libraries. In: PACT. IEEE (2011)
30. Saha, B., Zhou, X., Chen, H., Gao, Y., Yan, S., Rajagopalan, M., Fang, J., Zhang, P., Ronen, R., Mendelson, A.: Programming model for a heterogeneous x86 platform. In: PLDI (2009)
31. Saraswat, V.A., Sarkar, V., von Praun, C.: X10: concurrent programming for modern architectures. In: PPoPP (2007)
32. Sidelnik, A., Maleki, S., Chamberlain, B.L., Garzarán, M.J., Padua, D.: Performance portability with the chapel language. In: IPDPS. IEEE (2012)
33. Yan, Y., Grossman, M., Sarkar, V.: JCUDA: a programmer-friendly interface for accelerating java programs with CUDA. In: Sips, H., Epema, D., Lin, H.-X. (eds.) Euro-Par 2009. LNCS, vol. 5704, pp. 887–899. Springer, Heidelberg (2009)
34. Zhang, Y., Ding, W., Liu, J., Kandemir, M.: Optimizing data layouts for parallel computation on multicores. In: PACT (2011)

Topology-Aware Parallelism for NUMA Copying Collectors

Khaled Alnowaiser$^{(\boxtimes)}$ and Jeremy Singer

University of Glasgow, Glasgow, UK
k.alnowaiser.1@research.gla.ac.uk, jeremy.singer@glasgow.ac.uk

Abstract. NUMA-aware parallel algorithms in runtime systems attempt to improve locality by allocating memory from local NUMA nodes. Researchers have suggested that the garbage collector should profile memory access patterns or use object locality heuristics to determine the target NUMA node before moving an object. However, these solutions are costly when applied to every live object in the reference graph. Our earlier research suggests that connected objects represented by the *rooted sub-graphs* provide abundant locality and they are appropriate for NUMA architecture.

In this paper, we utilize the intrinsic locality of rooted sub-graphs to improve parallel copying collector performance. Our new topology-aware parallel copying collector preserves rooted sub-graph integrity by moving the connected objects as a unit to the target NUMA node. In addition, it distributes and assigns the copying tasks to appropriate (i.e. NUMA node local) GC threads. For load balancing, our solution enforces locality on the work-stealing mechanism by stealing from local NUMA nodes only. We evaluated our approach on SPECjbb2013, DaCapo 9.12 and Neo4j. Results show an improvement in GC performance by up to 2.5x speedup and 37 % better application performance.

Keywords: NUMA · Multi-core · Work-stealing · Runtime support · Garbage collection

1 Introduction

Managed runtime systems—such as the Java Virtual Machine (JVM) and Common Language Runtime (CLR)—successfully abstract low-level platform-specific details such as hardware configuration and memory management. However development efforts for these runtime systems may struggle to cope with rapid evolution and diversity in hardware deployments. Contemporary multicore processors are often designed with a distributed memory architecture to improve memory bandwidth. This architectural layout means that individual processor cores may incur non-uniform memory access (NUMA) latency. Therefore, multi-threaded applications running on several cores may access remote memory. A garbage collected runtime may cause non-determinism in data placement, which will lead

© Springer International Publishing Switzerland 2016
X. Shen et al. (Eds.): LCPC 2015, LNCS 9519, pp. 191–205, 2016.
DOI: 10.1007/978-3-319-29778-1_12

to unpredictable, suboptimal application performance, if the runtime system is not adapted to be aware of the underlying NUMA hardware.

A large body of research attempts to tackle data placement on NUMA architectures by means of improving locality and balancing allocation across memory nodes, e.g. [6]. A data placement policy that allocates data close to the core most frequently accessing it should minimize access time. However, locality-aware data placement policies could conflict with NUMA, perhaps through imbalance of access causing memory bus traffic saturation to some NUMA nodes. Other problems with NUMA imbalance include cache capacity issues, whereas using off-node caches may provide abundant memory space, e.g. [17].

In OpenJDK Hotspot (like many Java runtime systems) the generational Garbage Collector (GC) moves objects between spaces in the heap. For NUMA platforms, the existing memory placement and movement policies of the GC require re-engineering. Initially, the mutator threads use thread-local allocation buffers (TLABs) to allocate new objects in the young generation. Hotspot devolves memory mapping to the operating system. For example, Linux uses the *first-touch* policy as the default NUMA placement policy, which means that memory pages are mapped to the NUMA node associated with the core that first accesses a memory address in that page. As an advanced HotSpot configuration option, the user can choose a pre-defined JVM NUMA allocation policy (`-XX:+UseNUMA`) to map TLAB memory pages to local nodes.

Furthermore, GC threads also require local buffers, called promotion local allocation buffers (PLABs). A PLAB is used to move objects to the survivor spaces (in the young generation) and to the old generation. Mapping PLABs to NUMA regions remains the responsibility of the OS. Thus, the GC has the potential to *change* an object's NUMA node location after moving that object, which means subsequent mutator operations may incur remote access overhead. There is a need for topology awareness in the GC, which must take into account the NUMA architecture.

This paper extends our earlier work [1] which provided empirical observations of strong object locality in portions of the reference graph reachable from a single root reference. We refer to these graph components as *rooted sub-graphs*. In this paper, we modify the copying collector of the Hotspot JVM and implement a topology-aware parallel copying collector to preserve sub-graph locality and integrity. Our solution does not require any programmer intervention. We evaluated our algorithm with various benchmarks and the results show that leveraging rooted sub-graph locality improves substantially the GC performance (**up to 2.5x speedup**) and consequently improves application performance by **up to 37 %**.

In this paper, we describe the following key contributions to the HotSpot GC:

(a) We improve access locality by making the collector threads process *mostly* local objects.
(b) We improve work-stealing locality such that idle threads fetch work from local threads' queues.

2   Motivation

The existing ParallelScavenge copying GC in the Hotspot JVM uses conventional techniques for:

1. task generation: scanning memory areas that contain root references, e.g. mutator stacks, static areas, JNI handlers. At least one GC thread is used to scan each memory area. These task-generating threads enqueue root references locally, in a per-thread queue. *Our implementation distinguishes between root references and non-root references by storing them in different queues; the default scheme does not do this.*
2. distribution: each GC thread processes its own local queue of references—following references and processing (e.g. copying objects). *Our implementation directs references to appropriate queues, based on the underlying NUMA topology.*
3. load balancing: when a GC thread's local reference queue is empty, it randomly steals a single reference from the back of another thread's queue. This is a typical work-stealing approach. *Our implementation steals from nearer thread queues in terms of the NUMA topology, whereas the default scheme steals from an arbitrary queue in a NUMA-agnostic fashion.*

The key objective is to keep the GC threads busy collecting the heap regardless of the complex NUMA architecture. However, if a GC thread processes distant objects, it incurs remote memory access overhead. Further, the GC may relocate objects to a different NUMA node (e.g. during a copy-promotion); hence degrading mutator thread locality. Our topology aware GC scheme aims to alleviate both these problems.

Existing NUMA locality improvements for GC copying algorithms have a per-object granularity of work. Tikir and Hollingsworth [29] calculate the target NUMA node for an object copy by profiling thread access patterns to each object. Ogasawara [22] identifies the *dominant thread* of an object, which is likely to access the object most frequently. This analysis is based on references from thread stacks or the object's header.

Conversely, Alnowaiser [1] identifies *rooted sub-graphs* which contain a root reference and its descendant references in the reference graph. Rooted sub-graphs are shown to exhibit abundant locality, i.e. the majority of objects in a sub-graph are located in the same NUMA node as the root of that sub-graph. Selection of the *rooted sub-graph* as the work granularity for GC is appropriate for NUMA systems for two reasons:

1. When a GC thread processes a task, i.e. a rooted sub-graph, it is likely to be processing objects in a single NUMA region—ideally local for that GC thread.
2. If parallel GC threads operate in different NUMA regions on thread-local data, there is a reduction in cross-node memory traffic, reducing bus contention.

3   Topology-Aware Copying Collector

Our proposed topology-aware parallel copying collector leverages the locality that exists in rooted sub-graphs. Since we set the work granularity to be a rooted sub-graph, the main principle in our approach is to preserve the sub-graph integrity by processing its connected objects in a single NUMA node. As a result, a GC thread would move the entire rooted sub-graph to a single new location. For further locality gains, GC threads should process *local-node* root objects. We achieve this by organizing root objects according to NUMA nodes.

Moreover, when GC threads exhaust their local work queues, they should prefer to steal references from non-empty local queues of *sibling* cores, i.e. cores that are in the same NUMA node. This mechanism enables low access latency for work-stealing threads, and benefits from accessing shared resources (e.g. caches). Moreover, stolen objects will be moved to the same NUMA node as non-stolen objects in the same rooted sub-graph. Therefore the locality remains consistent.

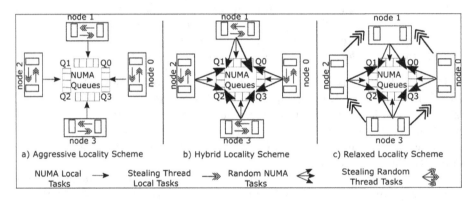

Fig. 1. Various topology-aware GC schemes. (a) aggressive scheme only processes local-node tasks (b) hybrid scheme distributes tasks across all nodes but steals from local node only. (c) relaxed scheme processes random tasks from any node

3.1   Data Structures

Figure 1 illustrates the data structures used in our scheme. At VM initialization, we create as many double-ended queues as there are NUMA nodes, to store root references for processing. Since GC threads run concurrently, we need to ensure that enqueue and dequeue operations are thread safe. For this purpose, we use the OpenJDK **Arora** queue which supports single producer/multiple consumers. GC threads pop root references from one end safely using atomic operations; however, the other end is guarded such that a thread must lock the queue before doing any enqueue operation.

To reduce lock contention on Arora queues, we buffer root references in thread-local queues. When a GC thread completes its root scanning task, it enqueues discovered root references into the corresponding Arora queue. The memory footprint of this design is small since the root set size is small compared to the live object set.

Threads that complete root scanning tasks obtain root references from Arora queues. In order to shorten the time between root scanning and enqueue operations, when a thread-local queue reaches a threshold length, the GC thread enqueues all references in that thread-local queue to the corresponding Arora queue. We set the threshold to 100 references.

3.2   Algorithm

Copying collection starts with a set of predefined tasks that are created in a sequential block of code. The VM thread, which runs the sequential code, populates a shared queue with three different kinds of tasks to handle the parallel copying collection:

1. *root scanning* tasks to discover roots in various JVM data areas.
2. *stealing* tasks to balance the load among threads
3. a *finalizer* task to terminate the parallel phase.

These tasks are present in the default ParallelScavenge GC, however we have modified their behavior to implement topology-awareness as follows. Root scanning threads classify roots according to NUMA nodes and insert the references into the appropriate local queue. Once a local queue reaches a threshold, the thread locks the corresponding Arora queue and enqueues all discovered references. Stealing threads compete on dequeuing a reference from non-empty queues. When references in Arora queues are consumed, threads attempt to acquire work from pending queues of NUMA-local threads. The thread that acquires the final task performs the parallel phase termination.

Listing 1.1. Topology-aware copying algorithm pseudo code

```
Task = acquire_gc_task()
switch (Task)
case scan_roots:
    for(all_root_areas){
        root = discover_roots()
        node = retrieve_root_node(root)
        enqueue_local_queue(root, node)
        if(queue(node)_size()>threshold)
            for(i =0; i<threshold; i++)
                enqueue_Arora_queue(root, node)
    }
case steal_work:
    node = get_thread_node()
    while(Arora_queue(node) != empty){
        ref = dequeue(node)
        follow(ref)
    }
    while(NUMA_local_queue(node) != empty){
        ref = dequeue()
        follow(ref)
    }
case final_task:
    wait_until_all_threads_terminate()
    hand_control_to_VM_thread()
    end
```

3.3   Optimization Schemes

We implement topology awareness for task distribution and work-stealing. However, retrieving an object's NUMA-specific location requires an expensive NUMA system calls. Therefore, we also explore various optimization schemes that preserve rooted sub-graph integrity but may not support locality for task distribution or work-stealing. Since we are optimizing two parallel techniques, we will have three optimization schemes, as illustrated in Fig. 1:

Aggressive: GC threads look up an object's NUMA node at task generation phase, and only steal references from NUMA-local threads as described in Sects. 3.1 and 3.2.

Hybrid: GC threads process roots randomly however they steal from sibling (NUMA-local) queues only.

Relaxed: GC threads process roots randomly and steal work from any queue.

4   Experimental Setup

4.1   System Configuration

We evaluated our work on an AMD Opteron 6366 system. The NUMA topology consists of eight nodes on four sockets, with 64 cores in total. NUMA nodes are connected by Hyper-Transport links with transmission speed up to 6 GB/s. Each node incorporates 64 GB RAM, i.e. 512 GB in total. The 64 cores are clocked at 1.8 GHz, and the machine runs Linux 3.11.4 64-bit. We set the OS memory policy to *interleaved*, which maps the memory pages to each memory node in a round-robin order. We use OpenJDK 8 for all our experiments. The 'original' JVM results use changeset 6698:77f55b2e43ae (jdk8u40-b06). All our modifications are based on this changeset.

4.2   Benchmarks

We use a variety of memory-intensive workloads to test our topology-aware copying collector:

Neo4j/LiveJournal: Neo4j is an embedded, disk-based, fully transactional Java persistence engine that stores data structures in graphs instead of tables [20]. The graph nodes and relationships are represented in the JVM heap. We use the LiveJournal social network data set, which consists of around 5 million nodes and 68 million edges [16]. We have a Java app that embeds Neo4j 2.2.1 as a library and queries the database to find all possible paths between two randomly selected nodes. The program uses 64 threads to drive the workload and uses a minimum of 150 GB heap size. The all-paths operation is repeated twice and the total execution time is reported.

DaCapo 9.12: We run applications from the DaCapo 9.12 benchmark suite [3] that are compatible with JDK8, namely: avrora, pmd, xalan, sunflow, h2, lusearch, and jython. The heap size for each program is set close to minimum and the input size is large.

SPECjbb2013: SPECjbb2013 [27] is a server business application that models a world-wide supermarket company. In our experiments, SPECjbb2013 executes the full workload with a heap size of 3 GB.

4.3   Evaluation Metrics

We use three different metrics to evaluate our GC implementation.

NUMA Locality Trace: Since our approach relies on rooted sub-graphs, we want to summarize quantitatively the NUMA locality of rooted sub-graphs. Our metric represents the locality richness in each sub-graph. To calculate the percentage of NUMA-local objects in a rooted sub-graph, we retrieve the NUMA node of the root and also the NUMA node of each descending object in the rooted sub-graph. For all rooted sub-graphs, the locality is recorded in an n-by-n square matrix, where n represents the number of NUMA nodes. Matrix element a_{ij} records the proportion of objects residing in node j that belong to a rooted sub-graph with root in node i.

We use the *Matrix Trace* property from Linear Algebra to calculate the NUMA locality of a program. The trace of an n-by-n square matrix A is defined by the sum of the elements on the leading diagonal, i.e.

$$tr(A) = a_{11} + a_{22} + ... + a_{nn} = \sum_{i=1}^{n} a_{ii} \qquad 0 \leq tr(A) \leq n \times 100 \qquad (1)$$

In our system with eight nodes, $tr(A) = 800$ represents perfect NUMA locality, whereas $tr(A) = 0$ means that no objects are allocated in the same node as the root. However, due to the memory allocation policy and program behavior, some NUMA nodes might not be used at all. Thus we define the relative NUMA Locality Trace metric such that:

$$loc(A) = \frac{tr(A)}{n \times 100}, \qquad 0 \leq loc(A) \leq 1 \qquad (2)$$

where n is the number of nodes that contain roots.

E.g. a program p uses six nodes for object allocation and $tr(p) = 450$, thus, $loc(p) = 0.75$ and we interpret the result as 75 % of objects are allocated in the same node as the root.

Application Pause Time and Total Execution Time: We measure and report the pause time caused by the (stop-the-world) GC and the end-to-end execution time of the JVM. All timing measurements are taken five times. We report arithmetic means, and plot 95 % confidence intervals on graphs.

Scalability: We run as many GC threads as the number of cores available to the system; however large heaps incur a scalability bottleneck. Roots available in the old generation are discovered by scanning the card table, which is a data structure used to record old-to-young pointers. As the heap size increases, the time consumed by scanning the card table grows; hence, we analyze the responsiveness of our optimization schemes to the increased heap size.

5   Evaluation

5.1   NUMA Locality Trace

Figure 2a shows the relative NUMA Locality Trace, see Sect. 4.3. For Neo4j/ Live-
Journal, we are unable to process all the data collected due to the huge size;
however, we use the data from the fifth GC cycle only as a sample of the application's GC phase. DaCapo/Sunflow obtains the best relative NUMA locality trace
results. Approximately, 90 % of objects are co-located in the same node as the
root. On the contrary, objects in DaCapo/h2 are dispersed across NUMA nodes
and rooted sub-graphs provide low locality traces: 42 %. For all benchmarks, the
relative NUMA locality trace is 53 % on average. These results differ from our earlier empirical study [1], which demonstrated higher locality. The main difference is
that we now examine rooted sub-graphs from the young generation in our samples.
This may suggest that we cannot rely on the locality features of rooted sub-graphs
to optimize the copying GC. However the following experiment gives more insight
on rooted sub-graph locality for different kinds of roots.

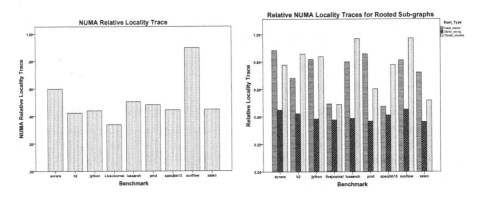

Fig. 2. (a) Relative NUMA Locality Traces for evaluated benchmarks. On average, 50 %
of objects are local within rooted sub-graphs. (b) Relative NUMA Locality Traces for
various root types: old-to-young, thread stacks, and class loader roots. An old-to-young
rooted sub-graph exhibits relatively low locality.

Recall that at the start of parallel GC, various root scanning tasks are
inserted in shared queues. These tasks direct the GC threads to different JVM
data areas which contain potential root references. These areas include mutator
thread-local stacks, card table (for old-to-young references), class loader data,
JNI handlers, etc. We calculate the NUMA Locality Traces for prevalent root
kinds and plot the results in Fig. 2b. For all evaluated benchmarks, the old-to-
young rooted sub-graphs consistently obtain low locality results, whereas other
roots show high locality.

These results suggest that aggressive locality optimization can be applied on
selected root types. In the next section, we show that GC performance increases
when applying locality optimization on *all root types except old-to-young references*. For old-to-young root, we randomly assign root references to any queue.

5.2   Pause Time and VM Time Analysis

Figures 3 and 4 plot the GC pause time and VM execution time results for the
Java benchmarks. Proposed topology-aware parallel techniques for task distribution and work-stealing outperform the default Hotspot ParallelScavenge GC
(labeled *org*).

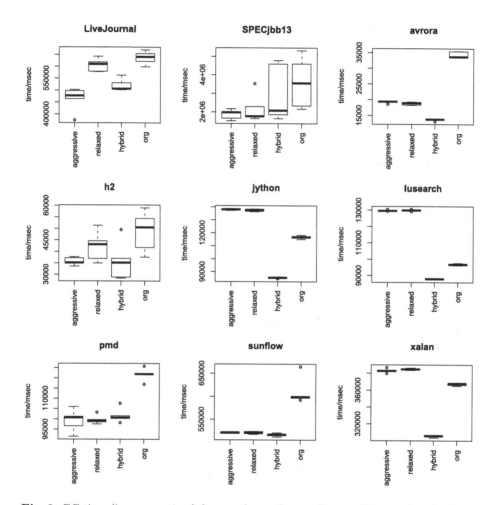

Fig. 3. GC time (i.e. pause time) for our three schemes. For small heaps (e.g. DaCapo
programs), hybrid scheme gives the best results, whereas aggressive scheme is more
effective for apps with larger heaps. (The default JVM is labeled Org.)

For programs with small heap sizes, represented here by DaCapo benchmarks, we observe that programs take the best advantage from Hybrid scheme.
Hybrid optimization scheme speeds up the GC performance by up to 2.52x and
never degrades it significantly. However, not all DaCapo programs follow the

same performance trend. For instance, DaCapo/avrora gains 2.5x GC speedup but the VM performance degrades by 31 %. Avrora simulates a number of applications running on a grid of micro-controllers. Previous studies [15,24], report that DaCapo/avrora incorporates extensive inter-thread communications and the application threads benefit from increased cache capacity. Thus, efforts to improve locality counteract this cache optimization.

We note that locality is vital to programs that have large heaps. Our approach improves Neo4j/LiveJournal GC performance by 37 %, 22 %, and 5 % for aggressive, hybrid, and relaxed optimization schemes respectively. With the aggressive scheme, SPECjbb2013 records improvement in GC and VM performance by 91 % and 20 % respectively.

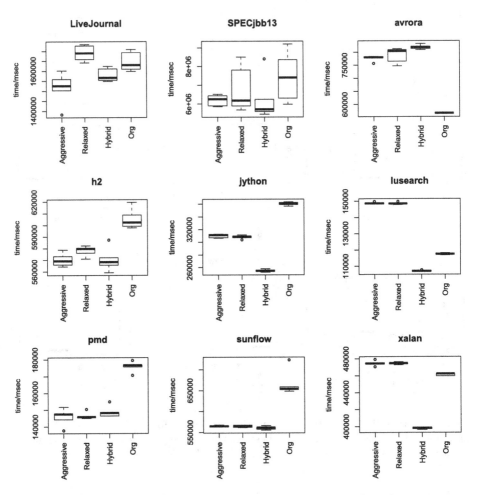

Fig. 4. VM time (i.e. end-to-end execution time) for our three schemes. At least one scheme provides better VM execution time than default (labeled Org) in most cases.

5.3 Scalability

When the heap size gets large, the copying collector might spend much time scanning roots for old-to-young references in the card table. Our experience is that many live objects are discovered through the card table; thus, the card table scanning accounts for the majority of GC pause time. On heap sizes above 100 GB, we found that card table handling often takes hundreds of seconds.

In this section, we study the scalability of our optimization schemes as the heap size increases. The experiments were run on Neo4j/LiveJournal with heap sizes of 100, 150, and 200 GB. Figure 5 shows the GC time and VM time scalability results. Ideally, as the heap size increases, the number of GC cycles decreases. However, the original GC implementation shows a slight increase in the GC time. We argue that this increase is due to the time consumed by processing the card table—in particular due to three factors. First, old-to-young rooted sub-graphs tend to be deep and require time for processing. Second, we have shown in Sect. 5.1 that such type of roots possess poor locality between objects; hence, incur significant remote access overhead. Third, deep sub-graphs are susceptible to work-stealing, thus, object connectivity will be broken and objects are scattered across NUMA nodes.

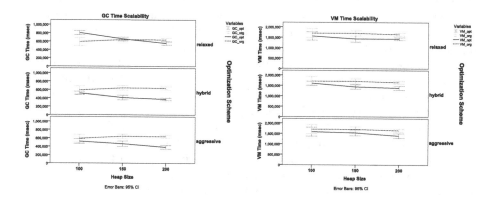

Fig. 5. GC (left) and VM (right) time scaling with heap size for Neo4j/LiveJournal. GC time decreases with heap size for our optimized versions, whereas the original implementation does not show any scaling.

Our three optimization schemes improve the second and third aspects and provide better scalability results. Preserving the rooted sub-graph integrity and enforcing topology awareness on work-stealing scales the GC time substantially. In fact, relaxed scheme which aims only at processing connected objects as a unit outperforms the original GC at 200 GB heap size. These results show that large heap sizes necessitate knowledge of the NUMA architecture to improve memory access behavior.

For VM scalability, the original JVM implementation provides a steady VM time over the three heap sizes and is not affected by the GC pause time. Hybrid and relaxed optimization schemes observe reduction in VM time but moderate scaling with increased heap size. Aggressive scheme follows the GC result's trend and obtains better scalability results.

6   Related Work

Prior work proposes allocating related objects close to each other to provide locality. Objects are co-allocated based on various criteria including temporal access patterns [5] and types [25]. Graph traversal order can improve object locality. Wilson et al. [30] suggest a hierarchical decomposition traversal order. This involves two different queues: small queues for descendant objects of some particular object in order to group them in a memory page, and a large queue to link these small queues. In our algorithm, we use two queues: NUMA queues for roots and local queues for rooted sub-graphs. Huang et al. [13] attempt to group frequently accessed fields in hot methods by sampling the program execution. At GC time, referents of hot fields are copied with their parents.

Thread-local heaps enforce local access to thread-specific objects [2,7,14, 18,28]. New objects are initially allocated in thread-local heaps until they are referenced by non-local objects. Such objects are promoted to a shared heap. Zhou and Demsky [32] implement master/slave collector threads and thread-local heaps. Each slave thread collects its own heap only. Any reference to a non-local object is sent to the master thread, which communicates with the appropriate thread to mark it live. In our algorithm, every GC thread is associated with a particular NUMA node and processes objects in that node only.

NUMA-aware collectors take into account object location before and after collection time. Tikir and Hollingsworth [29] sample memory accesses and move objects to the memory node of the thread accessing the object most frequently. Ogasawara [22] uses the dominant-thread information of each live object, e.g. thread holding the object lock, to identify the target memory node.

Connected objects in the object graph share various attributes. Hirzel et al. [12] examine different connectivity patterns with relation to object lifetime. They conclude that connected objects that are reachable only from the stack are shortlived; whereas, objects that are reachable from globals live for long time, perhaps immortally. In addition, objects that are connected by pointers die at the same time. Alnowaiser [1] studies the locality of connected objects and reports that the majority of connected objects, which form a sub-graph of a root, reside in the same memory node as that root.

Parallel GC algorithms aim to keep all cores busy processing the live object graph. The fundamental technique of task distribution is to create a per-thread work list that contains a set of tasks accessible by the owner thread. For load balancing, threads that complete processing their own queues steal tasks from non-empty queues [8,9,26,31]. However, such *processor-centric* algorithms do not consider object locality and may incur additional overhead for processing distant objects.

Memory-centric parallel GC algorithms take the object location into consideration. The heap is segregated into segments and each GC thread processes one or more segments. References to local objects in each segment are processed, whereas references to remote objects are pushed into a queue of the corresponding segment [4]. Alternatively, Shuf et al. [25] push references to remote objects into a shared queue enabling other threads to process them. For load balancing, GC threads need to lock unprocessed queues to trace live objects [21]. However, a memory segment boundary might not match the physical memory page size nor it is assigned to local threads; therefore, further locality improvements are required.

Work-stealing algorithms negatively affect object locality by separating child objects from their parents. Gidra et al. [10] remarks that disabling work-stealing improves program performance for some applications. Muddukrishna et al. [19] suggest a locality-aware work-stealing algorithm, which calculates the distance between NUMA nodes in a system with multi-hop memory hierarchy. An idle thread on a node attempts to steal work from the 'nearest' non-empty queues. Olivier et al. [23] propose a hierarchical work-stealing algorithm to improve locality. They enable one third of running threads to steal work on behalf of other threads in the same chip and push stolen work into a shared queue for local threads. Our approach allows threads to steal from local threads only, to preserve NUMA locality.

7   Conclusion

We have shown that a NUMA topology-aware copying GC based on per-node reference queues is able to preserve much of the rooted sub-graph locality that is inherent from mutator allocation patterns. Our improved copying GC has significant benefits—with improvements in GC performance up to 2.5x speedup and up to 37 % faster application runtime for non-trivial Java benchmarks.

We argue that further improvements are possible based on not only preserving locality of reference sub-graphs in single NUMA nodes, but also using local GC threads to operate on these sub-graphs. At present, we rely on expensive system calls to identify local work for GC threads—but cheaper techniques are presented in recent literature [11].

In summary, GC implementations should attempt to preserve intra-node reference graph locality as much as possible, to enable subsequent low-latency access times for both mutator and collector threads.

Acknowledgments. We would like to thank the University of Prince Sattam bin Abdulaziz for funding this research. We also thank the UK EPSRC (under grant EP/L000725/1) for its partial support.

References

1. Alnowaiser, K.: A study of connected object locality in NUMA heaps. In: Proceedings of MSPC, pp. 1:1–1:9 (2014)
2. Anderson, T.A.: Optimizations in a private nursery-based garbage collector. In: Proceedings of ISMM, pp. 21–30 (2010)

3. Blackburn, S.M., et al.: The dacapo benchmarks: Java benchmarking development and analysis. In: Proceedings of OOPSLA, pp. 169–190 (2006)
4. Chicha, Y., Watt, S.M.: A localized tracing scheme applied to garbage collection. In: Kobayashi, N. (ed.) APLAS 2006. LNCS, vol. 4279, pp. 323–339. Springer, Heidelberg (2006)
5. Chilimbi, T., Larus, J.: Using generational garbage collection to implement cache-conscious data placement. In: Proceedings of ISMM, pp. 37–48 (1998)
6. Dashti, M., Fedorova, A., Funston, J.: Traffic management: a holistic approach to memory placement on NUMA systems. In: Proceedings of ASPLOS, pp. 381–393 (2013)
7. Domani, T., Goldshtein, G., Kolodner, E.K., Lewis, E., Petrank, E., Sheinwald, D.: Thread-local heaps for Java. In: Proceedings of ISMM, pp. 76–87 (2002)
8. Endo, T., Taura, K., Yonezawa, A.: A scalable mark-sweep garbage collector on large-scale shared-memory machines. In: Proceedings of SC, pp. 1–14 (1997)
9. Flood, C., Detlefs, D., Shavit, N., Zhang, X.: Parallel garbage collection for shared memory multiprocessors. In: Proceedings of JVM (2001)
10. Gidra, L., Thomas, G., Sopena, J., Shapiro, M.: Assessing the scalability of garbage collectors on many cores. In: Proceedings of PLOS, pp. 1–7 (2011)
11. Gidra, L., Thomas, G., Sopena, J., Shapiro, M., Nguyen, N.: NumaGiC: a garbage collector for big data on big NUMA machines. In: Proceedings of ASPLOS, pp. 661–673 (2015)
12. Hirzel, M., Henkel, J., Diwan, A., Hind, M.: Understanding the connectivity of heap objects. In: Proceedings of ISMM, pp. 36–49 (2002)
13. Huang, X., Blackburn, S.M., McKinley, K.S., Moss, J.E.B., Wang, Z., Cheng, P.: The garbage collection advantage: improving program locality. In: Proceedings of OOPSLA, pp. 69–80 (2004)
14. Jones, R., King, A.: A fast analysis for thread-local garbage collection with dynamic class loading. In: Proceedings of SCAM, pp. 129–138 (2005)
15. Kalibera, T., Mole, M., Jones, R., Vitek, J.: A black-box approach to understanding concurrency in DaCapo. In: Proceedings of OOPSLA, pp. 335–354 (2012)
16. Leskovec, J., Krevl, A.: SNAP datasets: stanford large network dataset collection, June 2014. http://snap.stanford.edu/data
17. Majo, Z., Gross, T.R.: Memory management in NUMA multicore systems: trapped between cache contention and interconnect overhead. In: Proceedings of ISMM, pp. 11–20 (2011)
18. Marlow, S., Peyton Jones, S.: Multicore garbage collection with local heaps. In: Proceedings of ISMM, pp. 21–32 (2011)
19. Muddukrishna, A., Jonsson, P.A., Vlassov, V., Brorsson, M.: Locality-aware task scheduling and data distribution on NUMA systems. In: Rendell, A.P., Chapman, B.M., Müller, M.S. (eds.) IWOMP 2013. LNCS, vol. 8122, pp. 156–170. Springer, Heidelberg (2013)
20. Neo4J. http://www.neo4j.com/ (2015)
21. Oancea, C.E., Mycroft, A., Watt, S.M.: A new approach to parallelising tracing algorithms. In: Proceedings of ISMM, pp. 10–19 (2009)
22. Ogasawara, T.: NUMA-aware memory manager with dominant-thread-based copying GC. In: Proceedings of OOPSLA, pp. 377–390 (2009)
23. Olivier, S.L., Porterfield, A.K., Wheeler, K.B., Prins, J.F.: Scheduling task parallelism on multi-socket multicore systems. In: Proceedings of ROSS, pp. 49–56 (2011)

24. Sartor, J.B., Eeckhout, L.: Exploring multi-threaded Java application performance on multicore hardware. In: Proceedings of OOPSLA, New York, USA, pp. 281–296 (2012)
25. Shuf, Y., Gupta, M., Franke, H., Appel, A., Singh, J.P.: Creating and preserving locality of Java applications at allocation and garbage collection times. In: Proceedings of OOPSLA, pp. 13–25 (2002)
26. Siebert, F.: Limits of parallel marking garbage collection. In: Proceedings of ISMM, pp. 21–29 (2008)
27. SPECjbb2013: Standard Performance Evaluation Corporation Java Business Benchmark (2013). http://www.spec.org/jbb2013
28. Steensgaard, B.: Thread-specific heaps for multi-threaded programs. In: Proceedings of ISMM, pp. 18–24 (2000)
29. Tikir, M.M., Hollingsworth, J.K.: NUMA-aware Java heaps for server applications. In: Proceedings of IPDPS, pp. 108.b (2005)
30. Wilson, P.R., Lam, M.S., Moher, T.G.: Effective static-graph reorganization to improve locality in garbage-collected systems. In: Proceedings of PLDI, pp. 177–191 (1991)
31. Wu, M., Li, X.F.: Task-pushing: a scalable parallel GC marking algorithm without synchronization operations. In: Proceedings of IPDPS, pp. 1–10 (2007)
32. Zhou, J., Demsky, B.: Memory management for many-core processors with software configurable locality policies. In: Proceedings of ISMM, pp. 3–14 (2012)

An Embedded DSL for High Performance Declarative Communication with Correctness Guarantees in C++

Nilesh Mahajan[✉], Eric Holk, Arun Chauhan, and Andrew Lumsdaine

Indiana University, Bloomington, IN 47405, USA
{nnmahaja,eholk,achauhan,lums}@indiana.edu

Abstract. High performance programming using explicit communication calls needs considerable programming expertise to optimize. Tuning for performance often involves using asynchronous calls, running the risk of introducing bugs and making the program harder to debug. Techniques to prove desirable program properties, such as deadlock freedom, invariably incur significant performance overheads.

We have developed a domain-specific language, embedded in C++, called Kanor that enables programmers to specify the communication declaratively in the Bulk Synchronous Parallel (BSP) style. Deadlock freedom is guaranteed for well-formed Kanor programs. We start with operational semantics for a subset of Kanor and prove deadlock freedom and determinism properties based on those semantics. We then show how the declarative nature of Kanor allows us to detect and optimize communication patterns.

1 Introduction

Writing efficient parallel programs continues to be a challenge for the programming community. Large-scale parallel programs are usually coded using the partitioned address space model in which processes communicate by sending explicit messages using a standardized Message Passing Interface (MPI) library, which provides a highly portable interface.

Unfortunately, the most straightforward way to specify communication in MPI is usually not the most efficient. Consequently, MPI has grown to include a library of communication patterns that are carefully optimized for specific platforms. To enable further optimization MPI also includes asynchronous communication primitives. Utilizing the asynchronous communication primitives often involves a deep understanding of how a parallel program works and forces programmers to compromise readability by strewing communication primitives all over the unrelated computational code [7]. Moreover, ironically, such optimizations are highly platform-specific affecting the performance portability of the MPI code.

A. Chauhan—Currently at Google Inc.

© Springer International Publishing Switzerland 2016
X. Shen et al. (Eds.): LCPC 2015, LNCS 9519, pp. 206–220, 2016.
DOI: 10.1007/978-3-319-29778-1_13

Kanor takes a different approach. It is a domain-specific language (DSL) that allows programmers to specify communication patterns *declaratively*, at a high level, in Bulk Synchronous Parallel (BSP) style [11]. The semantics of the language are carefully defined to guarantee correctness properties, such as deadlock freedom and determinism, while allowing efficient execution. The language is highly *expressive*, able to succinctly describe all the existing MPI collective operations, and allowing users to create their own custom collectives that could be detected and optimized. The BSP style of Kanor also makes it amenable to source-level optimizations that are well understood [5], including those that exploit shared memory for efficient intra-node communication [9].

In this paper we describe a version of Kanor that has been implemented as a DSL embedded within C++. This allows Kanor to be compiled using standard C++-11 compilers. Since Kanor uses MPI underneath, existing programs using MPI can be converted to Kanor incrementally.

```
Topology topology;
rval[sndr]_at_ root << sval _at_ sndr |
  _for_each(sndr, topology.world) &
  _if (sndr % 2 == 0) _with toplogy;
```

Fig. 1. Example of a communication statement.

As an example of a communication statement consider the Kanor code in Fig. 1. The statement updates the variable `rval` at a Kanor process denoted by `root`. Only the processes with even process IDs send value stored in the variable `sval`. The receiver process set consists of a single process (`root`) and the sender process set consists of processes with even IDs, assuming that `Topology` defines integral type process IDs. The sender process set is formed with the help of Kanor constructs `_for_each` and `_if`, and `_with` specifies the topology. Finally, only the memory location `rval[sndr]` is updated with the value receiver from `sndr`.

As a slightly more realistic example, consider the MPI code in Fig. 2 where separate reductions are performed by even and odd processes with the sender processes sending different values. The functions `MPI_Isend` and `MPI_Recv` perform non-blocking send and blocking receive, respectively. This pattern can be written in other ways in MPI but the code will end up either using send and receive calls or MPI derived types and subcommunicator manipulations. Even with the new neighborhood collectives in MPI-3 standard, this pattern cannot be represented as a single function call. The programmer must also make sure the sent and received messages match and there is no deadlock. Various MPI implementations manage the temporary buffers differently so the deadlock bug might show up in some and not others. Finally, a better algorithm might be implemented with better knowledge of the communication pattern.

In contrast, in order to express this communication in Kanor, process sets, messages sizes, and memory locations can all be specified in a single communication statement. The operation can be viewed as a single parallel assignment of receiver memory locations by the senders. Kanor constructs are similar to list comprehensions seen in languages like Python and Haskell. The example communication in Fig. 2 can be expressed in Kanor succinctly, as shown in Fig. 3.

```
int rval;
std::vector<int> sbuff;
...
std::vector<MPI_Request> reqs;
int rmdr = me % 2;
for (int i = 0; i < nprocs; i++) {
  if (i % 2 == rmdr) {
      MPI_Request req;
      MPI_Isend(&sbuff[i], 1, MPI_INT, i, 0, MPI_COMM_WORLD, &req);
      reqs.push_back(req);
  }
}
MPI_Waitall(reqs.size(), reqs.data(), MPI_STATUSES_IGNORE);
for (int i = 0; i < nprocs; i++) {
  if (i % 2 == rmdr) {
      int r;
      MPI_Recv(&r, 1, MPI_INT, i, 0, MPI_COMM_WORLD, MPI_STATUS_IGNORE);
      rval += r;
  }
}
```

Fig. 2. Reduction using MPI; even and odd processors perform different reductions.

```
int rval;
kanor::CommBuff<int> sbuff;
...
Topology t;
rval _at_ rcvr << std::plus<int>() << sbuff[rcvr] _at_ sndr |
  _for_each(sndr, t.world) & _for_each(rcvr, t.world) &
  _if ((sndr % 2) == (rcvr % 2)) _with t & GLOBAL;
```

Fig. 3. Reduction is expressed much more concisely and clearly in Kanor.

In the rest of the paper, we describe the language and its semantics and show how those semantics lead to correctness guarantees. As an embedded DSL (EDSL), Kanor performs certain just-in-time optimizations at run-time and caches them to amortize the cost of the optimizations. We report experimental results that demonstrate that the overhead of Kanor is insignificant for the benchmarks we studied. This paper makes the following contributions.

- Design of Kanor as a DSL embedded within C++.
- An operational semantics for a subset Kanor and discussion of deadlock freedom and determinism properties.
- An approach for detecting collective communication patterns within Kanor.
- Performance evaluation of our collective detection approach.

2   Kanor Syntax

Figure 4 shows the BNF grammar for Kanor. A communication statement in Kanor consists of four parts: destination specification, operation, source specification, and condition. The operation is bracketed by the literal << and the condition is preceded by the literal |, which makes the communication statement read like set comprehension. The destination specification is any valid lvalue in C++ and source specification is any valid rvalue. If the source type is not assignable to the destination, compilation fails, as would be expected in standard C++. The operation bracketed by << can be any binary functor, which is applied to the source and the destination to update the destination. The operation may be omitted, in which case the operation defaults to identity operation. If specified the operation is assumed to be associative and commutative. Note that assigning multiple values to a single destination violates the condition of associativity, in which case the program's behavior is undefined.

The condition consists of a clauses separated by the literal &. A _for_each clause binds a process ID variable, *PVar*, to a set of process IDs (*ProcSet*). The set can be generated with the range *Beg* to *End*. An _if clause is used to filter out certain process IDs from a generated set; *Cond* is a boolean expression and may involve the *PVars* bound with a _for_each. The _let clause assigns a value *Val* to a *PVar*.

In destination and source specifications, Lval refers to an expression that evaluates to an lval, Rval to an expression that evaluates to an rval, and ProcIdExpr to an expression that evaluates to a valid process ID. The _with clause is used to specify a topology and provide certain hints to Kanor about the communication (see Sect. 4).

Kanor is sufficiently expressive to encode all the MPI collectives. Communication characteristics, such as, process sets, message lengths, and destination addresses can be specified as part of the statement itself. This means that a communication pattern like the MPI collective MPI_Alltoallv can be encoded in many ways with a Kanor communication statement. Some of the encodings are shown in Fig. 5.

$$
\begin{array}{lll}
CommStmt & ::= & DstSpec \ [<< Operation] << SrcSpec \ | \ Conditions \ [WithStmt] \\
DstSpec & ::= & Lval \ \_at\_ \ ProcIdExpr \\
SrcSpec & ::= & Rval \ \_at\_ \ ProcIdExpr \\
Conditions & ::= & Clause \ [\& \ Clause]* \\
Clause & ::= & ForEach \ | \ If \ | \ Let \ | \ TopoSpec \ | \ Hints \\
ForEach & ::= & \_for\_each(PVar, ProcSet) \ | \ \_for\_each(PVar, Beg, End) \\
If & ::= & \_if \ (\ Cond \ ) \\
Let & ::= & \_let \ (\ PVar, Val \ ) \\
WithStmt & ::= & \_with \ Hints \ [\& \ TopologyObject] \ | \ \_with \ TopologyObject \\
Hints & ::= & Hint \ [\& \ Hint]* \\
Hint & ::= & \text{GLOBAL} \ | \ \text{CORRESPONDING} \ | \ \text{SENDER} \ | \ \text{INVARIANT}
\end{array}
$$

Fig. 4. Formal syntax of Kanor. A communication statement expressed in Kanor is represented by the non-terminal, *CommStmt*.

All-to-All:

All Gather	`rb[s] _at_ r << sb _at_ s |` `_for_each(s, t.world) & _for_each(r, t.world) _with t;`
All Gatherv	`rb[Slice(dspls[s],counts[s])] _at_ r <<` `sb[Slice(0, counts[s])] _at_ s	... ;`
Reduce scatter	`rb[Slice(0, count[r])] _at_ r << std::plus<btype>()` `<< sb[Slice(displ[r], count[r])] _at_ s	... ;`

All-to-One:

Gather	`rb[Slice(s*blk_sz, blk_sz)] _at_ root` `<< sb[Slice(0, blk_sz)] _at_ s	... ;`
Gatherv	`rb[Slice(displ[s], counts[s])] _at_ root` `<< sb[Slice(0, counts[s])] _at_ s	... ;`
Reduce	`rb _at_ root << kanor::sum<btype> << sb _at_ s	... ;`

One-to-All:

Bcast	`rb _at_ r << sb _at_ root	... ;`
Scatter	`rb _at_ r << sb[Slice(r*blk, blk)] _at_ root	... ;`
Scatterv	`rb _at_ r << sb[Slice(displ[r], counts[r])] _at_ root	... ;`

Other:

Scan	`rb _at_ r << std::plus<btype>() << sb _at_ s |` `_for_each(s, t.world) & _for_each(r, s, t.world.size()) _with t;`
Exscan	`rb _at_ r << std::plus<btype>() << sb _at_ s |` `_for_each(s, t.world) & _for_each(r, s+1, t.world.size())_with t;`

Fig. 5. MPI collectives encoded in Kanor. In "One-to-All", `blk` refers to the size of `rb`.

Kanor makes extensive use of operator overloading for clean syntax and C++ expression templates [4] for performance. The users only need to include a single header, `kanor.h`.

3   Kanor Semantics and Properties

In order to make the language behavior precise we give a big-step operational semantics for a subset of Kanor. We have chosen to restrict ourselves to a subset of the entire language for space considerations and also to keep the proofs of determinism and deadlock freedom tractable. We call this restricted language K_T.

3.1   Semantics

The syntax for K_T is shown in Fig. 6. A K_T program consists of a sequence of commands denoted by c in the table. Traditional control flow constructs are represented by the **if** and **while** commands. Commands are sequenced with; (semi-colon): $c_1; c_2$ means that c_1 is executed before c_2. Variables, x, in the language represent memory locations that can be updated during execution of the program. Variables can be updated with the assignment command ($:=$) and with the communication command denoted by $comm$. Expressions can be arithmetic ($aexp$) or boolean ($bexp$).

$$
\begin{aligned}
aexp\ &::=\ n \mid x \mid a_0 \oplus a_1 \mid \textbf{me} \mid \textbf{np}\\
\oplus\ &::=\ + \mid \times \mid -\\
bexp\ &::=\ \textbf{true} \mid \textbf{false}\\
&\quad\mid a_0 \odot a_1 \mid b_0 \oslash b_1 \mid \neg b\\
\odot\ &::=\ < \mid > \mid \leq \mid \geq \mid =\\
\oslash\ &::=\ \wedge \mid \vee\\
cmd\ &::=\ \textbf{skip} \mid x := a \mid c_0; c_1\\
&\quad\ \textbf{if}\ b\ \textbf{then}\ c_1\ \textbf{else}\ c_2 \mid\\
&\quad\ \textbf{while}\ b\ \textbf{do}\ c \mid comm\\
comm\ &::=\ x_1 @\ p_1 \leftarrow op \leftarrow x_2 @\ p_2\\
&\quad\ \textbf{where}\ clause^* filter^*\\
clause\ &::=\ \textbf{foreach}(v, s\_exp)\\
s\_exp\ &::=\ \textbf{list}(a_0, a_1, ...) \mid \textbf{rep}(a_0, a_1)\\
&\quad\ \textbf{range}(a_0, a_1)\\
filter\ &::=\ \text{BExp expression}\\
op\ &::=\ \text{reduction op}
\end{aligned}
$$

Fig. 6. Formal syntax of K_T.

All K_T processes execute the same program similar to the single process multiple data (SPMD) model. Each process has its private memory, called that process's *store*. Each process starts with its own store with the variables me and np denoting the process rank and the total number of processes respectively. Communication can only be done with the $comm$ commands.

The operational semantics for K_T consist of local rules (Table 1) and communication rules (Table 2). The local semantics specify how processes compute values locally. Local process stores are modified with variable assignment denoted by the E-ASSIGN rule. The semantics for communication are specified by the E-COMM rule in Table 2. The communication command can be thought of as parallel assignment of receiver locations by sender values. The sender process s evaluates the expressions $(p_1, x_2, p_2, foreach(i, ...), ..., pred_1, ...)$ with the store σ producing an environment ρ_s (E-SENDABLES). ρ_s maps the sent variable (x_2) to a value (v_s) and also binds the generator-bound variables (i) to set of process IDs. The set of process IDs is generated after the evaluation of conditions $foreach(i, ...), ..., pred_1, ...$ Only the values of i that evaluate p_2 to s are stored in ρ_s. The operation $\uplus$ represents communication of data(ρ_s) from senders to receivers. The environment ρ_r is formed on receiver r, by combining mappings from ρ_s with $p_r = r$. All the sent variables are distinct from each other and their mappings are preserved in ρ_r. Finally, receiver r evaluates and updates memory location(s) x_1 by applying op to received values in the combined environment $\rho_r \oplus \sigma$. Application of op is a local computation on the receiver (E-APPOP). The environment ρ_r contains a set of values for x_2 received from different senders. Variable x_1 in σ is updated by combining all these values with operator (op). The updated store is denoted by σ_1.

Table 1. Local semantics in K_T.

$$\frac{\langle b_0 \mid \sigma \rangle \Downarrow_b t_0 \qquad \langle b_1 \mid \sigma \rangle \Downarrow_b t_1}{\langle b_0 \oslash b_1 \mid \sigma \rangle \Downarrow_b t} \text{ E-BOP}$$
$$\text{where } t = t_0 \oslash t_1$$

$$\frac{\langle a_0 \mid \sigma \rangle \Downarrow_a n_0 \qquad \langle a_1 \mid \sigma \rangle \Downarrow_a n_1}{\langle a_0 \oplus a_1 \mid \sigma \rangle \Downarrow_a n} \text{ E-AOP}$$
$$\text{where } n = n_0 \oplus n_1$$

$$\frac{}{\langle \textbf{skip} \mid \sigma \rangle \Downarrow \sigma} \text{ E-SKIP}$$

$$\frac{\langle a \mid \sigma \rangle \Downarrow_a n}{\langle x := a \mid \sigma \rangle \Downarrow \sigma \, [x \mapsto n]} \text{ E-ASSIGN}$$

$$\frac{\langle c_0 \mid \sigma \rangle \Downarrow \sigma_1 \qquad \langle c_1 \mid \sigma_1 \rangle \Downarrow \sigma_2}{\langle c_0; c_1 \mid \sigma \rangle \Downarrow \sigma_2} \text{ E-SEQ}$$

$$\sigma_1 := \sigma \left[x_1 \mapsto op \left(\sigma(x_1), \sum_{v \in \rho(x_2)} v \right) \right]$$
$$\frac{}{\langle (x_1, op, x_2) \mid \rho \oplus \sigma \rangle \Downarrow \sigma_1} \text{ E-APPOP}$$

$$\frac{\langle b \mid \sigma \rangle \Downarrow_b \textbf{true} \qquad \langle c_1 \mid \sigma \rangle \Downarrow \sigma_1}{\langle \textbf{if } b \textbf{ then } c_1 \textbf{ else } c_2 \mid \sigma \rangle \Downarrow \sigma_1} \text{ E-COND-T}$$

$$\frac{\langle b \mid \sigma \rangle \Downarrow_b \textbf{false} \qquad \langle c_2 \mid \sigma \rangle \Downarrow \sigma_1}{\langle \textbf{if } b \textbf{ then } c_1 \textbf{ else } c_2 \mid \sigma \rangle \Downarrow \sigma_1} \text{ E-COND-F}$$

$$\frac{\forall s \in P, \langle \textbf{foreach}(i, ...), ..., pred_1, ...) \mid \sigma \rangle \Downarrow_s R \qquad R_f \subseteq R}{\langle p_2 \mid \sigma \oplus R_f \rangle \Downarrow_s s \qquad \langle x_2 \mid \sigma \oplus R_f \rangle \Downarrow_s v_s \qquad \rho' := \rho \, [x_2 \mapsto v_s, i \mapsto v_2]}{\langle (p_1, x_2, p_2, \textbf{foreach}(i, ...), ..., pred_1, ...) \mid \sigma \rangle \Downarrow_s \rho'} \text{ E-SENDABLES}$$

$$\frac{\langle b \mid \sigma \rangle \Downarrow_b \textbf{false}}{\langle \textbf{while } b \textbf{ do } c \mid \sigma \rangle \Downarrow \sigma} \text{ E-WHILE-F}$$

$$\frac{\langle b \mid \sigma \rangle \Downarrow_b \textbf{true}}{\langle c \mid \sigma \rangle \Downarrow \sigma_1 \qquad \langle \textbf{while } b \textbf{ do } c \mid \sigma_1 \rangle \Downarrow \sigma_2}{\langle \textbf{while } b \textbf{ do } c \mid \sigma \rangle \Downarrow \sigma_2} \text{ E-WHILE-T}$$

Table 2. Communication semantics in K_T.

$$\frac{\forall r, s \in P, \exists p_{1s}, x_{2s}, p_{2s} \qquad \langle (p_{1s}, x_{2s}, p_{2s}, \textbf{foreach}(i, ...), ..., pred_1, ...) \mid \sigma \rangle \Downarrow_s \rho_s}{\biguplus \rho_s \Downarrow_r \rho_r} \text{ E-UNION}$$

$$\frac{\forall r, s \in P, \qquad \biguplus \rho_s \Downarrow_r \rho_r \qquad \langle (x_1, op, x_2) \mid \rho_r \oplus \sigma \rangle \Downarrow_r \sigma_1}{\langle x_1 @ p_1 \leftarrow op \leftarrow x_2 @ p_2 \textbf{ where } ... \mid \sigma \rangle \Downarrow_r \sigma_1} \text{ E-COMM}$$

3.2   Properties

We first define what well-formedness means for K_T programs. We assume K_T programs are well-formed in the ensuing discussion.

Definition 1. *Well-formedness K_T programs are said to be well-formed iff*

- *All processes participating in communication, C, execute C.*
- *All processes participating in communications, C_1 and C_2, execute C_1 and C_2 in the same order.*
- *There are no local errors, including the application of the reduction operator and ρ_s computation.*

First two requirements for well-formedness are the same as that for an MPI collective. The problem of checking well-formedness is undecidable in general.

Kanor does not provide syntactic support or semantic guarantees to ensure well-formedness. Well-formedness could be checked in limited cases (global knowledge) by the compiler, but not in general.

Determinism. We would like K_T programs to produce the same output on same inputs. This means that each K_T process starting with some initial configuration always ends up with the same final configurations on each run of the program. We say that K_T is deterministic if all programs satisfy this property. More formally, we say that K_T programs are deterministic if and only if for a given process set P, each process with an initial store $\sigma_p, p \in P$, all executions of the program c satisfy the following property: For each process $p \in P$, if two executions of c evaluate to final stores σ_1 and σ_2 then $\sigma_1 = \sigma_2$. Note that processes share the same program c but they can have different initial and final configurations (memory stores denoted by σ).

We divide the proof of determinism into two parts, proving that expression evaluation is deterministic and that the execution of commands is deterministic.

Lemma 1. K_T *expression evaluation is deterministic.*

- $\forall e \in AExp, \forall \sigma \in \Sigma, \forall n, n' \in \mathbb{Z}, \langle e, \sigma \rangle \Downarrow_a n \wedge \langle e, \sigma \rangle \Downarrow_a n' \Rightarrow n = n'$
- $\forall b \in BExp, \forall \sigma \in \Sigma, \forall t, t' \in \mathbb{B}, \langle b, \sigma \rangle \Downarrow_b t \wedge \langle b, \sigma \rangle \Downarrow_b t' \Rightarrow t = t'$

Proof. By induction on the structure of arithmetic expression e. The base cases are numeric constants n, **me** and **np**. The conclusion follows from reflexivity of integers. In case e is a variable x, x evaluates to a unique n in a given store σ. The inductive case $(a_0 \oplus a_1)$ follows from the deterministic nature of arithmetic operations. The proof for boolean expressions is similar.

A potential source of non-determinism is the communication command. The reduction operator might be non-commutative, e.g. assignment. If such an operator operates with different values on the same memory location, then the result might be non-deterministic. In this case, we make the operator application ($\Downarrow_s$) of rule E-APPOP in Table 2) deterministic by choosing a particular evaluation order. Also, we assume the network is reliable so that the $\uplus$ operator in E-UNION always produces the same environment after a union over the sent environments.

In the presence of commands like **while**, we cannot use induction on the structure of commands to prove determinism. Instead, we use induction on *derivation trees*. A *judgement* D of the form $c \Downarrow \sigma$ says that the command evaluates to final configuration σ without errors. The derivation of D starts by selecting the operational semantics rule (Tables 1 and 2) for which D is the consequent. The derivation then branches out, each branch representing a derivation for each premise of the selected rule. Derivation along a branch of ends when a rule with no premise is found. Thus the derivation for D forms a tree with D at its root. We prove determinism of command evaluation by induction over derivation trees.

Lemma 2. K_T *command evaluation is deterministic.* $\langle c \mid \sigma \rangle \Downarrow \sigma_1 \wedge \langle c \mid \sigma \rangle \Downarrow \sigma_2 \Rightarrow \sigma_1 = \sigma_2$

Proof. The most interesting case here is the rule E-COMM in Table 2. Let D be the derivation when c evaluates to σ_1 and D' be the derivation when c evaluates to σ_2. Derivation tree for D must have two branches (subderivations) from the root, one for rule E-UNION (D_1) and other for rule E-APPOP (D_2). At the end of D_1 we should get the store ρ_1 and at the end of D_2 we should get σ_1.

By inversion, since D' uses the rule E-COMM again with two subderivations D'_1 and D'_2 with stores ρ_2 and σ_2 respectively. By induction hypothesis on D_1 with D'_1, we have $\rho_1 = \rho_2$ and by induction hypothesis on D_2 with D'_2 and $\rho_1 = \rho_2$, we have $\sigma_1 = \sigma_2$.

A K_T program is a command with initial store. Hence, determinism of K_T programs follows from Lemma 2.

Deadlock Freedom. A message passing program might deadlock when a process blocks waiting for a message that is never sent. K_T programs are deadlock-free by construction.

Lemma 3. K_T *programs are deadlock free.*
$\forall c \in \mathbb{WC}, \forall p \in P, \langle c \mid \sigma_p \rangle \Downarrow \sigma'_p$ *where* $\mathbb{WC}$ *is the set of well-formed* K_T *programs.*

Proof. In well-formed K_T programs, application of the rule E-APPOP, is always successful across all processes. All other commands act locally and do not block, hence there is no deadlock. The proof follows similar pattern to the determinism proof. The induction is on the structure of derivations.

4   Optimizing Communication

Having established precise semantics and basic correctness of Kanor, we next identify opportunities to optimize it. Our core technique is based on inferring the collective operation at run-time the first time a communication statement is executed. Subsequent executions of the statement use the previously computed (cached) inference, which eliminates the overhead of the run-time inference of the pattern, which can take $O(n^2)$ time for n processes.

4.1   Communication Knowledge

In order to understand when and how collective patterns can be detected we need to define *communication knowledge* cases, which describe the extent to which the processes agree on the values of the expressions involved in a communication statement.

The receiver lval (*Lval* in *DstSpec* in Fig. 4) is computed on the receiver. Similarly, the sender rval is computed on the sender. This is necessary, because the lval might not make sense on the sender and rval might be meaningless on the receiver. However, the process sets—the sets of senders and receivers that are computed using *DstSpec*, *SrcSpec*, and *Conditions*—need to be computed by both the senders and the receivers in order for two-way communication to take place. If the sender and receiver process sets evaluate to exactly the same values on all the processes we call it the *global knowledge* case. This is the simplest of all cases.

It is possible that the receiver sets evaluate to different values on different processes. In such cases, Kanor assumes the communication to be sender-driven, i.e., the receiver process sets computed by senders take precedence[1]. Thus, the senders know which processes they are sending to, but the receivers may not know their senders. We call this the *sender knowledge* case. To illustrate it, suppose the sender process s computes the sender set S_s and receiver set R_s. The receiver process r computes the sender set S_r and the receiver set R_r. If $r \in R_s$ but $s \notin S_r$, the sender s still sends the message which must be received by r.

Finally, it is possible that the sender and the receiver processes agree on their corresponding receivers and senders, but other processes might not. Thus, if the communication statement requires process A to send data to B then both A and B agree on it, but a third process C might not, although, C knows that it is not involved in this communication. Such a case, which might be relatively rare compared to other cases, is called the *corresponding knowledge* case.

Note that there is no receiver knowledge case, since the communication in Kanor is sender driven. If sender expression evaluates to different values on different processes, it is still the senders' versions that take precedence.

It is possible to detect these cases using compiler analysis, however, that is beyond the scope of this paper. In this paper we assume that the users provide appropriate annotations with a communication statement (*Hint* in Fig. 4) to identify the knowledge case. For the rest of the discussion we assume global knowledge case, which is by far the most common. Other cases can also be handled similarly, but usually require additional communication. Assuming local computations are error-free, the global case guarantees well-formedness Definition 1. It is left to the programmer to make sure that non-global Kanor programs are well-formed.

4.2   Communication Invariance

A communication statement whose process set calculation depends on an enclosing loop's index may use different process sets in each iteration. Thus, certain aspects of a communication statement might change with each invocation. This is a property distinct from knowledge case.

We identify three core *characteristics* of a communication statement: *length* of the messages, the *contiguity* of the data in memory, and the *process sets* involved in sending and receiving data. We say that the communication is *invariant* if none of the communication characteristics change. Invariance of communication allows us to cache the communication pattern and reuse it in later instances of the same communication statement.

---

[1] This is motivated by the fact that one-sided *put* operations are usually more efficient than one-sided *get* operations.

If a communication statement is both global knowledge case and invariant then each process can independently infer the communication pattern and cache it, with the assurance that every other process will make an identical inference. The communication pattern is inferred using Algorithm 1 and cached for subsequent use. Our evaluation (Sect. 6) shows that the inference cost gets amortized quickly as message size increases.

```
1  Input: Communication Statement S
2  Output: Set of Collective Calls C
   // G is a directed graph, in which vertices are process IDs,
   // an edge connects sender to a receiver
3  G = build from S;
4  n = number of vertices in vertex set V(G);
5  if each vertex v in V(G) has degree n then
6      if send and receiver buffers contiguous then
7          C = {Alltoall};
8      else
9          C = {AllGather};
10     return;
   // build rooted collectives to be executed independently
11 foreach v in V(G) with no incoming edges do
12     if send and receiver buffers contiguous then
13         C = C ∪ {broadcast};
14     else
15         C = C ∪ {scatter};
```

Algorithm 1: Algorithm to detect MPI collectives.

5   Implementation Status

We have implemented Kanor as an embedded DSL in C++. We make use of operator overloading, template meta-programming and certain C++11 features, such as lambdas, to achieve this. The library will be released in open source.

Kanor process ranks are expressed as members of the `kanor::ProcID` class. Arithmetic and comparison operators are overloaded for the `ProcID` class. Programmers can use list comprehensions provided by Kanor to bind `ProcID` variables to sets. Other entities, including communication buffers and slices, are also provided as convenient Kanor classes. All communication is implemented using MPI as the underlying communication mechanism. This allows existing MPI programs to be converted to Kanor incrementally.

The implementation uses type traits to perform several compile-time checks, for example, to make sure that the sender and receiver expressions will evaluate to process IDs, and to make sure that the left hand side (receiver expression) is a valid lval. In order to implement communication pattern detection, carefully overloaded operators work together to construct an abstract syntax tree (AST) out of the communication statement. Once the AST is complete, Algorithm 1 is used to infer and cache the pattern as a lambda that can be invoked directly the next time. With the programmer-supplied hint the library generates optimized implementation for each knowledge case using expression templates.

6 Experiments

We evaluated the pattern identification and caching mechanism implemented in the library with several benchmarks. First set of benchmarks consists of well-known MPI collectives working with different process sets and buffer sizes. Each collective is executed in a loop. First iteration of the loop incurs detection and caching overhead. The runtime overhead for subsequent iterations is minimal compared to actual communication. We also evaluated our system on three other benchmarks, including one dense matrix kernel, Cholesky and two NAS parallel benchmarks, IS (Integer Sort), and FT (Fourier Transform) [1]. We selected Cholesky, where the matrix columns are cyclically distributed across processors, for an example of dense matrix computation with complex communication patterns. The NAS IS benchmarks models irregular communication seen in typical N-Body codes. NAS FT represents regular communication on a subset of processes.

The experiments were conducted on the Big Red II infrastructure at Indiana University. Big Red II is a Cray XE6/XK7 supercomputer with a hybrid architecture providing a total of 1,020 compute nodes. It consists of 344 CPU-only compute nodes, each containing two AMD Opteron 16-core Abu Dhabi x86_64 CPUs and 64 GB of RAM. It also has 676 CPU/GPU compute nodes, each containing one AMD Opteron 16-core Interlagos x86_64 CPU, one NVIDIA Tesla K20 GPU accelerator with a single Kepler GK110 GPU, and 32 GB of RAM. Big Red II runs a proprietary variant of Linux called Cray Linux Environment (CLE).

Micro Benchmarks. Figure 7 shows the results for the collective micro-benchmarks. Timings for six communication statements representing MPI all-toall, allreduce, broadcast, scatter, scatterv and gather are shown. The collectives were run for different message sizes, processors and loop iteration counts. We only show the results for 32 processors with variable sized messages of double precision values. Each vertical bar represents total time (in milliseconds) it took for the communication statement to finish. The bars are shown in groups of three. First bar shows the time taken by MPI collective. Next two bars show the time taken by an equivalent Kanor communication statement with caching enabled and disabled respectively. To enable caching, we provide the INVARIANT hint. With caching disabled (third bar in a group), the runtime incurs pattern detection overheads on each iteration. With caching enabled (second bar), the runtime incurs overheads related to the caching mechanism only. The pattern detection overheads (third bar) are considerable for small messages sizes and all-to-all patterns. Detection starts to match MPI for larger sizes. Kanor collectives with caching enabled, start to match MPI even for smaller message sizes.

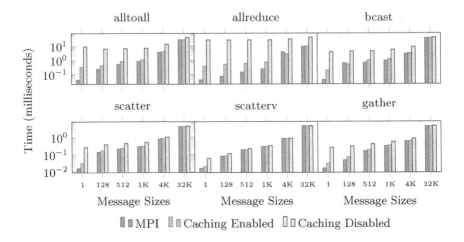

Fig. 7. Comparing Kanor implementations of MPI collectives to their counterparts for 32 processes.

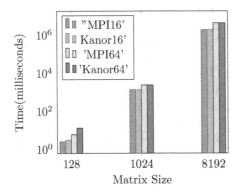

Fig. 8. Cholesky: Kanor vs MPI.

Application Benchmarks. The comparison results for Cholesky are shown in Fig. 8. In our implementation, the matrix columns are cyclically distributed and the main computation loop is strip-mined. A process operates on a block it owns and broadcasts the calculated column to downstream processes that require it. The message lengths may vary hence this is not an invariant communication statement. The computation time dominates the communication time so the detection overheads do not cause significant performance degradation.

Figure 9 shows the results of the NAS Integer Sort (IS) and Fourier Transform (FT) benchmarks. The benchmarks were run for classes S, W, A, B and C. IS processes send variable number of keys to other processes and the number of keys are not known a-priori. So an alltoall exchange happens to let the receivers of the number of keys they are receiving. Next an alltoallv actually sends the keys. The second alltoallv sends variable length messages, hence it is not an invariant communication. The detection and caching overhead shows up for smaller problem sizes (S, W). For larger sizes, the computation and communication time hides this overhead. Finally, FT is regular alltoall communication on a subset of processes and it is also invariant. Consequently, Kanor begins to match MPI even for smaller problem sizes.

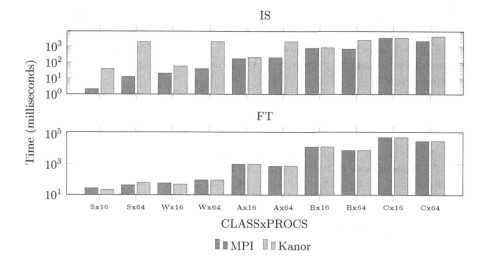

Fig. 9. Comparison of Kanor to MPI implementations of NAS Benchmarks Integer Sort (IS) and Fourier Transform (FT). NAS Benchmark class (S, W, A, B, C) denotes the size of the problem to be solved. Procs denote the number of processes used to solve the problem.

7 Related Work

Kanor's operational semantics were described in a previous paper [3]. This paper treats communication as parallel assignment, simplifying reasoning. Callahan et al. [2] detail small-step operational semantics for the BSPLib library. Gava et al. [6] give big-step operational semantics for a subset of BSPLib. Kanor communication statements are treated as parallel assignments in our approach. We do not work or reason with message queues which simplifies the semantics a lot.

Using expression templates [4] helps us pattern match AST nodes at compile time and inline code based on the match. This is in contrast to other embedding technique, used for example in Halide [10], that identifies AST nodes by casting pointers. New features provided in C++11 such as `static_assert` help us provide useful error messages in case the communication statement is ill-formed.

Collective detection efforts in MPI have mostly focused on analyzing traces of programs and detect patterns in them. Hoefler et al. [8] present an online algorithm to detect collective patterns in codes with point to point messages. Kanor communication statements enable easier detection of collectives. Also, we can detect reductions like allreduce.

8 Conclusion and Future Work

Declarative nature of Kanor allows programmers to write complex communication patterns including but not limited to MPI collectives. Well-formed Kanor programs are deadlock-free and deterministic. Kanor can identify and optimize communication patterns without expensive compiler analyses in the presence of global knowledge. We are currently focusing on implementing compiler analyses to automatically deduct hints as well as overlap computations with communication.

References

1. Bailey, D.H., Barszcz, E., Barton, J.T., Browning, D.S., Carter, R.L., Fatoohi, R.A., Frederickson, P.O., Lasinski, T.A., Simon, H.D., Venkatakrishnan, V., Weeratunga, S.K.: The NAS parallel benchmarks. Int. J. Supercomput. Appl. **5**(3), 63–73 (1991)
2. Callahan, D., Kennedy, K.: Analysis of interprocedural side effects in a parallel programming environment. J. Parallel Distrib. Comput. **5**(5), 517–550 (1988)
3. Cottam, J.A., Holk, E., Byrd, W.E., Chauhan, A., Lumsdaine, A.: High-level coordination specification: operational semantics for kanor. In: Workshop on Leveraging Abstractions and Semantics in High-Performance Computing (LASH-C; Workshop at PPoPP 2013), February 2013
4. Czarnecki, K., O'Donnell, J.T., Striegnitz, J., Taha, W.: DSL implementation in metaocaml, template haskell, and C++. In: Lengauer, C., Batory, D., Blum, A., Odersky, M. (eds.) Domain-Specific Program Generation. LNCS, vol. 3016, pp. 51–72. Springer, Heidelberg (2004)
5. Danalis, A., Pollock, L., Swany, M., Cavazos, J.: Mpi-aware compiler optimizations for improving communication-computation overlap. In Proceedings of the 23rd International Conference on Supercomputing, ICS 2009, pp. 316–325. ACM, New York (2009)
6. Gava, F., Fortin, J.: Formal semantics of a subset of the paderborn's BSPlib. In: Proceedings of the Ninth International Conference on Parallel and Distributed Computing, Applications and Technologies, PDCAT 2008, pp. 269–276. IEEE Computer Society, Washington, DC (2008)
7. Gorlatch, S.: Send-receive considered harmful: myths and realities of message passing. ACM Trans. Program. Lang. Syst. **26**(1), 47–56 (2004)
8. Hoefler, T., Schneider. T.: Runtime detection and optimization of collective communication patterns. In: Proceedings of the 21st International Conference on Parallel Architectures and Compilation Techniques (PACT), pp. 263–272. ACM (2012)
9. Jiao, F., Mahajan, N., Willcocok, J., Chauhan, A., Lumsdaine, A.: Partial globalization of partitioned address spaces for zero copy communication with shared memory. In: Proc. of the 18th International Conference on High Performance Computing (HiPC) (2011). doi:10.1109/HiPC.2011.6152733
10. Ragan-Kelley, J., Adams, A., Paris, S., Levoy, M., Amarasinghe, S., Durand, F.: Decoupling algorithms from schedules for easy optimization of image processing pipelines. ACM Trans. Graph. **31**(4), 32:1–32:12 (2012)
11. Valiant, L.G.: Bulk-synchronous parallel computers. In: Reeve, M. (ed.) Parallel Processing and Artificial Intelligence, pp. 15–22. John Wiley & Sons (1989)

Parallel Applications and Data Structures

PNNU: Parallel Nearest-Neighbor Units
for Learned Dictionaries

H.T. Kung[(✉)], Bradley McDanel, and Surat Teerapittayanon

Harvard University, Cambridge, MA 02138, USA
kung@harvard.edu, mcdanel@fas.harvard.edu, steerapi@seas.harvard.edu

Abstract. We present a novel parallel approach, *parallel nearest neighbor unit* (PNNU), for finding the nearest member in a learned dictionary of high-dimensional features. This is a computation fundamental to machine learning and data analytics algorithms such as sparse coding for feature extraction. PNNU achieves high performance by using three techniques: (1) PNNU employs a novel fast table look up scheme to identify a small number of atoms as candidates from which the nearest neighbor of a query data vector can be found; (2) PNNU reduces computation cost by working with candidate atoms of reduced dimensionality; and (3) PNNU performs computations in parallel over multiple cores with low inter-core communication overheads. Based on efficient computation via techniques (1) and (2), technique (3) attains further speed up via parallel processing. We have implemented PNNU on multi-core machines. We demonstrate its superior performance on three application tasks in signal processing and computer vision. For an action recognition task, PNNU achieves 41x overall performance gains on a 16-core compute server against a conventional serial implementation of nearest neighbor computation. Our PNNU software is available online as open source.

Keywords: Nearest neighbor · NNU · PNNU · Data analytics · Sparse coding · Learned dictionary · Parallel processing · Multi-core programming · Speedup · Matching pursuit · Signal processing · Computer vision · KTH · CIFAR

1 Introduction

In the era of big data, the need for high-performance solutions to support data-driven modeling and prediction has never been greater. In this paper, we consider parallel solutions to the nearest neighbor (NN) problem: given a set of data points and a query point in a high-dimensional vector space, find the data point that is nearest to the query point. NN is used in many data applications. For example, NN (or its extension of finding k nearest neighbors, kNN) is used to identify best-matched patterns in a set of templates [13]. NN also serves as an inner loop in popular feature-extraction algorithms such as matching pursuit (MP) [11] and orthogonal matching pursuit (OMP) [19].

© Springer International Publishing Switzerland 2016
X. Shen et al. (Eds.): LCPC 2015, LNCS 9519, pp. 223–237, 2016.
DOI: 10.1007/978-3-319-29778-1_14

A key operation in NN is the vector dot-product computation which computes the "closeness" of two vectors under cosine similarity. Exhaustive search of data points to find the largest dot-product value with the query point can quickly become prohibitively expensive as data size and dimensionality increase.

Developing efficient NN solutions for general data sets is known to be a challenging task. There is a vast amount of literature on this topic, including k-d trees [21], locality sensitive hashing [3], and nearest-neighbor methods in machine learning and computer vision [18]. For high-dimensional data, most methods in the literature usually do not outperform exhaustive NN search [6]. This is due to the fact that, in practical applications, the high-dimensional data space is commonly only sparsely populated. In our experiments, we find that this observation often holds for even a moderate dimensionality, such as 30.

In this paper, we consider parallel computing approaches to NN for applications in machine learning and data analytics. Particularly, we consider the problem of finding the nearest neighbor in a *dictionary* of atoms (features) learned from training data. We present a novel parallel scheme, *parallel nearest neighbor unit* (PNNU), offering a high-performance NN solution to this problem. By exploiting data characteristics associated with a learned dictionary, such as the dominance of a small number of principal components, PNNU realizes its high performance with three techniques:

T1. reducing the number of required dot-product computations,
T2. reducing the dimensionality in each dot-product computation, and
T3. parallel processing with low inter-core communication overheads.

For T1, we use a fast table look up scheme to identify a small subset of dictionary atoms as *candidates*. By carrying out dot-product computations only with these candidates, the query vector can quickly find its nearest neighbor or a close approximation. Our look-up tables are based on principal component analysis (PCA). For accurate candidates identification, we apply PCA to dictionary atoms rather than the original data set from which the dictionary is learned. The construction and usage of this fast table look up scheme is novel. For T2, we apply the same PCA technique to reduce dimensionality of the candidate atoms to lower the cost of computing their dot-products with the query vector. Finally, for T3, we show that multiple cores can each work on scalar projections of dictionary atoms on their respective dimensions independently without inter-core communication until the very end of the PNNU computation. At the very end, a simple and inexpensive reduction operation among multiple cores is carried out. The parallel processing enabled by T3 results in substantial speed-up gains on the already efficient computation brought by T1 and T2. Thus, PNNU does not suffer from a common drawback in parallel processing that good speedups are obtained only on more parallelizable but less efficient computations. We have implemented PNNU with these techniques in software for multicore computers, and our code is available as open source for public research use [10]. PNNU is written in C++ and contains language bindings and examples for Python and MATLAB making it simple to integrate into existing codebases.

2   Background: Learned Dictionaries and Spare Coding

A data-driven modeling and prediction task, such as those considered in this paper, generally involves two phases. The first phase is feature extraction, where we use clustering methods such as K-means and K-SVD [1] to learn a dictionary where atoms (features) are cluster centroids. These atoms are the most occurring, representative features of the data. The second phase is classification/regression, where we compute a sparse representation, via *sparse coding*, of an input data vector in the learned dictionary, and then based on the sparse representation perform classification/regression.

Mathematically, sparse coding is an optimization problem expressed as

$$\hat{\mathbf{y}} = \arg\min_{\mathbf{y}} \|\mathbf{x} - \mathbf{D}\mathbf{y}\|_2^2 + \lambda \cdot \psi(\mathbf{y}), \tag{1}$$

where $\mathbf{x}$ is an input data vector, $\mathbf{D}$ is a learned dictionary, $\hat{\mathbf{y}}$ is an sparse representation of $\mathbf{x}$, λ is certain constant and $\psi(\mathbf{y})$ is a sparsity constraint function. The choices of $\psi(y)$ are usually either the L_0-norm $\|\mathbf{y}\|_0$ or the L_1-norm $\|\mathbf{y}\|_1$.

Algorithms for sparse coding include those such as MP and OMP which greedily perform minimization under a L_0-norm constraint, and those such as Basis Pursuit [2] and LARS [4] which perform minimization under a L_1-norm constraint.

The inner loop in these algorithms is the NN problem for a learned dictionary: for a given input vector $\mathbf{x} \in \mathbb{R}^m$, find its nearest feature (atom) $\mathbf{d}_j$ in a $m \times n$ dictionary $\mathbf{D} = [\mathbf{d}_1\ \mathbf{d}_2 \ldots \mathbf{d}_n]$. In machine learning and data analytics applications, $\mathbf{D}$ is generally overcomplete with $m \ll n$, and that m and n can be large, e.g., $m = 100$ and $n = 4000$. In these cases, sparse coding is computationally demanding. The PNNU approach of this paper aims at alleviating this computational problem.

Convolutional neural networks (CNN) and convolutional sparse coding (CSC) have become popular due to their success in many machine learning tasks [9,12]. Interestingly, PNNU can help accelerate CSC. Convolution in CNN with Fast Fourier Transform has a complexity of $O(nm\log(m))$ as compared to $O(nm^2)$ for CSC. With PNNU, CSC's complexity cost is reduced to $O(\alpha\beta m^2)$ with a penalty to accuracy, for small α and β, which is discussed in detail in Sect. 5.

3   Parallel Nearest Neighbor Unit (PNNU)

In this section, we describe *parallel nearest neighbor unit* (PNNU) for a learned dictionary $\mathbf{D}$. The three subsections describe three techniques that make up the PNNU algorithm. The first technique T1 uses the Nearest Neighbor Unit (NNU) to reduce the number of dot-product computations. The second technique T2 reduces the cost of each dot-product computation via dimensionality reduction. The third technique T3 parallelizes NNU. These three techniques work in conjunction for high-performance nearest neighbor computation. That is, the first two techniques improves computation efficiency by reducing total cost of dot-product computations while the last technique further reduces the processing time via parallel processing.

3.1   Technique T1 (NNU): Identification of Candidates for Reducing Dot-Product Computations

Technique T1 concerns a novel table look-up method for identifying a small number of candidate atoms in $\mathbf{D}$ from which the nearest neighbor of a query data vector or a close approximation can be found. We call this the *nearest neighbor unit* or NNU. As Fig. 1 depicts, the naive exhaustive search involves $O(n)$ dot-product computations while NNU's candidate approach reduces this number to $O(m)$. This saving is significant for overcomplete dictionaries with $m \ll n$. As described below, the technique is divided into two steps: offline table preparation and online candidates identification.

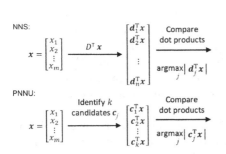

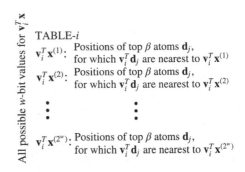

Fig. 1. A contrast between the naive exhaustive search and the NNU's candidates approach in the number of dot-product computations. The k candidates are a subset of D which are selected by NNU. Increasing the α and β parameters in NNU increases k, where $k \leq \alpha \cdot \beta$.

Fig. 2. Offline table preparation of content for TABLE-i associated with the top principal component $\mathbf{v}_i$ of $\mathbf{D}$ for $i = 1, 2, \ldots, \alpha$. For each possible w-bit value W for $\mathbf{v}_i^T\mathbf{x}$ the dictionary positions of the β atoms for which their scalar projections on $\mathbf{v}_i$ are nearest to W are stored at table location W.

NNULookup Table Preparation. We first compute principal components $\mathbf{V}$ for $\mathbf{D}$ by performing PCA [7] on $\mathbf{D}$, that is, $\mathbf{DD}^T = \mathbf{V}\mathbf{\Sigma}\mathbf{V}^T$ for a diagonal $\mathbf{\Sigma}$. We then form a sub-matrix $\mathbf{V}_\alpha$ of $\mathbf{V}$ by including the top α principal components for some $\alpha = O(m)$, which together explain the majority of data variations in $\mathbf{D}$, that is, $\mathbf{V}_\alpha^T = \left[\mathbf{v}_1^T, \mathbf{v}_2^T, \ldots, \mathbf{v}_m^T\right]^T$.

Based on $\mathbf{D}$ and $\mathbf{V}_\alpha$, we prepare content for α tables using $\mathbf{V}_\alpha^T\mathbf{D}$. As depicted in Fig. 2, for TABLE-i corresponding to $\mathbf{v}_i$, $i = 1, \ldots, \alpha$, we map each possible w-bit value of $\mathbf{v}_i^T\mathbf{x}$ to the dictionary positions of the β atoms $\mathbf{d}_j$, for which $\mathbf{v}_i^T\mathbf{d}_j$ are nearest to the $\mathbf{v}_i^T\mathbf{x}$ value.

To contain the table size, we aim for a small bit width w in representing $\mathbf{v}_i^T\mathbf{x}$. Specifically, we use the 16-bit IEEE 754 half-precision floating-point data type for all of our experimental results. Empirically, we have found that for many practical applications such as object classification for tens or hundreds of classes, $w = 16$ is sufficient. In this case, the tables can be easily fit in the main memory or even the L3 cache (4–8 MB) of today's laptops. However, this is no inherent restriction on the data type stored in the table and w can be increased when higher precision is required.

Note that our use of PCA here departs from the conventional application of PCA where principal components are computed from the raw data set, rather than the dictionary learned from this data set. Since dictionary atoms are cluster centroids learned by clustering methods such as K-means, they are denoised representation of the data. As a result, when PCA is applied to dictionary atoms, a smaller percentage of principal components can capture most of variations in the data, as compared to PCA applied to the raw data directly. This is illustrated by Fig. 3. The top 10 eigenvalues of the learned dictionary explain over 80.7 % of the variance, compared to 49.3 % for the raw data. Moreover, as shown in Table 1, NNU with applying PCA on a learned dictionary rather than the raw data gives results of substantially higher accuracy for an action recognition task. The use of PCA in this way, using the projection between $\mathbf{V}_\alpha$ and an input vector $\mathbf{x}$ to build a fast look up table, is novel and one of the largest contributions of this paper. (We note a similar use of PCA in [5] for a different purpose of preserving pairwise dot products of sparse code under dimensionality reduction).

NNULookup Algorithm. Given an input vector $\mathbf{x}$ we are interested in finding its nearest atom in $\mathbf{D}$. We first prepare search keys for $\mathbf{x}$, that is, $\mathbf{V}_\alpha^T \mathbf{x} = \left[\mathbf{v}_1^T \mathbf{x}, \mathbf{v}_2^T \mathbf{x}, \ldots \mathbf{v}_m^T \mathbf{x} \right]^T$. Next, for $i = 1, 2, \ldots, \alpha$, we use a w-bit representation of $\mathbf{v}_i^T \mathbf{x}$ as a key into TABLE-i, as depicted in Fig. 4. Note that these α table look

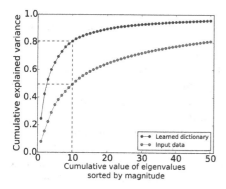

Fig. 3. Cumulative variance explained by PCA applied to the learned dictionary and raw input data for the action recognition task described in Sect. 5.1. The eigenvalues are sorted by magnitude and cumulatively summed to show total explained variance.

Table 1. Accuracy results of PNNU(α,β), for different α and β configurations, for the action recognition task described in Sect. 5.1 when applying PCA on a learned dictionary (PCA-D) versus applying PCA on the raw data (PCA-X).

	PCA-X	PCA-D
PNNU(1,1)	64.20 %	82.70 %
PNNU(1,5)	79.20 %	87.30 %
PNNU(1,10)	80.30 %	89.60 %
PNNU(5,1)	78.60 %	87.90 %
PNNU(5,5)	83.20 %	92.50 %
PNNU(5,10)	86.70 %	90.80 %
PNNU(10,1)	79.80 %	86.70 %
PNNU(10,5)	87.30 %	90.20 %
PNNU(10,10)	89.00 %	90.80 %

ups can be done independently in parallel, enabling straightforward parallelization (see Sect. 3.3). Finally, we identify candidates for the nearest neighbor of $\mathbf{x}$
by taking the union of the results from all α tables as illustrated in Fig. 5 for
$\alpha = 3$. Note that taking a union with the "OR" operator is amenable to efficient
hardware and software implementations.

For a given α and β, our table-lookup method will yield at most $\alpha\beta$ candidates. Increasing α and β will raise the probability that identified candidate
atoms will include the nearest neighbor. In Sect. 4 we show that this probability approaches 1 as α and β increase. Since tables can be accessed in parallel
(see Sect. 3.3 for PNNU), increasing α does not incur additional look up time
beyond the final low-cost reduction step. Additionally, since each look up produces β neighbors at the same time from each table, increasing β does not incur
additional look up time beyond the cost of outputting β values for the union
operation of Fig. 5.

$v_1^T x$ --→ TABLE-1: Positions of β atoms d for which $v_1^T d$ is nearest to $v_1^T x$

$v_2^T x$ --→ TABLE-2: Positions of β atoms d for which $v_2^T d$ is nearest to $v_2^T x$

$\vdots$

$v_\alpha^T x$ --→ TABLE-α: Positions of β atoms d for which $v_\alpha^T d$ is nearest to $v_\alpha^T x$

Atoms		1	2	3	4	5
Candidates			x	x	x	
Pooling with "OR"	⇑	⇑	⇑	⇑	⇑	⇑
TABLE-1			x	x		
TABLE-2			x		x	
TABLE-3			x	x		

Fig. 4. Online retrieval of content from tables.

Fig. 5. The union operation: pooling results from 3 tables with the "OR" operator.

3.2   Technique T2: Dimension Reduction for Minimizing the Cost of Each Dot-Product Computation

By technique T1, we can identify a set of candidate atoms that have a high
likelihood of containing the nearest neighbor of an input vector $\mathbf{x}$. Among these
candidate atoms, we will find the closest one to $\mathbf{x}$. The straightforward approach
is to compute the dot product between $\mathbf{x}$ and each candidate atom. In this
subsection, we describe technique T2 based on dimension reduction using the
same PCA on $\mathbf{D}$ as in technique T1, now for the purpose of lowering the cost
of each dot-product computation. For example, suppose that the original atoms
are of dimensionality 500, and after PCA we keep only their scalar projections
onto the top 10 principal components. Then a dot-product computation would
now incur only 10 multiplications and 9 additions, rather than the original 500
multiplications and 499 additions. Note that it is also possible to apply PCA
on raw data $\mathbf{X}$, but applying PCA on $\mathbf{D}$ is more natural to our approach, and
produces superior results on application accuracy as we demonstrate in Sect. 5.

Since PCA dimensionality reduction is a lossy operation, it is inevitable that
dot-products over reduced-dimension vectors will lower the accuracy of the

application result. In practice, we keep the top principal components whose eigenvalues can contribute to over 80 % of the total for all eigenvalues. In this case, as results in Sect. 5 demonstrate, the impact on accuracy loss is expected to be acceptable for typical applications we are interested in.

Note that in the preceding subsection, we use PCA to identify candidates. In this subsection, we use the same PCA to reduce dimensionality. These are two different usages of PCA. The former usage is novel in its role of supporting fast table look up for NNU, while the latter usage is conventional.

3.3 Technique T3: Parallel Processing with Low Inter-core Communication Overheads

This subsection describes the third technique making up PNNU. The NNU algorithm of technique T1 leads naturally to parallel processing. We can perform table-lookup operations for α dimensions in parallel on a multi-core machine. That is, for $i = 1, 2, \ldots, \alpha$, core i performs the following operations for an input data vector $\mathbf{x}$: (1) compute $\mathbf{v}_i^T \mathbf{x}$, (2) look up β values from table i based on $\mathbf{v}_i^T \mathbf{x}$, (3) compute β dot-product computations or reduced-dimension dot-product computations between the candidate dictionary atoms and $\mathbf{x}$, and (4) output the candidate atom which yields the maximum dot-product value on the ith dimension.

The final reduction step is performed across all cores (dimensions) to find the dictionary atom which yields the maximum dot-product value. We note that the table look-ups from multiple tables are carried out in parallel, so are the corresponding dot-product computations or reduced-dimension dot-product computations. We also note that this parallel scheme incurs little to no inter-core communication overhead, except at the final reduction step where α candidate atoms are reduced to a single atom that has the maximum dot-product value with $\mathbf{x}$. In Sect. 5, experiments show that this low communication overhead leads to large parallel speedups.

4 Probabilistic Analysis of PNNU

In this section, we analyze the probability P that for a given query vector $\mathbf{x}$, the PNNU algorithm finds the nearest neighbor $\mathbf{d}$ in a dictionary $\mathbf{D}$. Let $\mathbf{v}_1, \mathbf{v}_2, \ldots, \mathbf{v}_\alpha$ be the α top principal components of $\mathbf{D}$. We show that the probability P approaches 1 as α and β increase, satisfying a certain condition.

For a given $\epsilon \in (0, 1)$, let β_i be the least number of the nearest neighbors of $\mathbf{v}_i^T \mathbf{x}$ such that the probability that $\mathbf{v}_i^T \mathbf{d}$ is not any of the β_i nearest neighbors of $\mathbf{v}_i^T \mathbf{x}$ is less than or equal to ϵ. Given an α, for $i = 1, \ldots, \alpha$, let Y_i be an event that $\mathbf{v}_i^T \mathbf{d}$ is not any of the β nearest neighbors of $\mathbf{v}_i^T \mathbf{x}$, where $\beta = \max_{1 \leq i \leq \alpha} \beta_i$. Therefore, $\Pr(Y_i) \leq \epsilon$. Assume that Y_i are mutually independent. Then, we have $P = 1 - \Pr\left(\bigcap_{i=1}^{\alpha} Y_i\right) = 1 - \prod_{i=1}^{\alpha} \Pr(Y_i) \geq 1 - \epsilon^\alpha$. Thus, as α increases, and also β increases accordingly, ϵ^α decreases toward 0 and P approaches 1.

Consider using the parallel processing T3 technique of PNNU. Since we have low inter-core communication overheads, increasing α (the number of cores) does not impact the processing time significantly. Therefore, for a particular application, we can pick an ϵ and keep increasing α, and also β accordingly, until the probability $\Pr(A)$ is high enough.

To simplify the analysis, we have assumed that Y_i are mutually independent. Experimentally, we have found that this assumption holds well. For all experiments reported in this paper, $\Pr\left(\bigcap_{i=1}^{\alpha} Y_i\right)$ and $\prod_{i=1}^{\alpha} \Pr(Y_i)$ are reasonably close empirically. For example, in one experiment, these two numbers are 0.72 and 0.71 and in another experiment, they are 0.47 and 0.45.

5 Experimental Results of PNNU on Three Applications

In this section, we provide empirical performance results for PNNU on three applications: action recognition, object classification and image denoising. All three applications require the nearest neighbor computation. We replace the nearest neighbor computation with PNNU(α,β), where α, β denote different parameter configurations of PNNU. All experiments are run on a compute server using two Intel Xeon E5-2680 CPUs, with a total of 16 physical cores.

Algorithms to Compare. We consider both PNNU and PNNU without technique T2 (PNNU-no-T2). The latter involves more dot-product computations, but yields better application accuracy. We compare PNNU and PNNU-no-T2 (both serial and parallel implementations) with three other algorithms:

1. Straightforward method (S). This is the straightforward exhaustive search algorithm to find the nearest neighbor in terms of the cosine distance. If the input data vector is $\mathbf{x}$ and candidate atoms are the columns of $\mathbf{D}$, we compute $\mathbf{D}^T\mathbf{x}$. We call its serial implementation S. This method is the only algorithm in the comparison that is guaranteed to find the nearest neighbor of $\mathbf{x}$ in $\mathbf{D}$.
2. PCA-dimensional-reduction-on-dictionary (PCAonD(α)). For dimensionality reduction, we first perform PCA on $\mathbf{D}$ to get its top α principal components $\mathbf{V}_D^T$, that is, $\mathbf{D}\mathbf{D}^T = \mathbf{V}_\mathbf{D}\boldsymbol{\Sigma}\mathbf{V}_\mathbf{D}^T$ for some diagonal $\boldsymbol{\Sigma}$. Then during computation, instead of computing $\mathbf{D}^T\mathbf{x}$, we compute dot products $(\mathbf{V}_D^T\mathbf{D})^T(\mathbf{V}_D^T\mathbf{x})$ of reduced dimensionality. Note the parameter α specifies dimensionality of dot-product computations after PCA dimension reduction. In these experiments, we use $\alpha = 10$.
3. PCA-dimensional-reduction-on-data (PCAonX(α)). This is the same as the previous algorithm, but instead we compute PCA on the input data $\mathbf{X}$. Let $\mathbf{V}_X^T$ contain the top α principal components. We compute $(\mathbf{V}_X^T\mathbf{D})^T(\mathbf{V}_X^T\mathbf{x})$. Note the parameter α specifies the dimensionality of dot-product computations after PCA dimension reduction. We use $\alpha = 10$.

Performance Measures. We compare algorithms in terms of the following performance related measures, where an algorithm Y can be S, PCAonD, PCAonX, PNNU or PNNU-no-T2:

N: The number of arithmetic operations per query vector. This is the number of addition and multiplication operations each algorithm performs for a single query vector. For S, a dot-product between a query vector $\mathbf{x} \in \mathbb{R}^m$ and a dictionary $\mathbf{D} \in \mathbb{R}^{m \times n}$ incurs $n(2m - 1)$ arithmetic operations (nm for the multiplication and $n(m - 1)$ for the addition). For PCAonD(α) and PCAonX(α), it is $n(2\alpha - 1)$. For PNNU(α,β), it is bounded above by $\alpha\beta(2\alpha - 1)$. For PNNU-no-T2(α,β), it is bounded above by $\alpha\beta(2m - 1)$.

G: Efficiency gain. For an algorithm Y, its efficiency gain is the number of arithmetic operations of the straightforward method (N_S) over that of the algorithm Y (N_Y): N_S/N_Y.

T_s: Serial processing wall clock time in seconds. This is the time it takes for the serial implementation of the algorithm to run.

U_s: Serial speedup of an algorithm Y over the serial straightforward method. It is the wall clock serial execution time of the straightforward method over that of algorithm Y: T_{sS}/T_{sY}. This is a run-time realization of the theoretical efficiency gain G.

T_p: Parallel processing wall clock time in seconds. This is the time it takes for the parallel implementation of the algorithm to run.

U_p: Parallel-over-serial speedup. This is the parallel scaling performance of the algorithm. It is T_s/T_p.

U_t: Total performance gain of an algorithm Y over the serial implementation of the straightforward method: $T_{sS}/T_{pY} = U_s \times U_p$.

Q: Quality metric which is defined per application. For action recognition and object classification, we report the recognition/classification accuracy on the test set, i.e., the percentage of times the algorithm predicts the correct class labels. For image denoising, we report the peak signal-to-noise ratio (PSNR).

Performance Highlights. For each application, we will highlight the following points in our performance analysis:

1. A comparison of how PNNU performs compared to the simple PCA methods (PCAonX and PCAonD).
2. The algorithm and setting with the best quality metric (Q) compared to the straightforward method.
3. The algorithm and setting with the best total performance gain (U_t).

In the following we will explicitly mention these highlighted points for each application, and mark them with bold faces in the tables which report experiment results.

5.1 Application A1: Action Recognition

For the action recognition task we use a standard benchmark dataset, the KTH dataset [17], which is a video dataset consisting of 25 subjects where in each video a single subject is performing one of six actions (walking, jogging, running, boxing, hand waving and hand clapping). The dataset is split on subjects into a training and testing set. Features are extracted from each video using the same method as described in [20]. Features from each video consist of a variable number of columns, where each column is a 150-long feature vector. K-means is then performed on the training set to learn a dictionary of size 1000. Finally, each column from every video is then encoded with the learned dictionary using either conventional dot product or our PNNU approach. Each column is given a single atom assignment, and for a given video these column assignments are aggregated using a bag-of-words model. An SVM classifier with chi-squared kernel is then trained on the bag-of-words representation in order to obtain prediction results.

Table 2. The experiment results for the KTH dataset.

Algorithm	N	G	T_s	U_s	T_p	U_p	U_t	Q
S	299,000	1	692.89	1.00	108.48	6.39	6.39	**94.20 %**
PCAonX(10)	19,000	16	129.25	5.36	13.15	9.83	52.69	**77.50 %**
PCAonD(10)	19,000	16	128.40	5.40	13.24	9.70	52.34	**77.50 %**
PNNU-no-T2(1,1)	299	1,000	7.39	93.75	9.80	0.75	70.71	82.70 %
PNNU-no-T2(1,10)	2,990	100	28.80	24.06	20.41	1.41	33.94	89.60 %
PNNU-no-T2(5,1)	1,495	200	22.91	30.24	12.44	1.84	55.71	87.90 %
PNNU-no-T2(5,5)	7,475	**40**	75.30	**9.20**	16.73	**4.50**	41.41	**92.50 %**
PNNU-no-T2(5,10)	14,950	20	140.23	4.94	22.90	6.12	30.26	90.80 %
PNNU-no-T2(10,1)	2,990	100	19.24	36.01	10.44	1.84	66.35	86.70 %
PNNU-no-T2(10,10)	29,900	10	260.30	2.66	24.99	10.42	27.73	90.80 %
PNNU(1,1)	1	299,000	6.36	108.96	5.73	1.11	**120.95**	82.70 %
PNNU(1,10)	10	29,900	15.75	43.99	6.91	2.28	100.29	78.00 %
PNNU(5,1)	45	6,644	15.56	44.54	8.05	1.93	86.08	85.50 %
PNNU(5,5)	225	1,329	44.64	15.52	8.16	5.47	84.95	83.80 %
PNNU(5,10)	450	664	80.87	8.57	8.98	9.01	77.16	84.40 %
PNNU(10,1)	190	1,574	27.33	25.35	9.53	2.87	72.69	83.80 %
PNNU(10,10)	1,900	157	162.95	4.25	10.69	15.24	64.79	87.30 %

Table 2 shows the experiment results for the KTH dataset. The straightforward method, denoted as S, achieves the highest accuracy (Q) of 94.20 %. PCAonX(10) and PCAonD(10) both achieve accuracy (Q) of 77.50 %, which is in general substantially lower than PNNU configurations. Additionally, many PNNU configurations are strictly better in terms of both quality (Q) and total performance gain (U_t).

PNNU-no-T2(5,5) has an accuracy of 92.50 %, the closest to that of S, with an efficiency gain (G) of 40. This translates into a serial speedup (U_s) of 9.20x (the difference between G and U_s is due to both run-time overhead and G only counting arithmetic operations). The parallel speedup (U_p) is 4.50x, for a total performance gain (U_t) of 41.41x over the serial implementation of S.

Notably, PNNU(1,1) achieves the highest total performance gain (U_t) of 120.95x with accuracy (Q) of 82.70 %. This trade-off is good for applications that can accept a small reduction in quality in order to significantly reduce running time. As expected, PNNU-no-T2 achieves higher accuracy than PNNU at the expense of increased running time. We note this trend in other applications as well.

Though in general increasing α and β improves Q, it is not always the case. For instance, we observe a drop of 1.7 % in Q when going from PNNU-no-T2(5,5) to PNNU-no-T2(5,10). The reason for this is explained in the following example. Suppose given an input sample $\mathbf{x}$, the nearest atom to $\mathbf{x}$ is $\mathbf{d}^*$. Increasing β from 5 to 10 leads to finding the candidate atom $\mathbf{d}_{\beta=10}$ that is nearer to $\mathbf{x}$ than the candidate atom $\mathbf{d}_{\beta=5}$. Nonetheless, there is a chance that $\mathbf{d}_{\beta=10}$ is further away from $\mathbf{d}^*$ than $\mathbf{d}_{\beta=5}$. This results in the drop in Q. In general, when $\mathbf{x}$ is already close to $\mathbf{d}^*$, this phenomenon is unlikely to happen.

5.2   Matching Pursuit Algorithm with PNNU

The object classification and image denoising tasks rely on computing sparse codes. Before going into those applications, we introduce MP (Algorithm 1), the sparse coding algorithm that we use to compute sparse representations for these tasks. We modify the nearest neighbor computation section of MP to use PNNU and obtain MP-PNNU (Algorithm 2). For comparison with other algorithms, we just replace PNNU routine with other algorithms' routines of finding the nearest neighbor.

Algorithm 1. MP

1: **Input**: data vector $\mathbf{x}$, dictionary $\mathbf{D} = [\mathbf{d}_i, \ldots, \mathbf{d}_n]$, and the number of iterations L
2: **Output**: sparse code $\mathbf{y}$
3: $\mathbf{r} \leftarrow \mathbf{x}$
4: **for** $t = 1\ L$ **do**
5:    $i \leftarrow \arg\max |\mathbf{D}^T \mathbf{r}|$
6:    $y_i \leftarrow \mathbf{d}_i^T \mathbf{r}$
7:    $\mathbf{r} \leftarrow \mathbf{r} - y_i \mathbf{d}_i$
8: **end for**

Algorithm 2. MP-PNNU

1: **Input**: data vector $\mathbf{x}$, dictionary $\mathbf{D} = [\mathbf{d}_i, \ldots, \mathbf{d}_n]$, orthonormal basis $\mathbf{V}$, the number of iterations L, and PNNU
2: **Output**: sparse code $\mathbf{y}$
3: $\mathbf{r} \leftarrow \mathbf{x}$
4: **for** $t = 1\ L$ **do**
5:    $\mathbf{v} \leftarrow \mathbf{V}^T \mathbf{r}$
6:    $\mathbf{C} \leftarrow \text{PNNU}(\mathbf{v})$
7:    $j \leftarrow \arg\max |\mathbf{C}^T \mathbf{r}|$
8:    $i \leftarrow i$ s.t. $\mathbf{d}_i = \mathbf{c}_j$
9:    $y_i \leftarrow \mathbf{d}_i^T \mathbf{r}$
10:    $\mathbf{r} \leftarrow \mathbf{r} - y_i \mathbf{d}_i$
11: **end for**

The MP algorithm finds the column $\mathbf{d}_j$ in the dictionary $\mathbf{D}$ which is best aligned with data vector $\mathbf{x}$. Then, the scalar projection y_j along this $\mathbf{d}_j$ direction is removed from $\mathbf{x}$ and the residual $\mathbf{r} = \mathbf{x} - y_j \mathbf{d}_j$ is obtained. The algorithm proceeds in each iteration by choosing the next column $\mathbf{d}_j$ that is best matched with the residual $\mathbf{r}$ until the desired number of iterations is performed. We note that for each iteration, line 5 is the most costly nearest neighbor step. As we noted previously, for a $m \times n$ dictionary $\mathbf{D}$, exhaustive search will incur a cost of $O(mn)$ and thus can become prohibitively expensive when m and n are large. The MP-PNNU algorithm can mitigate this problem. MP-PNNU has the same overall structure as MP, except that in finding the best matched column $\mathbf{d}_j$, it uses the PNNU approach as described in Sect. 3.

5.3   Application A2: Object Classification

For the image object classification task we use the CIFAR-10 image dataset [8], an image dataset of 10 object classes. We randomly select 4,000 images from the training set and evaluate on 1,000 images from the test set (we ensure that the same number of samples are selected from each class). For each image, all 6 by 6 3-color-channel (RGB) patches are extracted sliding by one pixel, and therefore, each vector is 108 dimension long. We learn a 3,000-atom dictionary using K-SVD [1], a generalization of K-means, on the training patches. For encoding, we compare the classic MP (Algorithm 1) with MP-PNNU (Algorithm 2), setting $k = 5$ (number of coefficients) for both algorithms. Finally, we perform a maximum pooling operation over each image to obtain a feature vector. A linear SVM classifier is trained on the obtained training set feature vectors and testing set accuracy results are reported.

Table 3. The experiment results for the CIFAR-10 dataset.

Algorithm	N	G	T_s	U_s	T_p	U_p	U_t	Q
S	645,000	1	3,815.89	1.00	890.37	4.29	4.29	**51.90 %**
PCAonX(10)	57,000	11	1,492.36	2.56	187.27	7.97	20.38	30.40 %
PCAonD(10)	57,000	11	1,600.88	2.38	185.38	8.64	20.58	**33.10 %**
PNNU-no-T2(1,1)	215	3,000	38.2375	99.79	76.1259	0.50	50.13	33.90 %
PNNU-no-T2(1,10)	2,150	300	69.9699	54.54	86.6791	0.81	44.02	41.70 %
PNNU-no-T2(5,1)	1,075	600	65.3232	58.42	80.3086	0.81	47.52	40.20 %
PNNU-no-T2(5,5)	5,375	120	143.894	26.52	93.466	1.54	40.83	42.30 %
PNNU-no-T2(5,10)	10,750	60	241.786	15.78	113.46	2.13	33.63	45.10 %
PNNU-no-T2(10,1)	2,150	300	199.547	19.12	153.835	1.30	24.81	39.40 %
PNNU-no-T2(10,10)	21,500	**30**	971.899	**3.93**	115.558	**8.41**	**33.02**	46.60 %
PNNU(1,1)	1	645,000	76.8262	49.67	68.934	1.11	55.36	33.10 %
PNNU(1,10)	10	64,500	113.847	33.52	72.8819	1.56	52.36	34.10 %
PNNU(5,1)	45	14,333	114.627	33.29	65.21	1.76	**58.52**	37.30 %
PNNU(5,5)	225	2,867	227.224	16.79	85.5631	2.66	44.60	37.30 %
PNNU(5,10)	450	1,433	367.583	10.38	95.8492	3.84	39.81	36.30 %
PNNU(10,1)	190	3,395	165.41	23.07	121.995	1.36	31.28	35.80 %
PNNU(10,10)	1,900	5	724.173	5.27	108.528	6.67	35.16	39.10 %

Table 3 shows the experiment results for the CIFAR-10 dataset. The straightforward method S achieves the highest accuracy (Q) of 51.90 %. (This multi-class classification task is known to be difficult, so the relatively low 51.90 % achieved accuracy is expected for a simple algorithm like this [14].) PCAonX(10) and

PCAonD(10) achieve accuracy of 30.40 % and 33.10 %, respectively. Once again, we see that many PNNU configurations are strictly better in terms of both quality (Q) and total performance gain (U_t). PNNU-no-T2(10,10) has an accuracy of 46.60 %, the closest to that of S, with an efficiency gain (G) of 30. This translates into a serial speedup (U_s) of 3.93x, a parallel speedup (U_p) of 8.41x, for a total performance gain (U_t) of 33.02x over the serial implementation of S. PNNU(5,1) achieves the highest total performance gain (U_t) of 58.52x with accuracy (Q) of 37.30 %.

Table 4. The experiment results for denoising the Lena image.

Algorithm	N	G	T_s	U_s	T_p	U_p	U_t	Q
S	381,000	1	392.92	1.00	39.24	10.01	10.01	**32.34**
PCAonX(10)	57,000	7	48.27	8.14	13.59	3.55	28.90	**31.18**
PCAonD(10)	57,000	7	59.23	6.63	16.78	3.53	23.42	**31.20**
PNNU-no-T2(1,1)	127	3,000	5.98	65.68	5.42	1.10	72.51	25.88
PNNU-no-T2(1,10)	1,270	300	6.79	57.89	8.29	0.82	47.40	27.36
PNNU-no-T2(5,1)	635	600	11.25	34.91	8.66	1.30	45.35	29.05
PNNU-no-T2(5,5)	3,175	120	22.95	17.12	8.06	2.85	48.74	30.95
PNNU-no-T2(5,10)	6,350	60	35.85	10.96	10.47	3.42	37.53	31.58
PNNU-no-T2(10,1)	1,270	300	8.22	47.82	7.55	1.09	52.03	29.84
PNNU-no-T2(10,10)	12,700	**30**	31.46	**12.49**	7.53	**4.18**	**52.16**	**32.19**
PNNU(1,1)	1	381,000	4.55	86.33	4.89	0.93	**80.34**	**25.71**
PNNU(1,10)	10	38,100	5.64	69.61	5.28	1.07	74.41	25.80
PNNU(5,1)	45	8,467	6.77	58.07	5.42	1.25	72.45	28.71
PNNU(5,5)	225	1,693	11.14	35.28	5.49	2.03	71.60	29.87
PNNU(5,10)	450	847	14.88	26.41	5.68	2.62	69.23	30.17
PNNU(10,1)	190	2,005	6.76	58.11	5.26	1.29	74.75	29.67
PNNU(10,10)	1,900	201	25.96	15.13	5.96	4.36	65.95	31.64

5.4 Application A3: Image Denoising

In the previous subsections, we have shown that PNNU works well for classification problems. In this subsection, we showcase its performance at reconstruction, specifically, removing noise from an image of Lena [15]. First, a noisy version of the Lena image is generated by adding Gaussian noise with zero mean and standard deviation 0.1. This noisy image is then patched in the same manner as described in the previous subsection, using 8 by 8 grayscale patches, creating 64-dimensional vectors. These patches (roughly 250,000) are then used to learn a dictionary of 3,000 atoms using K-SVD with the number of sparse coefficients set to 5. The denoising process consists of encoding each patch with either MP or MP-PNNU. After encoding, each patch is represented as a sparse feature vector (sparse representation). To recover a denoised version of the input signal, the dot-product between the sparse vectors and learned dictionary is computed. Finally, the recovered patches are each averaged over a local area to form the denoised image. For our quality measure (Q), we report the peak signal-to-noise ratio (PSNR). A PSNR for a 8-bit per pixel image that is acceptable to human perception ranges between 20 dB and 40 dB [16].

Table 4 shows the experiment results for denoising the Lena image. From the table, we see that S achieves the highest PSNR (Q) of 32.34. PCAonX(10) and PCAonD(10) achieve similar PSNR of 31.18 and 31.20 respectively. In contrast with the other two applications, both algorithms perform reasonably well for this application. PNNU-no-T2(10,10) has PNSR (Q) of 32.19, the closest to that of S, with a G of 30, translating into a 12.49x speedup (U_s). Its parallel implementation (U_p) adds another 4.18x speedup, for a total performance gain (U_t) of 52.16x. Notably, PNNU(1,1) achieves the highest total performance gain (U_t) of 80.34x with PSNR (Q) of 25.71. This is good for scenarios where a rougher denoising result is acceptable for a significant gain in performance.

6 Conclusion

In this paper, we have described how nearest-neighbor (NN) is a key function for data analytics computations such as sparse coding. To enhance the performance of the NN computation, we have taken three orthogonal techniques: (T1) reduce the number of required dot-product operations; (T2) lower the cost of each dot-product computation by reducing dimensionality; and (T3) perform parallel computations over multiple cores. Noting that the gains from (T1), (T2) and (T3) complement each other, we have proposed a *parallel nearest neighbor unit* (PNNU) algorithm which uses a novel fast table look up, parallelized over multiple dimensions, to identify a relatively small number of dictionary atoms as candidates. Only these candidates are used to perform reduced-dimension dot products. PNNU allows the dot-product computations for these candidates to be carried out in parallel. As noted in Sect. 3.1, a key to the success of the PNNU approach is our application of PCA to dictionary atoms, rather than raw data vectors as in conventional PCA applications. This use of PCA to build a table lookup for the purpose of identifying the nearest candidate atom is novel.

We have validated the PNNU approach on multi-core computers with several application tasks including action recognition, image classification and image denoising. Substantial total performance gains (e.g., 41x) are achieved by software implementations of PNNU without compromising the accuracy required by the applications.

Other potential applications for PNNU are abundant. For example, large-scale data-driven deep learning can benefit from reduced dot product requirements in its computation. Mobile computing can benefit from speed and energy efficient implementation of sparse coding resulting from PNNU to allow sophisticated learning on client devices. In the future, we expect to implement PNNU as a hardware accelerator which can further speed up NN computations. In addition, we will explore integrated use of PNNU in conjunction with GPU accelerators.

Acknowledgments. This work is supported in part by gifts from the Intel Corporation and in part by the Naval Postgraduate School Agreement No. N00244-15-0050 awarded by the Naval Supply Systems Command.

References

1. Aharon, M., Elad, M., Bruckstein, A.: K-SVD: an algorithm for designing over-complete dictionaries for sparse representation. IEEE Trans. Sig. Process. **54**(11), 4311–4322 (2006)
2. Chen, S.S., Donoho, D.L., Saunders, M.A.: Atomic decomposition by basis pursuit. SIAM J. Sci. Comput. **20**(1), 33–61 (1998)
3. Datar, M., Immorlica, N., Indyk, P., Mirrokni, V.S.: Locality-sensitive hashing scheme based on p-stable distributions. In: Proceedings of the Twentieth Annual Symposium on Computational Geometry, pp. 253–262. ACM (2004)
4. Efron, B., Hastie, T., Johnstone, I., Tibshirani, R., et al.: Least angle regression. Ann. Stat. **32**(2), 407–499 (2004)
5. Gkioulekas, I.A., Zickler, T.: Dimensionality reduction using the sparse linear model. In: Advances in Neural Information Processing Systems, pp. 271–279 (2011)
6. Indyk, P.: Nearest neighbors in high-dimensional spaces (2004)
7. Jolliffe, I.: Principal component analysis. Wiley Online Library (2002)
8. Krizhevsky, A., Hinton, G.: Learning multiple layers of features from tiny images. Technical report, Computer Science Department, University of Toronto (2009)
9. Krizhevsky, A., Sutskever, I., Hinton, G.E.: Imagenet classification with deep convolutional neural networks. In: Advances in Neural Information Processing Systems, pp. 1097–1105 (2012)
10. Kung, H., McDanel, B., Teerapittayanon, S.: NNU Source Repository. https://gitlab.com/steerapi/nnu
11. Mallat, S.G., Zhang, Z.: Matching pursuits with time-frequency dictionaries. IEEE Trans. Signal Process. **41**(12), 3397–3415 (1993)
12. Mathieu, M., Henaff, M., LeCun, Y.: Fast training of convolutional networks through ffts. arXiv preprint arxiv:1312.5851 (2013)
13. Peterson, L.E.: K-nearest neighbor. Scholarpedia **4**(2), 1883 (2009)
14. Rifai, S., Muller, X., Glorot, X., Mesnil, G., Bengio, Y., Vincent, P.: Learning invariant features through local space contraction. arXiv preprint arxiv:1104.4153 (2011)
15. Roberts, L.: Picture coding using pseudo-random noise. IRE Trans. Inf. Theory **8**(2), 145–154 (1962)
16. Saha, S.: Image compression-from DCT to wavelets: a review. Crossroads **6**(3), 12–21 (2000)
17. Schuldt, C., Laptev, I., Caputo, B.: Recognizing human actions: a local svm approach. In: Proceedings of the 17th International Conference on Pattern Recognition, vol. 3, pp. 32–36 (2004)
18. Shakhnarovich, G., Indyk, P., Darrell, T.: Nearest-Neighbor Methods in Learning and Vision: Theory and Practice. MIT Press, Cambridge (2006)
19. Tropp, J.A., Gilbert, A.C.: Signal recovery from random measurements via orthogonal matching pursuit. IEEE Trans. Inf. Theory **53**(12), 4655–4666 (2007)
20. Wang, H., Klaser, A., Schmid, C., Liu, C.L.: Action recognition by dense trajectories. In: IEEE Conference on Computer Vision and Pattern Recognition, pp. 3169–3176 (2011)
21. Wess, S., Althoff, K.-D., Derwand, G.: Using k-d trees to improve the retrieval step. In: Wess, S., Richter, M., Althoff, K.-D. (eds.) EWCBR 1993. LNCS, vol. 837, pp. 167–181. Springer, Heidelberg (1994)

Coarse Grain Task Parallelization of Earthquake Simulator GMS Using OSCAR Compiler on Various Cc-NUMA Servers

Mamoru Shimaoka[1]([✉]), Yasutaka Wada[1,2], Keiji Kimura[1], and Hironori Kasahara[1]

[1] Advanced Multicore Processor Research Institute, Waseda University, 27 Waseda-machi, Shinjuku-ku, Tokyo 162-0042, Japan
shimaoka@kasahara.cs.waseda.ac.jp, {keiji,kasahara}@waseda.jp
[2] Department of Information Science, Meisei University, 2-1-1 Hodokubo, Hino, Tokyo 191-8506, Japan
yasutaka.wada@meisei-u.ac.jp
http://www.kasahara.elec.waseda.ac.jp/

Abstract. This paper proposes coarse grain task parallelization for a earthquake simulation program using Finite Difference Method to solve the wave equations in 3-D heterogeneous structure or the Ground Motion Simulator (GMS) on various cc-NUMA servers using IBM, Intel and Fujitsu multicore processors. The GMS has been developed by the National Research Institute for Earth Science and Disaster Prevention (NIED) in Japan. Earthquake wave propagation simulations are important numerical applications to save lives through damage predictions of residential areas by earthquakes. Parallel processing with strong scaling has been required to precisely calculate the simulations quickly. The proposed method uses the OSCAR compiler for exploiting coarse grain task parallelism efficiently to get scalable speed-ups with strong scaling. The OSCAR compiler can analyze data dependence and control dependence among coarse grain tasks, such as subroutines, loops and basic blocks. Moreover, locality optimizations considering the boundary calculations of FDM and a new static scheduler that enables more efficient task schedulings on cc-NUMA servers are presented. The performance evaluation shows 110 times speed-up using 128 cores against the sequential execution on a POWER7 based 128 cores cc-NUMA server Hitachi SR16000 VM1, 37.2 times speed-up using 64 cores against the sequential execution on a Xeon E7-8830 based 64 cores cc-NUMA server BS2000, 19.8 times speed-up using 32 cores against the sequential execution on a Xeon X7560 based 32 cores cc-NUMA server HA8000/RS440, 99.3 times speed-up using 128 cores against the sequential execution on a SPARC64 VII based 256 cores cc-NUMA server Fujitsu M9000, 9.42 times speed-up using 12 cores against the sequential execution on a POWER8 based 12 cores cc-NUMA server Power System S812L.

Keywords: Earthquake · GMS · OSCAR · Task parallelism · Compiler · scc-NUMA

© Springer International Publishing Switzerland 2016
X. Shen et al. (Eds.): LCPC 2015, LNCS 9519, pp. 238–253, 2016.
DOI: 10.1007/978-3-319-29778-1_15

1   Introduction

Earthquake simulation that simulates the propagation of seismic waves from hypocenters is important for minimizing the damage by natural disasters. Earthquake wave propagation is often formulated as wave equation, which is approximated by Finite Difference Method (FDM) or Finite Element Method (FEM). The precise simulation usually requires huge calculation time, studies of earthquake simulation have been trying parallelization of the program. Akcelik et al. [1] proposed an FEM earthquake simulation method parallelized by MPI. Their parallelized Simulator using 3000 processor cores showed 80 % parallel efficiency in weak scaling on the AlphaServer SC at the Pittsburgh Supercomputing Center (PSC). Aoi et al. [4] proposed the Ground Motion Simulator (GMS) and parallelized the GMS with GPGPU. They showed the parallelized GMS using 1024 nodes obtained 1028 times speed-up compared to 1 node in weak scaling on the TSUBAME2.0 in Tokyo Institute of Technology. Tiankai et al. [3] proposed the parallel octree meshing tool Octor and showed the evaluations of the parallel Partial Differential Equation (PDE) solver using octree mesh by the Octor on the AlphaServer SC at the PSC. They showed the solver using 2000 processor cores could speed-up earthquake simulation 13 times faster than that of using 128 processor cores in strong scaling. Those works achieve high parallel efficiency by hand parallelization. The hand parallelization needs deep knowledge of parallelization and long development periods and costs. Moreover, most existing studies achieve high parallel efficiency with weak scaling, but high parallel efficiency with strong scaling is more desirable than that with weak scaling. In these days, cache coherent Non Uniform Memory Architecture (cc-NUMA) is common architecture, this architecture requires additional tuning compared to Uniform Memory Architecture. Therefore, parallelization that is efficient on cc-NUMA by an automatic parallelizing compiler is expected for productivity and performance.

This paper proposes a parallelization method that includes modifying a sequential earthquake simulation program into a compiler friendly sequential program to assist automatic parallelization of the OSCAR multigrain parallelizing compiler [5,6]. Unlike the OSCAR multigrain parallelizing compiler, commercial compilers such as Intel Compiler and IBM XL compiler can utilize only loop parallelism. Slight sequential parts prevent us from achieving scalable speed-up in many core architecture. Therefore, multigrain parallelism offered by the OSCAR compiler is important.

In this paper, the proposed method parallelizes the earthquake simulator GMS, coarse grain task parallelism, as well as loop parallelism, is used. A locality optimization considering the boundary calculations of FDM, a locality optimization considering First Touch all over the program and an efficient task scheduling on servers using First Touch policy help to us get strong scaling speed-up.

The remainder of this paper is organized as follows. Section 2 introduces the earthquake wave propagation simulator GMS. Section 3 shows the proposed parallelization method. Section 4 gives speed-ups on five different cc-NUMA servers. The servers consist of the SR16000 VM1 (henceforth SR16000), the BS2000, the HA8000/RS440 (henceforth RS440), the SPARC Enterprise M9000 (henceforth M9000) and the IBM Power System S812L (henceforth S812L). Finally, Sect. 5 provides the conclusion.

2   The Ground Motion Simulator GMS

For effective disaster prevention planning, the importance of precise earthquake simulations is increasing. The Ground Motion Simulator (GMS) is the earthquake simulator developed by Aoi, Fujiwara in the NIED, and the GMS can precisely simulate for Japanese ground structure that we can download at J-SHIS [2]. The GMS consists of parameter generation tools, computation visualization tools and a wave equation solver, and we can download it from the URL in [7].

The GMS solves the wave equations in 3-D heterogeneous structure, and it uses Finite Difference Method to approximate the wave equations. One of the characteristics of the GMS solver is the use of staggered grids. For computation accuracy, grid points for displacement are shifted from grid points for stress a half grid in staggered grids. In staggered grids, second order difference operator is (1).

$$f'_i \simeq \frac{f_{i+1/2} - f_{i-1/2}}{\Delta x} \tag{1}$$

Fourth order difference operator that is higher accuracy than second order difference operator is (2).

$$f'_i \simeq \left(-1/24 f_{i+3/2} + 9/8 f_{i+1/2} \right.$$
$$\left. -9/8 f_{i-1/2} + 1/24 f_{i-3/2}\right)/\Delta x \tag{2}$$

Besides, the GMS solver uses discontinuous grids to accelerate the simulation. In discontinuous grid, as shown in Fig. 1, grids of near the earth's surface or Region I is three times smaller than that of a deeper region or Region II. It is because the grid spacing has to be smaller for precisely simulating waves of shorter wavelength. In the grids near the surface, the wavelength is shorter than that of the deeper region. By using discontinuous grid replace of uniform grid, the GMS solver reduces calculation for the deeper region.

In brief, the GMS solver is to calculate velocity and stress of each grid and each step by using external force as inputs.

In the GMS solver, external force can be added as velocity or stress and second order difference operator or fourth order difference operator can be used. This paper deals with the GMS solver in which external force is added as stress and fourth difference operator is used.

3   Coarse Grain Task Parallelization of the GMS

This section proposes a parallelization method for the GMS. Before parallelization, the sequential GMS solver written in Fortran 90 is changed into a sequential

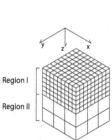

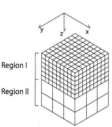

Fig. 1. Discontinuous grid in the GMS

Fig. 2. Macro task graph of the GMS main loop

FORTRAN 77 program. It is because the OSCAR compiler just supports FOR-TRAN 77 and the GMS uses Fortran 90 to use the I/O library HDF [8] though main parts are written in FORTRAN 77.

3.1 Coarse Grain Task Parallelization

This section shows how the OSCAR compiler [5,6] exploits parallelism in a program. The OSCAR compiler can exploit multigrain parallelism that uses loop parallelism, coarse grain task parallelism and statement level fine grain parallelism considering its parallelism. Coarse grain task parallelism in the OSCAR compiler means parallelism among three kinds of coarse grain tasks, namely Basic Blocks (BBs), Repetition Blocks (RBs) and Subroutine Blocks (SBs).

First, the OSCAR compiler decomposes a sequential source program to macro tasks in each nested level hierarchically. Then it makes macroflow graphs which represent data dependency and control flow among the macro tasks. Next, it analyzes and detects parallelism in the macroflow graphs by using Earliest Executable Condition analysis [5] that analyzes the simplest forms of conditions the macro tasks may start their execution considering control dependencies and data dependencies, and then generates macro task graphs. Next, it analyzes and detects parallelism in the macroflow graphs by using Earliest Executable Condition analysis [5] and then generates macro task graphs. Earliest Executable Condition analysis is to analyze the simplest forms of conditions the macro tasks may start their execution considering control dependencies and data dependencies. Macro task graphs represent parallelism among macro tasks. If the macro task graph has only data dependency edge, the macro tasks are assigned by static scheduling to processors or processor groups that are grouped logically by the compiler for hierarchical coarse grain task parallelization. If the macro task graph has any control dependency edges, the macro tasks are assigned to processors or processor groups at runtime by a dynamic scheduler. The dynamic scheduler is generated by the OSCAR compiler exclusively for the program [5] and embedded into the parallelized program automatically. Finally, the OSCAR compiler generates a parallelized Fortran program using the OSCAR API Ver2.0[11], which the ordinary product OpenMP compilers provided for the target machines can compile.

3.2   Modification of the GMS

Figure 2 shows the macro task graph in the main loop of the GMS. The macro task graph was generated by the OSCAR compiler and has 18 macro tasks and one exit task representing the end of the macro task graph. Solid edges in macro task graph represent data dependencies among macro tasks and broken edges in macro task graph represent control dependencies. There is parallelism among coarse grain tasks such as parallelism between SB3 and SB4 in Fig. 2. It is because of discontinuous grids of the GMS. In discontinuous grids, We can execute velocity calculation of the near surface grids or SB3 and velocity calculation of the grids in the deeper area or SB4 in parallel. After that, the boundary of the near surface grids and the grids in the deeper area is executed in SB5. There is similar parallelism for stress calculations. We can execute stress calculation of the near surface grids or SB11 and stress calculation of the grids in deeper area or SB12 in parallel.

Next, to increase coarse grain task parallelism, inline expansion is applied to all subroutines, or SBs in Fig. 2, in the main loop. Figure 3 is the macro task graph with 131 macro tasks for the main loop after the inline expansion of all subroutines. We extract very large coarse grain task parallelism as shown in Fig. 3. It is because coarse grain task parallelism inside the subroutines is taken out to the main loop level. By the inline expansion, task parallelism among the tasks in the SBs with dependency can be used. LOOP3 in Fig. 3 is originally in SB1 in Fig. 2, and DOALL10 in Fig. 3 is originally in SB3 in Fig. 2. Though SB1 and SB3 in Fig. 2 have dependency among them, LOOP3 and DOALL10 in Fig. 3 have no dependency among them. 60 macro tasks are analyzed to be DOALL or parallel loop in Fig. 3. Since we can split each DOALL loop into parallel macro tasks, much larger coarse grain task parallelism can be exploited.

Besides, to enhance loop parallelism and spatial locality, loop interchange and array dimension interchange are applied.

3.3   Data Distribution to Distributed Shared Memories Using First Touch

In cc-NUMA machines, how to distribute variables to memories is important to get good performance. Usually, cc-NUMA machines use first touch policy [12]. On first touch policy, a page is allocated to the memory nearest to the processor that first touched the page.

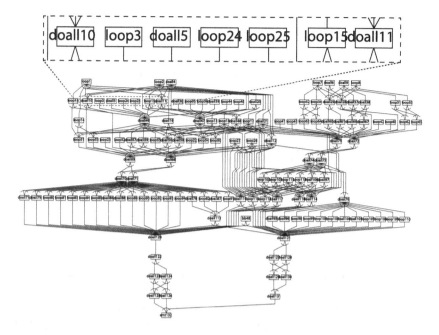

Fig. 3. Macro task graph after inline expansion

The GMS solver uses the Hierarchical Data Format (HDF) library [8] for file access. The HDF library is to allow us to manage large and complex data collections. The master thread executing the library first touches all input arrays of the original GMS solver. It forces cc-NUMA machines to assign those arrays to the distributed shared memory near the processor core that execute the master thread. It means that all processor cores access to the distributed shared memory near the processor core executing the main thread, and the heavy memory contention occurs.

To fully utilize distributed shared memories on cc-NUMA machines, in the proposed method, the input arrays are copied to new arrays with interchanged indexes to be first touched by each processor element. Figure 4 shows an example of the modification. Originally, an array A is first touched in a subroutine external_library_array_init and is used in a subroutine main_loop. Because the OSCAR compiler can't parallelize external library, a new array A_COPY is created and values of the array A are copied to the array A_COPY. Then, the subroutine main_loop uses the array A_COPY in place of the array A. In the GMS, 33 arrays are copied to be first touched by each processor element.

3.4 Task Scheduling on Cc-NUMA

The control dependencies in the macro task graph are represented as broken edges between tasks. There is no control dependency edge in Fig. 3. Therefore, the OSCAR compiler chooses static scheduling to schedule the macro tasks to processor elements.

```
program sample
  integer A(1000)
  integer A_COPY(1000)
  {copied array}
  call external_library_array_init(A)
  {a array is originally first touched here}
  do i=1,1000
    A_COPY(i)=A(i)
  enddo
  {copying the original array to a new array}
  call main_loop(A_COPY)
  {in main loop, the new array is used}
  do i=1,1000
    A(i)=A_COPY(i)
  enddo
  {copying the new array to the original array}
  call output_A(A)
end
```

Fig. 4. Example of the array copy for first touch

On cc-NUMA machines, access to a remote distributed shared memory is slower than that of a local distributed shared memory. So to improve the efficiency of parallel processing of the program, a scheduler that takes accounts of the first touch information was developed. By first touching the copied new arrays mentioned above, the arrays used for the main loop are first touched at the each copy loop, so the scheduler can know which processor element first touched the array. The static scheduler decides optimal processors to execute for each task using the first touch information, and then schedule ready tasks to its optimal processors in order of critical path length. Critical path length is the length of the longest path from any node to the exit node on a macro task graph.

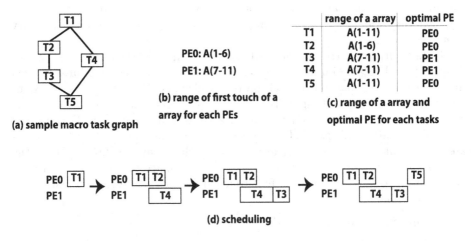

	range of a array	optimal PE
T1	A(1-11)	PE0
T2	A(1-6)	PE0
T3	A(7-11)	PE1
T4	A(7-11)	PE1
T5	A(1-11)	PE0

PE0: A(1-6)
PE1: A(7-11)

(a) sample macro task graph

(b) range of first touch of a array for each PEs

(c) range of a array and optimal PE for each tasks

(d) scheduling

Fig. 5. An example of the scheduling

Figure 5 is an example of the scheduling. Figure 5(a) is a macro task graph and (b) shows how PEs first touch variables. Figure 5(c) represents the range of arrays used by each task and the optimal PEs to which each task should be assigned considering the information of the first touch showed in (b). Finally Fig. 5(d) shows processing steps of the scheduling. In the third step of (d), the task T3 is assigned to PE1. The task T3 is not dependent on T4, so if the task T3 is assigned to PE0, the task T3 may start soon after the task T2 ended. But if the task T3 is assigned to PE0, access to a remote distributed shared memory would occur, so the scheduler assigns the task T3 to PE1. The scheduler restricts the tasks to be assigned to the optimal PE considering the first touch to reduce memory access overheads.

3.5   Locality Optimization of Boundary Calculations in FDM

Figure 6 is a source code of velocity calculation of the center grids or DOALL10 in Fig. 3 and that of boundary grids or DOALL11 in Fig. 3. The GMS use fourth order difference operator for FDM calculations. But the fourth order difference operator can't be used at the boundary of the grids in the GMS. Therefore, second order difference operator is used at the boundary. The DOALL10 and the DOALL11 have no dependency among them, but both loops access the almost same ranges of the arrays taking account of cache lines. Though cache reuse is expected by executing the both loops continuously [9, 10], the arrays used by the both loops are too large to be fully stored in L2 or L3 caches.

```
{calculation of the center area}
do i=2,ni-1
 do j=2,nj-1
  do k=2,nk-2
   ux(k,j,i)=(ux(k,j,i)+bbx*(
             +dtdx*(c0*(sxx(k,j,i+1)-sxx(k,j,i))
                  - c1*(sxx(k,j,i+2)-sxx(k,j,i-1)))
             +dtdy*(c0*(sxy(k,j,i)-sxy(k,j-1,i))
                  - c1*(sxy(k,j+1,i)-sxy(k,j-2,i)))
             +dtdz*(c0*(sxz(k,j,i)-sxz(k-1,j,i))
                  - c1*(sxz(k+1,j,i)-sxz(k-2,j,i))))
             )*aaqq
  enddo
 enddo
enddo
{calculation of the boundary}
do i=2,ni-1
 do j=2,nj-1
  do k=1,nk-1,nk-2
   ux(i,j,k)=( ux(i,j,k)+bbx*(
             +dtdx*(c0*(sxx(k,j,i+1)-sxx(k,j,i))
                  - c1*(sxx(k,j,i+2)-sxx(k,j,i-1)))
             +dtdy*(c0*(sxy(k,j,i)-sxy(k,j-1,i))
                  - c1*(sxy(k,j+1,i)-sxy(k,j-2,i)))
             +dtdz*(sxz(k,j,i)-sxz(k-1,j,i))  )
             )*aaqq
  enddo
 enddo
enddo
```

Fig. 6. Example of center and boundary calculations

In this section, the loop fusion is applied to the both loops to optimize the locality. To focus on ux in Fig. 6, the DOALL10 uses $ux(2: nk\text{-}2, 2: nj\text{-}1, 2: ni\text{-}1)$, and the DOALL11 uses $ux(1, 2: nj\text{-}1, 2: ni\text{-}1)$ and $ux(nk\text{-}1, 2: nj\text{-}1, 2: ni\text{-}1)$. Though the ranges of the array ux of the first loop don't overlap with that of the second loops, it is expected that $ux(1, j, i)$ and $ux(2, j, i)$ are allocated in the same cache line. The same is true of $ux(nk\text{-}2, j, i)$ and $ux(nk\text{-}1, j, i)$. By the loop fusion taking account of cache lines, memory access of the boundary calculation in FDM is expected to be sharply optimized.

Figure 7 is the macro task graph of the main loop after loop fusion. The proposed method fuses 12 loops into the four loops.

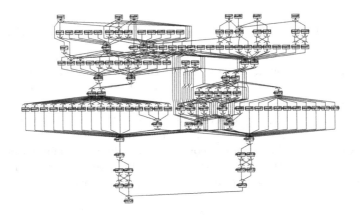

Fig. 7. Macro task graph after loop fusion

3.6 Generated Compiler Friendly Sequential Program and its Parallel Compilation

The proposed method applies above-mentioned modifications to the sequential GMS program. The modified sequential program is compiled by the OSCAR compiler and changed into parallelized Fortran program using the OSCAR API Ver2.0[11]. The OSCAR API is compatible with OpenMP. Therefore, compilers provided for target cc-NUMA machines can compile the program with the OSCAR API to the executable binary. In this paper, IBM XL Fortran compiler, Intel Fortran compiler and Sun Studio Fortran compiler compile the generated parallel programs.

4   Performance of the Parallelized GMS

This section evaluates speed-up of the parallelized GMS on five different cc-NUMA machines.

4.1   Evaluation Environments

The authors use the SR16000, the BS2000, the RS440, the M9000 and the S812L for the evaluations. Table 1 summarizes the specifications of the five servers.

The SR16000 is a POWER7 based 128 cores cc-NUMA machine. The SR16000 consists of four boards and the fully-connected network connects the four boards. Each board has four processors and the fully-connected network connects the four processors. The evaluations in Sects. 4.2, 4.3 and 4.4 use the SR16000. The authors bind the paralelized programs to the processor cores by the compact manner. The compact manner is to use processor cores in core number order.

The BS2000 is a Xeon E7-8830 based 64 cores cc-NUMA machine. The special feature of BS2000 is that it consists of four ordinary blade servers, however,

Table 1. Server Specifications

	SR16000	BS2000	RS400
CPU	POWER7	Xeon E7-8830	Xeon X7560
Frequency	4GHz	2.13GHz	2.27GHz
cores per 1 processor	8	8	8
L2 cache	256KB(1core)	256KB(1core)	256KB(1core)
L3 cache	32MB(1processor)	24MB(1processor)	24MB(1processor)
Processors	16	8	4
CPU cores	128	64	32
Memory	1TB	256GB	128GB
OS	RedHat Linux	RedHat Linux	Ubuntu
Version	6.4	6.1	14.04.1
Linux kernel version	2.6.32	2.6.32	3.13.0
Compiler	XL Fortran	Intel Fortran compiler	Intel Fortran compiler
Version	13.1	12.1.5	12.1.5
	M9000		S812L
CPU	SPARC64 VII		POWER8
Frequency	2.88GHz		3.026GHz
cores per 1 processor	4		12(1 DCM),6(1 chip)
L2 cache	6144KB(1processor)		512KB(1core)
L3 cache	none		96MB(1DCM),48MB(1chip)
Processors	64		1(DCM),2(chip)
CPU cores	256		12
Memory	512GB		64GB
OS	Solaris		RedHat Linux
Version	10		7.1
Linux kernel version			3.10.1
Compiler	Sun Studio Fortran compiler		XL Fortran
Version	12.1		15.1.1

Table 2. Number of grids in datasets

	Unit00420	Unit01680	Unit06720
Number of Grids in RegionI	$420 \times 420 \times 100$	$1680 \times 1680 \times 100$	$6720 \times 6720 \times 100$
Number of Grids in RegionII	$140 \times 140 \times 200$	$560 \times 560 \times 200$	$2240 \times 2240 \times 200$
Total Memory	0.8GB	12.2GB	195.2GB

just attaching the inter-blade coherent control module connecting the blades, the blades is changed into a cc-NUMA server. Because each processor can use three QPIs for inter-processor connection, some pairs of the processor are connected directly and the other pairs are connected with one hop or two hops. The evaluations in Sect. 4.3 use the BS2000. The authors bind parallelized programs to the processor cores by the compact manner.

The RS440 is a Xeon X7560 based 32 cores cc-NUMA machine. The RS440 consists of four processors each of which has eight cores, and QPIs fully connect each processor. The evaluations in Sect. 4.3 use the RS440. The authors bind parallelized programs to the processor cores by the compact manner.

The M9000 is a SPARC64 VII based 256 cores cc-NUMA machine. The M9000 consists of 16 boards each of which has 16 cores. Two crossbar switches connect eight boards to make a cluster, and then two clusters are connected to compose the M9000. The evaluations in Sect. 4.3 use the M9000. The evaluations use up to 128 cores of 256 cores for the OSCAR compiler can cope with up to 128 cores at present. The authors bind parallelized programs to the every other processor core to utilize L2 cache memory and main memory fully.

The S812L is a POWER8 based 12 cores cc-NUMA machine. The S812L has a Dual Chip Module (DCM) and a Dual Chip Module includes two chip each of which has six cores [13]. The evaluations in Sect. 4.3 use the S812L. Though S812L has eight slots for DIMM modules, the authors equipped four 16GB DIMM modules to S812L.

The evaluations use three data sets such as Unit00420, Unit01680 and Unit06720. Table 2 summarizes the number of grids in the data sets. The Unit01680 is medium size among them and used for Sects. 4.2 and 4.3. The Unit00420 is the smallest data set among them and used for Sect. 4.4. The Unit06720 is the biggest data set among them and used for Sect. 4.4.

4.2 Comparison of Commercial Compilers and the Proposed Method

The comparisons among the original GMS parallelized by commercial compilers provided for the servers, such as IBM XL Fortran compiler, Intel Fortran compiler and Sun Studio and the GMS parallelized by the proposed method are shown.

Figure 8 shows a summary of the comparison between XL Fortran compiler and the proposed method on the SR16000. On a one processor core, the sequential execution time by the proposed method is 1.65 times faster than the original sequential program. Speed-ups of the original GMS parallelized by XL Fortran compiler were 15.3 times using 32 cores, 10.3 times using 64 cores and 11.8 times using 128 cores. It means that XL Fortran compiler can find loop parallelism in the GMS, but it can't give us scalable speed-up for the GMS on 64PEs and 128PEs in the SR16000. Speed-up of the GMS parallelized by the proposed method using 128 cores was 156.3 times against the original sequential execution. Higher speed-up by the proposed method using 128 PEs is obtained. The first reason is that the parallelization by XL Fortran compiler can only utilize loop parallelism, besides the proposed method can utilize multigrain parallelism. The second reason is that the master thread first touches the most of arrays and those arrays are assigned to distributed shared memory near processor core that execute the master thread. Therefore, remote memory accesses of parallel execution by XL Fortran compiler occur frequently and the execution time gets long.

Figure 9 shows a summary of the comparison between Intel Fortran compiler and the proposed method on the RS440. The proposed method works 1.3 times faster than the original sequential execution. The speed-up ratio of Intel Fortran compiler using 32PEs is 17.8 times, and it means that Intel Fortran compiler can also find loop parallelism in the GMS. On the RS440, loop parallelization works well. But on cc-NUMA with the bigger number of cores like the SR16000 and the M9000, the distance between the core and the remote memory becomes farther. The parallelization of the initialization of the arrays and the coarse grain task parallelization which consider First Touch is thought to be indispensable on cc-NUMA with the big number of cores.

Figure 10 shows a summary of the comparison between Sun Studio and the proposed method on the M9000. The proposed method gives us 2.1 times faster execution than the original sequential execution. Moreover, the proposed method using 128PEs gets 211 times speed-up from the original sequential execution.

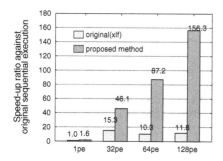

Fig. 8. XL Fortran compiler vs the proposed method on the SR16000 (Unit01680)

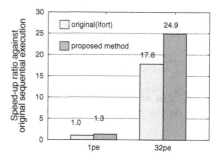

Fig. 9. Intel Fortran compiler vs the proposed method on the RS440 (Unit01680)

In Figs. 8, 9 and 10, the sequential executions of the proposed method get speed-up from the original sequential executions. This is because the locality optimization by the loop fusion described in Sect. 3.5.

4.3   Performance on the Five Different Cc-NUMA Servers

Speed-ups of the GMS parallelized by the proposed method from the sequential execution of the proposed method on the five different cc-NUMA servers are shown in Fig. 11. Speed-ups of the GMS on the SR16000 was 94.9 times using 128 cores, that with 64 cores on the BS2000 was 37.2 times, that with 32 cores on the RS440 was 19.8 times, that with 128 cores on the M9000 was 99.3 times, and that with 12 cores on the S812L was 9.42 times.

The BS2000 and the RS440 are relatively inexpensive servers compared to the SR16000 and the M9000, memory bandwidth of the former two servers are relatively narrow compared to the latter two servers. Therefore, speed-ups by parallelization on the former two servers tend to be limited by the memory bandwidth.

The speed-up of S812L is 9.42 times using 12 cores against sequential processing. The parallel efficiency of the S812L using maximum core is 9.42 ÷ 12 = 78.5 %, and it is higher than that of the RS440(61 %) and that of the BS2000(58 %).

On the SR16000 and the M9000, near 100 times speed-up using 128 cores can be obtained. It means that the proposed method successively utilize cc-NUMA machines.

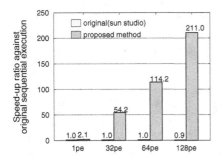

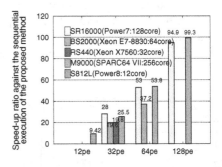

Fig. 10. Sun studio vs the proposed method on the M9000(Unit01680)

Fig. 11. SR16000 vs BS2000 vs RS440 vs M9000 vs S812L(Unit01680)

4.4   Evaluations with Various Data Sizes

Figure 12 summarizes the results of the evaluation with the various data sizes on the SR16000. The speed-ups on the Unit00420, a relatively small data set, were 25.0 times using 32 cores, 43.7 times using 64 cores and 75.7 times using

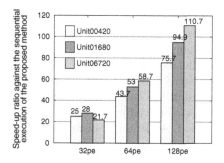

Fig. 12. Speed-up ratios of the proposed method with various data sets on the SR16000

128 cores. Even on the smallest data set, over 64 times speed-up or a half number of the cores used can be obtained. The speed-ups on the Unit06720 or the biggest data set were 21.7 times using 32 cores, 58.7 times using 64 cores and 110.7 times using 128 cores. Naturally, the results show that the bigger data size gives us better speed-ups because of the smaller ratio of remote memory access in the whole execution.

5   Conclusions

This paper has proposed a parallelizing optimization method of the earthquake simulator GMS. We can use earthquake simulations for damage predictions of earthquakes. By accelerating the earthquake simulations, it is expected that more exact damage prediction required for protecting more lives from disaster become possible. The proposed method modifies an original sequential Fortran program into parallelizing compiler friendly sequential Fortran program by hand to increase coarse grain task parallelism and data locality. The modifications by hand are the loop interchange and the array dimension interchange described in Sect. 3.2 and the array duplication described in Sect. 3.3 and the loop fusion described in Sect. 3.5. By the simple modifications, the OSCAR compiler can analyze coarse grain parallelism and data dependency among coarse grain tasks and generate a portable parallel program. In the proposed method, once users modify the original program into parallelizing compiler friendly sequential program, no further work is required to port to another shared memory servers.

The performance evaluations show 110.7 times speed-up using 128 cores against the sequential execution on the POWER7 based 128 cores cc-NUMA server Hitachi SR16000 VM1, 37.2 times speed-up using 64 cores against the sequential execution on the Xeon E7-8830 based 64 cores cc-NUMA server BS2000, 19.8 times speed-up using 32 cores against the sequential execution on the Xeon X7560 based 32 cores cc-NUMA server HA8000/RS440, 99.3 times speed-up using 128 cores against the sequential execution on the SPARC64 VII based 256 cores cc-NUMA server Fujitsu M9000, 9.42 times speed-up using 12 cores against the sequential execution on the POWER8 based 12 cores cc-NUMA server Power System S812L. Besides, the performance evaluation shows that the proposed method succeeded to obtain 13.2 times speed-up against the parallel execution by XL Fortran compiler using 128 cores on the SR16000 and 1.4 times speed-up against the parallel execution by Intel Fortran compiler using 32 cores on the RS440 and 211.0 times speed-up against the parallel execution by Sun Studio Fortran compiler using 128 cores on the M9000.

The proposed method is effective for programs with simple array access order like Finite Difference Method. Additional optimizations may improve the performance of programs with complex array access order parallelized by the proposed method. Finite Element Method often uses complex array access order.

This paper has shown the proposed parallelization method of the GMS using the OSCAR multigrain parallel compiler gives us scalable speed-ups with strong scaling on five different cc-NUMA servers.

Acknowledgment. The authors would like to thank the members of the Hitachi-Waseda collaborative research project and the Hitachi, Ltd. and the NIED for their support.

References

1. Akcelik, V., Bielak, J., Biros, G., Epanomeritakis, I., Fernandez, A., Ghattas, O., Kim, E.J., Lopez, J., O'Hallaron, D.R., Tu, T., Urbanic, J.: Highresolution forward and inverse earthquake modeling of terascale computers. In: Proceedings of the ACM/IEEE SC2003 (2003)
2. Aoi, S., Fujiwara, H.: 3-D finite difference method using discontinuous grids. Bull. Seismol. Soc. Am. **89**, 918–930 (1999)
3. Tiankai, T., David, R.O., Omar, G.: Scalable parallel octree meshing for terascale applications. In: Proceedings of ACM/IEEE SC2005 (2005)
4. Aoi, S., Nishizawa, N., Aoki, T.: Large scale simulation of seismic wave propagation using GPGPU. In: Proceedings of the Fifthteenth World Conference on Earthquake Engineering (2012)
5. Kasahara, H., Obata, M., Ishizaka, K.: Automatic coarse grain task parallel processing on SMP Using OpenMP. In: Midkiff, S.P., Moreira, J.E., Gupta, M., Chatterjee, S., Ferrante, J., Prins, J.F., Pugh, B., Tseng, C.-W. (eds.) LCPC 2000. LNCS, vol. 2017, pp. 189–207. Springer, Heidelberg (2001)
6. Obata, M., Shirako, J., Kaminaga, H., Ishizaka, K., Kasahara, H.: Hierarchical parallelism control for multigrain parallel processing. In: Pugh, B., Tseng, C.-W. (eds.) LCPC 2002. LNCS, vol. 2481, pp. 31–44. Springer, Heidelberg (2005)
7. GMS Homepage. http://www.gms.bosai.go.jp
8. The HDF Group. http://www.hdfgroup.org/
9. Monica, D.L., Edward, E.R., Michael, E.W.: The cache performance and optimizations of blocked algorithms. In: Proceedings of the Fourth International Conference on Architectural Support For Programming Languages and Operating Systems, pp. 63–74 (1991)
10. Apan, Q., Ken, K.: A cache-consciout profitability model for empirical tuning of loop fusion. In: 18th International Workshop, LCpPC 2005, Hawthorne, NY, USA, October 20–22, 2005, pp. 106–120 (2005)

11. OSCAR ApPI 2.0. http://www.kasahara.elec.waseda.ac.jp/api2/regist_en.html
12. Jaswinder, P.S., Truman, J., Anoop, G., John, L.H.: An empirical comparison of the Kendall Square Research KSR-1 and Stanford DASH Multiprocessors. In: Supercomputing 1993 Proceedings of the 1993 ACM/IEEE Conference on Supercomputing, pp. 214–225 (1993)
13. Cahill, J.J., Nguyen, T., Vega, M., Baska, D., Szerdi, D., Pross, H., Arroyo, R.X., Nguyen, H., Mueller, M.J., Henderson, D.J., Moreira, J.: IBM power systems build with the POWER8 architecture and processors. IBM J. Res. Dev. **59**(1), 1–10 (2015)

Conc-Trees for Functional and Parallel Programming

Aleksandar Prokopec[✉] and Martin Odersky

École Polytechnique Fédérale de Lausanne, Lausanne, Switzerland
aleksandar.prokopec@gmail.com

Abstract. Parallel algorithms can be expressed more concisely in a functional programming style. This task is made easier through the use of proper sequence data structures, which allow splitting the data structure between the processors as easily as concatenating several data structures together. Efficient update, split and concatenation operations are essential for declarative-style parallel programs.

This paper shows a functional data structure that can improve the efficiency of parallel programs. The paper introduces two Conc-Tree variants: the Conc-Tree list, which provides worst-case $O(\log n)$ time lookup, update, split and concatenation operations, and the Conc-Tree rope, which additionally provides amortized $O(1)$ time append and prepend operations. The paper demonstrates how Conc-Trees implement efficient mutable sequences, evaluates them against similar persistent and mutable data structures, and shows up to $3\times$ performance improvements when applying Conc-Trees to data-parallel operations.

1 Introduction

Balanced trees are good for *data-parallelism*. They can be easily split between CPUs, so that their subsets are processed independently. Providing efficient concatenation and retaining these properties is challenging, but essential for efficient declarative data-parallel operations. The following data-parallel program maps numbers in the given range by incrementing them:

```
(0 until 1000000).toPar.map(x => x + 1)
```

When the per-element workload is minimal, as is the case with addition, the overwhelming factor of the data-parallel computation is copying the data. Tree data structures can avoid the need for copying results from different processors by providing efficient concatentation. Another use case for trees is efficient parallelization of *task-parallel* functional programs. In the following we compare a *cons-list*-based functional implemenation of the sum method against the *conc-list*-based parallel implementation [16]:

```
1 def sum(xs: List[Int]) =          6 def sum(xs: Conc[Int]) =
2   xs match {                       7   xs match {
3     case head :: tail =>           8     case ls <> rs =>
4       head + sum(tail)             9       sum(ls) + sum(rs)
5     case Nil => 0 }               10     case Single(x) => x }
```

X. Shen et al. (Eds.): LCPC 2015, LNCS 9519, pp. 254–268, 2016.
DOI: 10.1007/978-3-319-29778-1_16

The first `sum` implementation decomposes the data structure `xs` into the first element `head` and the remaining elements `tail`. Sum is computed by recursively adding `head` to the sum of `tail`. This implementation cannot be efficiently parallelized. The second `sum` implementation splits `xs` into two subtrees `ls` and `rs`, and recursively computes their partial sums before adding them together. If `xs` is a balanced tree, the second `sum` implementation can be efficiently parallelized.

In this paper, we describe several variants of the binary tree data-structure called *Conc-Tree*, used to store sequences of elements. The basic variant is *persistent* [11], but we use Conc-Trees to design efficient mutable data structures. Traditionally, persistent data structures are perceived as slower and less efficient than imperative data structures. This paper shows that Conc-Trees are the basis for efficient *mutable* data structures for parallel computing. Data-parallel combiners [12,13] based on Conc-Trees improve performance of data-parallel operations. Functional task-parallel programming abstractions, such as Fortress Conc-lists [2], can be implemented using Conc-Trees directly. Concretely, the paper describes:

- Conc-Tree lists, with *worst-case* $O(\log n)$ time *persistent* insert, remove and lookup, and *worst-case* $O(\log n)$ *persistent* split and concatenation.
- Conc-Tree ropes, which additionally introduce *amortized* $O(1)$ time *ephemeral* append and prepend operations, and have optimal memory usage.
- Mutable buffers based on Conc-Trees, used to improve data-parallel operation performance by up to $3\times$ compared to previous approaches.

In Sect. 2, we introduce Conc-Tree lists. We discuss Conc-Tree ropes in Sect. 3. In Sect. 4, we apply Conc-Trees to mutable data structures, and in Sect. 5, we experimentally validate our Conc-Tree implementation. Finally, we give an overview of related work in Sect. 6.

2   Conc-Tree List

Trees with relaxed invariants are typically more efficient to maintain in terms of asymptotic running time. Although they provide less guarantees on their balance, the impact is small in practice – most trees break the perfect balance by at most a constant factor. Conc-Trees use a classic relaxed invariant seen in red-black and AVL trees [1] – the longest path from the root to a leaf is never more than twice as long than the shortest path from the root to a leaf.

The Conc-Tree data structure consists of several node types. We refer to Conc-Tree nodes with the `Conc` type. This abstract data type has several concrete data types, similar to how the functional `List` data type is either an empty list `Nil` or a `::` (pronounced *cons*) – element and another list. The `Conc` may either be an `Empty`, denoting an empty tree, a `Single`, denoting a tree with a single element, or a `<>` (pronounced *conc*), denoting two separate subtrees.

We show these basic data types in Fig. 1. Any `Conc` has an associated `level`, which denotes the longest path from the root to some leaf in that tree. The `level` is defined to be 0 for the `Empty` and `Single` tree, and 1 plus the level of

```
11 abstract class Conc[+T] {        27 case class Single[T](x: T)
12    def level: Int                 28 extends Leaf[T] {
13    def size: Int                  29    def level = 0
14    def left: Conc[T]              30    def size = 1
15    def right: Conc[T]             31 }
16    def normalized = this }        32
17                                   33 case class <>[T](
18 abstract class Leaf[T]           34    left: Conc[T], right: Conc[T]
19 extends Conc[T] {                 35 ) extends Conc[T] {
20    def left = error()             36    val level =
21    def right = error() }          37      1 + max(left.level,
22                                   38                right.level)
23 case object Empty                 39    val size =
24 extends Leaf[Nothing] {           40      left.size + right.size
25    def level = 0                  41 }
26    def size = 0 }                 42
```

Fig. 1. Basic Conc-Tree data types

the deeper subtree for the $<>$ tree. The `size` of a `Conc` denotes the total number of elements contained in the Conc-Tree. The `size` and `level` are cached as fields in the $<>$ type to prevent traversing the tree to compute them each time they are requested. `Conc` trees are persistent like cons-lists – they are never modified after construction. We defer the explanation of the `normalized` method until Sect. 3 – for now `normalized` just returns the tree.

It is easy to see that the data types described so far can yield imbalanced trees. We can construct arbitrarily large empty trees by combining the `Empty` tree instances with $<>$. We thus enforce the following invariant – the `Empty` tree can never be a part of $<>$. However, this restriction is still not sufficient – imbalanced trees can be constructed by iteratively adding elements to the right:

```
(0 until n).foldLeft(Empty: Conc[Int]) {
    (tree, x) => new <>(tree, new Single(x))
}
```

To ensure that the Conc-Trees are balanced, we require that the difference in `levels` of the left subtree and the right subtree is less than or equal to 1. This relaxed invariant imposes bounds on the number of elements. If the tree is completely balanced, i.e. every $<>$ node has two children with equal levels, then the subtree size is $S(level) = 2^{level}$. If we denote the number of elements as $n = S(level)$, it follows that the level of this tree is $level = \log_2 n$.

Next, if the tree is sparse and every $<>$ node at a specific $level$ has two subtrees such that $|left.level - right.level| = 1$, the size of a node at $level$ is:

$$S(level) = S(level - 1) + S(level - 2), S(0) = 1 \tag{1}$$

This is the familiar Fibonacci recurrence with the solution:

$$S(level) = \frac{1}{\sqrt{5}}(\frac{1+\sqrt{5}}{2})^{level} - \frac{1}{\sqrt{5}}(\frac{1-\sqrt{5}}{2})^{level} \tag{2}$$

The second addend in the previous equation quickly becomes insignificant, and the level of such a tree is $level = \log_{\frac{1+\sqrt{5}}{2}} n + \log_{\frac{1+\sqrt{5}}{2}} \sqrt{5}$.

From the monotonicity of these recurrences, it follows that $O(\log n)$ is both an upper and a lower bound for the Conc-Tree depth. The bounds also ensure that Conc-Trees have $O(\log n)$ lookup and update operations.

```
43 def apply(xs: Conc[T], i: Int) = xs match {
44   case Single(x) => x
45   case left <> right =>
46     if (i < left.size) apply(left, i)
47     else apply(right, i - left.size) }
48 def update(xs: Conc[T], i: Int, y: T) =
49   xs match {
50     case Single(x) => Single(y)
51     case left <> right if i < left.size =>
52       new <>(update(left, i, y), right)
53     case left <> right =>
54       val ni = i - left.size
55       new <>(left, update(right, ni, y)) }
```

The **update** operation produces a new Conc-Tree such that the element at index i is replaced with a new element y. This operation only allows replacing existing elements, and we want to insert elements as well. Before showing an $O(\log n)$ **insert** operation, we show how to concatenate two Conc-Trees.

Conc-Tree concatenation is shown in Fig. 2. The <> method allows nicer concatenation syntax – the expression xs <> ys concatenates two trees together. Note that this is different than the expression new <> (xs, ys) that simply links two trees together with one <> node – invoking the constructor directly can violate the balance invariant. We refer to composing two trees together with a <> node as *linking*. Creating a Conc-Tree that respects the invariants and that is the concatenated sequence of the two input trees we call *concatenation*.

The bulk of the concatenation logic is in the **concat** method in Fig. 2. This method assumes that the trees are *normalized*, i.e. composed from the basic data types from Fig. 1. In explaining the code in Fig. 2 we will make an assumption that concatenating two Conc-Trees can yield a tree whose **level** is either equal to the larger input Conc-Tree or greater by exactly 1. In other words, concatenation never increases the Conc-Tree **level** by more than 1. We call this the *height-increase assumption*. We will inductively show that the height-increase assumption is correct while explaining the recursive **concat** method in Fig. 2. We skip the trivial base case of merging **Single** trees.

The trees xs and ys may be in several different relationships with respect to their **levels**. First of all, the absolute difference between the **levels** of xs and ys could differ by one or less. This is an ideal case – the two trees can be linked directly by creating a <> node that connects them. Otherwise, one tree has a greater **level** than the other one. Without the loss of generality we assume that the left Conc-Tree xs is higher than the right Conc-Tree ys. To concatenate xs and ys we need to break xs into parts.

```
56 def <>[T](xs: Conc[T], ys: Conc[T]) = {
57   if (xs == Empty) ys
58   else if (ys == Empty) xs
59   else concat(xs.normalized, ys.normalized) }
60 def concat[T](xs: Conc[T], ys: Conc[T]) = {
61   val diff = ys.level - xs.level
62   if (abs(diff) <= 1) new <>(xs, ys)
63   else if (diff < -1) {
64     if (xs.left.level >= xs.right.level) {
65       val nr = concat(xs.right, ys)
66       new <>(xs.left, nr)
67     } else {
68       val nrr = concat(xs.right.right, ys)
69       if (nrr.level == xs.level - 3) {
70         val nr = new <>(xs.right.left, nrr)
71         new <>(xs.left, nr)
72       } else {
73         val nl = new <>(xs.left, xs.right.left)
74         new <>(nl, nrr)
75       } }
76   } else {
77     if (ys.right.level >= ys.left.level) {
78       val nl = concat(xs, ys.left)
79       new <>(nl, ys.right)
80     } else {
81       val nll = concat(xs, ys.left.left)
82       if (nll.level == ys.level - 3) {
83         val nl = new <>(nll, ys.left.right)
84         new <>(nl, ys.right)
85       } else {
86         val nr = new <>(ys.left.right, ys.right)
87         new <>(nll, nr)
88       } } } }
```

Fig. 2. Conc-Tree concatenation operation

Assume that xs.left.level $>=$ xs.right.level, in other words, that xs is left-leaning. The concatenation xs.right $<>$ ys in line 65 increases the height of the right subtree by at most 1. This means that the difference in levels between xs.left and xs.right $<>$ ys is 1 or less, so we can link them directly in line 66. Under the height-increase assumption, the resulting tree increases its height by at most 1, which inductively proves the assumption for left-leaning trees.

We next assume that xs.left.level $<>$ xs.right.level. The subtree xs.right.right is recursively concatenated with ys in line 68. Its level may be equal to either xs.level - 2 or xs.level - 3. After concatenation we obtain a new tree nrr with the level anywhere between xs.level - 3 and xs.level - 1. Note that, if the nrr.level is equal to xs.level - 3, then the tree xs.right.left level is xs.level - 2, by the balance invariant. Depending on the level of `nrr` we either link it with `xs.right.left`, or we link `xs.left` with `xs.right.left`, and link the resulting trees once more. Again, the resulting tree does not increase its height by more than 1. This turns the height-increase assumption into the following theorem.

Theorem 1 (Height Increase). *Concatenating two Conc-Tree lists of heights h_1 and h_2 yields a tree with height h such that $|h - max(h_1, h_2)| \leq 1$.*

The bound on the concatenation running time follows directly from the previous theorem and the implementation in Fig. 2:

Theorem 2 (Concatenation Time). *Concatenation of two Conc-Tree lists with heights h_1 and h_2 is an $O(|h_1 - h_2|)$ asymptotic running time operation.*

Proof. Direct linking in the concatenation operation is always an $O(1)$ operation. Recursively invoking `concat` occurs at most once on any control path in `concat`. Each time `concat` is called recursively, the height of the higher Conc-Tree is decreased by 1, 2 or 3. Method `concat` will not be called recursively if the absolute difference in Conc-Tree heights is less than or equal to 1. Thus, `concat` can only be called at most $O(|xs_{level} - ys_{level}|)$ times. □

These theorems will be important in proving the running times of the data structures shown later. We now turn to the `insert` operation to show the importance of concatenation on a simple example. The concatenation operation makes expressing the `insert` operation straightforward:

```
89 def insert[T](xs: Conc[T], i: Int, y: T) =
90   xs match {
91     case Single(x) =>
92       if (i == 0) new <>(Single(y), xs)
93       else new <>(xs, Single(y))
94     case left <> right if i < left.size =>
95       insert(left, i, y) <> right
96     case left <> right =>
97       left <> insert(right, i - left.size, y) }
```

Insert unzips the tree along a certain path by dividing it into two subtrees and inserting the element into one of the subtrees. That subtree will increase its height by at most one by Theorem 1, making the height difference with its sibling at most two. Merging the two new siblings is thus $O(1)$ by Theorem 2. Since the length of the path from the root to any leaf is $O(\log n)$, the total amount of work done becomes $O(\log n)$. The `split` operation is similar to `insert`, and has $O(\log n)$ complexity by the same argument.

Appending to a Conc-Tree list amounts to merging it with a `Single` tree:

```
def <>[T](xs: Conc[T], x: T) = xs <> Single(x)
```

The downside of appending elements this way is that it takes $O(\log n)$ time. If most of the computation involves appending or prepending elements, this is not satisfactory. We see how to improve this bound in the next section.

3   Conc-Tree Rope

In this section, we modify the Conc-Tree to support an amortized $O(1)$ time ephemeral append operation. The reason that `append` from the last section takes $O(\log n)$ time is that it has to traverse a path from the root to a leaf. Note that the append position is always the same – the rightmost leaf. Even if we could expose that rightmost position by defining the Conc-Tree as a pair of the root and the rightmost leaf, updating the path from the leaf to the root would take $O(\log n)$ time. We instead relax the Conc-Tree invariants.

We introduce a new Conc-Tree node called `Append`, which has a structure isomorphic to the `<>` node. The difference is that the `Append` node does not have the balance invariant – the heights of its `left` and `right` subtrees are not constrained. Instead, we impose the *append invariant* on `Append` nodes: the `right` subtree of an `Append` node is never another `Append` node. Furthermore, the `Append` tree cannot contain `Empty` nodes. Finally, only an `Append` node may point to another `Append` node. The `Append` tree is thus isomorphic to a cons-list with the difference that the last node is not `Nil`, but another Conc-Tree.

This data type is transparent to clients and can alternatively be encoded as a special bit in `<>` nodes – clients never observe nor can construct `Append` nodes.

```
98  case class Append[T](left: Conc[T], right: Conc[T])
99  extends Conc[T] {
100    val level = 1 + left.level.max(right.level)
101    val size = left.size + right.size
102    override def normalized = wrap(left, right)
103  }
104 def wrap[T](xs: Conc[T], ys: Conc[T]) =
105    xs match {
106      case Append(ws, zs) => wrap(ws, zs <> ys)
107      case xs => xs <> ys
108    }
```

We implement `normalized` so that it returns the Conc-Tree that contains the same sequence of elements as the original Conc-Tree, but is composed only of the basic Conc-Tree data types in Fig. 1. We call this process *normalization*. The method `normalized` in `Append` calls the recursive method `wrap`, which folds the trees in the linked list induced by `Append`.

We postpone claims about the normalization running time, but note that the previously defined `concat` method invokes `normalized` twice and is expected to run in $O(\log n)$ time – `normalized` should not be worse than $O(\log n)$.

We turn to the append operation, which adds a single element at the end of the Conc-Tree. Recall that by using `concat` directly this operation has $O(\log n)$ running time. We now implement a more efficient append operation. The invariant for the `Append` nodes allows appending as follows:

```
def append[T](xs: Conc[T], ys: Single[T]) = new Append(xs, ys)
```

Defined like this, `append` is a worst-case constant-time operation, but it has a negative impact on the `normalized` method. Appending n elements results

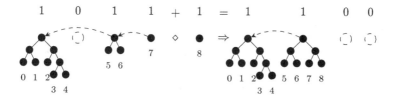

Fig. 3. Correspondence between the binary number system and append-lists

in a long list-like Conc-Tree on which `normalized` takes $O(n \log n)$ time. This `append` implementation illustrates that the more time `append` spends organizing the relaxed Conc-Tree, the less time a `concat` spends later.

Before attempting a different `append` implementation, note the correspondence between a linked list of trees of different `levels` and the digits of different weights in a standard binary number representation. This correspondence is induced by linking two Conc-Tree nodes of the same `level` with a new `<>` node, and adding two binary digits of the same weight. With binary numbers, counting up to n takes $O(n)$ computation steps, where one computation step is rewriting a single digit in the binary representation. Adding 1 is usually an $O(1)$ operation, but the carries chain-react and occasionally require up to $O(\log n)$ rewrites. It follows that adding n `Single` trees in the same way requires $O(n)$ computation steps, where a computation step is linking two trees with the same `level` together – by Theorem 2, an $O(1)$ operation.

We augment the append invariant – if an `Append` node `a` has another `Append` node `b` as the left child, then `a.right.level` `<>` `b.right.level`. If we now interpret the Conc-Trees under `Append` nodes as binary digits with the weight 2^{level}, we end up with the sparse binary number representation [11]. In this representation, zero digits (missing Conc-Tree levels) are not a part of the physical structure in memory. This correspondence is illustrated in Fig. 3, where the binary digits are shown above the corresponding Conc-Trees and the dashed line represents the linked list formed by the `Append` nodes.

Figure 4 shows the `append` operation that executes in $O(1)$ amortized time. The link operation in line 118, which corresponds to adding binary digits, occurs only for adjacent trees that happen to have the same `level`. The trees in the append list are in a form that is friendly to normalization. This list of trees of increasing size is such that the height of the largest tree is $O(\log n)$, and no two trees have the same height. It follows that there are no more than $O(\log n)$ such trees. Furthermore, the sum of the height differences between adjacent trees is $O(\log n)$. By Theorem 1 concatenating any two adjacent trees y and z in the strictly decreasing sequence t^*xyzs^* yields a tree with a height no larger than the height of x. By Theorem 2, the total amount of work required to merge $O(\log n)$ such trees is $O(\log n)$. Thus, appending in a way analogous to incrementing binary numbers ensures $O(\log n)$ normalization.

```
109 def append[T](xs: Conc[T], ys: Leaf[T]) =
110   xs match {
111     case Empty => ys
112     case xs: Leaf[T] => new <>(xs, ys)
113     case _ <> _ => new Append(xs, ys)
114     case xs: Append[T] => append(xs, ys) }
115 private def append[T](xs: Append[T], ys: Conc[T]) =
116   if (xs.right.level > ys.level) new Append(xs, ys)
117   else {
118     val zs = new <>(xs.right, ys)
119     xs.left match {
120       case ws @ Append(_, _) =>
121         append(ws, zs)
122       case ws =>
123         if (ws.level <= xs.level) ws <> zs
124         else new Append(ws, zs) } }
```

Fig. 4. Append operation

Note that the public **append** method takes a **Leaf** node instead of a **Single** node. The conc-lists from Sect. 2 and their variant from this section have a high memory footprint. Using a separate leaf to represent each element is inefficient. Traversing the elements in such a data structure is also suboptimal. Conc-Tree travesal (i.e. a **foreach**) must have the same running time as array traversal, and memory consumption should correspond to the memory footprint of an array. We therefore introduce a new type of a **Leaf** node, called a **Chunk**, that packs the elements more tightly together. As we will see in Sect. 4, this also ensures an efficient imperative **+=** operation.

```
125 case class Chunk[T](xs: Array[T], size: Int, k: Int)
126 extends Leaf[T] { def level = 0 }
```

The **Chunk** node contains an array **xs** with **size** elements. The additional argument **k** denotes the maximum size that a **Chunk** can have. The **insert** operation from Sect. 2 must copy the target **Chunk** when updating the Conc-Tree, and divides the **Chunk** into two if **size** exceeds **k**. Similarly, a **remove** operation fuses two adjacent **Chunks** if their total size is below a threshold.

The *Conc-Tree rope* has one limitation. When used persistently, it is possible that we obtain an instance of the Conc-Tree whose next **append** triggers a chain of linking operations. If we repetitively use that instance of the tree for appending, we lose the amortized $O(1)$ running time. Thus, when used persistently, the Conc-Tree rope has $O(\log n)$ appends. This limitation is overcome by another Conc-Tree variant called a *conqueue*, described in related work [12]. Conc-Tree ropes are nonetheless useful, since their simplicity ensures good constant factors and $O(1)$ ephemeral use. In fact, many applications, such as data-parallel *combiners* [13], always use the most recent version of the data structure.

```
127  class ConcBuffer[T](val k: Int) {
128    private var conc: Conc[T] = Empty
129    private var ch: Array[T] = new Array(k)
130    private var lastSize: Int = 0
131    def +=(elem: T) {
132      if (lastSize >= k) expand()
133      ch(lastSize) = elem
134      lastSize += 1 }
135    private def expand() {
136      conc = append(conc, new Chunk(ch, lastSize, k))
137      ch = new Array(k)
138      lastSize = 0 } }
```

Fig. 5. Conc-Buffer implementation

4 Mutable Conc-Trees

Most of the data structures shown so far were persistent. This persistence comes at a cost – while adding a single node has an $O(1)$ running time, the constant factors involved with allocating objects are still large. In Fig. 5, we show the ConcBuffer data structure, which uses Conc-Tree ropes as basic building blocks. This mutable data structure maintains an array segment to which it writes appended elements. Once the array segment becomes full, it is pushed into the Conc-Tree as a Chunk node, and a new array segment is allocated.

Although combiners based on growing arrays have $O(1)$ appends [13], resizing requires writing an element to memory twice on average. Conc-ropes with Chunk leaves ensure that every element is written only once. The larger the maximum chunk size k is, the less often is a Conc operation invoked in the method **expand** – this amortizes Conc-rope append cost, while retaining fast traversal. The ConcBuffer shown above is much faster than Java ArrayList or C++ vector when appending elements, and at the same time supports efficient concatenation. The underlying persistent Conc-rope allows an efficient copy-on-write snapshot operation.

5 Evaluation

In this section, we compare Conc-Trees against fundamental sequences in the Scala standard library – functional cons-lists, array buffers and Scala Vectors. In a cons-list, prepending an element is highly efficient, but indexing, updating or appending an elements are $O(n)$ time operations. Scala ArrayBuffer is a resizeable array known as the ArrayList in Java and as vector in C++. Array buffers are mutable random access sequences that can index or update elements with a simple memory read or write. Appending is amortized $O(1)$, as it occasionally resizes the array, and rewrites all the elements. An important limitation is that append takes up to 2 memory writes on average. Scala (and Clojure)

Vectors are efficient trees that can implement mutable and persistent sequences. Their defining features are low memory consumption and efficient prepending and appending. Current implementations do not have concatenation.

We compare different Conc-Tree variants: lists, ropes, mutable Conc-Buffers, as well as conqueues, described in related work [12].

We execute the benchmarks on an Intel i7 3.4 GHz quad-core processor. We start with *traversal* – we evaluate the `foreach` on persistent Conc-Tree lists from Sect. 2 and compare it to the `foreach` on the functional cons-list in Fig. 6A. Traversing the cons-list is tail recursive and does not use the call stack. Furthermore, Conc-Tree list traversal visits more nodes compared to cons-lists. Therefore, traversing the basic Conc-Tree list is slower than traversing a cons-list. On the other hand, the `Chunk` nodes ensure efficient traversal, as shown in Fig. 6B. For $k = 128$, Conc-Tree traversal running time is $2\times$ faster than that of Scala Vector. In subsequent benchmarks we set k to 128.

Appending is important for data-parallel transformations. While higher constant factors result in $2\times$ slower conqueue appends compared to *persistent* Vectors, *persistent* Conc-Tree rope append is faster (Fig. 6C). For comparison, inserting into a red-black tree is approximately $4\times$ slower than appending to a conqueue. In Fig. 6D, we compare Conc-Tree buffers against *mutable* Scala Vectors. Resizeable array appends are outperformed by all other data structures.

When it comes to *prepending* elements, cons-lists are very fast – prepending amounts to creating a single node. Cons-list have the same performance as *mutable* conqueue buffers, even though cons-lists are persistent. Both Scala Vectors and persistent conqueues are an order of magnitude slower.

Concatenation has the same performance for both persistent and mutable Conc-Tree variants. Concatenating mutable variants requires taking a snapshot, which can be done lazily in constant-time [14]. We show concatenation performance in Fig. 6F, where we repeat concatenation 10^4 times. Concatenating Conc-ropes is slightly more expensive than conc-list concatenation because of the normalization, and it varies with size because the number of trees (that is, non-zeros) in the append list fluctuates. Conqueue concatenation is slower (note the log axis) due to the longer normalization process. Concatenating lists, array buffers and Scala Vectors is not shown here, as it is a linear time operation, and thousands of times slower for the same number of elements.

Random access is an operation where Scala Vectors have a clear upper hand over the other persistent sequences. Although indexing a Scala Vector is faster than indexing Conc-Trees, both are orders of magnitudes slower than array random access. We note that applications that really need random-access performance must use arrays for indexing operations, and avoid `Vector` altogether.

We show *memory consumption* in Fig. 6H. While a Conc-Tree list occupies twice as much memory as a functional cons-list, using `Chunk` nodes has a clear impact on the memory footprint – arrays, Scala Vectors and Conc-Trees with `Chunk` nodes occupy an almost optimal amount of memory, where optimal is the number of elements in the data structure multiplied by the pointer size. Resizeable arrays waste up to 50 % of space due to their resizing policy.

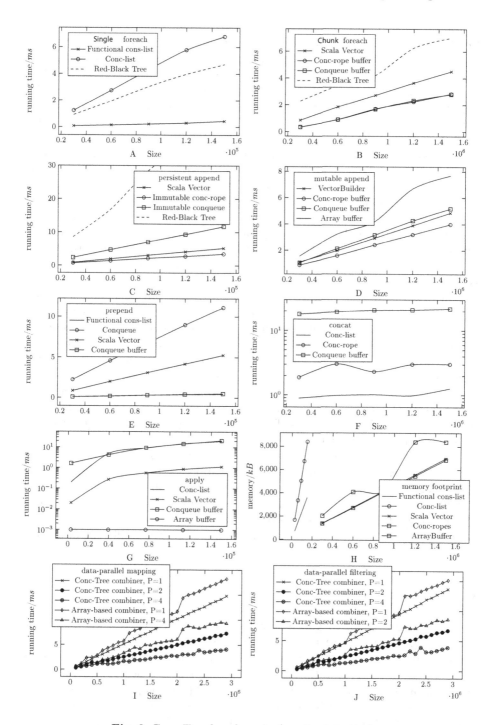

Fig. 6. Conc-Tree benchmarks (smaller is better)

Data-parallel operations are the main use-case for Conc-Trees. Scala collection framework defines high-level collection combinators, such as filtering, grouping, mapping and scanning. This API is similar to high-level data-processing APIs such as FlumeJava and Apache Spark. The example from Sect. 1 shows how to map numbers from a parallel range of numbers using the `map` operation. This `map` operation works by parts of the parallel range across different processors, and producing parts of the resulting collection in parallel. The lambda function `x => x + 1` is used on each input element to produce an output element. After independent processors produce intermediate collections, their results must be merged into a new collection. When the resulting collection is an array, intermediate array chunks cannot be simply linked together – instead, a new array must be allocated, and intermediate results must be copied into it. The array cannot be preallocated, because in general the number of output elements is not known in advance – in most data-parallel operations, a single input element can map into any number of output elements, determined after the lambda is run.

In the ScalaBlitz parallel collection framework [13,15], the unifying abstraction that allows expressing different parallel operations on Scala collections generically, is called a *combiner*. The combiner defines three generic operations: adding a new element to the combiner (invoked every time a new output element is created), merging two combiners (invoked when combiners from two different processors are merged), and producing the final collection (which is invoked once at the end of the operation). The arrays created from the parallel ranges in the `map` operation use a special array-based combiner, as described above.

We replaced the standard array-based combiner implementation in ScalaBlitz with Conc-Tree-based combiners, and compared *data-parallel map operation* performance with and without Conc-Trees in Fig. 6I, and *data-parallel filter operation* performance in Fig. 6J.

With Conc-Trees, performance of the data-parallel mapping is improved by $2 - 3\times$. The reason for this improvement is two-fold. First, array chunks stored inside Conc-Trees do not need bulk resizes, which array-based combiners periodically do. This is visible in Fig. 6I,J, where the array-based combiner has spikes at certain input collection sizes. Second, Conc-Tree-based combiners avoid copying each element twice, since intermediate Conc-Trees from different processors can be efficiently merged without copying.

6   Related Work

Standard programming language libraries come with resizeable array implementations, e.g. the `ArrayList` in the JDK or the `vector` in C++ standard template library. These are mutable data structures that provide $O(1)$ worst case time indexing and update operations, with $O(1)$ amortized time append operation. Although appending is amortized $O(1)$, each append on average requires two writes to memory, and each memory location is allocated twice. Concatenation is an $O(n)$ operation. Cons-lists have an efficient push-head and pop-head, but other operations are $O(n)$.

Ropes are heavily relied upon in the Xerox Cedar environment [5], where bulk rebalancing is done after the rope becomes particularly skewed. These ropes have an amortized $O(\log n)$ operation complexity. VList [3] is a functional sequence, with logarithmic time lookup operations. Scala Vector [4] is a persistent sequence implementation. Its dequeue operation has low constant factors, but requires $O(\log n)$ time. Scala Vector does not support concatentation, since concatenation support slows down other operations.

The idea of Conc lists was proposed in the Fortress language [2], where parallel programs are expressed as recursion and pattern matching on three types of nodes – empty, single element or conc nodes [16]. All Conc-Tree variants from this paper provide the same programming model as conc-lists from Fortress.

Relaxing the balancing requirements to allow efficient updates was first proposed by Adelson-Velsky and Landis, in the AVL tree data structure [1]. Okasaki was one of the first to bridge the gap between amortization and persistence through the use of lazy evaluation [9]. While persistent random access lists rely on binary number representations to achieve efficient append operations, they are composed from complete trees of different heights, and do not support concatenation as a consequence [11].

The recursive slowdown techniques were worked on by Kaplan and Tarjan [7]. Previously, persistent sequence data structures were proposed that achieve constant time prepend and append operations, and asymptotic constant time concatenation [8]. Although asymptotic bounds of these data structures are better than that of Conc-Trees, their operations have higher constant factors, and increased implementation complexity. The catenable real-time queues due to Okasaki allow efficient concatenation but do not have the balanced tree structure required for parallelization, nor support logarithmic random access [10]. Hinze and Paterson describe a lazy finger tree data structure [6] with *amortized* constant time deque and concatenation operations.

7   Conclusion

This paper introduces Conc-Tree data structures for functional parallel programming with worst-case $O(\log n)$ time splitting and concatenation. The Conc-Tree list comes with a worst-case $O(\log \frac{n_1}{n_2})$ time concatenation with low constant factors. The Conc-Tree rope provides an amortized $O(1)$ time append and prepend operations. In terms of absolute performance, persistent Conc-Trees outperform existing persistent data structures such as AVL trees and red-black trees by a factor of $3 - 4\times$, and mutable Conc-Trees outperform mutable sequence data structures such as mutable Vectors and resizeable arrays by $20 - 50\%$, additionally providing efficient concatenation. Data-parallel operation running time can be improved by up to $3\times$, depending on the workload characteristic.

When choosing between different Conc-Tree variants, we advise the use of ropes for most applications. Although Conc-Tree ropes achieve amortized bounds, ephemeral use is typically sufficient.

Besides serving as a catenable data-type for functional task-parallel programs, and improving the efficiency of data-parallel operations, the immutable nature of Conc-Trees makes them amenable to linearizable concurrent snapshot operations [12]. Inefficiencies associated with persistent data can be amortized to a near-optimal degree, so we expect Conc-Trees to find their applications in future concurrent data structures.

References

1. Adelson-Velsky, G.M., Landis, E.M.: An algorithm for the organization of information. Dokl. Akad. Nauk SSSR **146**, 263–266 (1962)
2. Allen, E., Chase, D., Hallett, J., Luchangco, V., Maessen, J.W., Ryu, S., Steele, G., Tobin-Hochstadt, S.: The Fortress Language Specification. Technical report, Sun Microsystems Inc., (2007)
3. Bagwell, P.: Fast Functional Lists. Deques, and Variable Length Arrays. Technical report, Hash-Lists (2002)
4. Bagwell, P., Rompf, T.: RRB-Trees: Efficient Immutable Vectors. Technical report (2011)
5. Boehm, H.J., Atkinson, R., Plass, M.: Ropes: An alternative to strings. Softw. Pract. Exper. **25**(12), 1315–1330 (1995)
6. Hinze, R., Paterson, R.: Finger trees: A simple general-purpose data structure. J. Funct. Program. **16**(2), 197–217 (2006)
7. Kaplan, H., Tarjan, R.E.: Persistent lists with catenation via recursive slow-down. In: STOC 1995, pp. 93–102. ACM, New York, NY, USA (1995)
8. Kaplan, H., Tarjan, R.E.: Purely functional representations of catenable sorted lists. In: Proceedings of the Twenty-Eighth Annual ACM Symposium on Theory of Computing, STOC 1996, pp. 202–211. ACM, New York, NY, USA (1996)
9. Okasaki, C.: Purely Functional Data Structures. Ph.D. thesis, Pittsburgh, PA, USA, AAI9813847 (1996)
10. Okasaki, C.: Catenable double-ended queues. In: Proceedings of the Second ACM SIGPLAN International Conference on Functional Programming, pp. 66–74. ACM Press (1997)
11. Okasaki, C.: Purely Functional Data Structures. Cambridge University Press, Cambridge (1998)
12. Prokopec, A.: Data Structures and Algorithms for Data-Parallel Computing in a Managed Runtime. Ph.D. thesis, EPFL (2014)
13. Prokopec, A., Bagwell, P., Rompf, T., Odersky, M.: A generic parallel collection framework. In: Jeannot, E., Namyst, R., Roman, J. (eds.) Euro-Par 2011, Part II. LNCS, vol. 6853, pp. 136–147. Springer, Heidelberg (2011)
14. Prokopec, A., Bronson, N.G., Bagwell, P., Odersky, M.: Concurrent tries with efficient non-blocking snapshots. In: PPopp 2012, pp. 151–160. ACM, New York, NY, USA (2012)
15. Prokopec, A., Petrashko, D., Odersky, M.: On Lock-Free Work-stealing Iterators for Parallel Data Structures. Technical report (2014)
16. Steele, G.: Organizing functional code for parallel execution; or, foldl and foldr considered slightly harmful. In: International Conference on Functional Programming (ICFP) (2009)

Correctness and Reliability

Practical Floating-Point Divergence Detection

Wei-Fan Chiang$^{(\boxtimes)}$, Ganesh Gopalakrishnan, and Zvonimir Rakamarić

School of Computing, University of Utah, Salt Lake City, UT, USA
{wfchiang,ganesh,zvonimir}@cs.utah.edu

Abstract. Reducing floating-point precision allocation in HPC prog
rams is of considerable interest from the point of view of obtaining higher
performance. However, this can lead to unexpected behavioral deviations
from the programmer's intent. In this paper, we focus on the problem of
divergence detection: when a given floating-point program exhibits different control flow (or differs in terms of other discrete outputs) with respect
to the same program interpreted under reals. This problem has remained
open even for everyday programs such as those that compute convex-
hulls. We propose a classification of the divergent behaviors exhibited
by programs, and propose efficient heuristics to generate inputs causing
divergence. Our experimental results demonstrate that our input generation heuristics are far more efficient than random input generation for
divergence detection, and can exhibit divergence even for programs with
thousands of inputs.

1 Introduction

Almost anyone writing a program involving floating-point data types wonders
what precision to allocate (single, double, or higher). There is a great temptation
to get away with single precision, as it can yield performance advantage of a
factor of 2.5 for CPU codes [20] or even higher for GPU codes [21,29]. Yet,
floating-point arithmetic is highly non-intuitive, causing non-reproducible bugs
and nightmarish debugging situations [8,10,24,25,28]. For instance, experts in
a recent project had to waste several days chasing a Xeon vs. Xeon-Phi floating-
point behavioral deviation where identical *source* code running on these machines
took different control paths for the same input [22].

Any program in which floating-point results flow into conditional expressions
can decide to take different control paths based on floating-point round-off. Also,
if a developer banks on a program meeting a specific post-condition, they may
find that the truth of the post-condition can depend again on floating-point
round-off. Such divergent behaviors ("divergence") have been widely discussed
in the literature. Kettner et al. [18] demonstrated that a geometric convex hull
construction algorithm can result in non-convex hulls under certain (manually

Supported in part by NSF Grants CCF 1421726 and ACI 1535032. This work was
also performed under the auspices of the U.S. Department of Energy by Lawrence
Livermore National Laboratory under Contract DE- AC52-07NA27344 (LLNL-
CONF-669095).

© Springer International Publishing Switzerland 2016
X. Shen et al. (Eds.): LCPC 2015, LNCS 9519, pp. 271–286, 2016.
DOI: 10.1007/978-3-319-29778-1_17

```
1: float8 a, b, c, d, e, f;
2: procedure FOO : → int
3:     if (a+b)+c > (d+e)+f then
4:         return  22;
5:     else
6:         return  33;
7:     end if
8: end procedure
```

(a) Illustrating Divergence and ABS

```
1: float8 x, y;
2: procedure VAR : → float8
3:     var = (x²+y²)/2−((x+y)/2)²;
4:     return var;
5: end procedure
6: Desired Post-condition: var ≥ 0;
```

(b) Illustrating GRT

Fig. 1. Motivating examples

generated) inputs. Problems due to inconsistency in geometric computations are described in great detail in the context of computer games [12]. The author of [27] suggests the use of "padding constants" followed by "thorough testing" as a practical solution to guard against the nasty surprises of divergence. With the increasing role of geometry in real life (e.g., manufacture of prosthetics using 3D printing, computer gaming, mesh generation, robot motion planning), divergence becomes a life-critical or resource-critical issue, and must be systematically tackled. While allocating higher floating-point precision can reduce the incidence of divergence, a programmer will not go this route (and suffer a slow-down) unless they have at least one piece of evidence (in the form of an input causing divergence – hereafter called *diverging input*) that this measure is necessary. We show that without systematic testing one can fail to find even one divergent behavior for many programs.

The hopelessness of manual reasoning can be highlighted through the program in Fig. 1a where, for simplicity, we consider 8-bit floating-point values. Let *float8* have one sign bit s, four bits of mantissa (or precision) m, and three bits of exponent e representing the value $(-1)^s \cdot 1.m \cdot 2^{e-4}$. One may not be surprised if told that this program may return 33 (under standard IEEE floating-point with round to nearest applied), while returning 22 if we used reals instead of float8. However, it is virtually impossible to manually obtain even one diverging input.[1] Purely random testing is ineffective for exhibiting divergence due to the huge state space it faces. There has been very little prior work on efficiently identifying diverging inputs. In this paper, we propose and evaluate methods to rapidly discover diverging inputs for many useful floating-point primitives. Such primitives are known to be used in many applications—for example, mesh generation.

We focus on the problem of developing efficient heuristics to generate diverging inputs. We assume that the user has identified *discrete features* (e.g., returning 22 or 33 in our example) as one of the key observable results from the

---

[1] $a = e = d = 1.0000 \cdot 2^{-3}$, $b = f = 1.0000 \cdot 2^2$, and $c = 1.0001 \cdot 2^{-3}$ causes divergence.

program.[2] Our algorithms then generate diverging inputs in a lower precision (say, 32-bit) computation.

While all divergences are attributable to some deviation in conversion of floating-point to discrete value such as deviation in control-flow, it is also well known (e.g., [7]) that many control-flow deviations do not cause divergence. In this paper, we describe divergence detection with respect to the user-given set of discrete features. Clearly, control-flow deviation is an extreme case in our definition: the discrete feature in that case is nothing but the full control-flow path.

The difficulty of identifying diverging inputs is due to (1) the sheer number of input combinations to be considered, (2) non-uniformity of floating-point number distribution, (3) the layers of floating-point operations (e.g., non-linear and transcendental operators and their associated rounding modes, catastrophic cancellations during subtraction [14]) that are involved before a conditional expression's truth value is determined, and (4) poor scalability of symbolic methods since floating-point arithmetic decision procedures are in their infancy. While our previous work [9] helps identify inputs that cause high round-off errors in floating-point functions, such methods cannot be directly used to identify diverging inputs. In this paper, we present an approach that addresses these difficulties by employing empirical search methods to efficiently discover diverging inputs. Ours is the first attempt to classify problems in this area into discernible groups, and provide heuristic approaches for input generation to trigger divergence. Our contributions in this paper are the following:

- Two approaches to trigger divergence in programs of interest to practitioners.
- A classification of programs into two categories, with corresponding new heuristics to trigger divergence in each category.

2   Overview of Our Approach

Given a program P and its input i, let $P_R(i)$ indicate the result of running the program on i under real number arithmetic. For simplicity, let vector i capture both the "data input" and "initial program state" of P. Let P_F be the floating-point version of P_R. We are interested in those inputs i under which $P_F(i) \not\equiv P_R(i)$, where $\equiv$ is some coarse equivalence relation since a programmer may not want bit-for-bit equality, but rather something higher level. We define $\equiv$ with the help of an abstract state space $A \subseteq U$ for some universe U, and an abstraction map α that maps into U. Then, a computation is divergent when $\alpha(P_F(i)) \neq \alpha(P_R(i))$.

Example 1: In the example of Fig. 1a, the relevant abstract state space is given by $A = U = \{22, 33\}$; we call the members of A discrete features (or discrete signatures). The input $a = e = d = 1.0000 \cdot 2^{-3}$, $b = f = 1.0000 \cdot 2^2$, and

---

[2] Real arithmetic is simulated by allocating very high precision. Typically we aim for 64- or 128-bit precision.

$c = 1.0001 \cdot 2^{-3}$ causes divergence. We now introduce our first search method called *abstract binary search* (ABS), which works as follows:

- We first use random testing to generate inputs i_1 and i_2 with signatures S_1 and S_2 under floating-point such that $S_1 \neq S_2$. In Fig. 1a, i_1 may under float8 result in signature 22 and i_2 in signature 33.
  Suppose i_1 results in 22 and i_2 in 33 under reals as well, and hence this is not a divergent situation.
- We use the discovered pair $\langle i_1, i_2 \rangle$ to bootstrap the binary search part of ABS. We compute the midpoint $mid = (i_1 + i_2)/2$ (taking /2 as a suitable way of finding the midpoint of two N-dimensional points) and proceed recursively with $\langle i_1, mid \rangle$ and $\langle i_2, mid \rangle$ as new pairs of inputs (details in Algorithm 1).
- If/when the floating-point signature output generated for mid differs from its real signature, we have located a diverging input and the algorithm terminates.

Example 2: We now introduce our second search method called *guided random testing* (GRT). Figure 1b computes the variance of x and y in terms of "mean of squares minus square of mean". Variances are non-negative, as captured by the given post-condition. We therefore choose $U = \{T, F\}$ to model Boolean truth, and $A = \{T\}$ to represent when the desired post-condition holds. In more detail, we have observed that for many problems (examples given in Sect. 4.2), the desired post-condition is of the form $(e_1 \geq 0) \wedge (e_2 \geq 0) \dots (e_n \geq 0)$, where e_i are expressions. GRT chooses one $e_i \geq 0$ conjunct, and it attempts to generate inputs that falsify it under floating-points (all conjuncts are assumed to be true under reals). In Sect. 3.2, we present a heuristic based on *relative errors* that helps find such inputs.

ABS vs. GRT: We recommend the use of GRT whenever a post-condition (always true under reals) has a chance of being violated under floating-points. On the other hand, ABS is recommended whenever such a post-condition does not exist, and one can bootstrap the process by quickly finding input i_1 and i_2 causing unequal signatures S_1 and S_2 under floating-points. The examples in this paper clarify further how we choose between these two search methods. We consider a more involved example next.

Example 3: Let P be a program computing a convex hull for a collection of points i. First, consider a simple case where i consists of five 2D points $\{\langle 0, 0 \rangle, \langle C, 0 \rangle, \langle C, C \rangle, \langle C, 2C \rangle, \langle 0, 2C \rangle\}$, where C and $2C$ are representable in floating-points. A convex hull algorithm is correct if the hull it returns is convex and encloses all the points (i.e., no point lies outside). According to this definition, there are two correct answers in this case:

- $\{\langle 0, 0 \rangle, \langle C, 0 \rangle, \langle C, C \rangle, \langle C, 2C \rangle, \langle 0, 2C \rangle\}$ or
- $\{\langle 0, 0 \rangle, \langle C, 0 \rangle, \langle C, 2C \rangle, \langle 0, 2C \rangle\}$.

In this example, one could either choose an exact listing of coordinates as the signature, or a more abstract signature such as the number of vertices in the convex hull. Whatever be our choice of signatures, we reiterate that in our approach (1) signatures are the only means of observing program behavior, (2) the signature returned by the real-valued computation is taken as the golden truth, and (3) divergence exists when the floating-point computation returns a different signature than the real computation.

Let the chosen signature be the number of vertices in the convex hull. Consider the input $\{\langle 0, 0 \rangle, \langle C, 0 \rangle, \langle C - \delta, C \rangle, \langle C, 2C \rangle, \langle 0, 2C \rangle\}$, where δ is very small, but $C - \delta$ is still representable in floating-points. For this input, our convex hull program returns 4 as the signature under reals. However, it may return 5 under floating-points due to round-off errors. This is an example of a divergent input according to our definition. We now summarize some of our observations:

- Signatures are a mechanism to mimic the "desired output".
- Some signatures (e.g., the count of the number of vertices in a convex hull) are *strong*, in that we observe empirically that one can arrive at diverging inputs fairly quickly.
- One can always choose the entire taken control-flow path as a signature. We empirically show that such signatures are typically *weak*, meaning that they make locating divergences very hard. Our experience shows that a good signature must ideally be a mapping into a small abstract space A.

3   Methodology

Given a program P and its input domain $\mathbb{I}$, we assume that each input $i \in \mathbb{I}$ is a scalar vector and $\mathbb{I}$ is convex. Let $i_X, i_Y \in \mathbb{I}$ be two inputs; then $\mathbb{I}$ is convex if all inputs *in-between* are also in $\mathbb{I}$: $\forall 0 \leq k \leq 1 . i_X * k + i_Y * (1 - k) \in \mathbb{I}$. The *midpoint* of i_X and i_Y is obtained by setting k to 0.5. A *signature*, as mentioned in the previous sections, is a discrete feature (or abstraction) of the concrete program output. Then, a *signature function* α maps program outputs under either floating-point or real arithmetic executions to abstract signature states.

For every input $i \in \mathbb{I}$, the output $P_F(i)$ of an execution under floating-points is supposed to have the same signature as the output $P_R(i)$ of an execution under reals. The *differential contract* of a program, which specifies when a divergence exists, is defined using the following predicate:

$$div(P, i) =_{def} \alpha(P_F(i)) \neq \alpha(P_R(i)). \tag{1}$$

Predicate *div* states that a divergence occurs when the signatures of real and floating-point outputs (i.e., executions) differ.

3.1   Abstract Binary Search (ABS)

Figure 2a illustrates how ABS detects divergence for the program in Fig. 1a. Here, the x-axis shows the values of $(a + b) + c$ and the y-axis the values of $(d + e) + f$. The diagonal separates the abstract signature state spaces of 22 and 33. ABS first finds a vector i_1 of values for inputs $a, \ldots, f$, whose abstract signature is 33 under both reals and floating-points (shown as point (1)). Then, it finds a vector

Algorithm 1. Abstract Binary Search (ABS)

```
1: procedure ABS (P, α, 𝕀)
2:     repeat                                          ▷ Find starting pair of points
3:         i_A = Random(𝕀)
4:         if div(P, i_A) then return i_A
5:         i_B = Random(𝕀)
6:         if div(P, i_B) then return i_B
7:     until α(P_F(i_A)) ≠ α(P_F(i_B))
8:     E = {⟨i_A, i_B⟩}                                ▷ Bootstrap binary search between end points
9:     while E ≠ ∅ do
10:        ⟨i_X, i_Y⟩ = Select(E)
11:        E = E \ {⟨i_X, i_Y⟩}
12:        if ∃i_M midpoint of ⟨i_X, i_Y⟩ distinct from i_X, i_Y then
13:            if div(P, i_M) then return i_M
14:            if α(P_F(i_X)) ≠ α(P_F(i_M)) then
15:                E = E ∪ {⟨i_X, i_M⟩}
16:            end if
17:            if α(P_F(i_M)) ≠ α(P_F(i_Y)) then
18:                E = E ∪ {⟨i_M, i_Y⟩}
19:            end if
20:        end if
21:    end while
22:    restart search                                  ▷ Optional restart step
23: end procedure
```

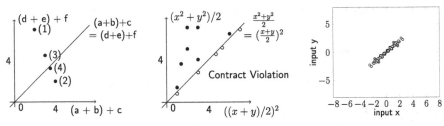

(a) Detecting Divergence in Fig. 1a using ABS

(b) Contract- and Non-violating Points for Fig. 1b

(c) Distribution of Diverging Inputs for Fig. 1b

Fig. 2. Applying ABS and GRT on examples from Fig. 1a and b

i_2 whose abstract signature is 22 under both reals and floating-points (shown as point (2)). The pair $\langle i_1, i_2 \rangle$ is the input of the subsequent binary search. (Note that ABS is typically not applicable on examples where finding points as above is extremely difficult, as Fig. 2b illustrates).

Our binary search method successively divides the N-dimensional space between vectors i_1 and i_2 by finding midpoints of these vectors (points (3) and (4) depict this N-dimensional binary search). It is highly unlikely that all points in this search sequence would all evaluate to the same abstract state under reals and floating-points. This is because it is also unlikely that the evaluations of the constituent expressions in the given program under reals, and their corresponding evaluations under rounding, would track each other perfectly with respect to the chosen discrete features.[3] As a consequence, ABS eventually encounters

---

[3] In practice, we do occasionally encounter a sequence whose discrete signatures match perfectly, and ABS exhausts all possible midpoints. In such cases, ABS is restarted with a different random seed.

a point (akin to point (4)) that lies at the borderline of the abstract spaces and causes a divergence.

The efficiency of ABS heavily depends on the chosen signature function. It must be possible to efficiently find — through a few random sampling steps — the initial points i_1 and i_2 that map to distinct abstract states. For example, it must be possible to efficiently locate points (1) and (2) in Fig. 2a.

Algorithm 1 gives pseudocode of ABS. As input it takes a program P, a signature function α, and the input domain $\mathbb{I}$, and it outputs a divergence-inducing input vector. The first phase of ABS (lines 2–7) finds the initial pair of points $\langle i_A, i_B \rangle$ satisfying $\alpha(P_F(i_A)) \neq \alpha(P_F(i_B))$ by employing random sampling. The second phase (lines 8–21) successively subdivides the space between a pair of points by removing a pair $\langle i_X, i_Y \rangle$ from E and seeking a divergence-inducing midpoint i_M. Under floating-point arithmetic, i_M can be equal to i_X or i_Y, which means we exhausted all midpoints, but could optionally restart. Otherwise, we determine which of the pairs $\langle i_X, i_M \rangle$ or $\langle i_M, i_Y \rangle$ are eligible for further search, and we add them to E. The while-loop of the second phase is guaranteed to terminate because floating-point domains are finite. The ABS procedure either returns a divergence-inducing input vector or timeouts (with the optional restart at line 22 using a different random seed). We rarely encountered timeouts in our empirical evaluation.

3.2 Guided Random Testing (GRT)

We designed GRT based on a key observation: a divergence occurs when one of the expressions in the signature has a high relative error; we now detail why this is so. The relative error of a value v is defined as $|\frac{v_R - v_F}{v_R}|$ [14]. In the example from Fig. 1b, the relative error of var must be high, and specifically greater than 1, when a negative variance is returned. Figure 2b illustrates that this is very rare by showing the space of contract (post-condition) violations and the space where the contract is met. Similarly, Fig. 2c shows all the diverging inputs obtained using a *satisfiability modulo theories* (SMT) solver [11].[4]

Let var_R (resp. var_F) be the variance computed under real (resp. floating-point) execution. Then, a divergence occurs when $(var_R \geq 0) \wedge (var_F < 0)$, which implies $var_R - var_F > var_R$. Thus, the relative error on var must exceed 1, meaning $|\frac{var_R - var_F}{var_R}| > 1$.

We have found that many problems amenable to GRT have a post-condition expressible as a conjunction $(e_1 \geq 0) \wedge (e_2 \geq 0) \wedge \ldots \wedge (e_N \geq 0)$, where e_i is a floating-point expression. Given such a formula, GRT aims to negate one of the conjuncts using guided random search. For this purpose, we employ our S3FP tool that efficiently maximizes a relative error of a given expression [9]. We now detail two approaches we investigated to drive the optimization.

---

[4] Current state-of-the-art SMT solvers work on micro-benchmarks with micro floating-point formats such as the program in Fig. 1b; they still cannot handle realistic floating-point programs used in our work.

Algorithm 2. Guided Random Testing (GRT)

```
1: procedure GRT (P, α, 𝕀)
2:     f_obj = ExtractObjective(α)
3:     while ¬Timeout() do
4:         i = Optimizer(P, 𝕀, f_obj)
5:         if div(P, i) then return i
6:     end while
7: end procedure
```

Single-term Objective: Choose one e_i from $e_1 \ldots e_N$ as the objective for triggering high relative error.

Multi-term Objective: Maximize $\sum_{i=1}^{N} err(e_i)$ such that

$$err(e_i) = \begin{cases} |rel\_err(e_i)| : |rel\_err(e_i)| < 1 \\ \quad\quad 1 \quad\quad : otherwise \end{cases},$$

where $rel\_err(e_i)$ is the relative error of expression e_i.

Algorithm 2 gives the pseudocode of GRT where we assume existence of a suitable function *ExtractObjective* that realizes either the single-term or the multi-term objective. Note that it if often convenient to provide a signature function that only loosely specifies program contracts, and falsifying such a contract does not always imply divergence (an example is provided in Sect. 4.2). Hence, each input vector returned by the optimizer (S3FP in our case) has to be checked to establish divergence using predicate *div*.

4   Experimental Results

We have evaluated ABS and GRT on a collection of realistic numerical routines. These routines regularly find applications in implementations of higher level algorithms such as Delaunay triangulation (often used for mesh generation) and other operations in high-performance computing [6]. Divergence detection for all benchmarks is achieved using differential contracts as stated in Eq. 1 and defined in Sect. 3. The only exception is the approximate sorting benchmark, which invokes an externally specified contract (see Sect. 4.2). As defined in Sect. 3, a differential contract is a comparison between signatures of outputs computed under reals and floating-points. We use high-precision floating-points to approximate reals, which is a technique employed in many floating-point analysis approaches (e.g., [3,9]). We categorize our benchmarks based on the signature model they follow.

4.1   ABS Benchmarks

Convex Hull: The algorithm takes a set of 2D points as input and outputs a 2D polygon. A coordinate of each point is a floating-point value in the range

$[-100, 100)$. The generated (convex) polygon must encompass all input points; we take the polygon vertex-count as our signature. We study four convex hull algorithms: simple [4], incremental [18], quick-hull [5], and Graham's scan [15]. The quick-hull and Graham's scan algorithms were taken from CGAL [6], which is a popular open-source geometric computation library.

Shortest Path: We implemented the well-known Floyd-Warshall shortest path algorithm [13], which calculates all-pair shortest paths for a graph. Our implementation takes a complete directed graph as input, and outputs a boolean value indicating the existence of a negative cycle. The input graph is represented as a sequence of floating-point edge-weights in the range $[-1, 10)$. The signature is the same as output: a boolean value indicating the existence of a negative cycle.

Intersection Between a 3D Line and Adjacent Triangles: This benchmark checks whether a 3D line intersects with two adjacent triangles. It takes six 3D points as input—four for the adjacent triangles and two for the line. The intersection scenario is one of the following types: the line (1) intersects with a triangle, (2) passes between the two triangles, and (3) neither. The signature indicates whether the intersection scenario is type (2), which is an unexpected scenario as described in related work [12]. This benchmark is taken from CGAL.

Geometric Primitives: These benchmarks, taken from CGAL, involve computing relationships between geometric objects, including a 2D triangle intersection test and several point-orientation tests. The triangle intersection test takes two 2D triangles as input, and determines if they intersect or not. Each point-orientation test takes a 2D/3D point and a 2D/3D shape as input, and determines if the point is inside/above or outside/below the shape. We collected four point-orientation tests: 2D point-to-triangle, 2D point-to-circle, 3D point-to-sphere, and 3D point-to-plane. All geometric primitives take a sequence of floating-point coordinates in the range $[-100, 100)$ as input. Their output is a boolean value indicating the relationship between geometric objects, which is also our chosen signature.

4.2 GRT Benchmarks

Variance Calculation: We implemented the naïve variance calculation, which is known to suffer from catastrophic cancellation effects [23]: $var(X) = E[X^2] - (E[X])^2$. Here, X is a random floating-point variable in the range $[-100, 100)$ and $var(X)$ is its variance. The post-condition states that the computed variance must be non-negative, and is captured with the signature $var(X) \geq 0$.

Exclusive Prefix Sum: The procedure takes an array $X_1, \ldots, X_N$ as input, and outputs a sequence of summations $Y_1, \ldots, Y_N$ such that $Y_1 = 0$ and $Y_i = \sum_{k=1}^{i-1} X_k$ for $2 \leq i \leq N$. If all input values are non-negative, exclusive prefix sum must output a monotonically increasing sequence. We implemented the naïve and two-phase scan [17] algorithms. We provide them with a sequence of floating-point values in the range $[0, 100)$ as input. Given output values $Y_1, \ldots, Y_N$, the post-condition is directly described in the signature function as:

$$(Y_2 \geq Y_1) \wedge (Y_3 \geq Y_2) \wedge \ldots \wedge (Y_N \geq Y_{N-1}). \qquad (2)$$

Standard and Approximate Sorting: These benchmarks bubble-sort a sequence of N floating-point values obtained using a procedure that introduces round-off errors. More specifically, we generate each value in the sequence to be sorted by summing over N floating-point values in the range $[-100, 100)$. Standard sorting judges the output sequence as correct when it is strictly non-decreasing, whereas approximate sorting allows for a bounded degree of mis-orderings, defined as follows. Given an unsorted input $X = X_1, \ldots, X_N$ and a sorted output $Y = Y_1, \ldots, Y_N$, let $Z = Z_1, \ldots, Z_N$ be the permutation vector. For example, if $X = \langle 7, 6, 8, 5 \rangle$ and $Y = \langle 5, 6, 7, 8 \rangle$, then $Z = \langle 3, 2, 4, 1 \rangle$. Let Z_F be the permutation vector under floating-points and Z_R under reals. We define the degree of misorderings d_{mis} as the mean-square of $Z_R - Z_F$. Then, our post-condition for approximate sorting is $d_{mis} \leq \sqrt{N}$. For standard sorting, our post-condition is $Y_1 \leq Y_2 \leq \ldots \leq Y_N$. We define a common signature function as Eq. 2.

For both types of sorting we use the above conjunctive signature. Hence, signature violations do not necessarily lead to post-condition violations for approximate sorting. Thus, an additional divergence check $d_{mis} < \sqrt{N}$ is required to confirm the inputs violating the differential contract. We call this additional divergence check an *externally specified contract*.

4.3 ABS Results

Table 1a shows our experimental results for ABS. Each run of ABS can restart multiple times to find an initial pair of points. All our experiments were performed on a machine with 12 Intel Xeon 2.40 GHz CPUs and 48 GB RAM. (We currently use only one processor of this multi-processor machine; parallelizing ABS and GRT is future work). We measure the efficiency of ABS using the number of inputs enumerated to trigger the first divergence within 30 min. To measure scalability, we experiment with large program inputs (thousands of input variables). Our experiments show that ABS efficiently detects divergences by enumerating just a few hundreds of inputs even for large input sizes. Furthermore, ABS usually restarts only a few times to find initial end points.

Discussion: As expected of dynamic analysis techniques that need to repeatedly execute programs, practical efficiency of our divergence detection methods is related to execution times of programs under test. For example, simple convex hull is an $O(N^3)$ algorithm, and its execution time becomes very long for large input sizes. Hence, ABS detected only 6 divergences over 10 runs for Conv. hull simple with 2000 input variables. When given extra time, more runs of ABS successfully detect divergences: Conv. hull simple $(1\,h)/(2\,h)$ in Table 1a denotes the result of running ABS for 1/2 hour(s).

ABS uses random search to find initial end points (see Algorithm 1), but programmers can provide hints to facilitate search. For our shortest path benchmark with input size of 2450, ABS failed to detect divergences in all runs since it

Table 1. Experimental results. *ISize* is the input size (i.e., the number of input floating-point values); *SRate* is the number of divergences detected in ten runs (each run either finds a divergence or timeouts after 30 min); *Samples* is the average number of inputs enumerated to trigger the first divergence, computed over runs that successfully found one (*N/A* denotes experiments that fail in all runs); *RT* is the number of divergences triggered using 1 million random inputs; *Restarts* is the average number of restarts over 10 runs of ABS.

Benchmark	ISize	SRate	Samples	Restarts	RT
Conv. hull simple	200	10/10	3.21e+2	0.2	0
	2000	6/10	3.66e+2	0	N/A
Conv. hull simple (1 hr.)	2000	9/10	4.61e+2	0	N/A
Conv. hull simple (2 hr.)	2000	10/10	5.16e+2	0	N/A
Conv. hull incremental	200	10/10	2.65e+2	0.1	0
	2000	10/10	5.60e+2	0.1	0
Conv. hull quick-hull	200	10/10	3.03e+2	0.1	0
	2000	10/10	4.68e+2	0.2	0
Conv. hull Graham	200	10/10	2.26e+2	0.0	0
	2000	10/10	6.09e+2	0.2	1
Shortest path	90	10/10	2.43e+2	5.7	0
	2450	0/10	N/A	N/A	0
Shortest path with manual hint	2450	10/10	1.27e+2	2.4	0
Line × Adjacent Triangles	18	10/10	8.19e+2	15.7	0
Line × Adjacent Triangles with manual hint	18	10/10	6.24e+2	5.5	0
Tri. intersection	12	10/10	3.86e+1	0.3	0
Pt. triangle	8	10/10	8.43e+1	1.2	0
Pt. plane (3x3)	12	10/10	5.02e+1	0.7	0
Pt. plane (4x4)	12	10/10	6.11e+1	1.0	1
Pt. circle (3x3)	8	10/10	2.64e+1	0	0
Pt. circle (4x4)	8	10/10	3.70e+1	0.3	0
Pt. sphere (4x4)	15	10/10	3.05e+1	0.1	1
Pt. sphere (5x5)	15	10/10	3.33e+1	0.2	1

(a) Experimental Results for ABS

Benchmark	ISize	SRate	Samples	RT
Variance est.	1000	10/10	1.28e+3	0
	10000	10/10	6.10e+2	0
Naïve scan (single)	1024	10/10	2.55e+3	0
	8192	10/10	1.03e+3	0
Naïve scan (multi)	1024	0/10	N/A	0
	8192	0/10	N/A	0
Two-phase scan (single)	1024	0/10	N/A	0
	8192	0/10	N/A	0
Two-phase scan (multi)	1024	0/10	N/A	0
	8192	0/10	N/A	0
Standard sorting (single)	4096	10/10	7.25e+2	70
	10000	10/10	2.42e+2	220
Standard sorting (multi)	4096	10/10	5.08e+2	70
	10000	10/10	1.19e+2	220
Approx. sorting (single)	4096	9/10	2.15e+4	0
	10000	7/10	2.06e+4	0
Approx. sorting (multi)	4096	10/10	4.63e+3	0
	10000	10/10	1.89e+3	0

(b) Experimental Results for GRT. The two-phase scan is divergence-free. The results of the naïve scan and sorting show the difference between selecting the single-term (*single*) and the multi-term (*multi*) objectives for optimization. The random testing results are the same for the two objectives.

failed to find initial end points: all randomly sampled inputs contained negative cycles. However, it is easy to manually provide an input which does not contain a negative cycle by assigning positive values to all edges' weights. Using this simple hint, ABS successfully detected divergences even in this case (see *Shortest path with manual hint* in Table 1a). Applying manual hints also improves ABS's efficiency of divergence detection. For our intersection check benchmark, we provided ABS with a manual hint causing different triangles to be intersected by the line (see *Line × Adjacent Triangles with manual hint* in Table 1a). Compared to the result that uses random search (see *Line × Adjacent Triangles*), with the manual hint ABS spent fewer enumerations to detect divergences.

Weak Signature Functions: Both ABS and GRT expect signature functions that satisfy Eq. 1. However, both methods could work even with signature functions that do not satisfy this equation. For example, for the convex hull

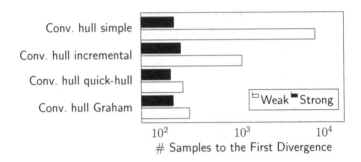

Fig. 3. Comparison of Using Strong and Weak Signature Functions with ABS

benchmarks we used a signature function that generates a boolean vector recording the point-orientation decisions made in the process of generating a convex
hull. We call such signature functions *weak signature functions*, while those satisfying the equation are *strong signature functions*. Figure 3 shows the comparison
between using the two types of signatures. The black bars indicate the usage of a
strong signature function (the number of the output hull vertices), and the white
bars the usage of a weak signature function (the decision sequence). The shorter
the bar, the fewer inputs enumerated by ABS were required to trigger the first
divergence, implying better efficiency of divergence detection. Our results show
that ABS can work with weak signature functions, but the efficiency is lower
than when using the strong ones.

4.4   GRT Results

Table 1b shows our experimental results for GRT. Benchmarks labeled with *sin-
gle/multi* denote the single-/multi-term objective applied to our optimizer (as
described in Sect. 3.2). The S3FP optimizer we use is an efficient tool for triggering high round-off errors [9]. Note that the random testing results under both
objectives are the same because objective selection and random testing are independent. GRT detects divergences in all our benchmarks except the two-phase
exclusive scan, which is expected since it is a divergence-free benchmark. The
results also suggest that GRT is scalable since it can handle large input sizes. It
is more efficient than random testing even for standard sorting. For example, for
the standard sorting with 256 input variables, GRT enumerates 5590 inputs on
average to trigger a divergence, while random testing needs over 300,000 inputs.

Discussion: While our dynamic analysis methods can precisely detect diverging
inputs, they cannot establish divergence-freedom when divergence is not possible in any feasible execution. For example, even though two-phase scan is a
divergence-free algorithm when inputs are non-negative, we cannot infer that
solely because GRT did not detect a divergence. (We omit the proof in this
paper; it can be done by a simple induction). Automatically proving divergence-
freedom can be done using static analysis techniques [7], which is complementary
to our work.

The results of the naïve scan and approximate sorting benchmarks indicate that the GRT's efficiency can be affected by optimization objective selection. Applying the single-term objective to the naïve scan can successfully detect divergences in all runs. On the other hand, applying the multi-term objective resulted in no detected divergences. However, the results for the approximate sorting show the opposite: applying the multi-term objective found more divergences than the single-term objective (29 over 30 runs versus 20 over 30 runs). As future work, we plan to explore heuristics for choosing a good optimization objective.

4.5 Random Testing

To demonstrate efficiency, we compare our methods with random testing, which is, to the best of our knowledge, the only divergence detection approach available to today's designers. In all our experiments, we randomly generated one million inputs for each input size, and column *RT* in Table 1 gives the number of divergences detected. At most one divergence was triggered in most of the benchmarks except the standard sorting. The results for *Conv. hull simple* with the input size of 2000 are not available because the execution time is very high (one million executions can take more than a week to finish). Our random testing results suggest that divergence is very difficult to detect without applying good search strategies such as ABS and GRT.

5 Related Work

In [7], the authors propose a verifier that attempts to prove that a set of user-specified axioms (e.g., Knuth's axioms for convex hulls [19]) cannot be violated by any control-flow path in a piece of code. Their work does not address floating-point directly; in fact, they treat all conditionals as non-deterministic selection statements, which can be unrealistic. Also, devising axioms for new problems is non-trivially hard. The scalability of their symbolic decision procedure is also in doubt (tool unavailable), and it can also generate false alarms (our method does not generate false alarms). Our approach is more practical, as it requires users to provide discrete features, and not an axiomatic specification.

Runtime instability detection could also be used to detect divergence [1]. This work does not address the task of generating inputs that can quickly induce divergence.

The authors of [16] propose a method for witnessing branch deviations across platforms. Their targeting problem is similar to the problem described in [22], and it is different from our targeting problem: witnessing discrete feature deviations between floating-point and real computations (which is called *divergence* in this paper). The key idea of their method is firstly using a SMT solver to find a candidate input, and then searching close inputs around the candidate and checking if any of them triggering a deviation. Our approach can address many practical scalability issues such as handling non-linear operations, and can be applied with equal ease even when source codes are unavailable.

White-Box Sampling: White-box sampling [2] was proposed for finding discontinuous program behaviors. In this work, a program is seen as a composition of continuous functions which have disjoint input domains. White-box sampling tries to discover all continuous functions by finding at least one input for each of their input domains. The approach of checking whether two inputs belong to the same continuous function's domain is by comparing the decision sequences generated in the executions. A decision sequence is composed with floating-point-decided discrete values, called discrete factors, like branch decision and float-to-int type casting. Such discrete factor sequence can be one of the weak signatures adopted by ABS (demonstrated in Sect. 4.3). Extracting discrete factor sequences from executions requires program instrumentation which is difficult to apply to large-scale programs (e.g. programs invoke dynamic linked libraries). However, ABS is not restricted to using discrete factor sequence as signature. ABS can treat programs as black boxes and adopt signature functions which directly observe program outputs.

Floating-Point Program Testing Methods and Dynamic Precision Analysis: Both our divergence detection method and dynamic round-off error estimation [9] are methods for testing floating-point programs. However, dynamic round-off error estimation merely triggers high error on a given expression while ABS and GRT automatically find inputs that cause divergence. We can see the both divergence detection and round-off error estimation are two methods for finding inputs triggering floating-point imprecision scenarios. The inputs are important for dynamic floating-point analyses to avoid overly underapproximating floating-point imprecision. Examples of dynamic floating-point analyses which use concrete inputs to profile precision are catastrophic cancellation detection [3], instability detection [1], auto-tuning [25], and synthesis [26].

6   Concluding Remarks

With the increasing pressure to reduce data movement, reducing floating-point precision allocation is a necessity. Also, the increasing platform heterogeneity is likely to increase the proclivity for program divergence — a definite impediment to achieving execution reproducibility. In this paper, we offer the first in-depth study of divergence. Our experimental results suggest that our new heuristics, namely ABS and GRT, are capable of handling many practical examples with well over 1000 inputs by quickly guiding input generation to locate divergence. For our future work, we plan to study heterogeneity-induced divergence scenarios.

References

1. Bao, T., Zhang, X.: On-the-fly detection of instability problems in floating-point program execution. In: OOPSLA, pp. 817–832 (2013)

2. Bao, T., Zheng, Y., Zhang, X.: White box sampling in uncertain data processing enabled by program analysis. In: OOPSLA, pp. 897–914 (2012)
3. Benz, F., Hildebrandt, A., Hack, S.: A dynamic program analysis to find floating-point accuracy problems. In: PLDI, pp. 453–462 (2012)
4. de Berg, M., Cheong, O., van Kreveld, M., Overmars, M.: Computational Geometry: Algorithms and Applications, 3rd edn. Springer-Verlag TELOS, Heidelberg (2008)
5. Bykat, A.: Convex hull of a finite set of points in two dimensions. Inf. Process. Lett. **7**(6), 296–298 (1978)
6. CGAL, Computational Geometry Algorithms Library. http://www.cgal.org
7. Chaudhuri, S., Farzan, A., Kincaid, Z.: Consistency analysis of decision-making programs. In: POPL, pp. 555–567 (2014)
8. Chiang, W.-F., Gopalakrishnan, G., Rakamarić, Z.: Unsafe floating-point to unsigned integer casting check for GPU programs. In: NSV (2015)
9. Chiang, W.-F., Gopalakrishnan, G., Rakamarić, Z., Solovyev, A.: Efficient search for inputs causing high floating-point errors. In: PPOPP, pp. 43–52 (2014)
10. Darulova, E., Kuncak, V.: Sound compilation of reals. In: POPL, pp. 235–248 (2014)
11. de Moura, L., Bjørner, N.S.: Z3: an efficient SMT solver. In: Ramakrishnan, C.R., Rehof, J. (eds.) TACAS 2008. LNCS, vol. 4963, pp. 337–340. Springer, Heidelberg (2008)
12. Ericson, C.: Real-Time Collision Detection, vol. 14. Elsevier, Amsterdam (2005)
13. Floyd, R.W.: Algorithm 97: shortest path. Commun. ACM **5**(6), 345 (1962)
14. Goldberg, D.: What every computer scientist should know about floating-point arithmetic. ACM Comput. Surv. (CSUR) **23**, 5–48 (1991)
15. Graham, R.L.: An efficient algorithm for determining the convex hull of a finite planar set. Inf. Process. Lett. **1**, 132–133 (1972)
16. Gu, Y., Wahl, T., Bayati, M., Leeser, M.: Behavioral non-portability in scientific numeric computing. In: Träff, J.L., Hunold, S., Versaci, F. (eds.) Euro-Par 2015. LNCS, vol. 9233, pp. 558–569. Springer, Heidelberg (2015)
17. Harris, M., Sengupta, S., Owens, J.D.: Parallel prefix sum (scan) with CUDA. GPU Gems **3**(39), 851–876 (2007)
18. Kettner, L., Mehlhorn, K., Pion, S., Schirra, S., Yap, C.: Classroom examples of robustness problems in geometric computations. Comput. Geom. Theor. Appl. **40**(1), 61–78 (2008)
19. Knuth, D.E.: Axioms and Hulls. LNCS, vol. 606. Springer, Heidelberg (1992). ISBN:3-540-55611-7
20. Lam, M.O., Hollingsworth, J.K., de Supinski, B.R., LeGendre, M.P.: Automatically adapting programs for mixed-precision floating-point computation. In: ICS, pp. 369–378 (2013)
21. Linderman, M.D., Ho, M., Dill, D.L., Meng, T.H.Y., Nolan, G.P.: Towards program optimization through automated analysis of numerical precision. In: CGO, pp. 230–237 (2010)
22. Meng, Q., Humphrey, A., Schmidt, J., Berzins, M.: Preliminary experiences with the uintah framework on intel Xeon phi, stampede. In: XSEDE, pp. 48:1–48:8 (2013)
23. Paganelli, G., Ahrendt, W.: Verifying (in-)stability in floating-point programs by increasing precision, using smt solving. In: SYNASC, pp. 209–216 (2013)
24. Panchekha, P., Sanchez-Stern, A., Wilcox, J.R., Tatlock, Z.: Automatically improving accuracy for floating point expressions. In: PLDI, pp. 1–11 (2015)

25. Rubio-González, C., Nguyen, C., Nguyen, H.D., Demmel, J., Kahan, W., Sen, K., Bailey, D.H., Iancu, C., Hough, D., Precimonious: tuning assistant for floating-point precision. In: SC, pp. 27:1–27:12 (2013)
26. Schkufza, E., Sharma, R., Aiken, A.: Stochastic optimization of floating-point programs with tunable precision. In: PLDI, pp. 53–64 (2014)
27. Shewchuk, J.R.: Adaptive precision floating-point arithmetic and fast robust geometric predicates. Discrete Comput. Geom. **18**(3), 305–363 (1997)
28. Solovyev, A., Jacobsen, C., Rakamaric, Z., Gopalakrishnan, G.: Rigorous estimation of floating-point round-off errors with symbolic taylor expansions. In: FM, pp. 532–550 (2015)
29. Taufer, M., Padron, O., Saponaro, P., Patel, S.: Improving numerical reproducibility and stability in large-scale numerical simulations on GPUs. In: IPDPS, pp. 1–9, April 2010

SMT Solving for the Theory of Ordering Constraints

Cunjing Ge[1]([⊠]), Feifei Ma[1], Jeff Huang[2], and Jian Zhang[1]

[1] Institute of Software, Chinese Academy of Sciences, Beijing, China
{gecj,maff,zj}@ios.ac.cn
[2] Department of Computer Science and Engineering, Texas A&M University,
College Station, USA
jeff@cse.tamu.edu

Abstract. Constraint solving and satisfiability checking play an important role in various tasks such as formal verification, software analysis and testing. In this paper, we identify a particular kind of constraints called ordering constraints, and study the problem of deciding satisfiability modulo such constraints. The theory of ordering constraints can be regarded as a special case of difference logic, and is essential for many important problems in symbolic analysis of concurrent programs. We propose a new approach for checking satisfiability modulo ordering constraints based on the DPLL(T) framework, and present our experimental results compared with state-of-the-art SMT solvers on both benchmarks and instances of real symbolic constraints.

1 Introduction

In the past decade, constraint solving and satisfiability checking techniques and tools have found more and more applications in various fields like formal methods, software engineering and security. In particular, Satisfiability Modulo Theories (SMT) solvers play a vital role in program analysis and testing. This work is motivated by the increasingly important use of SMT solving for symbolic analysis of concurrent programs.

It is well-known that concurrent programs are error-prone. Analyzing concurrent programs has been a big challenge due to subtle interactions among the concurrent threads exacerbated by the huge thread scheduling space. Among the broad spectrum of concurrency analysis techniques, symbolic analysis is probably the most promising approach that has attracted significant research attention in recent years [7,9,16–18,20,23,25,27,30]. Generally speaking, it models the scheduling of threads as symbolic constraints over *order variables* corresponding to the execution order of critical operations performed by threads (such as

This work is supported in part by National Basic Research (973) Program of China (No. 2014CB340701), National Natural Science Foundation of China (Grant No. 91418206, 91118007) and the CAS/SAFEA International Partnership Program for Creative Research Teams.

shared data accesses and synchronizations). The symbolic constraints capture both data and control dependencies among threads such that any solution to the constraints corresponds to a valid schedule.

A key advantage of symbolic analysis is that it allows reasoning about thread schedules with the help of automated constraint solving. By encoding interesting properties (such as race conditions) as additional constraints and solving them with a constraint solver, we can verify if there exists any valid schedule that can satisfy the property. Such an approach has been used for finding concurrency bugs such as data races [18,25], atomicity violations [30], deadlocks [7], null pointer executions [9], etc., and has also been used to reproduce concurrency failures [20,23], to generate tests [8], and to verify general properties [16,17]. In our prior work [18], we developed a tool called RVPredict, which is able to detect data races based on symbolic analysis of the program execution trace.

Despite its huge potential, symbolic analysis has not been widely adopted in practice. The main obstacle is the performance of constraint solvers. For real world applications, the size of complex constraints can be extremely large that is very challenging for existing SMT solvers to solve. For example, for data race detection in RVPredict, the number of constraints is cubic in the trace size, which can grow to *exascale* for large programs such as Apache Derby[1], the traces of which contain tens of millions of critical events [18]. We provide an illustrative example for RVPredict in Sect. 2.

To improve the scalability of symbolic analysis for analyzing concurrent programs, we need highly efficient constraint solvers. Fortunately, we note that the symbolic constraints in many problems [9,16–18,20,23,25] take a simple form. Each constraint consists of conjunctions and disjunctions of many simple Boolean expressions over atomic predicates which are just simple *ordering* comparisons. An example is: $O_1 < O_2 \wedge O_3 < O_4 \wedge (O_2 < O_3 \vee O_4 < O_1)$. Here each variable O_i denotes the occurrence of an event; and the relation $O_i < O_j$ means that event e_i happens before event e_j in certain schedules. A constraint like this is called an *ordering constraint* (OC). The relational operator could also be $\leq$, $\geq$, etc. However, the specific value difference between variables is irrelevant, because in many applications we do not concern about the real-time properties among events. Therefore, to solve ordering constraints, it is not necessary to use the full (integer) difference logic (DL), which is the most efficient decision procedure used by existing solvers for OC.

In this paper, we study properties and decision procedures for ordering constraints (OCs). The theory of ordering constraints is a fragment of difference logic, which can be decided by detecting negative cycles in the weighted digraph. However, we find that detecting negative cycles is not essential to the consistency checking of ordering constraints. In fact, the problem is closely related to the decomposition of a digraph into its strongly connected components. Based on Tarjan's strongly connected components algorithm, we propose a linear time decision procedure for checking satisfiability of ordering constraints, and investigate how to integrate it with the DPLL(T) framework. We have also

---

[1] http://db.apache.org/derby/.

initially $x=y=0$ resource $z=0$	
Thread $t1$	Thread $t2$
1. *fork t2*	
2. *lock l*	
3. $x = 1$	
4. $y = 1$	
5. *unlock l*	
	6. { //*begin*
	7. *lock l*
	8. $r1 = y$
	9. *unlock l*
	10. $r2 = x$
	11. *if*$(r1 == r2)$
	12. $z = 1$ (**auth**)
	13. } //*end*
14. *join t2*	
15. $r3 = z$ (**use**)	
16. *if*$(r3 == 0)$	
17. *Error*	

Fig. 1. An example with a race (3,10).

initially $x = y = z = 0$	
1. *fork*$(t1, t2)$	
2. *lock*$(t1, l)$	
3. *write*$(t1, x, 1)$	
4. *write*$(t1, y, 1)$	
5. *unlock*$(t1, l)$	
	6. *begin*$(t2)$
	7. *lock*$(t2, l)$
	8. *read*$(t2, y, 1)$
	9. *unlock*$(t2, l)$
	10. *read*$(t2, x, 1)$
	11. *branch*$(t2)$
	12. *write*$(t2, z, 1)$
	13. *end*$(t2)$
14. *join*$(t1, t2)$	
15. *read*$(t1, z, 1)$	
16. *branch*$(t1)$	

Fig. 2. A trace corresponding to the example

developed a customized solver for SMT(OC), and conducted extensive evaluation of its performance compared with two state-of-the-art SMT solvers, Z3 [5] and OpenSMT [3], on both benchmarks and real symbolic constraints from RVPredict. Though not optimized, our tool achieves comparable performance as that of Z3 and OpenSMT both of which are highly optimized. We present our experimental results in Sect. 6.

The rest of the paper is organized as follows. We first provide a motivating example to show how ordering constraints are derived from symbolic analysis of concurrent programs in Sect. 2. We then formally define ordering constraints and the constraint graph in Sect. 3 and present a linear time decision procedure for OC in Sect. 4. We further discuss how to integrate the decision procedure with the DPLL(T) framework to solve SMT(OC) formulas in Sect. 5.

2   Motivation

To elucidate the ordering constraints, let's consider a data race detection problem based on the symbolic analysis proposed in RVPredict [18].

The program in Fig. 1 contains a race condition between lines (3,10) on a shared variable x that may cause an authentication failure of resource z at line 12, which in consequence causes an error to occur when z is used at line 15. Non-symbolic analysis techniques such as happens-before [10], causal-precedes [28], and the lockset algorithm [19,26] either cannot detect this race or report false alarms. RVPredict is able to detect this race by observing an execution trace of the program following an interleaving denoted by the line numbers (which does not manifest the race). The trace (shown in Fig. 2) contains a sequence of events emitted in the execution, including thread *fork* and *join*, *begin* and *end*, *read* and *write*, *lock* and *unlock*, as well as *branch* events.

The constructed symbolic constraints (shown in Fig. 3) based on the trace consist of three parts: (A) the must happen-before (MHB) constraints, (B) the locking constraints, and (C) the race constraints. The MHB constraints encode the ordering requirements among events that must always hold. For example, the *fork* event at line 1 must happen before the *lock* event at line 2 and the *begin* event of $t2$ at line 6, so we have $O_1 < O_2$ and $O_1 < O_6$. The locking constraints encode lock mutual exclusion consistency over *lock* and *unlock* events. For example, $O_5 < O_7 \lor O_9 < O_2$ means that either $t1$ acquires the lock l first and $t2$ second, or $t2$ acquires l first and $t1$ second. If $t1$ first, then the *lock* at line 7 must happen after the *unlock* at line 5; otherwise if $t2$ first, the *lock* at line 2 should happen after the *unlock* at line 9.

The race constraints encode the data race condition. For example, for (3,10), the race constraint is written as $O_{10} = O_3$, meaning that these two events are un-ordered. For (12,15), because there is a *branch* event (at line 11) before line 12, the control-flow condition at the *branch* event needs to be satisfied as well. So the race constraint is written as $O_{10} = O_3 \land O_3 < O_{10} \land O_4 < O_8$, to ensure that the *read* event at line 10 reads value 1 on x, and that the *read* event at line 8 reads value 1 on y. The size of symbolic constraints, in the worst case, is cubic in the number of reads and writes in the trace.

Putting all these constraints together, the technique then invokes a solver to compute a solution for these unknown order variables. For (3,10), the solver returns a solution which corresponds to the interleaving 1-6-7-8-9-2-3-10, so (3,10) is a race. For (12,15), the solver reports no solution, so it is not a race.

The symbolic constraints above are easy to solve, since the size of the trace is small in this simple example. However, for real world programs with long running executions, the constraints can quickly exceed the capability of existing solvers such as Z3 [5] as the constraint size is cubic in the trace size. As a result, RVPredict has to cut the trace into smaller chunks and only detects races in each chunk separately, resulting in missing races across chunks. Hence, to scale RVPredict to larger traces and to find more races, it is important to design more efficient solvers that are customized for solving the ordering constraints. Although we focus on motivating this problem with RVPredict, the ordering constraints are applicable to many other concurrency analysis problems such as replay [23], failure reproduction [20], concurrency property violation detection [9,17], model checking [16], etc.

We next formalize the ordering constraints and present our algorithm to solve this problem with a linear time decision procedure.

3   Preliminaries

Definition 1. *An **ordering constraint** (OC) is a comparison between two numeric variables. It can be represented as $(x \; op \; y)$, where $op \in \{<, \leq, >, \geq, =, \neq\}$.*

A. MHB	$O_1 < O_2 < \ldots < O_5$
	$O_{14} < \ldots < O_{16}$
	$O_6 < O_7 < \ldots < O_{13}$
	$O_1 < O_6 \wedge O_{13} < O_{14}$
B. Locking	$O_5 < O_7 \vee O_9 < O_2$
C. Race (3,10)	$O_{10} = O_3$
Race (12,15)	$O_{15} = O_{12}$
	$O_3 < O_{10} \wedge O_4 < O_8$

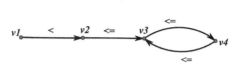

Fig. 3. Symbolic constraints of the trace

Fig. 4. Example 1

The theory of ordering constraints is a special case of difference logic, where the constant c in the difference theory atom $((x - y) \; op \; c)$ is restricted to 0.

Definition 2. *An SMT formula ϕ over ordering constraints, i.e., an **SMT(OC) formula**, can be represented as a Boolean formula $PS_\phi(b_1, \ldots, b_n)$ together with definitions in the form: $b_i \equiv x \; op \; y$, where $op \in \{<, \leq, >, \geq, =, \neq\}$. That means, the Boolean variable b_i stands for the ordering constraint $(x \; op \; y)$. PS_ϕ is the* propositional skeleton *of the formula ϕ.*

Without loss of generality, we can restrict the relational operators to $<$ and $\leq$. In other words, the problem at hand is a Boolean combination of atoms of the form $x < y$ or $x \leq y$.

A set of ordering constraints can be naturally represented with a directed graph.

Definition 3. *Given a set of ordering constraints, the **constraint graph of the ordering constraints** is a digraph $G = \{V, E\}$ which is constructed in the following way:*

1. *For each variable x_i, introduce a vertex $v_i \in V$.*
2. *For each constraint $x_i < x_j$, introduce an edge $e_{i,j}^< \in E$ from v_i to v_j.*
3. *For each constraint $x_i \leq x_j$, introduce an edge $e_{i,j}^\leq \in E$ from v_i to v_j.*

Definition 4. *The **out-degree** of a vertex v of digraph G is the number of edges that start from v, and is denoted by **outdeg**(v). Similarly, the **in-degree** of v is the number of edges that end at v, and is denoted by **indeg**(v).*

Example 1. Consider a set of ordering constraints: $\{x_1 < x_2, \; x_2 \leq x_3, \; x_3 \leq x_4, x_4 \leq x_3\}$. Figure 4 shows the constraint graph constructed by Definition 3. The variables $\{x_1, x_2, x_3, x_4\}$ are represented by the nodes $\{v_1, v_2, v_3, v_4\}$, respectively, and outdeg$(x_3) = 1$ and indeg$(x_3) = 2$.

Recall that difference logic also has a graph representation. A set of difference arithmetic atoms can be represented by a weighted directed graph, where each node corresponds to a variable, and each edge with weight corresponds to a difference arithmetic atom. Obviously the constraint graph of ordering constraints can be viewed as a special case of that of difference logic, where all weights can only take two values. The distinction between ordering constraints and difference logic seems to be slight. However, in the rest of the paper we will show how this minor difference leads to a new decision procedure with lower time complexity.

4   The Decision Procedure for Ordering Constraints

It is well known that DL can be decided by detecting negative cycles in the weighted directed graph with the Bellman-Ford algorithm [24]. The complexity of the classical decision procedure for DL is $O(nm)$, where n is the number of variables, and m is the number of constraints. As a fragment of difference logic, ordering constraints can be directly checked with the aforementioned algorithm. However, through exploring the structure of the constraint graph of ordering constraints, we observe that detecting negative cycles is not essential to the consistency checking of OC. In this section, we propose a new way to check the inconsistency of OC, which needs only to examine the constraint graph in linear time.

Before presenting the decision procedure for OC, we first introduce some theoretical results on OC and its constraint graph.

Lemma 1. *If digraph G has no cycle, then G has a vertex of out-degree 0 and a vertex of in-degree 0.*

Proof. We prove this lemma via reduction to absurdity. Assume for each vertex v of G, $outdeg(v) > 0$. Let v_1 be a vertex in V. Since $outdeg(v_1) > 0$ by the assumption, there exists an edge e_1 which starts from v_1 and ends at v_2. Since $outdeg(v_2) > 0$, there exists an edge e_2 which starts from v_2 and ends at v_3, and so on and so forth. In this way, we obtain an infinite sequence of vertices $\{v_1, \ldots, v_k, \ldots\}$. Note that $|V|$ is finite, there must exist a cycle in this sequence, which contradicts the precondition that G has no cycle. The proof of case of in-degree is analogous.

Lemma 2. *Given a set of ordering constraints α, if its constraint graph G has no cycle, then α is consistent.*

Proof. Based on the acyclic digraph G, we construct a feasible solution to the variables of α in the following way:

(1) Set $i = 0$, and $G_0 = G$.
(2) Find the set V_i' of vertices of in-degree 0 in $G_i = (V_i, E_i)$. For each vertex v_t in V_i', let the corresponding variable $x_t = i$.
(3) Let $E_i' = \{e | e \in E_i$ and e starts from a vertex in $V_i'\}$. Construct the subgraph G_{i+1} of G_i by $G_{i+1} = (V_{i+1}, E_{i+1}) = (V_i - V_i', E_i - E_i')$.
(4) Repeat step (2) and (3) until G_i is empty.

We now show that this procedure terminates with a solution that satisfies α. Note that G is acyclic and each G_i is a subgraph of G, so G_i is acyclic. According to Lemma 1, we have $|V_i'| > 0$ every time the iteration reaches step (2). Therefore, this procedure will terminate.

Consider two adjacent vertices v_p and v_q with an edge $\langle v_p, v_q \rangle$. As long as v_p remains in the current graph G_i, $\text{indeg}(v_q) > 0$. Hence v_p must be deleted earlier than v_q, and we have $x_p < x_q$. In general, for an arbitrary pair of vertices $(v_p$ and $v_q)$, if there exists a path from v_p to v_q, namely $\langle v_p, v_{p_1}, \ldots, v_{p_k}, v_q \rangle$, then we have $x_p < x_{p_1} < \cdots < x_{p_k} < x_q \Rightarrow x_p < x_q$.

Theorem 1. *Given a set of ordering constraints α and its constraint graph G, α is inconsistent if and only if there exists a maximal strongly connected component of G that contains an $e^<$ edge.*

Proof. $\Longleftarrow$ Let G' be a maximal strongly connected component of G which contains an $e^<$ edge $\langle v_1, v_2 \rangle$. Since v_1 and v_2 are reachable from each other, there exists a path from v_2 to v_1 in G'. Without loss of generality, we assume the path is $\{v_2, \ldots, v_n, v_1\}$. The path and the edge $\langle v_1, v_2 \rangle$ form a cycle in G', which implies that $x_1 < x_2 \leq \cdots \leq x_n \leq x_1$. Thus $x_1 < x_1$, and α is inconsistent.

$\Longrightarrow$ We prove this via reduction to absurdity. Suppose every maximal strongly connected component of G does not contain an $e^<$ edge. Consider an arbitrary pair of vertices v_p and v_q that are reachable from each other. Since v_p and v_q belong to a maximal strongly connected component, there only exist $e^\leq$ edges in the path from v_p to v_q, then $x_p \leq x_q$. On the other hand, we have $x_p \geq x_q$. As a result, $x_p = x_q$. Let $G_s = (V_s, E_s)$ be a maximal strongly connected component of G. We could merge vertices of V_s into one vertex v and obtain a new graph $G' = (V', E')$, where $V' = (V - V_s) \cup \{v\}$ and $E' = \{\langle v_i, v_j \rangle | \langle v_i, v_j \rangle \in E, v_i \notin V_s, v_j \notin V_s\} \cup \{\langle v, v_j \rangle | \langle v_i, v_j \rangle \in E, v_i \in V_s, v_j \notin V_s\} \cup \{\langle v_i, v \rangle | \langle v_i, v_j \rangle \in E, v_i \notin V_s, v_j \in V_s\}$. In addition, $x = x_i, \forall v_i \in V_s$. Consider the following way to construct a solution to α. For each maximal strongly connected component of G, we merge it into a vertex and finally obtain $G' = (V', E')$. Note that such G' is unique and acyclic. We could construct a solution from G' by Lemma 2.

We now show the solution constructed by this procedure satisfies α. That is, for each pair of vertices (v_p, v_q), if there exists a path from v_p to v_q, then $x_p \leq x_q$. Furthermore, if there exists an $e^<$ edge in a path from v_p to v_q, then $x_p < x_q$. Let v_p and v_q map to v_p' and v_q' of G'. If $v_p' = v_q'$, then $x_p = x_p' = x_q' = x_q$. Otherwise, there exists a path from v_p' to v_q'. By Lemma 2, $x_p = x_p' < x_q' = x_q$. Hence $x_p \leq x_q$ always holds. If there exists an $e^<$ edge in a path from v_p to v_q, then v_p and v_q cannot be in the same maximal strongly connected component. Therefore, $v_p' \neq v_q' \Rightarrow x_p < x_q$. It can be concluded that α is consistent since the solution satisfies the constraints of α.

Example 2. Recall in Example 1 that there are 3 strongly connected components $\{\{v_1\}, \{v_2\}, \{v_3, v_4\}\}$. If we add a constraint $x_3 \leq x_1$, the resulting constraint graph is shown in Fig. 5. There is only one strongly connected component, which

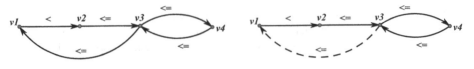

Fig. 5. Example 2   **Fig. 6.** Example 3

itself is a connected graph. Since $\langle v_1, v_2 \rangle$ is an $e^<$ edge, the conjunction of ordering constraints is inconsistent by Theorem 1. The conflict $x_1 < x_1$ can be drawn from $\{x_1 < x_2,\ x_2 \leq x_3,\ x_3 \leq x_1\}$.

Theorem 1 suggests that, to check the consistency of ordering constraints, we can decompose its constraint graph into maximal strongly connected components and then examine the edges. We use Tarjan's algorithm [29] to find the maximal strongly connected components in our ordering constraints theory solver. It produces a unique partition of the graph's vertices into the graph's strongly connected components. Each vertex of the graph appears in exactly one of these components. Then we check each edge in these components whether it is an $e^<$ edge. Therefore the consistency of conjunctions of ordering constraints can be decided in $O(n + m)$ time.

5   Integrating DP_{OC} into DPLL(T)

5.1   The DPLL(T) Framework

DPLL(T) is a generalization of DPLL for solving a decidable first order theory T. The DPLL(T) system consists of two parts: the global DPLL(X) module and a decision procedure DP_T for the given theory T. The DPLL(X) part is a general DPLL engine that is independent of any particular theory T [13]. It interacts with DP_T through a well-defined interface. The DPLL(T) framework is illustrated in Fig. 7. We assume that the readers are familiar with DPLL components, such as Decide, BCP, Analyze and Backtrack. The component TP represents theory propagation, which is invoked when no more implications can be made by BCP. It deduces literals that are implied by the current assignment in theory T, and communicates the implications to the BCP part. Although theory propagation is not essential to the functionality of the solving procedure, it is vital to the efficiency of the procedure. The component Check encapsulates the decision procedure DP_T for consistency checking of the current assignment. If inconsistencies are detected, it generates theory-level minimal conflict clauses.

5.2   Theory-Level Lemma Learning

We now discuss how to integrate the decision procedure DP_{OC} into the DPLL(T) framework. In DPLL(T), the decision procedure is called repeatedly to check the consistency of (partial) assignments. To avoid frequent construction/destruction of constraint graphs, at the beginning of the solving process, we construct the

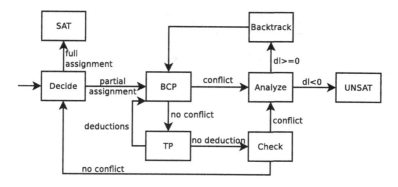

Fig. 7. The DPLL(T) Framework

constraint graph G of the set of all predicates in the target SMT(OC) formula. In this graph, each edge has two states: an edge is **active** if its corresponding boolean variable is assigned a value (true, false); and is **inactive** if its corresponding boolean variable is undefined.

Notice that initially all edges are inactive. When the solver finds a partial assignment α, the edges in G corresponding to α are activated. Hence the constraint graph G_α of the ordering constraints of α consists of every active edge in G, and is a subgraph of G. The decision procedure DP_{OC} checks the consistency of α based on G_α.

Example 3. Consider a formula $PS_\phi(b_1, b_2, b_3, b_4, b_5) = (b_1 \wedge (\neg b_2) \wedge (b_3 \vee b_4 \vee b_5))$, $\{b_1 \equiv x_1 < x_2, b_2 \equiv x_3 < x_2, b_3 \equiv x_3 \leq x_4, b_4 \equiv x_4 \leq x_3, b_5 \equiv x_3 \leq x_1\}$. Figure 6 shows the constraint graph G_β of all predicates in this formula with a possible partial assignment β, $\{b_1 = True, b_2 = False, b_3 = True, b_4 = True, b_5 = Undefined\}$. Note that $\{\langle v_1, v_2 \rangle, \langle v_2, v_3 \rangle, \langle v_3, v_4 \rangle, \langle v_4, v_3 \rangle\}$ are active and $\langle v_3, v_1 \rangle$ is inactive. Actually, the graph of Example 1 is a subgraph of G_β, which can be constructed by choosing all active edges in G_β.

To maximize the benefits of integration, the OC solver should be able to communicate theory lemmas to the SAT engine, including conflict clauses and deduction clauses at the OC theory level. We next discuss two such techniques.

Minimal Conflict Explanation. According to Theorem 1, the OC solver detects an inconsistency of the current assignment if it finds an $e^<$ edge in a strongly connected component of the constraint graph G. Without loss of generality, we assume the $e^<$ edge is $e = \langle v_1, v_2 \rangle$, and denote the strongly connected component by G'. The inconsistency is essentially caused by a cycle that contains e. Note that all paths from v_2 to v_1 are in G'. Hence we only have to find a shortest path from v_2 to v_1 in G' instead of G. The shortest path from v_2 to v_1 and the edge $e = \langle v_1, v_2 \rangle$ form a shortest cycle with an $e^<$ edge, corresponding to the minimal conflict that gives rise to the inconsistency. Therefore, we generate theory-level conflict clauses according to such cycles.

Algorithm 1. Tarjan's Algorithm Combined With Theory Propagation

---

Tarjan() initialize v, S, *index*, *scc*;
for each v *that* v.*index is undefined* **in** V **do**
  | Tarjan_DFS(v);

Tarjan_DFS(v) v.index, v.lowlink $\leftarrow$ *index*, *index* $\leftarrow$ *index* $+$ 1, S.push(v);
for each *active edge* $\langle v, w \rangle$ **in** E **do**
  | **if** w *is not visited* **then**
  | | w.father $\leftarrow$ v;
  | | **if** $\langle v, w \rangle$ *is an* $e^<$ *edge* **then**
  | | | w.nf $\leftarrow$ v.nf $+$ 1;
  | | **else**
  | | | w.nf $\leftarrow$ v.nf;
  | | Tarjan_DFS(w);
  | | v.lowlink $\leftarrow$ min(v.lowlink, w.lowlink);
  | **else if** w **in** S **then**
  | | v.lowlink $\leftarrow$ min(v.lowlink, w.index);

if v.*lowlink* $=$ v.*index* **then**
  | **repeat**
  | | s, t $\leftarrow$ S.pop(), s.scc $\leftarrow$ *scc*;
  | | **while** t.*father is defined* **do**
  | | | t $\leftarrow$ t.father;
  | | | **if** $(\langle s, t \rangle$ *or* $\langle t, s \rangle$ *is inactive)* **and** *(s.nf $>$ t.nf or $\langle s, t \rangle$ is an* $e^<$
  | | | *edge)* **then**
  | | | | generate TP clause from s to t by father vertex records;
  | | **until** ($s = v$);
  | *scc* $\leftarrow$ *scc* $+$ 1;

Theory Propagation. In order to improve performance, we apply a "cheap" theory propagation technique. Our theory propagation is combined with the consistency check to reduce its cost. However, it is an incomplete algorithm.

Algorithm 1 is the pseudocode of the whole consistency check procedure. It is mainly based on the Tarjan algorithm on the graph $G' = (V, active(E))$. Like the original Tarjan algorithm, the *index* variable counts the number of visited nodes in DFS order. The value of v.index numbers the nodes consecutively in the order in which they are discovered. And the value of v.lowlink represents the smallest index of any node known to be reachable from v, including v itself. The *scc* variable counts the number of strongly connected components. And the attribute scc of a vertex records the strongly connected component it belongs to. S is the node stack, which stores the history of nodes explored but not yet committed to a strongly connected component.

We introduce two values for a vertex v, v.father and v.nf, for theory propagation. The value of v.father represents a vertex w, that the DFS procedure visits v through edge $\langle w, v \rangle$. Assume the DFS procedure starts from vertex u. Then

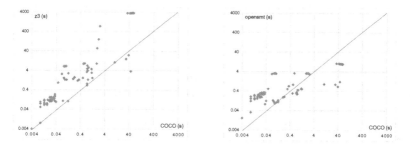

Fig. 8. Experiments on instances generated from RVPredict

we can generate a path from u to v by retrieving the father attribute of each vertex on this path from v. The number of $e^<$ edges on this path is recorded by v.nf. We add two parts into the original Tarjan algorithm. In Algorithm 1, the statements from line 7 to line 12 record the "father" and the "nf" attribute of w. The loop from line 23 to line 27 recursively checks the vertex t by retrieving father records from s. We can obtain a path p_{ts} from t to s in this way. If t.nf$<s$.nf, there exists at least one $e^<$ edge on this path. Thus p_{ts} and edge st compose a negative cycle if t.nf$<s$.nf or st is an $e^<$ edge. We can determine the assignment of the Boolean variable which corresponds to the edge ts or st and generate the Boolean clause of this deduction.

In Example 3, our algorithm starts from v_1, and then applies a DFS procedure. When the algorithm visits the last vertex, v_4, we have v_4.nf $= v_3$.nf $= v_2$.nf $= v_1$.nf $+ 1$. Then the algorithm starts popping stack S and constructing strongly connected components. At vertex v_3, we find v_1 is the father of v_3.father, $\langle v_3, v_1 \rangle$ is inactive and v_3.nf $> v_1$.nf, so we deduce that $b_5 \equiv \langle v_3, v_1 \rangle$ should be *False* and generate a clause, $(\neg b_1) \vee b_2 \vee (\neg b_5)$.

6   Experimental Evaluation

We have implemented our decision procedure in a tool called COCO (which stands for **C**ombating **O**rdering **CO**nstraints) based on MiniSat 2.0[2]. We have evaluated COCO with a collection of ordering constraints generated from RVPredict and two series of QF_IDL benchmarks (diamonds and parity) in SMT-Lib[3], which are also SMT(OC) formulas. The experiments were performed on a workstation with 3.40 GHz Intel Core i7-2600 CPU and 8 GB memory. For comparison, we also evaluated with two other state-of-the-art SMT solvers, i.e., OpenSMT[4] and Z3[5]. The experimental results are shown in Figs. 8 and 9. Note that each point represents an instance. Its x-coordinate and y-coordinate represent the running

[2] N. Eén and N. Sörensson. The MiniSat Page. http://minisat.se/.
[3] They are available at: http://www.cs.nyu.edu/~barrett/smtlib/.
[4] The OpenSMT Page. http://code.google.com/p/opensmt/.
[5] The Z3 Page. http://z3.codeplex.com/.

Table 1. More details about the "Hard" instances.

Instance		OpenSMT			COCO			Z3
Name	Dims	TS sat calls	TS unsat calls	Time(s)	TS sat calls	TS unsat calls	Time(s)	Time(s)
Harness_1	19783	40460	1	9.489	21664	12775	59.768	—
Harness_2	19783	41278	1	9.929	18703	12011	50.937	—
JigsawDriver_3	1548	5796	0	0.892	12797	15604	10.447	10.549
JigsawDriver_7	1548	6198	0	0.848	997	1671	0.538	8.813
BubbleSort_3	1195	36989	71	0.868	47643	52508	30.708	15.761
JGFMolDynA_1	7718	11448	0	3.028	3	17	0.074	2.64
JGFMolDynA_2	7718	12914	4	2.972	2214	3181	2.522	748.207
BoundedBuffer_39	828	5640	1	0.500	787	1109	0.312	1.196
BoundedBuffer_40	828	11464	47	0.444	2621	2924	0.830	1.360
BoundedBuffer_41	828	5537	1	0.500	3256	3327	1.252	1.640
main_15	9707	12882	1	3.228	2132	2122	2.184	158.214

times of COCO and Z3/OpenSMT on this instance, respectively. All figures are in logarithmic coordinates.

Figure 8 shows the results on instances that are generated from RVPredict. Our tool performs well on some small instances. It takes dozens of milliseconds for COCO to solve them. Z3 usually consumes more time and memory than COCO, and it fails to solve some large instances, due to the limit on memory usage. For such instances, we regard the running time of Z3 as more than 3600 s. Nevertheless, on some larger instances OpenSMT is more efficient. Our investigation of OpenSMT reveals that it adopts an efficient incremental consistency checking algorithm and integrates minimal conflict with a theory propagation technique, which COCO currently does not fully support. The advantage of theory propagation is that it allows the solver to effectively learn useful facts that can help reduce the chances of conflicts. On the instances generated from RVPredict, theory propagations are very effective, because the Boolean structures of the SMT(OC) formulas are quite simple.

Table 1 gives more details on some "hard" instances in Fig. 8. "TS sat calls" and "TS unsat calls" represent the number of satisfiable/unsatisfiable calls of the theory solver, respectively. "Dims" denotes the number of numeric variables, i.e., dimension of the search space. The running times of both OpenSMT and COCO are closely related to the dimension of the instance and the number of calls of the theory solver. An unsatisfiable call of the theory solver causes backtracking and retrieving reasons; so it consumes much more time than a satisfiable call. Notice that OpenSMT hardly encounters unsatisfiable calls. Its theory propagation procedure greatly reduces the number of unsatisfiable calls. On the contrary, COCO even encounters more unsatisfiable calls than satisfiable calls in some circumstances, because its theory propagation is incomplete.

Figure 9 shows the experimental results on SMT-Lib benchmarks "diamonds" and "parity". It appears that OpenSMT is often slower than COCO, and Z3 performs well in these cases, in contrast to Fig. 8. OpenSMT only applies the incremental algorithm which cannot skip steps, so it checks consistency incrementally whenever it makes decision or propagation. On instances that contain complicated Boolean components, like some SMT-Lib benchmarks, OpenSMT is not so efficient, because it has to backtrack often and applies the consistency checking algorithm step by step again even with complete theory propagations. On the other hand, Z3 tightly integrates many strategies, some of which are hand-crafted and fall outside the scope of DPLL(T), such as formula preprocessing, which COCO does not implement. These may be the reasons for the good performance of Z3 in Fig. 9.

In addition to the running time, we also compared the memory usage of these three solvers. It turned out that COCO always occupies the least memory. The memory usage of OpenSMT is about 5 to 10 times as much as that of COCO, and Z3 consumes tens of times even hundreds of times higher memories than COCO. The detailed data are omitted, due to the lack of space.

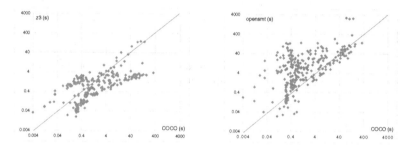

Fig. 9. Experiments on QF_IDL benchmarks in SMT-Lib

To summarize, COCO achieves better scalability than Z3 on the real instances generated by RVPredict. On the other hand, when comparing COCO with OpenSMT, there seems no clear winner. The incremental decision procedure with complete theory propagation enables OpenSMT to perform well on many instances generated by RVPredict, whereas it results in poor performance of OpenSMT on the classical SMT-Lib instances. Besides, our current tool has potential to achieve better performance as we have not designed a complete theory propagation, as demonstrated by OpenSMT, and many other optimization strategies used by Z3.

7   Related Work

As we mentioned earlier, there has been a large body of work on solving (integer) difference constraints. See, for example, [4,12,22,24]. Nieuwenhuis and Oliveras presented a DPLL(T) system with exhaustive theory propagation for solving SMT(DL) formulas [24]. They reduced the consistency checking for DL to detecting negative cycles in the weighted digraph with the Bellman-Ford algorithm [24].

The complexity of this decision procedure is $O(nm)$, where n is the number of variables, and m is the number of constraints. In [4] Cotton and Maler proposed an incremental complete difference constraint propagation algorithm with complexity $O(m + nlogn + |U|)$, where $|U|$ is the number of constraints which are candidates for being deduced. However, to check the consistency of conjunctions of constraints, the incremental algorithm has to be called for each constraint. Therefore, the complexity of the whole procedure is even higher. In contrast, the complexity of our decision procedure for ordering constraints is only $O(n + m)$.

Besides, there are some works consider extending a SAT solver with acyclicity detection. [21] deals with a conjunction of theory predicates, while our work is concerned with arbitrary Boolean combinations of ordering constraints. Due to the existence of the logical connectives (OR, NOT) of SMT(OC) formulas, the equality and disequality relations can be represented by inequality relations. We only have to consider two types of edges ($e^{>=}$ edge and $e^{>}$ edge) in our graph, which is more simple than four types of edges in [21]. Moreover, our theory propagation exploits the information from Tarjans algorithm. [14,15], and recent versions of MonoSAT [2] all rely on similar theory propagation and clause learning techniques. [2], for example, also uses Tarjan's SCC during clause learning in a similar way as this paper. However, they don't have a notion of $e^{<}$ edges versus $e^{<=}$ edges, and they couldn't support distinction of $e^{<}$ edges versus $e^{<=}$ edges without significant modifications.

8   Conclusion

Satisfiability Modulo Theories (SMT) is an important research topic in automated reasoning. In this paper, we identified and studied a useful *theory*, i.e., the theory of ordering constraints. We demonstrated its *applications* in symbolic analysis of concurrent programs. We also presented *methods* for solving the related satisfiability problems. In particular, we gave a decision procedure that has a lower complexity than that for the difference logic. We have also implemented a prototype tool for our algorithm and compared its performance with two state-of-the-art SMT solvers, Z3 and OpenSMT. Although our current implementation is not optimized, it achieves comparable performance as that of Z3 and OpenSMT which have been developed for years and are highly optimized. We explained why a particular tool is more efficient on certain problem instances. In our future work, we plan to further improve the performance of our approach by developing incremental and backtrackable decision procedures with more efficient theory propagation.

References

1. Barrett, C., Conway, C.L., Deters, M., Hadarean, L., Jovanović, D., King, T., Reynolds, A., Tinelli, C.: CVC4. In: Gopalakrishnan, G., Qadeer, S. (eds.) CAV 2011. LNCS, vol. 6806, pp. 171–177. Springer, Heidelberg (2011)

2. Bayless, S., Bayless, N., Hoos, H.H., Hu, A.J.: SAT modulo monotonic theories. In: AAAI (2015)

3. Bruttomesso, R., Pek, E., Sharygina, N., Tsitovich, A.: The OpenSMT solver. In: Esparza, J., Majumdar, R. (eds.) TACAS 2010. LNCS, vol. 6015, pp. 150–153. Springer, Heidelberg (2010)

4. Cotton, S., Maler, O.: Fast and flexiable difference constraint propagation for DPLL(T). In: SAT (2006)

5. de Moura, L., Bjørner, N.S.: Z3: An efficient SMT solver. In: Ramakrishnan, C.R., Rehof, J. (eds.) TACAS 2008. LNCS, vol. 4963, pp. 337–340. Springer, Heidelberg (2008)

6. Dutertre, B., De Moura, L.: The Yices SMT solver. Technical report (2006)

7. Eslamimehr, M., Palsberg, J. Sherlock: Scalable deadlock detection for concurrent programs. In: FSE (2014)

8. Farzan, A., Holzer, A., Razavi, N., Veith, H.: Con2colic testing. In: ESEC/FSE (2013)

9. Farzan, A., Madhusudan, P., Razavi, N., Sorrentino, F.: Predicting null-pointer dereferences in concurrent programs. In: FSE (2012)

10. Flanagan, C., Freund, S.N.: Fasttrack: efficient and precise dynamic race detection. In: PLDI (2009)

11. Ganesh, V., Dill, D.L.: A decision procedure for bit-vectors and arrays. In: Damm, W., Hermanns, H. (eds.) CAV 2007. LNCS, vol. 4590, pp. 519–531. Springer, Heidelberg (2007)

12. Gange, G., Søndergaard, H., Stuckey, P.J., Schachte, P.: Solving difference constraints over modular arithmetic. In: Bonacina, M.P. (ed.) CADE 2013. LNCS, vol. 7898, pp. 215–230. Springer, Heidelberg (2013)

13. Ganzinger, H., Hagen, G., Nieuwenhuis, R., Oliveras, A., Tinelli, C.: DPLL(T): fast decision procedures. In: Alur, R., Peled, D.A. (eds.) CAV 2004. LNCS, vol. 3114, pp. 175–188. Springer, Heidelberg (2004)

14. Gebser, M., Janhunen, T., Rintanen, J.: SAT modulo graphs: acyclicity. In: Fermé, E., Leite, J. (eds.) JELIA 2014. LNCS, vol. 8761, pp. 137–151. Springer, Heidelberg (2014)

15. Gebser, M., Janhunen, T., Rintanen, J.: Answer set programming as SAT modulo acyclicity. In: ECAI (2014)

16. Huang, J.: Stateless model checking concurrent programs with maximal causality reduction. In: PLDI (2015)

17. Huang, J., Luo, Q., Rosu, G.: Gpredict: Generic predictive concurrency analysis. In: ICSE (2015)

18. Huang, J., Meredith, P.O., Rosu, G.: Maximal sound predictive race detection with control flow abstraction. In: PLDI (2014)

19. Huang, J., Zhang, C.: PECAN: persuasive prediction of concurrency access anomalies. In: ISSTA (2011)

20. Huang, J., Zhang, C., Dolby, J.: CLAP: Recording local executions to reproduce concurrency failures. In: PLDI (2013)

21. Kroening, D., Weissenbacher, G.: An interpolating decision procedure for transitive relations with uninterpreted functions. In: Namjoshi, K., Zeller, A., Ziv, A. (eds.) HVC 2009. LNCS, vol. 6405, pp. 150–168. Springer, Heidelberg (2011)

22. Kim, H., Somenzi, F.: Finite instantiations for integer difference logic. In: FMCAD (2006)

23. Lee, D., Said, M., Narayanasamy, S., Yang, Z., Pereira, C.: Offline symbolic analysis for multi-processor execution replay. In: MICRO (2009)

24. Nieuwenhuis, R., Oliveras, A.: DPLL(T) with exhaustive theory propagation and its application to difference logic. In: Etessami, K., Rajamani, S.K. (eds.) CAV 2005. LNCS, vol. 3576, pp. 321–334. Springer, Heidelberg (2005)

25. Said, M., Wang, C., Yang, Z., Sakallah, K.: Generating data race witnesses by an SMT-based analysis. In: Bobaru, M., Havelund, K., Holzmann, G.J., Joshi, R. (eds.) NFM 2011. LNCS, vol. 6617, pp. 313–327. Springer, Heidelberg (2011)

26. Savage, S., Burrows, M., Nelson, G., Sobalvarro, P., Anderson, T.: Eraser: A dynamic data race detector for multi-threaded programs. In: TOCS (1997)

27. Sinha, N., Wang, C.: On interference abstraction. In: POPL (2011)

28. Smaragdakis, Y., Evans, J., Sadowski, C., Yi, J., Flanagan, C.: Sound predictive race detection in polynomial time. In: POPL (2012)

29. Tarjan, R.: Depth-first search and linear graph algorithms. SIAM J. Comput. 1(2), 146–160 (1972)

30. Wang, C., Limaye, R., Ganai, M., Gupta, A.: Trace-based symbolic analysis for atomicity violations. In: Esparza, J., Majumdar, R. (eds.) TACAS 2010. LNCS, vol. 6015, pp. 328–342. Springer, Heidelberg (2010)

An Efficient, Portable and Generic Library for Successive Cancellation Decoding of Polar Codes

Adrien Cassagne[1,2]([✉]), Bertrand Le Gal[1], Camille Leroux[1],
Olivier Aumage[2], and Denis Barthou[2]

[1] IMS, University of Bordeaux, INP, Bordeaux, France
{bertrand.gal,camille.leroux}@ims-bordeaux.fr
[2] Inria/Labri, University of Bordeaux, INP, Bordeaux, France
{adrien.cassagne,olivier.aumage,denis.barthou}@inria.fr

Abstract. Error Correction Code decoding algorithms for consumer products such as *Internet of Things* (IoT) devices are usually implemented as dedicated hardware circuits. As processors are becoming increasingly powerful and energy efficient, there is now a strong desire to perform this processing in software to reduce production costs and time to market. The recently introduced family of Successive Cancellation decoders for Polar codes has been shown in several research works to efficiently leverage the ubiquitous SIMD units in modern CPUs, while offering strong potentials for a wide range of optimizations. The P-EDGE environment introduced in this paper, combines a specialized skeleton generator and a building blocks library routines to provide a generic, extensible Polar code exploration workbench. It enables ECC code designers to easily experiments with combinations of existing and new optimizations, while delivering performance close to state-of-art decoders.

Keywords: Error correction codes · Polar codes · Successive cancellation decoding · Generic programming · Code generation · Domain specific language · SIMDization

1 Introduction

Error correction coding aka channel coding is a technique that enables the transmission of digital information over an unreliable communication channel. In today's communication systems, hardware digital circuits are in charge of performing the encoding (resp. decoding) of transmitted (resp. received) information. These custom Error Correction Code (ECC) circuits lack flexibility and suffer from very long, expensive development cycles. In order to improve the system flexibility and to reduce time to market, and as a consequence from the strong performance increase of low power general purpose processors such as found in IoT devices, researchers recently suggested implementing channel decoders in software. Moreover, it is also much needed to be able to run such

© Springer International Publishing Switzerland 2016
X. Shen et al. (Eds.): LCPC 2015, LNCS 9519, pp. 303–317, 2016.
DOI: 10.1007/978-3-319-29778-1_19

algorithms on high end, high performance processors to shorten the computationally intensive algorithm validation process. During such a process, long sequences of information are encoded with the studied algorithm, altered with a controlled random noise, decoded, and compared with the initial sequence to assess the error correcting power. Indeed, some classes of decoding algorithms can take advantage of modern CPU features such as SIMD units, and even many/multi-cores, making the software approach even more desirable.

In this paper, we focus on the software implementation of Successive Cancellation (SC) algorithm for a recent family of error correction codes: Polar Codes [2]. As an alternative to hardware implementation, several recent software implementations were proposed in the literature in order to demonstrate that polar codes decoding can be efficiently implemented on a multi-core CPUs (x86, ARM). These software implementations take advantage of various optimizations that were first proposed for hardware implementations. However, depending on the processor micro-architecture and instruction set, some optimization techniques may not work equally on distinct processors. New optimization techniques may be designed. Some optimization combinations may be less successful than others. As a result, the optimization space of polar decoder implementations is wide, and its exploration non trivial.

For this reason, we propose a new polar decoder experimentation framework named P-EDGE (Polar ECC Decoder Generation Environment), which combines a specializing skeleton generator with a building block library of elementary polar code processing routines. The algorithm-centric skeleton generator is fully independent from the hardware architecture enabling high-level algorithmic optimization to be implemented in a portable manner. The architecture-centric building block library is fully independent from the generated skeleton instance, enabling architecture porting effort and low-level routine optimization to be concentrated on a small set of short functions. P-EDGE enables separation of concerns between algorithmic and architecture optimizations. The panel of evaluation experiments we conducted shows the high flexibility of our framework. The performance evaluation results we obtained, nearing and sometime outperforming state-of-the-art handwritten implementations, confirm that the benefit from this high flexibility is not cancelled by an expensive penalty.

The remainder of this paper is organized as follows. Section 2 details the context and relevant characteristics of the general polar code decoding process, as well as the large optimization space resulting from its implementation. Section 3 presents our proposed framework as well as the architecture independent skeleton generator. Section 4 provides implementation details on the architecture dependent building blocks. Section 5 talks about the achieved related works in the domain. Section 6 shows experiments and performance results. Section 7 concludes the article.

2   Successive Cancellation Decoding of Polar Codes

Error correction codes are widely used in digital communication and data storage applications. The encoding process consists in adding some redundant information (parity check bits) in order to strengthen the message against transmission errors. On the receiver side, the decoder estimates the transmitted bits based on (i) the received sequence and (ii) the knowledge of the encoding process. Polar Codes were recently proposed in [2]. Similar to state of the art LDPC codes [4,9] and Turbo codes [3], polar codes can achieve very good error correction performance. However, a very large codelength ($N > 2^{20}$) is required in order to approach to the theoretical error correction limit proved by Shannon [13]. The challenge is then to design polar codes decoders able to decode several millions bits frames while guaranteeing a compelling throughput. Assume we want to transmit K bits over a noisy communication channel. The encoding process appends $N - K$ parity check bits before the resulting N bits codeword can be transmitted over the channel. On the receiver side, the noisy sequence Y is a vector of N real values each corresponding to *a priori* beliefs on the transmitted bits. These beliefs are in the form of a Log-Likelihood-Ratio (LLR). Using the knowledge of the encoding process, the decoder job is to estimate the transmitted N-bit codeword based on a received sequence of N LLRs.

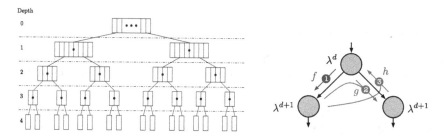

Fig. 1. (a) Tree layout. (b) Per-node downward and upward computations.

The SC decoding algorithm can be seen as the traversal of a binary tree starting from the root node. For a codelength $N = 2^m$, the corresponding tree thus includes $m+1$ node layers, indexed from $d = 0$ (root node layer) down to $d = m$ (leaf nodes layers). As the tree is initially full, each layer d contains 2^d nodes, each node of that layer d containing 2^{m-d} LLRs (λ) and 2^{m-d} binary values denoted as *partial sums* (s). At initialization, LLRs received from the channel (Y) are stored in the root node. Then, the decoder performs a pre-order traversal of the tree. When a node is visited in the downward direction, LLRs of the node are updated. In the upward direction, partial sums are updated. Figure 1b summarizes the computations performed in both directions. The update functions are:

$$\begin{cases} \lambda_c & = f(\lambda_a, \lambda_b) & = sign(\lambda_a.\lambda_b).\min(|\lambda_a|, |\lambda_b|) \\ \lambda_c & = g(\lambda_a, \lambda_b, s) = (1 - 2s)\lambda_a + \lambda_b \\ (s_c, s_d) & = h(s_a, s_b) & = (s_a \oplus s_b, s_b). \end{cases} \quad (1)$$

The f and g functions both generate a single LLR. The h function provides a couple of partial sums.

Before recursively calling itself on the left node, the algorithm apply the f function, respectively, before calling itself on the right node the g function is applied. At the end (after the recursive call on the right node) the h function is applied. The f and g functions use the LLRs (read only mode) from the current node n_i in order to produce the new LLR values into respectively left and right n_{i+1} nodes. The h function, in the general case (non-terminal case), reads the bits from the left and right n_{i+1} nodes in order to update the bit values of the n_i node. For the terminal case, the h function reads the LLRs from itself and decides the bit values.

Leaf nodes are of two kinds: *information bit* nodes and *frozen bit* nodes. When a frozen bit leaf node is reached, its binary value is unconditionally set to zero. Instead, when an information leaf node is reached, its binary value is set according to the *sign* of its LLR (0 if LLR is positive, 1 otherwise). Once every node in the tree has been visited in both directions, the decoder eventually updates partial sums in the root node and the decoding process is terminated. At this point, the decoding result is stored in the root node in the form of a N-bit partial sum vectors.

2.1   Code Optimization Space

The previous decoder algorithm has a number of characteristics of interest for its optimization. Generating decoders able to take advantage of this optimization space is the key for high performance decoders:

- The tree traversal is sequential, but f, g and h are applied element-wise to all elements of the LLR and bits in the nodes and their children. As there is no dependence between computations involving different elements of the same node, these node computations can be parallelized or vectorized (cf. the *intra-frame* strategy introduced in [5]),
- Frozen bits fully define their leaf values, hence some part of the traversal can be cut and its computation avoided, depending on the location of the frozen bits. More generally, the tree computation can be versioned depending on these bits (cf. [1,12]),
- The decoder can be specialized for a particular configuration of frozen bits, as frozen bit locations do not change for many frames,
- Similarly, multiple frames can be decoded concurrently, with parallel or vector code. Such *inter-frame* optimizations can increase the decoding throughput, however at the expense of latency, which is also one important metric of the application (cf. [8]).

Beside optimizations coming from the computations in the tree, several representations of LLR may lead to different error correction performance. LLR for instance can be represented by floats or integers (fixed point representation), LLR from different frames can be packed together.

Finally, usual code optimizations, such as unrolling or inlining can also be explored. For instance, the recursive structure of the tree computation can be fully flatten, depending on the size of the codelength.

3   The P-EDGE Framework

We now presents the framework we designed to study, experiment with, and optimize the decoding of *polar codes*. While our contributions focus on the decoding stage, a whole encoding/decoding chain is required for testing and validation purpose, and we therefore give an overview of our communication chain.

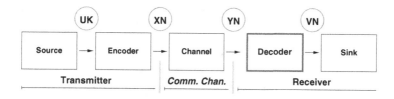

Fig. 2. The communication chain.

Figure 2 depicts the whole communication chain of our framework. The chain stages are organized as the following main segments:

The **Transmitter** segment is made of two Stages: (1) The source signal generator stage (*Source*) produces the vector of information bits U_K to be transmitted. (2) The polar encoding stage (*Encoder*) inserts parity check redundancy bits into information vector. For every packet of K information bits, a total of N bits are produced (information+redundancy bits). The resulting N-bit vector (X_N) is transmitted over the communication channel.

The **Communication channel** segment simulates a noisy communication, adding additive white Gaussian noise to the frames, producing the real vector Y_N from the binary vector X_N.

The **Receiver** segment is made of two Stages: (1) The *Decoder* stage produces a binary vector V_N from Y_N along using the algorithm described above. (2) The *Sink* stage eventually compares the K information bits (V_K) in V_N with U_K in order to count the number of remaining binary errors after the decoding is performed. The more effective the error correction code is, the closer the V_K bits should be from the U_K bits. Resilient errors may come from (1) inherent limitations in the polar code construction, (2) sub-optimal decoding algorithm, (3) a high noise power in the communication channel. Moreover, while testing new algorithm implementations or optimizations, an abnormally high error rate can also be the sign of a bug.

3.1   The P-EDGE Decoder Generator

Specialized Decoder Skeletons and Building Blocks Library. The tree structure at the heart of SC decoders is fully determined by the parameters of a given code instance: the code size, the code rate ($R = K/N$), position of the frozen bits. All these parameters are statically known at compile time. Thus, the recursive tree traversal code structure and the corresponding tree data structure are challenging to vectorize and to optimize for a compiler. Our Polar ECC Decoder

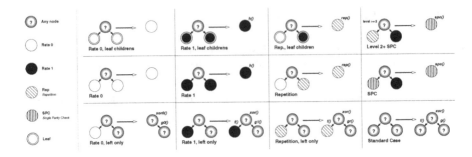

Fig. 3. Subtree rewriting rules for processing specialization.

Generation Environment (P-EDGE) builds on this property to provide a general framework for polar decoder design, generation and optimization. Beyond the *code parameters*, Polar decoders can be tweaked and optimized in many different orthogonal or loosely coupled ways: *Elementary* type (floating point, fixed point), *Element containers* (array size), *Data layout* (bit packing techniques), *Instruction Set* (x86, ARM), *SIMD* support (scalar, intra-frame or inter-frame processing vectorization), *SIMD instruction set variant* (SSE, AVX, NEON), as well as the set and relative priorities of the *rewriting rules for tree pruning*. Our framework enables to quickly experiment the different combinations of all optimizations. The decoder code thus results from two distinct parts:

- An architecture independent *specialized decoder skeleton* generated by our decoder generator, from a given frozen bits location input. Starting from the naive, recursive expression of the computational tree, we apply successively cuts and specializations on the tree. They are described through a set of rewriting rules, that can be customized according to the specificities of the decoder and to the constraints in term of code size for instance.
- A library of architecture dependent *elementary computation building blocks*, corresponding to the implementation variants of the f, g and h functions (fixed or floating point versions, scalar or vector versions, ...). These blocks do not depend on the frozen bits location and can therefore be used by any specialized skeleton.

This separation of concerns between high-level specialized algorithmic skeletons and low-level arithmetic routines, enables both ECC experts to focus on optimizing algorithm skeletons and architecture experts to focus on writing highly optimized routines, without interferences.

Decoder Generation. The decoder generator first builds the binary tree structure as shown in Fig. 1a from the frozen bit location input. Each internal node has a tag indicating the type of processing required at that node (recursive children processing, $f/g/h$ functions to be applied or not). This tag is initially set to *standard*, corresponding to the canonical processing described in Fig. 1b.

For some sub-tree pattern configurations, the processing to be performed at the root of such sub-trees can be simplified, or even skipped completely,

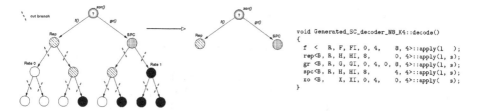

```
void Generated_SC_decoder_N8_K4::decode()
{
    f   <  R, F, FI, 0, 4,   8, 4>::apply(l   );
    rep<B, R, H, HI, 8,      0, 4>::apply(l, s);
    gr <B, R, G, GI, 0, 4, 0, 8, 4>::apply(l, s);
    spc<B, R, H, HI, 8,      4, 4>::apply(l, s);
    xo <B,    X, XI, 0, 4,   0, 4>::apply(  s);
}
```

Fig. 4. Generation process on a small binary tree ($N = 8$). The tree is cut and the computations are versioned according to the location of the frozen bit. The final code generated is in the right.

for instance when a node only has two frozen bit leaf children. To exploit such properties, the decoder generator repeatedly applies the set of sub-tree rewriting rules listed in Fig. 3 using a depth first traversal to alter the node tags, until no rewriting rule applies anymore.

Each rewriting rule defines a subtree pattern *selector*, a new *tag* for the subtree root, and the f, g, and h *processing functions* to be applied, simplified or skipped for this node in the resulting decoder. A *null* f (resp. g) function cuts the left (resp. right) child of the node. From an implementation point of view, a rule is defined as a class, with a **match** function, and a set of functions f, g, and h. The current set of rewriting rules can thus easily be enriched with new rules to generate even more specialized versions.

Patterns on the first two rows result in cutting away both children. For instance, the first rule, named *Rate 0, leaf children*, cuts the two frozen bit leaf children of the parent node, and tag it as *Rate 0* (white node). Processing is completely skipped on this node since the values of the bits are unconditionally known. The *Repetition* rules match subtrees where only the rightmost leaf is black (tag *Rate 1*), the others being frozen bits. In this case, the whole subtree is cut and replaced by a more simple processing. Moreover a single, specialized *rep* function is applied on the node instead of the three functions f, g and h. The third line describes partial cuts and specialization. For instance, the rule "Repetition, left only" specializes the g and h functions to use, but does not prune the recursive children processing.

Rewriting rules are ordered by priority (left to right, then top row to bottom row in Fig. 3), thus if more than one rule match an encountered subtree, the highest priority rule is applied. The priority order is chosen such as to favor strongest computation reducing rules over rules with minor impact, and to ensure confluence by selecting the most specific pattern first. Rules selectors can match on node tags and/or node levels (leaf, specific level, above or below some level). A given rule is applied at most once on a given node.

Finally, once the tree has been fully specialized, the generator perform a second tree traversal pass to output the resulting decoder. An example of such a tree specialization process together with the generator output is shown in Fig. 4.

4   Low Level Building Blocks

The main challenge in implementing P-EDGE's architecture dependent building blocks is to provide enough flexibility to enable varied type, data layout
and optimization strategies such as intra-frame SIMDization (intra-SIMD) and
inter-frame SIMDization (inter-SIMD), without breaking the high level skeleton abstraction. To meet this requirement, our building block library heavily
relies on generic programming and compile time specialization by the means of
C++ templates, in a manner inspired by *expression template* techniques [15].
Template specializations provide node functions. Figure 4 gives a example of a
generated decoder for $N = 8$, calling template instances of the node functions.
B: partial sum type; R: LLR/λ type; F/G/H/X: Scalar standard SC function versions; FI/GI/HI/XI SIMD versions. Remaining template parameters are offsets
and chunk sizes to control data layout.

```
template <typename R>                    template <typename R>
R f_seq(const R& la,                     mipp::vec f_simd(const mipp::vec& la,
        const R& lb)                                      const mipp::vec& lb)
{                                        {
  auto abs_la  = (la >= 0) ? la : -la;     auto abs_la  = mipp::abs <R>(la            );
  auto abs_lb  = (lb >= 0) ? lb : -lb;     auto abs_lb  = mipp::abs <R>(lb            );
  auto min_abs = std::min(abs_la, abs_lb); auto min_abs = mipp::min <R>(abs_la, abs_lb);
  auto sign    = (0 < la*lb) - (la*lb < 0);auto sign     = mipp::sign<R>(la,      lb  );
  auto lc      = (R)sign * min_abs;        auto lc      = mipp::neg <R>(min_abs, sign );

  return lc;                               return lc;
}                                        }
```

Fig. 5. Example of the C++ implementation of the f function in P-EDGE (the sequential version is in the left whereas the SIMD one is in the right).

A single SIMD set is needed because *SIMD routines are common to both
intra-SIMD and inter-SIMD*. In the later case, the generated decoder packs as
many frames together from the frame stream as the vector size in a transparent
manner. In both cases, offsets are fully precomputed at compile time. **Intra-
SIMD** exploits SIMD units without increasing the decoder latency, since it still
processes frames one at a time and thus preserves fine grain frame pipelining.
However, at leaf nodes and nearby, too few elements remain to fill SIMD units.
For instance, 4-way SIMD registers are fully filled only at level 2 and above. Thus,
Intra-SIMD will only be effective on trees that can be heavily pruned from these
numerous scalar nodes. **Inter-SIMD** does not suffer from this problem, since
SIMD register lanes are filled by LLRs and bits from multiple frames instead.
However, the decoder needs to wait for enough frames to arrive, which increases
latency, and to interleave the LLRs from these frames (*gather*) before proceeding.
It also needs to de-interleave the resulting data (the bits) after decoding (*scatter*).
Refer to [8] for more details about the interleaving process.

The framework instantiates scalar or SIMD functions as appropriate (hence
the two sets of functions). These two sets of functions are *independent* on the element type. Scalar functions are datatype-parametered templates.

SIMD functions use the template-based MIPP intrinsics wrapper library developed by one of the authors to benefit from SSE, AVX and NEON flavors SIMD instruction sets in a portable and extensible manner. As an example, the generic scalar and SIMD implementations of the f function are shown in Fig. 5. We also tried an auto-vectorized approach but even if all the routines were well vectorized (from the compiler report), the performance was, at least, 3 times slower than the MIPP handwritten versions.

The decoder stores its state using two data buffers, one for the LLR values (λ) and the other for the bits (partial sums s). The "logical" tree layout is implemented as a simple and efficient *heap* vector data layout. Traversing the tree therefore corresponds to moving through the array, at different offsets and considering different index intervals. The LLR offset is computed from the graph depth d (or the node vertical indexing) as follows:

$$off_\lambda(d = 0) = 0, \ off_\lambda(d > 0) = \sum_{i=1}^{d} \frac{N}{2^{i-1}}. \tag{2}$$

Given l the lane (or the node horizontal indexing), the bit offset is determined as follows:

$$off_s(d, l) = \frac{N}{2^d} \times l. \tag{3}$$

The LLR buffer size is $2N$ and the bit buffer is N, for a frame of N bits. Thus, the memory footprint per frame is:

$$mem_{fp} = N \times (2 \times sizeof(LLR) + sizeof(bit)). \tag{4}$$

LLRs element size is 4 bytes (float) or 1 byte (fixed point numbers). The Inter-SIMD version also employs a *bit packing* memory footprint reduction technique [8] to pack several bits together by using shifts and masking instructions.

5   Related Works

Polar codes [2] keep on gaining attention from circuits and systems designers. The practical interest of these codes comes from the possibility to implement them efficiently in software. Software implementations were proposed in [5] on x86 processor targets, using SIMD instructions to speed-up single frame decoding (intra-frame parallelism). In addition to SIMD optimizations, the tree pruning step described in Sect. 3 was also applied to the decoder in [12]. Moreover, fixed point representation was implemented in order to speed up the decoding process. This modification of the data format has a negligible impact on error correction quality while enabling better throughput. The authors proposed to improve the throughput performance by auto-generating the source code of their floating point decoders [11]. A second set of works [8] has considered an another way to take advantage of SIMD processing capabilities. Authors focused on inter-frame parallelism using both SIMD and multi-thread parallelization. Indeed, this approach enables constant parallelism level during the overall decoding process, at the cost of an increased latency. Throughputs achieved using this approach and the associated implementation optimizations were about ×4 to ×8 times higher than [5]. An ARM-based implementation was also explored in [7] to enable low power consumption software decoding for a potential use on consumer devices.

The P-EDGE philosophy differs from these previous approaches by promoting separation of concerns and genericity as first class objectives to enable experimenting with multiple optimization strategies. Results presented in Sect. 6 show that these objectives are not incompatible with performance.

Concerning automatic generation of high performance libraries, ATLAS generator [18], LGen [14] and SPIRAL [10] are examples for linear algebra libraries and signal processing domains, all resorting to autotuning to find the best version. LGen and SPIRAL generate optimized code from a Domain Specific Language (DSL). A different generative approach is adopted by Eigen [6] or uBLAS [17]. While Eigen focuses on structural recursion, it is applied to matrices and not to trees. They use C++ templates to optimize the code at compile time. Comparatively, the technique presented in this paper combines the two generative approaches: the generator produces code from an initial formulation, optimized by rewriting rules. The second step also optimizes code from C++ templates.

6 Evaluation

In this section we first describe the protocol we used, after that we provide a performance comparison between the state-of-the-art and P-EDGE. At the end we discuss the exploring capabilities of our framework.

Table 1. Performance evaluation platforms.

	x86-based	ARMv7-based	prev. work arch. [11]
CPU	Intel Xeon E31225 3.10 Ghz	ARM Cortex-A15 MPCore 2.32 GHz	Intel Core i7-2600 3.40 GHz
Cache	32KB L1I/L1D, 256KB L2 L3 6 MB	32KB L1I/L1D, L2 1024KB No L3	32KB L1I/L1D, L2 256 KB L3 8 MB
Compiler	GNU g++ 4.8	GNU g++ 4.8	GNU g++ 4.8

The platforms used for performance evaluation are shown in Table 1. Unless stated otherwise, each measure is obtained as the best of ten runs of a 10 s simulation, taking into account frame loading and result storing. SNR (Signal Noise Ratio) is set to 2.5 dB for tests with 1/5 and 1/2 rates, and to 4.0 dB for the 5/6, 0.84, and 9/10 rate tests. Colors differentiate the codes rates of the Polar Code, point shapes differentiate decoder types (Intra-SIMD vs Inter-SIMD).

6.1 Comparison Between P-EDGE and the State of the Art

Figure 6 shows P-EDGE intra-frame throughput on different architectures. Our generic framework performance outperforms previous work decoder results (between 10 % and 25 % higher). This is confirmed in Table 2 which compares P-EDGE with the state-of-the-art result samples for some specific rates reported in [11]. The throughput of the inter-frame implementation is shown in Fig. 7 for different architectures. Again, the results confirm that our generic approach overtakes handwritten code (also between 10 % and 25 % higher on x86).

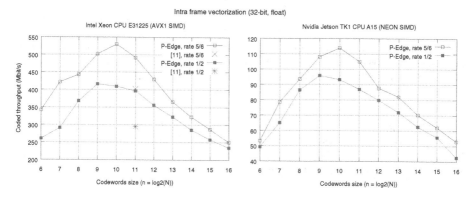

Fig. 6. Performance comparison between several code rates of 32-bit floating point decoding stages (running on the Intel®Xeon®CPU E31225 and, respectively, on the Nvidia®Jetson TK1®CPU A15).

Table 2. Comparing P-EDGE with a state-of-art software polar decoder, for codes of rate 0.84 and rate 0.9, using Intra-SIMD. The two cross marks show state-of-the art performance results reported in [11], for comparison.

(N, K)	Decoder	Info T/P (Mb/s)	Latency (μs)
(16384, 14746)	prev. work [11]	292	50
	this work	341	43
(32768, 27568)	prev. work [11]	220	125
	this work	241	114
(32768, 29492)	prev. work [11]	261	113
	this work	293	101

For all the test series, the bandwidth first increases with codeword size, as the tree pruning becomes increasingly more effective with larger trees. The effect is stronger for Intra-SIMD where pruning also results in removing inefficient scalar nodes. However, beyond a codeword size point which depends on the architecture and on the selected SIMD version, performance decreases again due to L1 cache

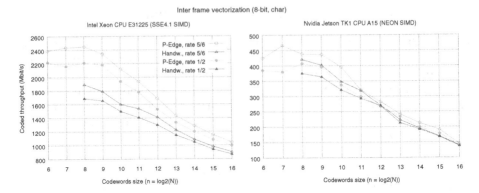

Fig. 7. Performance comparison between several code rates of 8-bit fixed point decoding stages (running on the Intel®Xeon®CPU E31225 and, respectively, on the Nvidia®Jetson TK1®CPU A15). Circles show P-EDGE results. Triangles show our former "handwritten" implementation results [8].

Table 3. Code size (in KB) of the generated decoders depending on the number of bits N per frame (code respectively compiled with AVX1 instructions for the 32-bit decoders and with SSE4.1 instructions for the 8-bit decoders). For comparison, code size without compression are shown in parentheses.

Decoder	$N = 2^6$	$N = 2^8$	$N = 2^{10}$	$N = 2^{12}$	$N = 2^{14}$	$N = 2^{16}$
inter 32-bit, $R = 1/2$	1 (7)	2 (24)	7 (**77**)	9 (**254**)	19 (**736**)	**40 (2528)**
inter 32-bit, $R = 5/6$	1 (4)	2 (19)	4 (**53**)	7 (**167**)	16 (**591**)	32 (**1758**)
intra 32-bit, $R = 1/2$	1 (4)	3 (16)	9 (**56**)	8 (**182**)	19 (**563**)	**38 (1947)**
intra 32-bit, $R = 5/6$	1 (3)	3 (13)	6 (**38**)	7 (**126**)	20 (**392**)	27 (**1365**)
inter 8-bit, $R = 1/2$	1 (5)	2 (22)	7 (**72**)	8 (**252**)	17 (**665**)	**36 (2220)**
inter 8-bit, $R = 5/6$	1 (4)	2 (18)	4 (**51**)	6 (**191**)	14 (**461**)	26 (**1555**)

misses, not only L1D but L1I as well. Indeed, decoders are generated as straight-line code (no recursive calls), with all node computations put in sequence. This improves performance for small to medium codeword size, up to the point where the compiled binary exceeds the L1I cache size. We mitigated this issue by reducing decoder binary sizes using two compression techniques: (1) in the generated code, we moved the buffer offsets from template arguments to function arguments, which enabled the compiler to factorize more function calls than before (improvement by a factor of 10), (2) we implemented a sub-tree folding algorithm in the generator, to detect multiple occurrences of a same sub-tree and to put the corresponding code into a dedicated function (improvement by a factor of 5 for $N = 2^{16}$, the compression ratio increases with the size of the tree).

Table 3 shows the binary code size of the decoders depending on N. The results which exceed the 32 KB of the L1I cache are highlighted in bold font. Sub-tree folding was enabled starting from $N = 2^{12}$ because there is an overhead (at run-time) when using this technique. P-EDGE decoder code sizes without compression are shown in parentheses: we can observe a huge improvement, until $N = 2^{14}$ the code size never exceeds the L1I cache anymore.

6.2 Exploring Respective Optimization Impacts with P-EDGE

In this sub-section the compression techniques have been disabled.

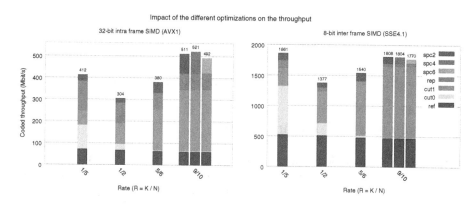

Fig. 8. Throughput depending on the different optimizations for $N = 2048$, for intra-frame vectorization on the left and intra-frame vectorization on the right, resp. (on the Intel®Xeon®CPU E31225).

The tree pruning step has a dramatical effect in general. For example, the reference code for a rate of $1/2$ has 2047 nodes, whereas only 291 nodes remain in the pruned version. However, the individual effect of each rewriting rule is not trivial. The plots in Fig. 8 show the respective impact of several rewriting rules (cuts, repetitions, single parity checks (SPC)), with $N = 2048$ and multiple code rates, for Intra-SIMD and Inter-SIMD respectively. The purpose of the plots is to show that no single rewriting rule dominates for every code rate, and that the respective impact of each rule may vary a lot from rate to rate, making the case for the flexible, extensible architecture of P-EDGE. Indeed, P-EDGE's rewriting rule set can also be enriched with rules for specific ranges of code rate. For instance, the rule *Single Parity Check (SPC)* has been applied with different level limits for $9/10$ code rate, where it has a significant impact and may benefit from fine tuning.

A comparison between the performance of the different decoder instances obtained from the same code is shown in Fig. 9. Only codeword sizes of more than 2^8 are shown, as smaller sizes are of little interest in practice. One can see that for a given bit rate, *the best version depends on the codeword size*. Inter-SIMD dominates for a $1/2$ rate, while Intra-SIMD dominates for a $5/6$ rate on code size larger than 2^{12}. This shows the interest of having both intra-frame and inter-frame SIMD in the same framework.

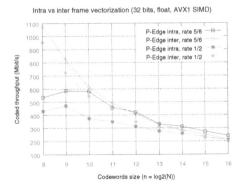

Fig. 9. A focus on 32-bit floating point P-EDGE decoder instances performance on large codeword size, *considering the decoding time only* (on Intel Xeon CPU E31225).

7   Conclusion and Future Works

In this paper, we have developed a framework that enables exploring optimizations for Successive Cancellation decoders of the Polar Codes family while enforcing a clear separation of concerns between the generic, abstract algorithmic level and the low-level architecture dependent on building block implementations. The benefits in terms of software design and flexibility are not overshadowed by prohibitive run-time performance results. On the contrary, the use of a specialized skeleton generator to produce optimized compile-time decoders enables performance levels to match, and even to exceed state of art implementations.

Future work will in priority be dedicated to a more in-depth performance analysis, for instance by applying the *Roof-line* model [19] or even better the *Execution-Cache-Memory* (ECM) model [16], would also give us much more insight about the remaining code optimization head-room, as the algorithm tend to be inherently memory bound. Finally, we intend to stress-test the genericity of our framework on other decoder variants from the Polar Codes family.

Acknowledgements. This study has been carried out with financial support from the French State, managed by the French National Research Agency (ANR) in the frame of the "Investments for the future" Programme IdEx Bordeaux - CPU (ANR-10-IDEX-03-02). The authors would also like to thank Guillaume Berhault for the helpful discussions.

References

1. Alamdar-Yazdi, A., Kschischang, F.: A simplified successive-cancellation decoder for polar codes. IEEE Commun. Lett. **15**(12), 1378–1380 (2011)
2. Arikan, E.: Channel polarization: a method for constructing capacity-achieving codes for symmetric binary-input memoryless channels. IEEE Trans. Inf. Theory **55**(7), 3051–3073 (2009)

3. Berrou, C., Glavieux, A., Thitimajshima, P.: Near shannon limit error-correcting coding and decoding: Turbo-codes. 1. In: IEEE International Conference on Communications, 1993. ICC 1993 Geneva. Technical Program, Conference Record, vol. 2, pp. 1064–1070, May 1993
4. Gallager, R.G.: Low-density parity-check codes (1963)
5. Giard, P., Sarkis, G., Thibeault, C., Gross, W.: Fast software polar decoders. In: 2014 IEEE International Conference on Acoustics, Speech and Signal Processing (ICASSP), pp. 7555–7559, May 2014
6. Gottschling, P., Wise, D.S., Joshi, A.: Generic support of algorithmic and structural recursion for scientific computing. Int. J. Parallel, Distrib. Syst. (IJPEDS) **24**(6), 479–503 (2009)
7. Le Gal, B., Leroux, C., Jego, C.: Software polar decoder on an embedded processor. In: Proceedings of the IEEE International Workshop on Signal Processing Systems (SIPS 2014), pp. 1–6. Belfast, October 2014
8. Le Gal, B., Leroux, C., Jego, C.: Multi-gb/s software decoding of polar codes. IEEE Trans. Sig. Process **63**(2), 349–359 (2015)
9. MacKay, D.J.: Good error-correcting codes based on very sparse matrices (1999)
10. Puschel, M., Moura, J., Johnson, J., Padua, D., Veloso, M., Singer, B., Xiong, J., Franchetti, F., Gacic, A., Voronenko, Y., Chen, K., Johnson, R., Rizzolo, N.: Spiral: code generation for DSP transforms. Proc. IEEE **93**(2), 232–275 (2005)
11. Sarkis, G., Giard, P., Thibeault, C., Gross, W.: Autogenerating software polar decoders. In: 2014 IEEE Global Conference on Signal and Information Processing (GlobalSIP), pp. 6–10 (2014)
12. Sarkis, G., Giard, P., Vardy, A., Thibeault, C., Gross, W.: Fast polar decoders: algorithm and implementation. IEEE J. Sel. Areas Commun. **32**(5), 946–957 (2014)
13. Shannon, C.: A mathematical theory of communication. Bell Syst. Tech. J. **27**(379–423), 623–656 (1948)
14. Spampinato, D.G., Püschel, M.: A basic linear algebra compiler. In: Proceedings of Annual IEEE/ACM International Symposium on Code Generation and Optimization, pp. 23:23–23:32, CGO 2014. ACM, New York (2014). http://doi.acm.org/10.1145/2544137.2544155
15. Stroustrup, B.: The C++ Programming Language, 4th edn. Addison-Wesley Professional, Boston (2013)
16. Treibig, J., Hager, G.: Introducing a performance model for bandwidth-limited loop kernels. CoRR abs/0905.0792 (2009). http://arxiv.org/abs/0905.0792
17. Walter, J., Koch, M.: ublas. www.boost.org/libs/numeric
18. Whaley, R.C., Petitet, A., Dongarra, J.: Automated empirical optimizations of software and the atlas project **27**(1–2), 3–35 (2001)
19. Williams, S., Waterman, A., Patterson, D.: Roofline: an insightful visual performance model for multicore architectures. Commun. 52(4), 65–76. ACM (2009). http://doi.acm.org/10.1145/1498765.1498785

Author Index

Printed in the United States
By Bookmasters